CONJUNCTIONS

Bi-Annual Volumes of New Writing

Edited by
Bradford Morrow

Contributing Editors
John Ashbery
Martine Bellen
Mei-mei Berssenbrugge
Mary Caponegro
Brian Evenson
William H. Gass
Peter Gizzi
Robert Kelly
Ann Lauterbach
Norman Manea
Rick Moody
Howard Norman
Karen Russell
Joanna Scott
David Shields
Peter Straub
John Edgar Wideman

Published by Bard College

D0099278

EDITOR: Bradford Morrow
MANAGING EDITOR: Micaela Morrissette
SENIOR EDITORS: Benjamin Hale, Joss Lake, J. W. McCormack, Edie Meidav,
    Nicole Nyhan, Pat Sims
COPY EDITOR: Pat Sims
ASSOCIATE EDITOR: Jedediah Berry
PUBLICITY: Darren O'Sullivan, Mark R. Primoff
EDITORIAL ASSISTANTS: Matthew Balik, Elena Botts, Kaitlynn Buchbaum,
    Brigid Fister, Adela Foo, Gilad Jaffe, Julie Jarema, Kelsey Johnson, Tessa
    Menatien, Chloe Reimann, Zoe Rohrich, Jay Rosenstein, Anna Sones,
    Nicholas Wetherell

CONJUNCTIONS is published in the Spring and Fall of each year by Bard College,
Annandale-on-Hudson, NY 12504.

SUBSCRIPTIONS: Use our secure online ordering system at www.conjunctions.com,
or send subscription orders to CONJUNCTIONS, Bard College, Annandale-on-
Hudson, NY 12504. Single year (two volumes): $18.00 for individuals; $40.00 for
institutions and non-US. Two years (four volumes): $32.00 for individuals; $80.00
for institutions and non-US. For information about subscriptions, back issues, and
advertising, contact us at (845) 758-7054 or conjunctions@bard.edu. *Conjunctions*
is listed and indexed in JSTOR and Humanities International Complete and
included in EBSCO*host*.

Editorial communications should be sent to Bradford Morrow, *Conjunctions*,
21 East 10th Street, 3E, New York, NY 10003. Unsolicited manuscripts cannot be
returned unless accompanied by a stamped, self-addressed envelope. Electronic
and simultaneous submissions will not be considered. If you are submitting from
outside the United States, contact conjunctions@bard.edu for instructions.

Cover design by Jerry Kelly, New York. Cover art by Zach Horn (www.zachhornart
.com): *The Garden of Nocturnal Delights*, 2015. Acrylic on canvas, 50 x 62 in.
© Zach Horn 2016; all rights reserved by the artist.

Conjunctions e-books of current and selected past issues are distributed by Open
Road Integrated Media (www.openroadmedia.com/conjunctions) and available for
purchase in all e-reader formats from Amazon, Apple, B&N, Google, Indiebound,
Kobo, Overdrive, and elsewhere.

Retailers can order print issues via Ubiquity Distributors, Inc., www.ubiquitymags
.com, 607 Degraw Street, Brooklyn, NY 11217. Telephone: (718) 875-5491. Fax: (718)
875-8047.

Printers: Edwards Brothers Malloy, Circle Press

Typesetter: Bill White, Typeworks

ISSN 0278-2324

ISBN 978-0-941964-82-1

Manufactured in the United States of America.

Bard   FICTION PRIZE

Bard College invites submissions for its annual Fiction Prize for young writers.

The Bard Fiction Prize is awarded annually to a promising, emerging writer who is a United States citizen aged 39 years or younger at the time of application. In addition to a monetary award of $30,000, the winner receives an appointment as writer-in-residence at Bard College for one semester without the expectation that he or she teach traditional courses. The recipient will give at least one public lecture and will meet informally with students.

To apply, candidates should write a cover letter describing the project they plan to work on while at Bard and submit a C.V., along with three copies of the published book they feel best represents their work. No manuscripts will be accepted.

Applications for the 2017 prize must be received by June 15, 2016. For further information about the Bard Fiction Prize, call 845-758-7087, or visit www.bard.edu/bfp. Applicants may also request information by writing to the Bard Fiction Prize, Bard College, Annandale-on-Hudson, NY 12504-5000.

Bard College PO Box 5000, Annandale-on-Hudson, NY 12504-5000

COMING UP IN THE FALL

Conjunctions:67
OTHER ALIENS
Coedited by Bradford Morrow and Elizabeth Hand

Who or what is an alien? Someone or something simply unknown to us, a being manifest from an incomprehensible territory? From the depths of the ocean, the deeps of space, an unmapped land far from home? Does otherness emerge from physical displacement, or psychic and spiritual displacement, or does it emerge from other sources? Must difference inevitably provoke fear and mistrust or does it sometimes elicit curiosity instead, firing the drive to explore and understand and even love? "Alien" is a powerful and flexible word. Aliens are Other, aliens are the stuff of science fiction and fantasy, aliens are traditional literary figures who, when we witness our "normal" lives through their strangers' eyes (think Frankenstein), cause us to see ourselves anew. Indeed, we become the unfamiliar ones.

Other Aliens brings together works of literary science and speculative fiction with innovative short stories, poetry, and essays that explore the vast precincts of unfamiliarity, of keen difference, of weirdness and not belonging. In this special issue, readers will encounter travelers on the cusp, on the edge, out there—beings as different as a California aquarium octopus named Clyde who follows his deadly instincts; a classic robot who achieves consciousness; a semitranslucent skyman named Xander who falls in love with an earthbound organic blueberry farmer, who, in turn, gives birth to a loving girl with vampiric habits. *Other Aliens* will feature new work by some of our most imaginative writers, including Julia Elliott, Peter Straub, S. P. Tenhoff, and Benjamin Hale, along with many others.

TABLE OF CONTENTS

AFFINITY:
THE FRIENDSHIP ISSUE
Edited by Bradford Morrow

IN MEMORIAM

C. D. Wright

January 6, 1949–January 12, 2016

In Friendship

EDITOR'S NOTE

ALONG WITH LOVE, FRIENDSHIP is the most universal, enlivening, challenging, mercurial, and genuine of human experiences. Whereas blood kinship is fated—our ancestors are our ancestors, like them or not, and so it is with parents and siblings—friendships are forged with people we choose, and continue to choose. People who become, in essence, a free-will kind of family, which, like our blood family, can be a strong source of happiness and, sometimes, of grand miseries. A friend is also one who becomes, as Aristotle proposed in his *Nicomachean Ethics*, essentially "another self." But just as we have the capacity both to embrace and torment ourselves, so can Aristotle's other selves do the same. Friendship, like selfhood, is a complex enterprise, a mixed bag.

This issue is a gathering of writings that address some of the myriad ways in which we encounter one another as friends. The nimble dance between love and friendship is part of the dialogue. Staunch friendships and fraught ones. False friendships and fading ones. Friendships brought into being in the cauldron of illness, friendships that make us feel most alive. Friendships between people long dead and friendships that are still going strong. It's a theme about which, over the millennia, much has been written, but one I believe readers of this issue will find framed and investigated in new ways.

Many of us involved with *Conjunctions*, writers and readers alike, unexpectedly lost a very dear friend earlier this year in the extraordinary poet, publisher, teacher, and longtime contributor to these pages, C. D. Wright. It is to her that *Affinity* is dedicated.

—Bradford Morrow
April 2016
New York City

An Anatomy of Friendship
Rick Moody and Darcey Steinke

October 18, 2015

DEAR DARCEY,

WHERE DID OUR FRIENDSHIP START, and does talking about where a friendship starts have meaning for what a friendship is? Isn't the process more important than the time line? Yesterday I was trying to mend a wall in the yard, the destruction of which has been caused by the hill in the back moving ever so slightly. Or that is my guess. We imagine that hills are fixed, but my observation is that they're always moving or eroding just a bit according to the machinations of time and the elements. Friendships move in a similar way. That is my argument for today.

It was in Bennington, VT, or near Bennington, VT, or that is my recollection. And I know that it was Jill Eisenstadt who introduced us. It's funny how sometimes you are close with someone, and then, in turn, you become closer with her friends. I used to see Jill a lot on the street when I was living in Park Slope, but I never sat down and had a cup of coffee with her, even though back in the nineties, when she introduced me to you, I considered her among my dearest friends. We used to do a lot of running in the park together. Now she swims, because of her bad knees. And I live in Queens.

Anyway, I think it was a dinner party during the summer when she and I were teaching high-school kids at Bennington College, which I did between 1991 and 1998, along with Helen Schulman, and a bunch of other people. Jill knew about it, because she was a Bennington alum, and at some point she hooked me up with the job. I'm not sure it was 1991 that we met at this dinner, but I also don't think it was as late as 1994. Maybe you remember.

I knew a little about your work. *Suicide Blonde* had come out relatively recently. I hadn't read it in full, nor *Up Through the Water*. But somehow I was cowed by your reputation. I remember someone saying that you were glamorous, but in a way this is, even in recollection, making that elementary mistake of confusing the book and its character with the author. You were married to Michael then, and I remember being at some house, off campus, for the dinner, and Michael was there, and the two of you radiated a certain kind of contemporary, self-confident monogamy that I found enviable. You guys were both smart, affable, and funny. I felt like a lesser light by comparison, like an angel from a much lower rung. I can't even remember how much I talked to you even, because I was busy feeling not as interesting as you were. I can kind of recall a dining room and a table, and a certain number of faces (more than six), but not one thing about who else was there.

Is feeling less competent than your friend a good basis for a friendship? I don't know if it's good, but it's what we had at the outset, at least as I recall it. I must have contrived with Jill to get her to invite us to a couple more things together. I must admit I wanted to get to know you a bit, more than if you were just another writer in Brooklyn. You were living in Brooklyn Heights then, and so was I, so I guess maybe we did something together, via Jill or otherwise, and then there was a party at your place, which I remember vividly, because I talked with Michael about *Selected Ambient Works, Volume II*, by Aphex Twin. He didn't really think it was so great, he said, right before putting on *No Quarter* by Jimmy Page and Robert Plant. Was that a thing that anyone wanted to hear at a party? And what did I know about it? If that is right, that he played that album, it was 1994, and I probably had already published *The Ice Storm*. I remember that Michael said *The Ice Storm* was just proving I could be "professional," and therefore less good than *Garden State*. One always remembers remarks like that.

But it's disappointing that I can't remember *exactly* how our friendship started. Except that I am so happy about it now that I sort of don't care so much how it started, just that I'm glad for what it is. It was a slow-moving thing at first, and that is maybe how important friendships go. They meander along until you have some shared purpose.

Love,
Rick

Rick,

I was trying to think when we first met too. I kept getting a picture of us sitting outside at a table talking. In my mind's eye this table is set up in front of my apartment on Hicks Street there in Brooklyn Heights but that's not possible. But what I remember from that first lunch is your hair (which frankly was fantastic!). And also the sense I had that you HAD mixed me up with Jesse, the narrator of *Suicide Blonde*. I remember you seemed a little disappointed that I was maybe a little less depraved and a little bit more wholesome than you thought! Also you were interested in God. I was interested in God too. Very few people that we knew at this time were interested in God. This made me want to stay close to you.

But let me go back to Bennington. I do remember we came to visit Jill and her saying, Let me get Rick; he wants to meet you. I had read *Garden State*. I think Jill got me to read it. I really loved it. Partly because it seemed to be about something I was interested in then, the idea of people who stayed in their hometown versus people who left. At that time I was most likely feeling sort of proud of myself for leaving my hometown and coming to the city. You seemed very smart to me and also vulnerable. A combination I have always been drawn to. In my mind you had on white tennis shorts but this can't be true.

You were at a few parties at our apartment on Hicks Street. We had so many parties in those days! Through my grandmother we'd lucked into a big prewar rent-controlled apartment and it was party central there for a while. I remember Moby DJing once. And a female writer, who will remain nameless, shooting up and then passing out in the bathroom. Michael, my first husband, had been a local rock star in Portland, Oregon, and so had many strict ideas about music. He was making a Wax Trax! record at about that time. The one with "Mind the Gap" on it. House music was new then.

My main memory of you from the early part of our friendship is seeing you on the street trying to hail a taxi, either on your own or with Jeffrey Eugenides or Donald Antrim. Just you standing in the dark outside a *Paris Review* party or in Brooklyn trying to get a cab into the city. You seemed to me like a rocket that had already been launched. Even when you pretended to be relaxed I could tell you were thinking. You tried all the time. I liked this a lot.

About a year in, as you say, we started to have our Friday afternoon cabbage soup lunches at the Long Island Restaurant. Which was the greatest place. The red booths! Remember them? Now it's gentrified and I am sure nice, but remember that lovely women who ran the place, she was so kind to us. Once you put your palm against the vinyl and said, "I could write about these all day long!" We started to talk about God in earnest then. It was, for me, a deeply meaningful phase. Even more so in retrospect.

Love,
Darcey

October 31, 2015

Dear Darcey,

It's a measure of the way the particular friendship under scrutiny *works* that I am willing to talk about the theological part of all this in public, in writing, at all. The way our friendship works, it seems to me, is that I am challenged by you, both by your model and by what you actually say, and then I attempt to rise to the occasion. In the process, I believe I am made better as a person. I can't say that I always like this about our friendship, the growth-opportunities portion of it, or I have not liked it at certain times, but I have always ultimately gone in the direction I was meant to go, it seems, finding the gratitude at some later date, and so I will do now with the theological part of the discussion.

I don't remember when I really understood the extent that spiritual feeling played in your life, and as I'm mostly *not* in the habit of talking about this subject with everyone I meet, I'm not sure how we brought it up. But by the time we were having lunch at the Long Island Restaurant, on Atlantic Avenue, it was the preeminent theme of our friendship.

I know that I was at this dinner in this stretch of months, sponsored by, I think, Karen Rinaldi, who was Donald Antrim's girlfriend at the time (either then or just before then), and there was, at this Rinaldi-hosted dinner, some hand-wringing about the Religious Right. It would have been during the first Clinton term, when these culture wars were far less brutal than they got later on, but still. *What to do.* I had an epiphanic idea that night that I should try to sponsor some kind of literary project about the Religious Left, that stratum of the

11

religious establishment that was abolitionist, suffragist, antiwar, and strongly pro Civil Rights, over some hundred and fifty years. That part of mainstream American religious life I found deeply admirable, beginning with Emerson and including John Brown and Martin Luther King Jr. And so I was thinking, after the dinner party, about to whom I could talk about this idea, and I remember thinking very much that I wanted to talk about it with you.

This is how we came up with the idea to make the anthology called *Joyful Noise*, which we then worked on at lunch on Fridays for more than a year. I can't remember when we started work on it, but I remember telling my family that we had sold the book right after my sister had died (twenty years ago tomorrow), and then I know that the book came out in 1997. I don't know if I started wanting to talk about spiritual matters with you because I thought it was a promotable topic of conversation, but as I have (increasingly) felt that it was nobody's business but mine, especially in literary circles, I can't but imagine that there was something about the way we discussed this stuff that was useful to us both. Maybe it was one of these challenges, coming from you.

You often led with "I was a minister's daughter," and after a time I met the minister in question, and your brothers, and it's clear how much that legacy defined you, but that's not the part of the spiritual experience I was interested in. I wasn't even, really, interested in Lutheranism, which was what you practiced with your dad and his various parishes. I was interested in the part of spiritual experience that was keen about God, but terribly uncertain, the part that didn't even know whether, from a congregational perspective, you could *do* liberal Protestantism anymore. The part that felt some class of experience out there associated with God, but didn't know how *religion* was part of it. The part that was always looking around the corner for some new way to express this feeling, whether it was interviewing Kurt Cobain, or seeing a lot of new conceptual art, which were things you had done.

Working on the book became the way to talk about this stuff. In the end, I feel sort of mixed about the book itself, as if I could do a lot better if we did it now, but I also feel that doing what we did enabled us to get to be closer friends. There are pieces in *Joyful Noise* that still seem very important to me: your piece, Barry Hannah's piece, Lucy Grealy's piece, Lydia Davis's, and so on. I wish we had included William Vollmann! (I am mad we got talked out of that.)

The lady at the Long Island Restaurant was a symbol of all this. It seems to me we tried a few other restaurants in the area, which has plenty of them, and then one day we were there, at your suggestion. It must have been a bar at one point, because it looked more like a bar than like a restaurant, and it was perpetually empty, and it was all vinyl (and I used that red vinyl in *Purple America*), and the proprietrix always came over and said, "Well, today I have some cabbage soup," or something similar. Seems like it was always some kind of soup, and then maybe if you were nice she would make something else, a grilled cheese or something, but I don't think we ever had anything else. Once we discovered her, avatar of the infinite, imitator of Christ, we never went anywhere else, and we just ate what she gave us. Rightly so. We gave her a book at one point too, right? I think when we had a finished book we gave it to her, and I remember her being a bit flustered, like she wished we wouldn't make a big deal out of it, that we had basically commissioned and edited an entire anthology in her restaurant, the restaurant that would *definitely* go out of business when the neighborhood finished gentrifying, or when she got too old, as she assuredly did not long after.

Those were some great days, when I think back on them. If I were to say what I learned from those lunches, I would probably adduce your essay for *Joyful Noise*, which is about Mary's labor, and which you were able to write after experiencing labor yourself, as an example of what education in the *Joyful Noise* project was like. In many quarters, it seems, it would be heretical to write about Mary's labor, but why? Is not Mary's labor, in its way, a most beautiful thing to think about? About how like every other childbirth, in mean circumstances, it must have been, and yet how important too? As they all are, these childbirths.

Love,
Rick

Rick:

I do think part of the reason our friendship has lasted so long and has been so kinetic is in part because we challenge each other. I met you at a time when, though I was thinking of having a baby, I was deeply committed to my writing and worried what having a family might do to my artistic life. At that time I still stayed up late writing and smoking cigarettes. I thought of it as my Joan Didion routine. I was writing a lot for *Spin* then and I flew around some and wrote about rock stars, David Koresh and Waco, and Norwegian Black Metal. But I was worried all that was about to change and I think your commitment to your work really inspired me. And that continues through the years. I feel sometimes after I talk to you I want to throw myself down on the ground with my head pressed up against a book and recommit myself to fiction.

As to how we got started taking about religion, I remember you telling me a story about a hard time you had in prep school. The main thing I remember is you saying that you had a breakdown and you hid under a table and a priest was trying to get you to come out. After this you felt more interested in the divine. I have thought of this now and then, the large lovely wood table, the teenage you hiding underneath and refusing to come out, the patient priest trying to convince you to come. Maybe this is misremembered but to me that story was and is very compelling, the hiding from and mistrust in religion but also the loneliness and the longing.

We talked some too about how annoying it was that nobody thought of religion as an intellectual subject at that time. This was particularly true at the sort of parties I went to then. It was just verboten. I remember once being at a party with a bunch of music critics, and the very smart and wonderful Bob Christgau, when I mentioned something spiritual, said to me, "So you believe in a man with a long gray beard in a white dress," and I just sort of lost it. All the historical theological thought, what religion meant to the civil rights movement, the great thinkers, Thomas Merton, Simone Weil, Rabbi Heschel, got reduced to this idea that I was a soft-brained moron believing in a version of Santa Claus.

So I was very interested in your idea of pushing back. I think before we started *Joyful Noise*, though, we read novels that may or may not have had a religious theme and talked about them. I remember a heated discussion on Endo's *Deep River*, which at that time was a favorite of mine. I remember we talked about Simone Weil some too. We read *Gravity and Grace*. Our exchange of ideas about religion was the first I had with another writer. Since then I have had many; over the years I have sought them out. Ours had something very alive about it.

You mention your sister. Another landmark in our friendship was the fact that your sister died and then my daughter, Abbie, was born a week later. When you called me to tell me she had died I was very pregnant and to hear you sobbing on the phone just obliterated me. Also, the details of her putting her kids to bed and the very maternal and domestic way it happened haunted me. I had Abbie just a few days later and I remember calling you on the hospital phone to tell you. I was so anxious to tell you about new life coming into the world. During that call you told me about the plans for your sister's funeral and I told you about my labor. It was a conversation with so much honesty and rawness.

Love,
Darcey

November 15, 2015

Darcey,

I'm writing this on the plane to Seattle, while on book tour, an adventure that I feel both lucky to undertake and about which I am extremely apprehensive. I don't want to do what I have to do this week, the glad-handing, and I feel the cost of doing it. I don't feel like myself when I am touring. I feel simulated, artificial, other than myself. I feel reduced to an animal that can merely *survive*. That is the extent of it. And yet I also feel like I am lucky to have the chance to meet the readers.

And: there's no way not to talk about how you and I got to be the kind of friends that we got to be without talking about the portion of our friendship when we were in love, in the eros sense, but I don't know if I can do it without real regret, or some balancing of real regret and great joy. I learned so much from going through what we went through, even though I also feel awful about it. In a way I was hoping that you would go first in writing about this part.

I remember that we were in a taxicab going back to Brooklyn one day when you started crying. I remember there was a time before this, some weeks before, when you had described telling someone that I was your "intellectual boyfriend," and rather than dwelling on this with any rational sense of what was happening, I kind of filed it away and tried to pretend to myself that the phrase did not presage anything much. But then we were in the taxi, and I don't know what we were talking about, but you were suddenly crying. And when I asked what you were crying about, you said, "I think I am in love with you." Or words to that effect. It was pretty close to that sentence. And then I remember that you wanted to get out of the cab immediately, you almost flung yourself out of the cab, without allowing me to console you, nor to talk more about what you'd said.

I think I went after you. I know at some point I lodged a reply, which was, "Well, I *always* loved you." That was the comeback as I recollect it. A face-to-face reply, not a telephone reply, maybe? In those days we talked on the phone a lot.

It's no coincidence that I was grief-stricken at that time, as far as I recollect it. Something happened to me when my sister died, and some of the moral framework that I thought I had, that I thought I could rely on, *lapsed*, and I sort of stopped caring whether I was as morally upright as I had been before. I couldn't understand the purpose of moral thinking, because I thought my sister's death was pointless, arbitrary, and the effect of it on many people I loved was unthinkable and devastating. If there was a moral operating principle to creation, to the ontology of it all, it seemed to me then, if there was a God, then God had somehow blinked on November 1, 1995. It's not that I set out to do things that were pointless and arbitrary, as befitted the way I thought about God and God's works for a while, it's that I stopped caring. It was obvious to me that I had *always loved you*, and I didn't see any reason to do otherwise.

The situation was a dishonor to us both because we were both involved with other people. It's a dishonor because we knew better, and we had the ethics to discuss doing better, but we failed to do better. We could have done better, even if it hurt, even if it was costly to us. But we didn't do these things. So the failure part of it was uppermost in my mind. That I was failing. That I should not have been doing what I had done. That whatever ethics I was practicing in church, or alleging to practice, I was not practicing them very rigorously in real life.

But maybe, just a little bit, there was a point to this too. A humble purpose to it. I remember your saying to me, one time, in this period, "My soul wants your soul." Which is one of the most wonderful things anyone ever said to me. In many ways, I was so hurt then that I didn't know if I could live up to this remark. But let's say, just for the sake of the conversation, that you were really telling the truth then. Then maybe the eros-not-agape part of the whole thing was something that we had to go through to come out the other side? Maybe we couldn't really care about each other the way we do now if we had not gone through that?

I suffered both with you and in the absence of you, in this period. It lasted until I went to Yaddo at one point, for a residency (I must have been starting *The Black Veil* then, because I know you had already read *Purple America*), and you visited, and I felt stuck with this awful feeling that I was not smart enough nor adult enough nor perfect enough to get out from under everything, all the entanglements of the real world, as opposed to this intense but slightly sequestered place we had got ourselves into, in order to be *together*. I was afraid, and selfish about it, because I was afraid, and this was mixed up with the feeling that we had dishonored ourselves, and we needed to stop. And so we stopped. Most of the blame for it falls on me, I believe. On that point, I could go on and on.

It is part of the Song of Songs that one should mix up the ecstatic with the spiritual, that the two kinds of ecstasy are consubstantial. But maybe this is like the incarnations of the Buddha—they are all great, all these incarnations, but some are greater than others, and to rest in eros, thinking it was the ultimate destination, thinking it *was* our friendship, that was rank vanity, with which I was much afflicted in those days. We were all done with that part by, what, the late nineties, and then we had to weather all the transition out of it. You had a child, for example. A lovely, excellent child.

Love,
Rick

Rick:

I remember well the car ride. It was cold out and we both had on big coats and gloves. I remember you saying something about going away, maybe to Yaddo and I started to cry. It was one of those very surprising cries that just started up without warning. And I did tell you that I loved you. I had not till that moment thought this in the front of my brain, but the way it hurt me, the idea that you were going away, made it all suddenly clear how I felt. But what I remember most was that we both had our gloves on still and we held hands with our gloves on for a few moments. And I always remember that as a sort of image of the whole thing. That there was a deep connection but we could never completely connect in the romantic love sphere.

The context that made my own life morally wobbly then was that my marriage was in deep trouble. Not that this is an excuse, it's not. Abbie, my daughter, was two when this happened. And while for a while I was very happy in my marriage, with the birth of my daughter things changed. I felt out of sync with my partner and very lonely. We spent so many beautiful hours together, Abbie and I. It was almost like loving her I realized what love could really be, and I wanted more from a partner. Also we were very emotionally intimate, you and I, and that also made me realize I wanted more from a lover.

I can see now that in some ways I wanted an escape hatch from my life and myself.

After the car ride I think there was only a few weeks of actual connection. I knew it was wrong—I remember thinking we could be friends still, trying to meet as friends, but that never worked out once the proclamations were made. I remember this happened over and over again. You went to Yaddo, which was good. And I did come and visit once. I was up near Saratoga to do some research on my Millerite, *Great Disappointment* book, which is of course very ironic. That was also the time I realized, while I did love you, you were not the answer to my problems with my marriage and my life in general. You were sort of closed off and distant then and that was hard for me. I remember driving away from Saratoga and listening to Leonard Cohen on the radio and feeling in a sort of free fall. It was a relief in a way but very scary. I knew then I would have to make changes to my life myself without the support of someone else.

It sounds crazy but I have always been grateful to you for this. I know I could have jumped to someone else without really looking at myself closely, what I wanted and who I was, but that did not happen and it's been a great gift to me. Also just the open feeling I had with you at times, I remember talking to you and feeling that, after a long time, I finally sounded like myself again. It was like the very pitch of my voice had changed and I recognized myself. What happened between us was very powerful. It was the first step leading me toward a new and bigger life.

I went away to be the writer-in-residence at the University of Mississippi then. And thank goodness for that. That time gave me the space away from my marriage to figure things out and also away from you to get over you and the idea of you and me together. I was so lonely that year but what a beautiful year it was. I was broken open and I experienced so much, the blues, I also read like a maniac.

Also Abbie and I had a sort of magical time going across the street from our house to Faulkner's and chasing rabbits. It was idyllic and profound. I remember one night I had put her to bed and I was reading, I think, a book of Thomas De Quincey's essays and I had the feeling there was a presence in the room, it was like my loneliness had broken off from me and hovered nearby, but my loneliness was also transfigured—I knew then that my daughter and I would be all right.

When I got back from Mississippi, I rented an apartment for Abbie and me in Fort Greene. I don't remember how we started to put it back together as friends. Do you? I do remember you coming to that apartment and we played our guitars together a few times. I was starting my band Ruffian then with my friends. I also remember that I interviewed you at the New School. We might have read together a few times. I remember you and your partner were moving toward marriage in those years and I wondered about that for you.

I was angry at you still for a while. What bothered me was that you sometimes minimized what happened between us and this hurt me. I knew too that it was not going to work, that it should be over but I also felt it was BIG, and I sort of wanted that honored somehow. I see now that to calibrate the Bigness might have meant getting into it all again.

The lovely thing is now, while admitting it was fucked up, we can also sort of honor it.

The thing that has always been remarkable about our friendship is that whenever I see you I feel transported back to this spot where frankly "my soul wants your soul." And not in a romantic way. Which is crazy beautiful and very rare.

Love,
Darcey

Darce,

It's just a couple of days before Christmas, and it's true that I have Christmas to blame for my slow response time here, and I also have the fact that my wife is pregnant and not feeling well at all. These would be good reasons to be preoccupied. But there's also the fact that I have been feeling low about my behavior during the period we have been writing about most recently, and I feel there's a way that I have not sufficiently apologized. In a way, I know this is not entirely true, because I have amended my behavior in ways that I am proud of, and have become, I feel, *a real adult*, which I don't know if I would have said of myself in the late nineties. But I still feel dumb about what happened, about not honoring what happened, as you say, and I feel I did the stupidest possible thing at the time, which was to spurn a heartfelt connection for no reason but that intimacy was painful to me in those days. I regret it a lot.

The question of how we rounded the corner on all of that is an interesting and meaningful question. My recollection is that partly there was the work of *Joyful Noise*, which went on for a while. We were known, for a spell, as literary people who had something to say about religion (which made my publishers nervous), and we got to be on panels of the like-minded. I know we did that panel at St. Luke in the Fields for Roger Ferlo, which led to my being in his Dante class, and then becoming a parishioner there. And then were on that panel at NYU which concerned new thinking about faith. I was on that panel, in fact, the faith panel, and at a celebration of Kathy Acker's work in the same week. The concerns of the two panels could not have been more disparate. (And yet I still think of myself as a guy who both loves Kathy Acker and the New Testament.) The Acker panel had Kim Gordon on it, and Richard Foreman, and a bunch of other eminences, but it did not compare, in terms of weirdness, to the new-thinking-about-faith panel, which in my recollection was full of people with a tentative grasp on the real world! If you had told me there were bipolar sufferers and schizophrenics in the audience, I would not have been surprised. But the Acker panel just had celebrities. I *loved* that we journeyed to the much more dangerous and surprising place together, you and me.

Anyway, we did that, all the stuff relating to the anthology, and then we did some music stuff together for a while. I remember you were in Ruffian, and then you and I played together on a *Tin House* event of some kind, which must have been in 1999 or so. I remember we were talking a lot about music there for a while. It was before I was playing in the Wingdales, so it was sort of an area of great fertility for me. I was thinking a lot about music. And somewhere in that span we did a joint appearance in Oxford, Mississippi, which did provide the occasion on which the two of us went and sat out on the lawn in front of Faulkner's house for the afternoon. There were a couple of things that were memorable about that trip. I remember you finding my airport-related anxiety irritating (you told me so!), which was a rare moment of your getting impatient with me, and I remember telling you that I was going to marry the woman who became my first wife, which you took in stride, and then I remember sort of asking somehow if our friendship was going to have to change because I was getting married, and you saying, more or less, "Well, of course." And I was really disappointed by that! Maybe not the perfect kind of way to be thinking about someone who is not your wife when you're about to get married, I'll hazard.

But the apex of the trip to Oxford was going to Al Green's church in Memphis, and attending the service. Truly one of the great experiences of my life. I didn't quite know what a musical ministry was until we went there. All the improvised testifying and everything. It was incredibly powerful. And I remember Al looking at us, you and me, at one point and saying "You all got the light! You people there, you got the light!" Or some such. It was maybe one of the only times in my life I felt really sufficient as a spiritual being, because Al Green said so.

My supposition was that we put in a lot of work, in this period of the early twenty-first century, to become friends who were not lovers. In my life, this has not always worked at all. And there was ample reason to suppose that it would not work this time. But I feel like we both put in a lot of work. And it required respect and real forbearance and spiritual effort, and it required putting other people ahead of one's own wishes, at least on my end of things. I so delighted in our conversation and our area of shared interests that I really wanted to solve the impediments to our being friends and moving forward. I wanted to survive my own mistakes.

I suppose the truly transformative moment came when you announced that you were getting remarried.

I'm leaving out a lot of ligamentary passages in this span of years— like you had your problems at the New School in this span, and I got really lost with addictive behavior for a few years in there too—but somehow there was a sense of shared purpose that had to be nurtured in order that we could become something like what we are now, and that sense of purpose and mutual respect that came from working on stuff together and not shrinking from that. I have had people in life who say that I am in some ways *impossible* to be friendly with if you don't work with me in some capacity. My bandmates have said that. And after *Joyful Noise* came out in paperback and during the years that followed we instituted some of the right kind of boundaries, and *worked together* on various things, at various times, and I

21

really loved that. I love it still. I loved making an anthology with you, I loved singing with you, I loved reading your books in manuscript, all of that.

Merry Xmas,
Rick

Rick:

Now it's between Christmas and New Year's, the twenty-ninth to be exact, and I am staying with my husband in my mother-in-law's assisted-living complex in Richmond, Virginia. We took the long and lovely train ride yesterday from Penn Station. I love the train, how you can look into people's backyards and see their overturned bird-baths, woodpiles, laundry blowing on the line.

I have also been terrible at establishing friendships with people I have been linked with romantically. Mostly I have had little interest in doing so. With us, the fact that we were friends first helped and also that we both did work at it. In the years we came back together we gave each other a lot of room.

As you look back on your life things shake out some and you see who you really loved, who really loved you, also who the people were that you had deep connections with whether it worked out or not. About ten years ago, I remember this started to happen to me and it was at first painful, as I had to be honest about how often I had thrown away love.

I want to say again that while the period we are writing about was one of the hardest in my life, I was a single mother with a toddler and writing financially is not the most stable career in the world, it was also a time of great beauty. I ached a lot, not just in my mind but in my body too. But I did a lot of things I am very proud of besides getting our friendship back on track, I bought a house in Lefferts Gardens, I started my memoir, *Easter Everywhere*, I learned to play the guitar, I got a spiritual director, a small, intense Episcopal nun, named Sister Leslie. I realized all the ways my life had been false and I tried to make it better.

It's interesting to me how several times in this conversation you have mentioned worrying about how faith will seem to your readers, you worrying and also your publisher too. This is something I have thought about lately a lot. All my writing has to do in one way or another with my faith and doubt and interest in the spiritual realm and I do think this fact has maybe hurt the trajectory of my books some. I know we have Marilynne Robinson, I like some of her work a lot, but I also feel though she lives now at this time she is more involved in an older 1950s type of faith. I am interested in how to be a person of faith and also love Sonic Youth and David Lynch films, and also Kathy Acker. Did you know that when I interviewed Kurt Cobain for *Spin* (when *In Utero* came out) he was reading Kathy Acker and he said he got ideas for guitar riffs from her prose! Anyway, this question is not really a choice for me, I always write about a person pushed around by the spirit.

Do you remember at our very first reading for *Joyful Noise*, after we read, a young woman stood up, she had dyed black hair and was punkish. She asked us "How did you find the courage to talk about God?" This has always stuck with me. And frankly, to my mind, is enough reason for the whole project.

It was a joy to be in Oxford together, a place I love so much. I remember Richard Howorth, the owner of Square Books, coming up to you in the bookstore when we were there and saying, "Rick, I have always wanted to have you in the store." And I loved the idea that having writers in a bookstore sort of makes the store more holy! Also, we got to go to Faulkner's house and it's fixed up now but then it still had like Faulkner's crappy plastic shoe rack and his handwritten numbers above the phone in the kitchen. I am not big on going to writers' houses, but there was such a feeling of anxious unease in that house that is so familiar to me. It's the general mood of the writer's life.

I don't think of meeting my current husband Mike or marrying him as affecting our relationship. But that is my side of things. I had been single for maybe five years when he came to stay with me, as a friend; he had once written a story about me for the Roanoke newspaper and we had kept in touch. He was on a story. He had ridden up from the South with a bus full of people who had gotten bad mortgages and who were going to bust into the Citibank board meeting. So that was pretty exciting to me, to hear the story of this from a serious investigative reporter. We got married six years ago and I understand now, in my second marriage, why people do it. I do think that new intimacies change and shake up and maybe even supplant older ones. And maybe this did happen some with us.

What I like about our friendship now is that while we don't see each other a ton in person, we are sort of always in touch, connected in a loose but firm way. We check in. I have called on you in the last years when I had trouble with a romantic stalker and also when I was having trouble with my novel *Milk,* I remember we met and I told you the whole arc of the book in very overreaching thematic ways and you looked at me and said, *OK, just tell me the story.* And your focused attention really helped me, just that little exchange got me out of my grandiose ideas and back on the fragile human story.

Love,
Darcey

January 18, 2016

Hey Darce,

It is the new year and again I have been very slow. I have been thinking about the meaning of this exchange. I'd been working on a mass, I might have told you, with composer Daniel Felsenfeld, which premiered on December 30. It went well, and it was one of those things (they don't happen often enough in the creative life), where the only problem with the project is that it *ends.* Then I never know what to do with myself afterward. Anyway, in the audience was that priest from Old First Presbyterian, Daniel Meeter, his name is. For whom you and I did that panel discussion, which must have been maybe four years ago or so? I'm guessing here. Daniel Meeter came to the premiere because he knew both Danny and me.

The Rev. Meeter had a profound reaction to the piece. He was crying a little bit, I think it's fair to say, and he sort of got right up in my face and said something like: "You can't possibly know how important these words you've written are!" Of course I agreed, because it would not have been sporting to disagree, although I work hard to try to know exactly how important (and unimportant) my words are most of the time. I was just glad the piece happened, but I also *did* think about the words, you know, a little bit. Anyway, I bring him up because for me the really important night with you, in the period of our trying to put our friendship back together, when I really knew that I had let go of most of the preconceptions I had about you and me and all that went before, was that night that we did the panel for the

24

Rev. Meeter at Old First Presbyterian. We went out for dinner before-hand, and that's when I finally told you that my first marriage was over with. And you looked at me in this way that I sort of took as a mime-world synonym for "I've waited for this announcement for a while." I'm not sure it was judgmental, I didn't take it that way, but more just a recognition that something long delayed had happened, and that you had suspected it would happen.

There's a way that some social things are never understood, the value of social things is never understood, until in the nexus of friend-ship. Or: the meaning of what we do, in the world, is never really clear until it is *discussed*. The language is the way that events begin to *mean*. And there was every reason for you to have feelings on this subject of my marriage, long ago, but what I thought that night was that there was this way that our friendship was sort of solving the problem of my marriage, that night, and I felt some real gratitude for you for letting me take as long as I took, but also for your telling me the truth about my life. It was a powerful feeling of gratitude that I felt then.

You can go a long way as a fiction writer trying to describe these things, and still not get them exactly right. A burden was removed, I suppose, from our friendship—my delusion about my relationship. But also enough time had passed for that burden to no longer be quite so burdensome. I had the feeling that I have had since: of how much I owe you and how much I care about you. And it was moving because it didn't have anything to do with eros, even invoking eros is rude at this point (though I'm trying hard to get the words to do exactly what I want them to do to describe the particular surfeit of human emo-tions), but really just what I imagine friendship is, now, in my gallop-ing toward old age, just knowing someone for a really long time, and really meeting them periodically *where they are*, and not where you need them to be, and feeling powerful feelings of contentment that your friendship is still going and that you can still do things together and see each other, and that many of the failed parts, the parts that you personally have fucked up, can in some way be forgiven, or at least set aside, and you can go on, somehow relying on a person. Like when Melville visited Hawthorne when he was consul in England. It was England, right? And it had been years since they were so close (so close that some people think they were lovers), and Melville came to visit him while abroad, and it was strange, because time had passed, and there had been misunderstandings, but also a recognition of in-debtedness and mutual impact, a recognition of friendship.

Maybe part of what we're describing here is *reconciliation*. At St. Paul's Chapel, where I go these days, they used to bring out this cross from Coventry Cathedral every week, and remind us all about reconciliation after WWII. (This in part because St. Paul's is across the street from the World Trade Center, where reconciliation is *much needed*.) I often found that cross really moving (and Hazel, my daughter, often did too). But that doesn't mean in the really vexing difficulties with people that I easily feel, *Hey, let's figure out how to work this out! We can do it! We're adults!* I do not always feel that way. Sometimes I feel like it's not my fault, and I don't feel like it's all my responsibility, the reconciliation. But what's a blessing, I guess, is when you don't have any doubt about wanting to repair the past, when you just feel a big uncomplicated tidal surge of love, and you know that you don't give a shit about all the trouble, or the friction, and you know you want to find a way. I have had that feeling with you a lot. I was looking at some interview we did together, not long ago, in *Bomb*. I just stumbled on it, and I thought, *My God, I just really love that Darcey Steinke*. I mean, this does a disservice to the feeling, because it wasn't expressed in facile language, but just a tremendous warmth at all we have done together, and still do together, when we can, despite all that happened, and despite our busy lives now.

What is friendship then? It's that arrangement in which love really is, from this vantage point, unconditional, and in which everyone blows it at some point, and no one is perfect, over the course of many, many years. It's unconditional love + time.

Maybe you should get to have a last word, if you like!

Love always,
Rick

Rick:

It is the day after the big snowstorm. Snow, like lace, covers my kitchen window where I write to you. I just got back from DC and the National Zoo where I met a sixty-eight-year-old elephant named Ambika. I wanted to get to know her for a book I am working on about menopause and killer whales. Because elephants are so wrinkly and droopy, it was hard to see her as old, but when her keeper pointed out her frayed cabbage-leaf ears and how her forehead was more pronounced, I could tell she was an elder. In hearing about her life, how she was born in India, captured, and made to work at a logging camp, before being shipped to America and then driven around the country in a truck to visit elementary schools, how when she finally came to the zoo fifty years ago, she was chained by the leg in a small cement room, it all made me think of the length of a life—an animal life, a human life, which is also an animal life.

Your last response really moved me. I knew about your mass, yes, you sent me the text and I thought it was very beautiful. Your mass tried to get at what we are talking about here, the pain and the love and the disappointment and the joy and how these things are all connected, not separated out from each other. It's like human tissue connects them all. It's not so much I was waiting to hear about your marriage ending but that I wanted more for you. I did not at that point want anything romantic at all, but I still wanted more for you as to what love is and can be. We differed on this subject early on. I really believed in the soul-to-soul connection when it comes to romantic love, that it's a singular thing between two people and that sex is also most meaningful taken in these terms as well. For me the movement forward in our relationship was that night but also this summer when I heard from you, after you read the *Bomb* interview. I knew when I heard from you that, because of the love you have now with Laurel, you are able to see what happened between us more clearly. That's what I was trying to get at in my last installment, that as time moves forward you are always seeing your life and relationships in new ways, you are realizing what actually took place. This is one of the best things about moving through time, telling yourself your own story in different ways, forgiving yourself and others.

This is also why friendship is so sacred, you carry a love for someone through time. And I do feel this about you. I think ultimately our staying connected was the most important thing about us. It was hard to figure this out at first, what we meant to each other, in what configuration we were supposed to be.

Whenever I see you I always think of that scene from *Death Comes for the Archbishop* by Willa Cather. A priest, who is the main character, hears that his friend, a Native American chief, had lost a child. The priest rushes to his friend. When he arrives the chief comes out and says, "My Friend Has Come." There is such gratitude and need in that line. We need each other so deeply sometimes it's

27

hard to bear. I feel sad when I see you sometimes, the sadness of the past, of so much time being gone, but I also feel our hard-won connection is visceral, is real. I am FOR you. And I know you are FOR me. This is no small thing. I am grateful.

Love,
Darcey

From Huck Out West
Robert Coover

HUCK AND TOM IN MINNYSOTA

IT WAS UP IN MINNYSOTA that Tom made up his mind to give over cowboying and take on the law. Becky Thatcher was the daughter of a judge and maybe she give him the idea how to set about doing it. Before that him and me was mostly adventuring round the Territories without no thoughts about the next day. We run away from home all them years ago because Tom was bored and hankered to chase after what he said was the noble savages. At first they was the finest people in the world and Tom wanted to join up with them, and then they was the wickedest that ever lived and they should all get hunted down and killed, he couldn't make up his mind. Some boys in a wagonload of immigrants we come across early on learnt us how to ride and shoot and throw a lasso so that we got to be passing good at all them things.

That story turned poorly and we never seen what was left of them afterward, but ending stories was less important to Tom than beginning them, so we was soon off to other adventures that he thought up or read about in a book or heard tell of. Sometimes they was fun, sometimes they warn't, but for Tom Sawyer they was all as needful as breathing. He couldn't stand a day that didn't have an adventure in it, and he warn't satisfied until he'd worked in five or six.

Once, whilst we was still humping mail pouches back and forth across the desert on our ponies, I come on a rascally fellow named Bill from near where we come from. He was also keen on adventures and he was heading back east to roust up a gang of bushwhackers in our state to kill jayhawks over in the next one. The way he told it, he had a bunch of swell fellows joining his gang and he wondered if Tom and me might be interested. With the war betwixt the states starting, there were lots of gangs forming up and making sport of burning down one another's towns, which seemed like sure enough adventures, not just something out of books, so maybe we was looking in the wrong place. But when I told Tom about it the next time we

29

crossed up at a relay station, he says he reckoned he'd just stay out west and maybe get up a gang of his own, because he couldn't see no profit in going back. But I knowed that warn't the real reason. The real reason was he couldn't be boss of it.

It was while we was on one of his adventures in the New Mexico Territory that Tom got the notion to go watch the hangings in Minnysota, a notion that would change everything. The Pony Express company had suddenly gone bust the year before when the cross-country tellygraph come in. We never even got our last paychecks, so we paid ourselves with ponies and saddles, which was how I got Jackson. I'd named Jackson after an island in the big river where my life took a change because, with me and Tom setting out on our western adventures, it was a-changing again and I wanted to mark that.

Jackson's Island was where me and Jim met up when we was both running away, so naming the pony Jackson was also a way of remembering our grand adventures on that river all them years ago. The last time I seen Jim was one of my sorrowfullest days ever, and I seen more'n a few. We'd brung Jim out west with us when we'd left home, Tom and me, but when we hired on as riders for the Pony, we didn't know what to do with him. The war had not yet started up, and though Jim was a free man, the bounty hunters didn't always mind such particulars. Sometimes we had to pretend he was OUR slave, and we always had to be on the watch-out he didn't get stole.

The Pony Express Stables, however, was hiring only skinny young white orphans, and though Jim was surely an orphan, he come up short on the other requirements. The station keeper said if we wanted the job, we had to get rid of him. I says we have to look for another job, but they paid fifty dollars a month, which was more money than a body could tell what to do with, so Tom said we didn't have no choice and he sold him to a tribe of slaveholding Indians. "It's the right thing to do, Huck," Tom said after he'd gone and done it. "Jim's used to being a slave and he's probably happier when he has someone telling him what to do. And besides, they're more like his own kind." Tom was surely right as he most always was, but it made my heart sink into my bootheels to see how sad Jim was that day. I waved at him and he looked at me like he was asking me a dreadful question, and then he was gone, with a rope round his neck. Tom bought us new riding boots with the money.

We was both broke, money just falling out of my pockets somehow, whilst Tom was spending his up shipping long tellygrams back to Becky Thatcher. He wanted all his adventures wrote down like the ones he'd read in books and she knowed how to read and write and was the sort of cretur who would be impressed by his hifalut'n style and not have nothing else to do, so she got elected. She couldn't write back to him because there warn't nowheres to write to, but that warn't no matter, there warn't nothing she'd have to say that would interest him.

Riding, wrangling, and shooting was what we done best and our backsides had got so leathery toting mail a body could strop razors off them, so we hired on to guard wagon trains and run dispatches and handle horses and scout for whichever armies and exploring parties we come upon, and we had a tolerable good time of it. Back home we was Rebs, I guess; out here we mostly worked for the Union, though we warn't religious about it. Fact is, that time back in the New Mexico adventures we started out scouting for the Rebs, who was trying to cut a route through the Territory to California to get at the gold and silver; but we got lost and ended up instead scouting for the Union army and having to shoot at our most recent employers. Tom thought that improved the adventure considerable, adding what he called a pair a ducks, which Becky, if he wrote to her about it, maybe understood better'n me.

One a the Union colonels was a hardshell parson who had such a strong conviction about the afterlife that he believed in shipping all his prisoners off there to populate it, sending along with them all their ponies, mules, grub, garb, weapons, and wagons, just so's they'd feel at home when they got there, he says. He needed a lot a shooting and burning for this holy work and we was volunteered to supply it. Tom was a good soldier and done as he was told. I warn't and didn't always and didn't then. So I was oftenest in trouble while Tom palled around with the bosses. And it was whilst he was setting down with the parson over fresh roasted horse meat and the colonel's private sin supply, as he called his jug of whiskey, that Tom learnt that they was laying out intentions up in Minnysota to hang more'n three hundred Sioux warriors all at the same time. The parson thought this was the splendidest idea since the Round Valley massacres and Tom says it was something he had to see.

Tom loved a good hanging, there warn't nothing that so lifted his spirits, and he never missed one if it was anywheres in the neighborhood. I warned him about getting too close to them things, some day they may decide it's his turn, and he says, "Well, if that happens, Huck, I'll only be sorry I can't watch." And then he grinned under the new mustache he was growing and says, "But you're invited, Huck."

31

The notice of that quality hanging party up in Minnysota had Tom so feverish he couldn't set down, lest it was in the saddle heading north. "Just think of it, Huck! Over three hundred injuns all swinging and kicking at the same time! It'd be something to see! You could say you was THERE!" I druther be able to say I warn't there. Gallows always make me feel powerful uncomfortable and clumsy, like I might stumble and fall into one of them scratchy loops by happenstance. But Tom, like always, had his way, and soon we was making the long trek north.

Tom was afraid we'd be late and miss everything, so we clipped along at a fair pace, but it warn't anything like galloping across the plains. Winter was a-coming on, there was north winds and snow, worse weather than I ain't never seen before or since, not even in the Black Hills. We heaped blankets on us and on our horses and stuck our chins out and blew up at our noses to keep them from freezing up and dropping off. The days was ever shorter and seemed like night, even at noon, and we didn't always know, famous scouts that we was, where we was going.

The people along the way was good to us, though. They fed us and our horses and let us sleep in their barns and pointed us toward the hanging grounds when we was misdirected. They all said they wished they was going with us, and told us horrible stories about what them filthy heathens had done to them and to people they knowed, and some of the stories was maybe true. They was all good Christians and said they prayed they'd hang every last one of them red hyenas, they was just pisoning the earth.

Then come the bad news. They was only going to hang thirty-nine of them; the president had let the rest off. The people was madder'n blazes. The president and his spoilt wife was living high and mighty off in the East somewheres and couldn't understand the feelings out here. They said they ought to make room on the gallows for that ugly string a bones. They was sorry they had voted for him. He had let them down and ruint their Christmas.

It was Tom's opinion that the president was a bumbler who ain't got the brains nor the guts for the job and who was only against slavery because it won him votes. And now that he'd stumbled the country into a war, he was too dumb to know what to do next. When I says that it seems like everybody wants to shoot him, and that'd be a pity, Tom says, "Well, that's just what makes this country so exciting, Huck. Just like in the time of King Arthur, and all them kings in the Bible."

"Was that the same time?"

"Almost. We was born too late, Huck. This is what we got."

I agreed it warn't much and sejested we turn back and go where it was warmer, but Tom wouldn't have none of it. It was still the biggest hanging ever and he wanted to be there, though you could see he was awful disappointed.

When we finally rode in, the sun was already gone down. Tom trotted us straight into town, afeard we might a missed it. A monstrous big gallows stood plumb in the middle of an open square betwixt the main street and the river, and there was crowds with lanterns milling about it in the dark, but the saloons was all closed and everything was stiller than it should ought to be. There was candles in some of the windows. People was dressed up in their Sunday best and some of them was singing happy church songs, but we was pretty sure it warn't a Sunday. Tom was anxiouser than I'd seen him since we left the New Mexico Territory. He was sure we'd fetched up there too late and he was pegging at me for always moving too slow. "You don't have no respect for the BUSINESS of the world, Huck," he says. When he asked if the hangings had already happened, though, they called him a damfool and said you don't hang even injuns on Christmas Day. Christmas Day! We didn't know that. "Happy Christmas!" they said, and we said it back. Tom looked mighty relieved. "After sunup tomorry," they told us. "We're stayin' up all night to git the best places."

We was most about starved, cold to the bone, and dog-tired. We couldn't a-stayed up all night if we was ordered to nor else face a firing squad. Tom was carrying a letter for the preacher of a church in that town, signed by "The Fighting Parson," which described Tom as a hero in the noble battles against Rebs, Indians, and unbelievers, and me as his stable boy, and the preacher welcomed us and fed us a hot stew with something like meat in it and blessed us and prayed over us in his quavery way and let us sleep under our blankets on church pews. He lived in a little room off of it. It was my first time in a church since I was held captive by the Widow Douglas and her sister Miss Watson, churches comforting me about the same as gallows do, though I felt a surge a spiritual gratefulness when I was able to stretch out at full length for a whole night. Tom stayed up to write another immortal tellygram for Becky by lamplight, but without no help from his stable boy.

The next morning, Tom was up and out well before the sun was, but I waked slower and stayed for bread and coffee with the preacher by the light of his whale-oil lamp, setting at his rough-hewed pine

33

table with him. He was scrawny and old, fifty year and more, with stringy gray hair down to his shoulders and dark pouches under his eyes like empty mochilas. He had a way of talking about Jesus and his friends like they was close kin of his, and praying come more natural to him than breathing done. He wore a raggedy black suit and peered over bent spectacles festooning the tip of a nose so thin and bluish it looked like a dead man's nose.

He seen that I warn't in no hurry to attend the day's revelments and, after mumbling a few more praise-the-Lords, he let it out that he had preached against the hangings and all his congregation had upped and walked out on him. He knowed he shouldn't a done it, and he was sorry about it, but he couldn't help it. One of his deacons told him he resked getting lynched himself and he should best get out of town. He would a done, too, but he didn't have no place to go. He'd been waiting for them to come after him ever since and was scared to answer the door when me and Tom knocked the night before. But he was glad that he done so. He wondered now if maybe we could stay and help protect him. He couldn't pay nothing, he says, but he would pray for our souls three times a day, or even up to six times if we wanted.

I told him we'd be leaving before them poor devils was even cold, and he shuddered and muttered that it was an ungodly thing they was doing, and the baby Jesus only a day old. He said them fellows and their families was starving to death. The federal agents wouldn't let them have no food without the guvment paid them and the guvment was too busy and broke fighting a war, so they could just starve, they didn't like them anyway, and it would be the guvment's fault. Them poor people was always getting pushed around and almost didn't have no place to live no more. Finally they got desperater than they could stand and they fought back and, when it was over, hundreds of Santee Sioux was taken prisoner and put straight on trial by the army without any lawyers or jury nor even no one to translate for them so they could know what everyone was talking about. As the preacher laid open the story, his nose flared up in splotches and a kind of sparkly light come into his pale blue eyes. You could see there warn't no hope for him.

The little town set on a shallow river like a shrinked-down version of St. Petersburg back home. The walk to the middle of it shouldn't of took more'n a minute, but there was thousands of people to squeeze past on the streets. The night before, the streets was frozen mud. That morning, with all the tramping of them, they was just plain mud. It was the most people I ever seen clumped up together in one place. Some of them was locals, but most warn't. A few was looking scared, others angry, some was laughing and cussing. The saloons was all shut till after the hangings, but most everybody was carrying flasks under their coats, which they sucked at from time to time and whooped for the pleasure of it. They was having a grand party. I hain't seen nothing like it since in that river town when everybody come running to watch old man Boggs get shot by the Colonel.

The gallows was a giant open box with nooses hanging like Christmas ribbons, ten to a side, and it was set on oak timbers eight foot high so's there'd be room for the bodies to drop without hitting the ground. It also give everybody all the way down to the river a good view when it got light enough. It was the lonesomest thing I ever seen. It turned out from people talking that another prisoner had been pardoned, so there was an extra halter for whoever wanted it, and folks was volunteering each other and shoving them toward the gallows and hee-hawing. They said they better hurry and string up the rest of them devils, or they'd all get off and go back to killing and raping decent white folk again.

I didn't have no trouble finding Tom. He was standing on a special raised platform near to the gallows hobnobbing with the quality. Now and then the crowd let out a big cheer and the man standing alongside of Tom in a black swallowtail coat raised his top hat and smiled and waved at everybody, and Tom smiled and waved too. Tom had trimmed his mustache and scraped his cheeks clean. The polished-up spurs on his boots shone bright as new silver. He was wearing his slouch hat and buckskin shirt and was smoking a seegar somebody must a gave him. He looked a western gentleman all over. When he took notice of me, he made a sign to come up and join him, but I shook my head. I seen all I wanted to see. He said something to the fellow in the hat beside him and stepped down off the platform and made his way over to me. The crowd respected him and opened up to let him through.

"Huck! Where you been? It's about to start! I got us the bulliest place to watch, so close you can almost reach out and touch a body hanging there. But you got to come now. It's starting up!"

I could hear them, somewheres further off, making some awful racket which might a been singing. "I seen you up there with all them high hats and was wondering what lies you had to tell to get invited."

"Lies! Huck, how you talk! I only let them know we was famous scouts and injun fighters from out west and showed them the parson's

35

letter and I mentioned that you was the legendary H. Finn, breaker of wild horses, and all that was nearly mostly true."

You could see the prisoners by then, past the caps of the soldiers standing in two lines leading to the gallows. They was tied up and wearing what looked like rolled-up muslin meal sacks on their heads, which give them a comical aspect. They warn't moving too slow, but they warn't moving too fast nuther. Their faces was painted and they was singing to beat the band, but you couldn't hardly hear them because of all the hooting and hollering of the crowd.

"Who's that big-bug beside you up there, the one been collecting all the cheers?"

"Why, that's the persecuting lawyer, the one who got over three hundred savages sentenced to death. And they would've hanged them all too, he says, if we didn't have such a weak injun-loving president. He says the heathen Sioux has got to be slayed to the last man and anybody who'd spare them is an enemy to his race and to his nation. That fellow ain't had to shoot nobody nor get shot at, but still he's the biggest hero here today. Ain't that something?"

"If that's him, he warn't nothing fair. Them people had been getting badly misused. And they warn't allowed no lawyers nor no—"

"FAIR! Stuff! You've clean missed the POINT, Huck! Ain't NOTH-ING fair, starting with getting born and having to die. THAT ain't fair. But a body can't do no more about it than them poor condamned injuns can. You can only live out what you got as fierce as you can and it don't matter when or where it ends." The prisoners was being marched toward the steps up to the platform. They was still chanting and singing their "hi-yi-yis" and the crowd was still trying to drown them out with whooping and cussing. Some was hollering out church songs. They was all around us and you couldn't hardly hear nothing else. "Besides, Huck, they're only injuns, who are mostly all ignorant savages and murderers and cannibals."

"What? They're all cannibals?"

"Ever last one of them, Huck. Come on now, it's—"

"You sold Jim to cannibals?"

"Well, wait, there's two kinds of injuns, the ones that keep slaves and the ones that's cannibals." The prisoners in their white night-caps was starting up the steps, and folks was growing quiet, letting them sing if they wanted to. "But hurry! This is HISTORY, Huck! You don't want to miss it!"

"Tom? Huckleberry? Is that you?" It was Becky Thatcher, completely out of the blue, pushing through the thick crowds. It took a moment to reckanize her because she'd growed up some and warn't sporting yaller pigtails no more. Tom's jaw dropped like its hinges was broke, and I s'pose mine was hanging too. "My laws! How you boys have changed! All that face hair! That long, stringy beard makes you look a hundred years old, Huck!"

Tom had hauled his jaw back up, but he was struck dumb. He probably hain't never planned on his audience visiting him head on. He turned and walked off without nary a word. Up on the gallows they was unrolling them muslin bonnets into hoods that covered their painted faces. Some of them was holding hands.

"Tom! Wait!" Becky called out, and went chasing after him.

I should a stayed and watched, like Tom said, but that extra noose and the drumrolls was giving me the fan-tods. I seen the Minnysota River in front of me, and it called me down to walk it a stretch like rivers do. It still warn't yet noon and soon as the hangings was over I was ready to saddle up and light out whilst there was still daylight, but Tom was having a high time and I misdoubted he'd want to leave till he'd lined out a few more adventures.

I felt comfortabler down by the shore. A river don't make you feel less lonely but it makes you feel there ain't nothing wrong with being lonely. The Minnysota was a quiet little wash, near shallow enough to walk across without getting your knees wet, but a flat-bottom steamboat run on it, and it was setting out there then with a passel of whooping gawkers on it, watching the hangings through spyglasses. It had started freezing up at the shore, and soon walking across it would be all a body could do.

Past the steamboat landing, the shore was low and woodsy like a lot of the islands in the big river back home, and it got me to thinking about other ways a body might blunder through life. By piloting a riverboat for a sample. That would be ever so splendid, and just thinking on it lifted some my sunk spirits. But probably I warn't smart enough. Well, I could do the loading. Folks running away from the war was saying the whole river back home was on fire and the bullets was flying like mosquitoes in August, but in this nation a body can get shot anywhere, and getting shot on the river beats getting shot in the desert every time.

The day warn't hardly more'n begun when I got back to the church, but it was already growing dark and puckering up like it might snow some more. The preacher warn't around. Maybe he was hiding somewheres from all the right-minded townsfolk. I found a morsel of bread on his pine table and though it was at least a week old and worse even than the hardtack we got fed at the army forts, I borrowed it and went and stretched out on a pew under a heap of blankets to gnaw on it.

The next thing I knowed, Tom was setting there talking to me. I judged it was Tom. He seemed more like a spirit, appearing so sudden like that and in such a place. He had a candle, and the light from it made his face sort of come and go. "What I wanted to tell you, Huck, is that there is two kinds of injuns," Tom says, if it was Tom. "There's the ones who slaughter white folks and roast them for supper, and there's the ones they call friendlies who ain't cannibals. The friendlies respect the white man and try to act just like him, which is why some of them keep slaves and eat with forks, and lots of them is even Christians." I believed Tom like I always done, but I didn't believe him. I was glad he come back, but I didn't know why he'd waked me up to tell me that. Then I seen the others. Becky Thatcher. The preacher. Tom's horse. "Huck, I'm gonna leave you for a time," Tom says.

It turned out him and Becky was getting hitched by the preacher, and me and the horse was the witnesses. Tom was giving the horse to the preacher as pay for marrying them, and him and Becky was taking the steamboat upriver the next day on its final journey of the year to connect up with the big riverboats headed down toward St. Petersburg. "You can come and see us off," he says.

The news shook me, but I done my best not to show it. Nuther me nor the horse said nothing, though the horse wagged his head about like he was looking for the way out. Well, he'd never been to church before and he didn't know how to behave. It sure warn't the place to be dropping what he was dropping, but he didn't know that. Becky had bought some beer with her pappy's money to celybrate the wedding with and after the preacher had gone and took the horse with him, the three of us set there in the church and drunk it. She'd also found some doughnuts and jelly somewheres to go with it. The hotels was jam full, Becky said, but a gentleman give up his room for them. She was staring at Tom like he was the most amazing thing she ever seen.

"You missed something great, Huck, when you left," Tom says. "One a them injun braves starts yelping out that if we found a white man's body with his head cut off and stuffed up his own backside, he was the one who done it. And he beat his chest with his tied-up fists and somehow got his britches down and wagged his naked backside at everybody. Ain't that a hoot?" Becky was blushing and excused

38

herself to step outside a minute and Tom leaned close and says, "I learnt something here, Huck, about the law and how it makes some folks poor and some folks powerful rich and famous. I want me some a that power, Huck. Judge Thatcher will learn me. I'll come back and I'll find you wherever you are and we'll have adventures again. But they'll be better ones."

When they'd left, I blanketed me and Jackson and we headed south.

HUCK FINN'S BANDIT DAYS

When Tom Sawyer left me alone in the West, I carried on like before, hiring myself out to whosoever, because I didn't know what else to do, but I was powerful lonely. I wrangled horses, rode shotgun on coaches and wagon trains, murdered some buffaloes, worked with one or t'other army, fought some Indian wars, shooting and getting shot at, and didn't think too much about any of it. I reckoned if I could earn some money, I could try to buy Jim's freedom back from the Cherokee Nation, but I warn't never nothing but stone broke. The war was still on, each side chasing and killing the other at a brisk pace clean across the Territory, and they both needed a body like me to scout ahead for them, watch over their stock at night, pony messages to the far side of the fighting, clean their muddy boots, and help bury the dead, of which there warn't never no scarcity, nuther boots nor dead.

Out in these parts both armies warn't tangling so much with each other as they was with the natives, who kept getting in their way like mischeevous rascals at a growed-ups' party. I was riding generly on the Northern side because that was where I found myself. They called theirselves Abolitionists and what they was mostly abolitioning was the tribes. Every time they ruined a bunch of them, they ended up with herds of captured ponies, and somebody had to put saddles and bridles on the ones that warn't summerly executed and break them in the white man's fashion, and I could help do that. I s'pose I was having adventures like before, but without Tom to make a story out of them, they didn't feel like it. They was more like a kind of slow dying, and left me feeling down and dangersome.

Fetched low like that, I fell in with a band of robbers, though I didn't want for nothing to rob, except maybe a shot a whiskey or a beer. I'd been hired on to guard a stagecoach from the East on its way up the Oregon Trail to Frisco, hauling a load a mail-order brides for gold miners who'd struck it rich out there, but I fell dead asleep just when the coach was set upon by a masked gang. When the shouting and hallooing begun, I couldn't hardly think where I was or even who I was. The bandits yelled out they don't kill women, it ain't in the books like that, so everybody could just leave their money and julery and weapons and run away and tell everybody they'd been robbed by the Missouri Kid and his murdrous gang, the Pikers, though if anybody wanted to stay and get shot, they could do that.

Whilst the Pikers was busy collecting their riches, I mounted old Jackson, ducked my head, and slid in with the others, but the ladies was mad at me for not trying to save them and they give me away. The bandits grabbed me off Jackson and tied me up, and when the others was galloped off, they begun arguing about what to do with me. Some of them wanted to write a direful warning on my backside with their sheath knives and hang me from a tree for a lesson to passing strangers, others wanted to ransom me for money. "He won't ransom for two cents," one of them says, "and his butt ain't big enough to carve even half a cussword on it. We'll jest have to shoot him." They was all finally agreed that was the best way, and the Missouri Kid he cocked his pistol and asked me what my name was so's they'd know what to write on my gravestick.

When I told him, the others all laughed because of how long it was and hard to spell, but the Kid he staggered back like he'd been smacked in the jaw and says, "Huckleberry Finn! I cain't BELIEVE it! Is that really YOU behind that raggedy beard, Huck? This is MOST amaz'n!" He pulled off his mask to show me a gashly face with a broke nose and one eye whited over and a thick black beard sprouting round a loose scatter a chipped teeth. "It's ME, Huck! BEN ROGERS! Don't you 'MEMBER me? We was in Tom Sawyer's robber gang together, back when we was jest mean little scamps!"

He untied me and give me a happy punch on the arm. Ben Rogers! It did feel good to find someone I knowed out in all that miserable wilderness, even if he was a bandit and a body couldn't hardly reckonize him. "Gol DANG it, Huck!" There was tears in Ben's good eye. He says he's been so horrible lonesome for me and Tom and all the others from back home he most can't stand it, and he begged me to travel with him and his boys for a spell. He says the Pikers only rob from the rich and give to the poor, specially poor orphan children, but they don't know nobody poorer than what they are and they ain't met up yet with no orphans before me, so they mostly give it to theirselves so's not to waste it. "C'mon, Huck! It'll be jest like old times!" Ben says I don't have to do nothing I don't want to, except promise to bury him if he gets killed and be sure to tell everybody back home about the Missouri Kid and what all he done. He says I can add a few stretchers if I want to, and I says I could do that.

So I become a highwayman and me and Ben Rogers rode together for a time, working the Platte River immigrant trails with his Missouri Piker gang, and I helped hold up the kind of wagons and coaches I used to ride shotgun for. Ben and me talked about the fun we had in the old days back on the Big River, and he told me all his adventures since then, saying I should maybe be writing some of them down whilst he could still recollect what he just said. He says he lost the eye when an old prewar pistol backfired on him, but I could say it was because of a fight he got into with a hundred Mexican bandits along the Rio Grande. He says he ain't never been there, but he heard it was as mighty as the Big River and twice as muddy.

I ain't had no adventures since Tom left, so I told him about me and Tom riding the Pony Express together, which made Ben whistle out his beard and say it was the most astonishing thing he ever heard in all his born days. I told him about the Fighting Parson's righteous slaughter of the tribes and about riding northards in the winter with Tom to see all them poor Santees get hung. Ben says he wished he'd seen that, and I says I most wished I hain't.

One evening, when the Pikers was holed out on a woodsy island in the middle of the river, me and Ben moseyed off to a saloon a few miles away that I knowed from the Pony days to have a drink and buy some bottle whiskey for the others. There was thousands a birds fluttering through the twilighty air, making a body restless, and fish was a-jumping and plopping in the still river like they wanted the birds to pay them more mind. The saloon was fuller of loose women than I recollected, and Ben, scratching his black beard, says he had a weakness for their kind and he warn't leaving till he'd got close acquainted with at least six of them. Serviceable ones ain't easy to come by out in the wilderness, he says, so a body had to store up a few extra to fill in for the off days.

We had a good time that night and was tolerable drunk when we rode back, Ben personating a Big River steamboat and its bells, making wide turns on his horse and singing out a load a ting-a-ling-lings and chow-ch-chow-wows, the wolves and coyotes yipping and howling along with him. On the island, though, there warn't nobody singing. All Ben's gang had been murdered by a rival gang. The rivals was called the Boss Hosses and all the corpsed bodies had horseshoe nails hammered into their chests or backsides. Ben cussed and wailed and fired off shots into the trees around. Then we left the island and went back to the saloon because Ben says he has to dunk his sorrows. One of the two rival gangs was Union, the other Confederal. I disremember now which was which, but it probably don't matter none.

We still had some swag left, and Jim had been worrying my mind, so I sejested we go see if we can buy him back from the Indians who bought him. Ben didn't know who Jim was and, when I told him, he says he ain't going to resk his neck for no dad-blame slave. I says it was Tom's idea of a bully adventure, and maybe we might could even turn a profit off him. Ben still warn't convinced, but he finally agreed when I told him how friendly the Cherokee maidens was. Mainly I s'pose he was scared and sad after the massacre of his gang by the Boss Hosses, and just only didn't want to be left alone. I reckoned after he met Jim, he'd like him like I liked him and would forgive him and wouldn't want to sell him back into slavery again.

Ben Rogers warn't no cleverer at hanging on to money than I was and by the time we fetched up at the border of the Cherokee Nation, we only had two dollars left. We spent one of them on a bottle a whiskey to carry along like a gift, and that left us just a dollar. Ben says it warn't near enough and he wanted to go spend it on more practical things like women, but I reckoned a dollar might buy us an elbow or an ear and they could maybe borrow us the rest.

The Cherokee Nation warn't a tribe a feather-headed natives in wigwams. They was all Southern gentlemen, living very high off the hog. They wore puffy silk cravats and stiff high collars and growed magnolia trees and tobacco and had slaves picking cotton in their fields, though I couldn't see Jim amongst them.

The chief come out from his white mansion in his creamy pants and black frock coat, and I raised my hand and says, "How!" and give him the bottle a whiskey. He took one taste, spit it out, and throwed the bottle away.

Ben yelped in protest and run to pick it up. "Tarnation! Who the blazes does that dang barrel organ monkey think he IS?" he roared. I tried to shush him up, but he went right on cussing and hollering and calling that Indian every name he could think of.

I didn't know no Cherokee, so I says to them as clear as I could, "Me looking for slave Negro name Jim."

They all busted out laughing. They took my dollar and passed it around like a joke, give it back to me. "We only accept Confederate money here," the chief says, gripping his coat lapels in both hands and peering down at me like a judge. "You boys Abolitionists?"

"No, sir! That slave belonged to my family back on the river, but he run off on us. My pap and uncle sent me and my cousin out here to try and hunt him down."

"Well, you're out of luck," the chief says. "We reckoned he was a runaway and there might be somebody like you turning up to claim him, so we sold him to some white bounty hunters, and they put him in chains and took him off east."

A little Cherokee girl about twelve years old was smiling up at Ben from behind one of the tall white pillars of the chief's big house. "Hah!" Ben says. "There's one!" She squeaked in fright and run away and Ben went a-chasing after. I yelled at him to come back, we was going now, but he cocked his good eye at me over his shoulder and shouted, "You can see how spunky she is, Huck! Won't take me a minute!"

"You'd better rein in your cousin," the chief says coldly, fingering the little gold cross hanging round his neck.

"That won't be easy," I says. "He suffered a dreadful head wound at Vicksburg near where our families' plantations is, and he's been crazy like that ever since. You can see how he was half blinded by it. I hope, sir, you can forgive him his trespasses."

"I can, but her father probably cannot."

He couldn't. He clove Ben's head in with a tomahawk. They brung the body, throwed it over his horse, and chased us out of there with war whoops and horsewhips and gun shots.

So I rode out in the desert and dug a hole for Ben's remainders and told the hole I'd let everybody back home know about the Missouri Kid. Then I rolled him into it and kicked some dirt in to cover him up and went back to killing buffalos and guarding wagon trains again. My bandit days was over.

THE HANGING OF HUCK FINN
Fourteen Years Later

Gulch history got made by 'lowing me the novelness of a trial, but they didn't lose no time in their charging, convicting, and condamning drills. After my licking, they hauled me up out a the mud and got right to it. Dawn warn't even completely broke. They was dragging me straight to the hanging tree where that country boy was a-dangling, but Eyepatch stopped them and says that warn't sivilized, they had to give testimony and take a vote, and THEN hang me.

Eyepatch he was the persecuter, his pal Bill whose hand I shot was chairman of the jury, and his other pal Pegleg, who was earless and couldn't read or write, was who they give me like a lawyer. Yaller Whiskers was the judge and the jury was all the scoundrels left over, mostly sick red-eyed immigrants just raising up from the mud or crawling out a their shackly wagons, not knowing what they was s'posed to be doing or even where in creation they was, but madder'n hell. To keep order in the court, Eyepatch hired on them two ugly pock-faced robbers who nearly done poor old Deadwood in, and they watched over the trial doings like turkey buzzards with clubs in their claws and their hat brims down over their beaks.

One a the robbers raised up his gold fob watch and says it's time to get the blamed thing over with. Bill told his jury to ca'm down or he'd see personal to them being horsewhipped. There was some loud cussing in objection to his pronouncement, some declaring it was just as toothless as he was and stunk even worse, but Bill fired off some shots into the air with his good hand, and that settled the matter.

Eyepatch shoved a thumb in his waistband and raired back and declared that I was an arched crinimal who was on trial for the gashly Bear-Claw Murder. He held up my good-luck neckless and says they found it fastened like a noose round old Zeb's throat, his both eyes popping their last pop, and all his traps and his packhorse stole, and he asks me if the neckless was mine. I says I give it to Zeb for good luck, and he says to shut up and answer his question: was it mine? I says it was, but—and he cut me off again and says it didn't bring nuther of us much luck, did it? And them loafers all had a good hoot.

I was in a tight place. Zeb's killers was my accusers and judges, but if I raired a fuss and said so, Eyepatch'd just laugh and turn the others loose on me. They was only looking for an invite, feeling monstrous sick and unhappy. I couldn't spy half a friend among them.

"And whar did this string a heathen julery come from, genlmen a the jury? Why, from them filthy iggorant Sooks who the killer has been pallin' round with! You want to know whar your vegilanty rifles has got to? Ask them war-pathin' redskins that give him this neckless in thanks for all he done for 'em! Finn ain't only a cold-bloody murderer, genlmen, he's a traiter to all white Christians everywheres! He's a traiter to YOU'N ME!"

His rising voice had all them rapscallions roused up and it warn't sure he could hold them back if they took after me. Already I was getting punched and kicked by the nearest ones. Worse, Eyepatch was right in parts, I couldn't deny it. Helping Eeteh the way I done so's we'd be free to leave together was a low-down thing. Ain't never done a low-downer thing. But what was the low-downest of all was I warn't sorry for it. I would hive them rifles for him all over again. I only wished I hain't been such a fool as to go and get caught. That was the most low-downest thing I done: letting Eeteh down. I was feeling terrible worried and sorry about him, but at least they warn't passing his head around like a trophy, so maybe he got away.

"And that ain't ALL!" Eyepatch says. "Him and his brother and his dog catched the POX and they didn't TELL no one—did any a you ever hear of it? NO! Them flat-heads went on recklessly spreadin' their mortal sickness round THE WHOLE TERRITORY! They wanted everybody to catch it like they catched it theirselves! Now the brother is dead, the dog is dead, only this KILLER is still a-kickin'! But, genlmen"—he looked around at them all with his glittery one eye—"he only's got JEST ONE KICK LEFT!"

They was all a-whooping and hollering for justice and saying they had to hang me NOW! They had a terrible itch in their pants and couldn't wait no more. Yaller Whiskers had a hammer for a gavel, and he was belting a stump with it like he was trying to split it for kindling, and yelling for them to just hang on, ding-bust it, they'll all get their chance.

"And even THAT ain't all!" hollered Eyepatch above the ruckus. There still warn't much light in the sky. The day was slow at waking up like it was afraid to open its eyes. "He also shot our jury boss when there warn't no warrant for it and ruint his hand so bad the pore man cain't even pan for gold no more! Jest look at it! Hold it up thar, Bill! Ain't that the horriblest mess you ever seen? If Finn ain't been such a bad shot, he would a killt him, cuz he's a natural-born crippler and killer! Why, jest last night he give our feller Gulch citizen Deadwood an unmerciless hiding that peart nigh destroyed the ole rip!"

"That ain't so!" I says, though I knowed better than to say nothing at all. Huck, I says to myself, you ain't never going to learn.

Eyepatch he only smiled his cold gold smile at me and signaled to his jury chairman to go for Cross-Eyes. They fetched the old toothless prospector on his plank and set him down and Eyepatch pointed at me and asked him if I was the one who give him his awful thrashing. Deadwood raired his head an inch or two and aimed one or t'other of his crossed eyes at me, groaned and nodded, and he fell back and they carted him away again. "I cain't hardly believe how any human person could be so despicable crool and mean!" Eyepatch says. "Such a varmint don't DESERVE to live!" Them two robbers was shaking their heads sadfully, like they couldn't believe it nuther.

If all them red-eyed immigrants reckoned I was the one who beat up Deadwood, they also reckoned I doctored him afterward, because when they seen that his bandages was ripped from their own missing shirts, they shouted that if they catched the new-monia and died, there'd be even more murders to hang me for. Others was cussing me out for pisoning Zeb's whiskey, saying I was the worse killer since Ulysses Grant, nor else Robert Lee, they warn't all agreed which one was prime.

Eyepatch says Zeb was toting some a that pison in a fancy box which probably his killer hid there to be shut of it after he stole everything else. When they smelt its horrible stink, he says, they poured it out so's it wouldn't harm nobody never again, hoping only it didn't kill off all the trees.

"You oughtn't a done that," I says. "That was his mother."

"Sure it was," says Eyepatch, "and you're my sister." And they all fell about snorting and hee-hawing.

I asked Pegleg why he don't point out the bullet holes in Zeb's back, which was what killed him, and he spit a gob and says, "What bullet holes?" The old whiskey-maker's body was still a-drooped over the mare's back and them holes was in plain view.

"You can see how desprate he is, yeronner," Eyepatch says to Yaller Whiskers with a meloncholical smile, fingering his badge, "unloosing bare-face lies like that to try'n save his wretchid hide whilst losing forever his pit-black soul."

The jury thought that was the splendidest thing that they ever heard and they clapped their hands together in testimony of it, leastways those of them that warn't back to sleep again or throwing up or drifting off to attend to the biling disturbance in their bellies, grabbing their guts and holding up two fingers to ask Bill's permission.

My lawyer he stuffed a plug of chaw in his jaws and says I should ought to plead guilty. I says I warn't guilty a nothing and I ain't saying I was. "The defender says he's guilty, Judge," Pegleg says, and Yaller Whiskers rapped the hammer down on the tree trunk, and says there ain't nothin' for it, I got to be hanged till I'm completely mortified, the trial was done and over.

They swarmed over me again. I thought I was about to join that rube in the tree and my heart was in my throat, but they fetched me

along to Zeb's shack and throwed me in it. The chinless mule-
toothed prospector who struck the gold fleck the day before was
posted at the door with an old shotgun, looking like he'd only made
it partways into the new day and warn't inclined to go no further. His
mustaches hung like sad stringy curtains around his big front teeth.

The old whiskey shack stunk more'n it commonly done, not only
of sick and privies and stale whiskey like always, but also from a
couple of carcasses laying about and starting to go off. They'd stay
there till somebody decided they wanted the shack for theirselves,
and then they'd get throwed in the woods for the wolves to supper
on. Which was where I was headed. Wolf vittles. My feelings was
sunk low and such thoughts warn't of a nature to raise them up
again.

Mule Teeth was soon tipping back in a chair, taking a snooze, the
shotgun leaning against the wall, and I judged I could walk out past
him and just keep on going. He half opened one bloodshot eye under
his floppy hat brim and seen me calculating. "I know what you're
thinkin'," he drawls from under his two monster teeth. "I don't sejest
you try it. I don't give a keer, one way or t'other, and I ain't goin' to
stop you, but they's a posse a hongry bounty hunters out thar jest
a-waitin' for sumthin live to shoot at." He raised the other eyelid
halfway up and struggled slow to his feet like his bones was made a
lead. "C'mere. Look at behind all them wagons and trees. See 'em?"
I seen them. All watching my way. "I don't reckon you done what
they say you done, and I'm nation sorry for you, but there ain't nothin' I kin do, nor not you nuther."

"It warn't me who killed Zeb. It was that one-eyed persecuter and
his pals who done it."

"I know it," he says, sinking dozily back into the chair. He slurped
noisily and says he judged the Cap'n was setting to take over here,
him and the judge together,and my hanging was their ticket for that,
so it didn't matter whether I done nothing crinimal or not. Mule
Teeth was right. The rule a law warn't about such matters. Eyepatch
and his pals was rich now after robbing Zeb, and they was calculating how to use the law to get richer. Mule Teeth says that like enough
they was the ones who robbed all my goods too, because there warn't
nothing left down by the crick except the tepee poles.

Mule Teeth called Eyepatch Cap'n on account of that's what he
was in the Confederal Army in the recent troubles. He lost his eye at
the Battle of Shiloh, and he come out west after that to help the Rebs
cut a trail to California through the New Mexico Territory to where

the gold was. Leastways, that's what Mule Teeth says that Eyepatch says. Me and Tom was scouting down there for the Rebs back then so, until we got lost and ended up scouting for the Union instead, us and Eyepatch was maybe traveling together. But though I seen plenty one-eyed bandits like old Ben Rogers, I ain't got no recollection of any long-haired one-eyed captains. Lying come easy to Eyepatch. Most probably he was a plain deserter, living off of robbing and killing like other ordinary runaway soldiers.

When Mule Teeth warn't drowsing under his hat, him and me talked away the morning. It was my last one and it seemed as how there must probably be liver things to do with it, even penned up in a smelly old shack, but I couldn't think of them. It was just only a morning like any other morning and it slipped by like they all done.

The bounty hunters was still outside, watching the open door, hoping I'd make a run for it, so I held my nose and stayed back in the shadows in case them fellows' fingers got itchy. Mule Teeth told me about having to pay extra for prostytutes on account of his teeth, and asked me what it was like to kiss a woman because ain't none a them ever allowed him to do that. I says I ain't done much kissing neither, because there warn't nothing romantic about most a the women I knowed, except for one maybe, and my Crow wife she didn't have no nose and was uncomfortable about a body getting anywheres close to the area.

"You had a squaw?"

"For a while, till she cussed me out one day and walked out a the tepee and never come back."

"You lived with injuns? That's innaresting," he drawls and slurps again. "They say a squaw's business runs sidewise 'stead of fore'n aft. Is that how you found it?"

"No, just ordinary," I says. I was worried to know more about Eeteh and Ne Tongo, but this didn't seem the right way to get at it. "Old Man Coyote, though, had a wife with one that was like the mouth of a coiled-up snake that swallowed you down in like a whirlpool."

"That must of been fun. But who was Old Man Coyote?"

"They have stories about him. A friend told me."

"Injun friend?"

"Fellow who used to help the owner of this shack trade with the tribes."

"The one you murdered. Or they say you did."

Out a-front the shack, men was hacking away at the foot of the hanging tree, making the dead country jake jiggle and dance on his rope like a puppet till his straw hat fell off. Mule Teeth says they was chopping the tree down to knock up a gallows there. "The persecuter and the judge reckon it ain't possible to sivilize a place without you got a proper insterment to hang a body. The coffin-maker's busy a-buildin' it, so you still got a little time. Wisht I could find somethin' to help you pass it better, but we pretty much drunk the camp dry last night, and I'm anyways dead sick from it and ain't got no stake left to buy nothin'. Don't even have a dang chaw to share."

I asked him what he done with the gold fleck the yaller-whiskered land surveyor helped him find. "I give it back to him," he says. Yaller Whiskers was setting up a table in the street and there was already a line of immigrant prospectors waiting to buy one of his hand-drawn survey maps. "The judge only borry'd it to me to set out his bony-fydies, as he called 'em, so's he'd fetch a fair price for his maps." Yaller Whiskers was drawing pictures fast as he could, but new-comers was rolling in by the minute, he couldn't keep up. He was finally only putting a few marks down on each page, and yelling cusswords whenever a body complained.

Meantimes, the tree with the rube still hanging in it got cut down and dumped upstream in the Gulch where all the other dead trees was. The coffin-maker had already built sections of the new gallows, and now he set to hammering it all up together where the tree had stood. A lantern-jawed picture-taker in a billed cap and black frock coat was setting up his camera in front of it.

The bran-new street out a-front was so packed with immigrant miners, wagons, horses, and oxen, you couldn't hardly move. The men was all excited and grinning ear to ear about the chance of watching a body get stringed up. Fingers was pointed at me in Zeb's shack. They didn't know who I was nor what I was s'posed to be hanged for, but that warn't no matter. Eyepatch was right: the gallows was going to make the Gulch more sivilized-looking.

A preacher come to see me about my soul, and how I could save it by fessing up to murdering old Zeb even if I ain't done it. It was that chubby land-surveyor-banker-dentist-judge Yaller Whiskers again, only now he was a preacher. There warn't nothing that fellow couldn't do if he set his mind to it. He was wearing the hanged man's floppy straw hat, which was the same color as his bushy whiskers. With his dusty clothes, he made a body think of a small round haystack with eyes. He wanted us to pray together to some of the same dead people the Widow Douglas and her sister Miss Watson was always carrying on with, and see if we couldn't strike a deal with the Lord about my soul before I danced the hempen jig, as he called it, and flew off to Providence, or some place even more unpleasanter.

"Praying ain't never worked for me, Reverend," I says, "and I ain't got no soul to barter with. Maybe I used to have one, but if I did, it got drownded on the Big River, nor else it was stole by a couple a royal bamboozlers like yourself who didn't have none a their own."

The preacher he got a little hot under the collar then like he done when he was a judge and says he won't be talked at so disrespectable. He says he should a sentenced me to a hundred lashes besides only getting hanged—he would a gratefully laid on the lashes himself, before, during, or after the hanging. He was going to go right now and fetch his horsewhip to the ceremonials, in case he got a chance to use it, and, given my rascally nature, he allowed he surely would.

The more Yaller Whiskers carried on, the madder he got. He remembered me of old pap when he went to ripping and cussing like all fury, swearing to cowhide me directly as he got sober, and that made me smile, which made Yaller Whiskers so sore, he whiffed his pudgy fists around a-front my face till his cheeks was red and he throwed the rube's straw hat at me and kicked at my knees and yelled, "What're you laughin' at, you goddam sneak-thief injun lover?"

Then he ca'med down and picked up the straw and set it back on, saying he was sorry, and he went back to being a preacher again. Sin always got him riled up like that, he says, he just didn't have no tolerance for it. But he had to learn himself more Christian forbaring, it went with being a man a the cloth, he says, though he probably didn't know no more'n I done what cloth he was talking about.

It was nigh noon. Yaller Whiskers and Mule Teeth tied my hands behind my back and took me by the elbows and walked me out to the gallows, tromping through the gumbo and the thickening crowds. All the busy hammering and sawing and hollering stopped when we stepped out a the shack, and people begun running toward the gallows, pushing and a-shoving to get the up-frontest places. I warn't customed to being much noticed of a rule, but they was all gaping at me and didn't want to look at nothing else. Some was laughing or shouting out cusswords, but most was only staring with their eyes wide open like they was trying to eat me with their eyes.

That army drummer was at it again, banging out a march, and we was stepping along to it, the crowds opening up as we come on them. Eyepatch was a-waiting for us by the gallows in his black shirt, his black bandanna knotted round his head, his gold teeth and earrings and tin star glinting in the midday sun. He looked like he might a washed his hair for the grand occasion, nor else he only greased it. His pals Pegleg and Bill was standing longside him, Bill with a nasty three-tooth sneer on his face.

The lanky coffin-maker in the tall black hat was there, looking monstrous proud of what he'd made. One of his empty body boxes was propped up against the contraption, and the picture-taker was aiming his camera at it. So I warn't going to be throwed into the Gulch, after all. I was going to be a famous murderer and bandit with white eyes and a stretched neck, laying in a pine box. Maybe they'd even get to see me back in St. Petersburg.

The preacher he says he'll ask for mercy because of middlegating circumstances, if he could think of any. Though I knowed it wouldn't make no matter, I hoped Mule Teeth might furnish some. "We fetched you the prisoner, Cap'n," Mule Teeth says, and when Eyepatch asks him if I repented of my vilence whilst he was guarding me, Mule Teeth says I did not. "Fact is, Cap'n, he bragged about it, goddamming everybody and you in partickler. He's a liar and a traiter and he pals around with hoss-tile hucksters. Got a squaw with a business that sucks a body in like quicksand." That done it. Like my mean old pap used to say, it's the ones who talk lazy and drawly you got to watch out for. Eyepatch nodded. It was all up for me.

It was earless Pegleg who took over then and led me up the steps. The drummer had stopped his pounding and was commencing a drumroll. The drumroll was scary, but warn't near so as the wooden peg knocking loud and hollow up the stairs ahead a me. Whilst climbing them, I recollected that crazy injun in Minnysota who Tom said dropped his pants and wagged his naked behind at all the gawkers. I wished I could do something owdacious like that, but I was too scared and downhearted. I didn't never want to die, and now that it was happening I didn't want it more'n ever.

There was a powerful lot of steps to climb. The picture-taker in the long frock coat had moved his camera on its long skinny legs and was watching me through it. That chap with the fiddle was twanging away sorrowfully and whining through his nose something about jumping off into the other world. I was thinking about Ne Tongo, who won't understand what happened to me or where I went off to. How do you explain that to a horse?

From up on the platform I could see all the tents and lean-tos, the muddy streets, the half-built shanties and storefronts, the long line of incoming wagons stretching back into the hills. Many of the newcomers was hopping out a their wagons and running toward us with big grins on their faces. Others was galloping in on horses. They didn't know what was happening, but they didn't want to miss nothing.

Pegleg stood me onto the trapdoor and fitted the scratchy rope round my neck. "Kin I have the next dance?" he asks with a mean grin. I warn't able to grin back. I was feeling desperately lonely and wished there was somebody to hold my hand. But I was all alone. Did you ever notice, Eeteh says to me one day, how making a world always begins with loneliness? The Great Spirits could invent all the suns and moons and rivers and forests they wanted, but it warn't never enough. They was still lonely. There warn't nobody to talk to and nothing was happening. So they had to make us loafers to kill so's to liven up the passing days.

One of the arriving immigrants was galloping in on a high white horse with a passel a friends behind him. He was fitted out in bleached doeskin and a white hat, with white kid gloves and a red bandanna tied round his throat, gleaming silver spurs on his shiny boots. He had big bushy mustaches ear to ear and long curly hair, twinkling eyes. Puffing on a fat seegar. Coming for a laugh. "HANG HIM QUICK!" Eyepatch shouted. Pegleg drawed his pistol with one hand and reached for the lever with t'other and I dropped. My throat got snagged and then there was a shot and I kept on dropping, landing hard on the ground under the gallows. Then more shots, and Pegleg come falling through the trapdoor and landed on top of me. That seegar-smoker must a shot the rope!

Only one man I knowed could do that. He was grinning down at me from his white horse. "Hey, Huck," he says, flicking some ash off his seegar. It was Tom Sawyer! His own self!

Useful Knots and How to Tie Them
Rachel Blau DuPlessis

THE MEDIUM

There is yearn, then there is yarn.
A strand is strung
from a number of yearns
twisted together.

Rope is twined
in a long building
by pulling cordage
out of sheer matter in
the endless twists of
how it matters, that it matters.
And what matters.
Space stands in for time.
Stringently.

THE OVERHAND KNOT

The overhand is
the simplest and smallest
of all knot forms
and the beginning
of many more difficult ones.

INSTRUCTION. OR FAILURE

This is one more lump
of the humped rope
inarticulate, snarled.
Stand ambiguates bight,

end skeins twist.

Quick or careless tightening
results in a useless tangle.
If you do not follow the pattern,
you may get a different knot.
Even no knot at all.

OLDER TRACTION POINTS

Climbing
up fibrous ladders
and rope sways together,
you, and me, and others, specific,
needy, all unsortable,
there the ropy sway of acrobatic mountaineers
corded together, strung in a line,
toggled, cramponed.

And the climbing.
And the holding.
Bare ruinous coirs
threading athwart time.
There is everything to begin.
But it seemed as if nothing can or will or could
(tense problem)
(begin).

COMRADESHIP

It is node of
tightened snags;
is a knot garden;
is a splay of quipu;
is many-colored shimmers drawn
with embroidery silks
around padded trapunto;
is "a more or less complex, compact intersection
of interlaced cord, ribbon, rope, or the like."

It is a power bundle
of peerless conjure and conjecture.
Impossible to do one metaphor only
from the sheer joy.
Of being like this.

But eventually one wakes
shaking out those silver streamers
from the nub, examining
their beauty, regarding them
suspiciously. Yet always
a little fondly.

Other moments
stayed vivid
in such flashes
as shoelaces.
Shoelaces!
What little tie will hold
when you are brought
to this edge?

THE FISHERMAN'S KNOT

Strings follow knots,
knots demand strings,
and journeys capitulate
to restlessness.
Sounds start how-where
in birds, chk-warble,
or in the silences
of fish flickering,
but they exist for you only
when you hear them.

Unless you begin thinking
of real birds, real fish,
actual water enchained and linked.
Of really being here.
Then your sense

of implication becomes
quite a bit more complicated.

Now seeing at least two
separate lines clearly,
or, as *you* say, clearly,
to tie, lay the two ends together
each pointing in the opposite direction.
Tie an overhand knot in the end of each
around the standing part of the other.

When drawn tight
the two knots slide together
and will not slip.
This will hold different strings
and extend them by
reciprocal pressures along the juncture.
The many times we want to use this
might surprise you.

THE CAT'S-PAW

A forty-five-foot train runs like a river
from her Red Dress.
Foldings and loopings of material
matter
more than rufflings,
though there are rutchings
aplenty.
Then there is sheer
length to consider.

One is forced to reflect
on a Dress that Big.
Extent is flooded by its flag-bright color,
a red paint poured, pooling in sunlight.

If I were an engineer
I would schedule
site assessments,

public hearings,
maybe (though conceding
nothing) recalibrations.
But even without them, the ambition is clear.
A high wind roars in the valley of the seam.

The Cat's-Paw is a hook hitch for heavy loads.
One grasps the two bights held well apart
twisting each away from you.
The strength occurs
in the double twist
and the oppositional direction
of their bearings.

The two loops thus formed
are brought together, tensile, vivid,
and placed over one hook.

THE WALK ON A BLOCKED PATH

Itchy.
Just as the raw brown twine
with the key is, on my neck.
I walked along the obstructed path.
There was a drop on one side.
Twig piles and shagged-off branches
had been left thickly on the path
to prevent more erosion.
But this
became a further impediment, tangle
crisscrossed and cracking under foot.

Snakes hid in the side patches,
I, banging with a peeled stick
from the same woods
in which I was enmeshed.
I tripped. I pitched down.
I blamed myself.

Rachel Blau DuPlessis

Being

a) in the middle
of a woods, a
wayward, I
would design a way
with words,
but only stuttering
way-off words.

b) steadfast with the key still
hung around my neck
the twine itching
as I walked the key
to the hidden mailbox
with its little keyhole.

THUS

The two struggled by design.
Neither could see the witless
witness, affirm the with-ness they denied,
though they were two ends
of the same rope,
wrestling with
themselves
locked into, snarled up, and
roused beyond by power and by
seeking it. Or seeking
to be overcome
by contact and searing.

CROSS AND TWIST

Is this possible—
being given, and driven by the knot?
this set of tracks
these woven intersections, intricate lines,
the turn and fold,
and the monumental desire and failure?

The ropes are scrolls
the scrolls are ropes,
Their rubric words remain bright red.
And these almost invisible bumps and swellings?
Nodules of commentary.

ANY REGRETS?

It was all necessary,
the desire, the loss, the itch, the anger,
the impossible push,
the separated cartilage.
And what now?
Acknowledge
that it was all necessary?
Or just refuse to concede?

STRING THEORY

Inside there are three strong stands
on which one's past is tied:
carrick bend
(for heavy ropes
that cannot be tightened by hand)
sheet bend
(unties easily
without injuring rope fibers)
and sheepshank
(used to shorten rope).

So bright and clear
in this billowy air,
there is no sense of solidity,
no sense of crux or knot.
Yet it is all knot,
knots to which one is apprenticed,
knots pulling contradictions tight,
spun solids spiraling into void,

wads of matter,
the efficiency of the splice,
the memorable torque:

it was all there
although also all air.

ANOTHER METAPHOR

In the closet
the basket falls over.
nineteen spools of silky thread—
all the faded thread that chance had left here—
have rolled into a corner

noisily on those wooden spools
the way they
knock about and ricochet
down the already tangled
warp of strangeness
pink notions, green cotton
mercerized,
thick black coat thread
a few pearly shirt buttons thrown in,
a hook, an eye, an allegory, a clew,
ball of old yarn rolled out
and traveling toward the center of the labyrinth.

Yards of yarn
loops of line,
texted and tangled
the wild loose threads, their unintended knots.
How did they manage such a colorful mix
from random thread spools knocking together in corners?
How could we not honor this urge for entanglement?

And intransigence—the thing that ties double knots.
Meaning that: first things are tied, then untied,
first raveled, then unraveled,
a joke

like flammable and inflammable.

So bound by the twine
that unwound in this labyrinth
quickened by the mystery of maze
we get tightened anew in the center of words,
clotted like blood and snared at the core
of former days.

—June–October 2007; November 2015

NOTE. The found language in this poem, including its title, is from the pamphlet "Useful Knots and How to Tie Them," a free handout from the Plymouth Cordage Company in Plymouth, Massachusetts, copyright 1946, and distributed by Louis E. Helm Marine Company in Wethersfield, Connecticut, in the 1950s. "A more or less complex, compact intersection of interlaced cord, ribbon, rope, or the like" is the dictionary definition of knot from *The American Heritage Dictionary*. The Red Dress that makes an appearance in one section is by the artist Beverly Semmes, 1992, seen in the Hirshhorn Museum and Sculpture Garden, Washington, DC.

North Brother Island: cottage overlooking East River.
Courtesy NYC Municipal Archives.

Where You Go I'll Go
Elizabeth Gaffney

15 SEPTEMBER 1907
Blue and bright white, a sparkling day. I am out of gray yarn.

SOMETIMES SHE DAYDREAMED of bodies washing ashore. Or maybe those weren't dreams.

The boat had sunk three years ago, before she ever came to the island. A thousand women and children drowned or burned when the steamer *Slocum* went down just off North Brother Island, a thousand souls, a thousand ghosts.

She glanced over to see if Tyrone could see them too, smell them, but he slept on, twitching and farting.

She stared out the windows at the riverscape, vaster than any possible from the city. Not quite the coast of Ireland, what with the oil tanks across the water, in the Bronx, but the air was damp enough to let the skin breathe. And here she sat, leading a life of indolence, when her mother'd never rested an hour straight.

It was a dream, a life of ease—if only she had chosen it.

It was a nightmare, a foreign prison—which might have been tolerable if only Freddie were with her. They might have enjoyed the quiet together, except for those sodden limbs scudding. And if only Carrie Bowen weren't out there among them, little Carrie, skipping along the shore like it was the coast of Maine, counting the bodies the same way she used to count anything—lobster boats, seagulls, lady's slippers.

Four hundred eighty, four hundred eighty-one, four hundred eighty-two. Mary tried to calculate how many minutes it would have taken the child to count to a thousand.

She wondered how she'd survive without company other than ghosts. Reading, knitting, housekeeping—for what?

They said she'd sickened people. Clearly a lie, for only such a very few of the people she'd cooked for had ever taken ill. People did take sick just on their own, after all. If the miasmas got to them. It wasn't the cook's fault. It was the doctors'. They were the ones who couldn't help when Carrie was stricken, and Mary'd been made the devil. Now here she was, forbidden to cook or break bread with anyone.

There were twelve windows, nine panes each, 108 little window-lets. She'd counted them and she'd cleaned them with sheets of *The New York Times*. Flashing in the sun, the windows wrapped around three sides of her one-room cottage. You couldn't ask for a brighter, airier place, but somehow the light just made the loneliness louder. She looked at the sweater in her basket, still short an arm and no yarn left. More was on the way but for now she got out her tatting instead and peered through loops of white thread at her own hand.

2 NOVEMBER 1907
Greenish and greasy, like dishwater, overcast. A strange woman knocking at my door.

She peered through loops of white thread—the curtain she'd tatted—at a woman's face.

"I've brought you a parcel. May I come in?"

"Set it on the step," said Mary.

"I'd like to speak with you too, if I might. Would you walk with me to the ferry landing? It isn't cold."

"Ah, so they haven't given up on the samples, after all. You shy or just tactful?"

It made her sick, what the doctors wanted from her, a scoop of her own waste every day.

"I don't know anything about samples, Miss Mallon. I'm nothing to do with samples."

"What *are* you to do with then?" Mary wrapped her stole more firmly around her shoulders.

"I work at the hospital—I'm a nurse—but only here to be sociable. I heard about you. And, well, you see, I've already had the typhoid myself."

Mary looked at her, pondering whether she was genuine. "Have you then."

A warm day, for fall. The stones crunched under their feet.

"I'm on the children's ward. I gather you've worked with children."

"The families I worked for had them, so I fed them, washed them, scolded them, and put them to bed at night."

"We have many children here, not enough matrons."

"I thought you were a nurse."

"I am a nurse. They need more care than nurses can give."

"You're asking something of me?"

"We could use your help with lessons, reading to."

"You don't worry I'll make them sick? "

"They're sick already. And you're not going to cook their meals. What they need is kindness."

"Who says I'm kind?"

"What you are is *here*. Here when their mothers can't be."

"I've never been sick a day in my life, you know. I'm not sick now. I'm as strong as an ox. It's madness that I'm here."

"You're clearly in good health. And of course you don't want to be here. But consider this: it's a gift to the children that you are. That's the wonder of it."

"Some wonder, locked up on quarantine island."

"You must be so bored, with just your needlework, a few magazines."

"I've got Tyrone, haven't I?" Mary nodded her chin at the yellow dog who loped along beside them.

"By the way, I'm Addie. Adelaide Offspring."

"Are you then? Good for you. Don't guess I need any introduction."

"No, Miss Mallon. You're known to me. That's why I came."

2 JANUARY 1908
Cold, pale sky, like shreds of white lace on the ceiling of the heavens.

"I came because I wanted to say how pleased I am. How well it seems to be going—your work with the children."

"Milk and two sugars," muttered Mary.

"Why, yes, that's right. *Thank you.*"

"Never forget how a person takes her tea," said Mary.

"So, how are the children? Are you enjoying them?"

"Ah, well. Most of them are brats, but that's children for you. I like the one called Gwennie. She has pluck. I'd like to see her make it home."

Addie smiled. "She might yet."

"Best thing for her'd be to go home to her mother."

"The rules are hard. Speaking of which, how stands your appeal?"

"Wrote to the judge again. Told him I sailed to this country for freedom, not to live in a jail when I've done no crime."

"Any reply?"

"None yet."

65

"It's smells good in here. Baking?"

"Raisin tart," said Mary, thinking of Carrie Bowen, whose favorite it had been. And then she hesitated. "Care for a slice?"

Addie swallowed. "Yes, thank you. I think I would."

When she finished it, she smiled. "Would you cut me another, Mary? It's delicious."

25 JANUARY 1908
Sky is oatmeal today, dull and lumpy, snow coming.

"Won't you cut me another, Mary?" begged Gwennie, holding up the chain of paper dolls, little boys in short pants joined at the toes and the hands. "But make it girls this time—girls in dresses, with pigtails!"

"Oh, you! Girls are more difficult, you know."

But she'd cut out girls for Carrie Bowen. She could do them just as deftly as boys. Her reluctance came from the last chain she'd made for Carrie, the one the girl had colored in so carefully, when she was ill—collars on their dresses and rosy cheeks and all, perfect in a way that paper dolls weren't meant to be.

Mary had crumpled them and watched them flare up in the grate when she was cleaning the sickroom afterward.

"*Please*, Miss Mary, won't you try?"

So Mary folded a sheet of newsprint like an accordion and took up her sewing scissors. Snip, snip. It didn't take her long. She handed one end to Gwennie, took the other herself, and shook the cutouts gently till they bridged the gap between them like a merry gang of school-girls, heels and skirts flying in the wind.

"When can *I* go out and play, Mary?"

"Soon enough. It's too cold now. First you need to rest, rest and drink your broth, little one."

Gwennie was feverish and shallow of breath. Her hands were translucent. She couldn't make it to the toilet without help, much less go outdoors. She was as trapped and alone as Mary.

No visitors. No visitors at all to North Brother Island. Only in-mates—patients, doctors, nurses, and workers. Thank God for Addie, Mary thought, remembering how annoyed she'd been the first day she came. Addie had given her the chance to work with the children. And Addie sat with her as the sun dropped behind the pipes and tanks of the oil yard and the shadows rose—keeping at bay the ghosts of the *Slocum*. Now they came only on the weekends when Addie wasn't there to discuss the news or play backgammon.

Mary didn't know why she enjoyed the games with Addie so much. Addie always let her win, like she was some child. Every time, she told Addie, *Play for the win, this time.* And Addie would start out as if she had a strategy. Mary'd think she had a chance of losing. But every time Addie would pass up some obvious move. She couldn't bring herself to send Mary, so trapped there on North Brother Island, back to the start.

So why was it so suspenseful, when it wasn't a surprise?

2 MARCH 1908
White ice rimming dark channels. Gwennie passed last night.

It wasn't a surprise. She'd been vanishing by degrees all winter. Coughing her useless cough, too weak to get anything up. Her mother never got to say goodbye, but Mary did. Gwennie looked an angel, dressed to be buried with the best of Mary's tatted collars round her neck.

Addie and Mary walked all that morning, round and about in as good a circuit as they could hope to do on their rotten little island with its overgrown shores and icy crusts of snow, not to mention the raspberry prickers, which seemed to have been sharpened by the ice.

Back at the cottage, Mary opened Addie's basket: more white thread and more gray wool, for more sweaters for more orphans—and the Sunday paper and also a piece of mail she'd picked up at the office.

It was Freddie. He'd been in jail. *I dreamed of you, when I found the wherewithal to dream,* he wrote. So now he knew what it was like to be cooped up. When she finished the letter, she thought a moment, then read it aloud to Addie.

"I envy you," she said.

"How could you envy me?"

"Because you have Freddie."

"I haven't his flesh. I haven't his child. I haven't even his company, damn it," she said. "All I have is the thought of him. No—all I *really* have here, Addie, is you."

"And I have you," said Addie, reaching for her hand.

Mary knew the others on the island shunned Addie now.

*

67

Elizabeth Gaffney

Rain smacks windowpanes, night seems to have crept up into afternoon—and yet it is strangely warm.

"For you, Mary," said Addie as she folded her sopping umbrella, extending a canvas bag.

The bag was heavy, and Mary smiled. Her *Ladies' Home Journal* and whiskey, the one notable absence in her weekly box of provisions.

"Help pass a dreary afternoon, won't it now?" asked Addie.

"I'd take a dram to scare off the damp."

"What are you making today, Mary?"

"Just socks, socks for the children. I had nothing but remnants, and socks are the thing to get rid of them. Now I can get back to sweaters."

"What about a blue for once? Or red?"

"Gray's what the nuns require. It's suitable for either sex, and the children have nothing to squabble over, if they're all alike, now do they? But if you brought me some red, I'd knit *you* a shawl. Red would become you."

Addie blushed. "I could hardly stand it if a shawl for me took you away from your calling."

"I bore of gray."

Addie smiled. "To red then!"

"To red!"

They laughed and topped up their glasses. Then Mary put the needles down and shook out the paper. After a few minutes, she looked up.

"Another ferry wrecked."

"What? Where?"

"Oyster Bay. But they saved all souls. Every one."

"Why, it's a miracle then."

"How is it that some gain by miracles and others are neglected?"

"You'll have to ask your nuns."

"They've got no answers, just more nonsense to do with Job. I'd sooner ask Tyrone."

They looked at the dog, licking his groin, and laughed. Mary reached down to scruffle his jowls, and he groaned.

*

19 FEBRUARY 1910
Pink, orange, blue, and flaming gold. Is it possible I'll miss this view?

The ferry heaved against the pilings of the small pier. Addie stood beside her, watching.

Mary thought about the letter that had come, granting the thing she'd dreamed of—freedom. Now she felt queasy.

The ghosts of the *Slocum* were there in the wavelets that broke against the shore. She was glad to be leaving them behind. But as for the ghost of Carrie Bowen, Mary knew it would come with her, wherever she went.

The violent dawn had dimmed to a simple blue-sky day streaked with thin clouds. A fish hawk screeched.

Her trunk was packed and buckled, and the hospital porter wheeled it ahead of her to the gangway. Tyrone was on a lead by her side.

"I never thought it'd be you leaving *me*, Mary." Addie's eyes on the far shore.

"We can see each other anytime now. Weekends, even!"

"Of course we can. We can meet in the city. I'll take the bus."

"Or I will."

But they both of them knew they wouldn't.

Mary was going home. To Fred, Fred, who had waited for years and was waiting even now, on the other side of the water.

Would he still love her, three years older and a different person than she'd been when the Health Department snatched her? Would she feel the old yearning when she smelled his skin?

"Mary?"

Mary turned and Addie kissed her, for the first time in all those three years. And there it was: a yearning right through her body, right where it didn't belong.

As the ferry backed away from the pier, Addie wrapped the red shawl round herself and waved. Tyrone barked, and Mary barked too: a word, a farewell, almost a plea.

15 JANUARY 1915
Ferry ride back to North Brother took five minutes, a lifetime. Sun beat the cold away. And I am back with the bodies—and her.

Addie.

As she made her way from the ferry with her carpetbag in hand, she remembered walking arm in arm with Addie on the pebbled path, their skirts swishing as they strode. She'd dreamed so many nights of Addie.

What if those weren't dreams?

She peered from outside the door through the loops of white thread of the curtain she'd tatted years before. Inside, everything exactly as she'd left it, just dustier.

"I came back," she said to Addie that afternoon.

"Oh, Mary," said Addie and wrapped her in her arms.

But later, it was, "How could you do it? You cut their lives short just to work."

"I didn't do anything. It was no surprise, that outbreak, not with the conditions there. It wasn't ever my fault."

"But Mary, a lying-in hospital? You swore you wouldn't work as a cook."

"I did it for you," she whispered.

Addie groaned, the red shawl dangling slack from her shoulders.

Mary thought of Freddie with his rough beard and whiskey tongue. At least he believed in her innocence.

In the slapping tide, the ghosts of the *Slocum* were joined by Carrie Bowen and a new row of women great with child.

"Addie?" Mary pleaded. "It wasn't me. It isn't true. It can't be."

And after a time, Addie replied, "No, of course not, Mary. It's madness."

"*Madness*," said Mary

"I've missed you, my darling," said Addie quietly and took Mary's hands.

Mary looked up.

NOTE. Mary Mallon was quarantined on North Brother Island from 1907 to 1910, after being identified as an asymptomatic typhoid carrier and the cause of several out-breaks in and around New York City. On North Brother Island, she met and was befriended by Adelaide Jane Offspring, a nurse who worked at the quarantine hospital. Mallon repeatedly petitioned in writing for release from custody and was eventually granted her freedom in 1910, on the condition that she never again work as a cook. In 1915, however, during a typhoid outbreak among the patients at the Sloane Hospital for Women, she was discovered working in the kitchens under the name of Mrs. Brown. Mallon, who never believed she was a vector of the disease, was arrested and returned to her cottage quarantine for the remainder of her life. The friendship between Mary Mallon and Adelaide Offspring lasted from 1907 to Mallon's death on the island in 1938. Offspring, who was retired by then, returned to the island to nurse Mary Mallon in her last week of life.

Roll for Initiative

Andrew Ervin

I SET UP MY SCREEN and get out my maps and dice. "Roll for initiative," I say.

A good dungeon master doesn't kill the players in his charge. He lets them kill themselves. That's how I see it anyway. I don't mean to suggest that I'm a great DM. On the contrary, if the last three weeks have taught me anything it's that I don't know what I'm doing. I never should have agreed to this.

Having the party sacrifice their own lives—be it through inaction or poor decision-making—will be the only way to end this reunion. It will also provide the illusion of free will while in actuality I've been in charge of their fates the entire time.

I am sitting at the head of my dining-room table. To my right sit Jamin and Carlo and across from them is the new guy, Gregor. He lives at the end of the street. Dig Doug is at the opposite end of the table.

Jamin's a dwarf fighter and Carlo rolled a half-elf wizard. Gregor is playing a wood elf rogue and Dig Doug is a human cleric. They will all be dead soon.

All the lights are on and the detritus of five pizzas covers the table. Gregor is eating a slice with a knife and fork. I'm on my second IPA or maybe my third. Moira has taken the boys to a neighbor's house to use the pool and watch movies on an outdoor screen. They know that daddy is a big nerd.

Dig Doug has eaten enough of Moira's hummus to spackle the garage. He will die first.

For tonight's session I found my copy of the "Queen of the Demonweb Pits" module in the attic and spent a few hours redrawing parts of it because Carlo has probably committed every word to memory. Instead of spiders I have skeletons. The Demonweb is now a series of catacombs. Using graph paper I remade the Spidership into a skull shape. Because I didn't run them through "Vault of the Drow" first I will need to fudge the start. No big deal.

Queen Lolth is going to destroy them. She can only be hit with magic weapons and she can dispel magic each round. I will enjoy every moment of their agony.

I want their characters to die so slowly and with such humiliation that they never ask me to play again. In a matter of hours—by midnight tonight—every man at this table will have unfriended me on Facebook.

Nevertheless I should have read more of the *Dungeon Master's Guide* before now so Carlo would stop lawyering me about the rules. Except of course that I've already put far too much time into this game. Not to mention the inconvenience for Moira.

She and I have known Jamin and Carlo since college. I had not seen them again until they begged me to run this campaign. Dig Doug graduated the same year that Moira and I did but I don't remember him playing with us back then. The fact that he's the most polite member of the group will not save his skin.

Looking over the assembled party it occurs to me that as far as my social life goes, my greatest ambition is to have a series of lifelong friends whom I am never—and I mean *never*—required to spend time with.

I roll a d20 behind my screen: seven. I have a habit of rolling for initiative right away so the players don't know when there is danger lurking beneath their feet. "I rolled an eighteen," I tell them. "What did you guys get?"

I write down their order of attack. Not that it matters. I push back my chair and go to the kitchen for another beer.

Our deck overlooks the yard and Wissahickon Valley Park. The lawn glows with lightning bugs. My son Harry still thinks they are will-o'-the-wisps. He and Jason have an authentic, full-sized tepee at the edge of the property in which they play European Occupiers and Lenni-Lenape. Harry once came inside crying because his brother put smallpox in his sleeping bag. I think it was baking soda.

Here's why I never should have agreed to do this.

Twenty years ago me and Jamin and Carlo lived in the same dorm. The Main Line was never exactly a hotbed of intellectual stimulation and I had what we will call trouble adjusting to life away from home. That antisocial behavior lasted until my sophomore year when I got accepted to join Jamin and Carlo's three-nights-a-week campaign. My first character was a half-orc assassin. The rules were different then.

Everything was different then.

Those guys were a year ahead of me. Their game—and it remained *their* game no matter how long I participated in it—ran until the winter break before they graduated. They had a rolling roster of temporary players, all of whom got kicked out after a week or two. The three of us and Farley were the only regulars.

The idea for this new campaign started a month ago on Facebook. Like all rational and sentient beings, I hate Facebook with a frothy passion. And like all rational and sentient beings, I check it at least twice an hour.

Carlo had posted a scanned-in photograph from an old session. The four of us sit around the common-room table. Carlo's head sticks up like whack-a-mole from behind his DM screen. There must be three hundred dice on the table, several dozen painted miniatures, a *Fiend Folio*, and at least two copies of the 144-page, Elric- and Cthulhu-era *Deities and Demigods*. Farley is wearing a Viking helmet. He was the smartest person I've ever met. He made the people around him smarter, even us idiots. We look happy.

Within minutes of the photo going up, Dig Doug sent me a friend request. What I normally do in these situations is accept the request and then unfriend the person a few days later. I never got the chance. Doug began pestering all of us to put together a campaign like we had in college and then Jamin and Carlo jumped in.

We have to do it, they said.

It will be like old times, they said.

I held out as long as I could, but every excuse I could muster soon dried up. Even Moira said I should do it.

It will do you some good, she said.

There was no way I was about to venture into whatever dank werebear cave I assumed Jamin and Carlo were still living in. Their dorm room had squirmed with month-old take-out cartons. I can still smell it. They run a hobby shop in a strip mall out in the Brandywine Valley. It must take them an hour to get to Manayunk. That's without Schuylkill traffic.

My wife said she would be cool with having everyone over as long as she didn't need to clean up after us. She knows what Carlo and Jamin are like.

I look out over our manicured yard. According to the *Monster Manual*, will-o'-the-wisps are riddled with despair. They are agents of evil.

Moira and I hooked up for the first time the night Farley crashed my Honda.

*

Back at the table, Queen Lolth grows ever more hungry. I get myself situated. "You are in a tavern," I say.

"Seriously?" Jamin asks. His hair is so dirty it looks wet.

"Yes."

"You suck at this," he says.

"Why isn't Carlo DMing?" Dig Doug asks.

"Ask Carlo," I say. "You are fully rested and have all your hit points back. A tall humanoid in a hooded cape stands at the bar with his back to you, but you get the sense he's aware of your presence."

"I conduct a perception check," Gregor says. This is his first campaign. He and his wife are German. They are the closest thing to friends we have in the neighborhood. Moira is at their place right now.

"I'm already DMing two games," Carlo says.

"He wanted to do it anyway," Jamin says, "but I talked him out of it. My mistake."

"Roll perception."

"Fourteen."

"All day?"

"Add your modifier and prof bonus."

"I thought Germans were supposed to be fastidious about rules."

"*Sechzehn.*"

"You perceive that he is tense but not necessarily aggressive."

"Sex what?"

"That's not how perception works."

"Perception is more for seeing things that are hidden."

"Jesus, fine. Whatever. You don't perceive anything being hidden in the tavern."

"How many people are inside?"

"Do you mean people or humanoids?"

"Humanoids, I guess."

"Try attacking them with Preparation H."

"That's hemorrhoids."

"I roll a saving throw against ass pain."

The game will go on like this for several more hours and then they will all die.

"Queen of the Demonweb Pits" is one of the most challenging modules ever published and my modifications make it even deadlier. The party needs to be balanced, which I suppose this one is, but there should be at least eight characters. Tough shit. It's a TPK waiting to happen.

The humanoid at the bar is Cropaz, an emissary from the village council who has come in search of adventurers for hire. The party's job tonight is to travel to the nether plane and descend into Lolth's lair and retrieve the town's sigil. First, however, they must make peace with the huntsmen of the Feywild, in whose protected land they will find the portal to Lolth's massive royal lair. Cropaz gives them each a healing potion and the choice of weapon upgrades from the local armory. They set off.

What the guys don't yet know is that the only way to return from the abyssal plain is by opening a locket around Lolth's neck. It will be impossible to escape until she lies dead. If they are to return to the village and collect their rewards they must first defeat her and her handmaidens.

They will not make it back.

During one finals week Farley heard about an off-campus bash some Bryn Mawr students were throwing. Twelve women had rented a mansion next to a golf course. They were getting evicted at the end of the month. The party had been going on for a week. Even Jamin and Carlo agreed to go. It was my turn to be designated driver.

A loose jazz combo huddled around a baby grand covered in puma-spot watermarks. A card game involved bowling pins and shots of rum. The Rolling Rock pony races had begun in the dining room and in the kitchen six two-person coed teams played Edward Fortyhands with their khakis and boxer shorts and panties at their ankles. Smoke clung to the windows. As usual, people gravitated toward Farley. He reached for the duct tape and I went out back for some air. A moderate snow fell on the skinny-dippers and empty kegs bobbing in the pool. The cold chewed through my flannel shirt.

The irony, of course, is that I did stay sober.

The combo played all the notes around "Stormy Weather" without stepping on the actual melody. I wandered through the huge house, past the murmuring stoners and half-dressed mating rituals in progress. My boredom felt like a jail sentence for trumped-up charges. Up on the third floor I heard classical music behind a closed door. Solo cello. I stood still and the hardwood stopped creaking beneath my boots. The door flew open. "What are you doing?" Moira asked. "Go away."

I didn't know yet that her name was Moira. She was the only other not-drunk person on the premises.

As soon as I said, "You're really good," it occurred to me that the music was still playing behind her.

"At what?"

"I'm sorry to bother you," I said. "I don't really like my friends even when they're sober. I'm bored out of my skull."

"It's Starker performing Bach," she said. To this day she still indulges me with that same not-smiling smile. "I'm studying, but you can come in if you promise to be quiet."

She had a dress on that buttoned all the way up the front and ragg wool socks. The oak door groaned on its hinges.

"The dwarf feels a kind of trembling in the earth," I say.

"That's lowercase *e*, right?"

"As in Middle-earth."

"Fine, from the ground. The big thing beneath your feet."

"I am rolling for perception: four. *Scheiße.*"

"Your rolls suck."

"You can use my dice."

"You are not very perceptive."

"It's impossible to localize the vibration but it might be growing in intensity."

"Is that an icosahedron in your sack or are you just happy to see me?"

"I cast mage armor. It lasts eight hours."

The front door opens before I can have them roll again for initiative. Jason runs into the dining room and yells, "Neeeeerds!" at us and retreats giggling up the stairs.

Harry comes in and scavenges for leftover pizza. He is wrapped in a wet SpongeBob towel. Red juice covers his mouth. He grabs the Beholder miniature and floats it over the table making spooky sounds. The Beholder is his favorite monster. The Gelatinous Cube is his other favorite. And the will-o'-the-wisps out back. They are all his favorite.

The atmosphere changes when Moira comes in. "You, get in the tub," she tells Harry. The sari she's wearing clings to the wet bathing suit underneath. My wife is still extremely attractive—even more beautiful now than when we were in school. "Let Daddy play his nerdy game," she says.

"Hey, Moira," Jamin says.

"Hello, guys. How's the game going?"

"Your husband is a terrible dungeon master."

"The hummus was excellent, thank you."

"I require a new set of dice."

"Kobolds are dicks."

"Language!" Moira says.

Jamin shouldn't be allowed around children.

"Sorry—jerks. Kobolds are jerks."

"Harold, upstairs now!"

Harry grabs a bouquet of Twizzlers and marches up to his watery fate. My wife goes to the kitchen. She fills the kettle and puts it on. The sliding door opens and closes.

"You're a lucky man," Dig Doug says.

"Kobolds are dicks," Harry yells down the stairs.

We listened to the *Cello Suites* on repeat. Moira, still dancing in those days, had control of every motion and intake of breath. János Starker performed a series of small miracles. The winter sky brightened a little bit.

A pair of Doc Martens shook the floorboards down the corridor. I detangled myself from Moira and poked my head out the door. "Keep it down," I said. "People are sleeping."

"We need to get back," Benjamin said. He had trouble standing. "I have a chemistry exam in—shit—two and half hours."

Even asleep, Moira seemed composed and graceful. The semester was almost over, the mansion about be emptied. If I left I might never see her again. The night's spell could be broken forever.

"Are you OK to drive?"

"Not even close."

From Bryn Mawr to Villanova is a straight shot on Lancaster Ave. Two miles, tops.

"Get Farley to do it," I said. I threw him my car keys. They hit him in the chest and fell to the floor. He swayed on his feet to pick them up. I closed the door.

The kettle whistles and Moira comes inside for a moment and then rejoins the will-o'-the-wisps.

That mansion burned down a few years ago. There are condos there now.

Lolth's skeletal minions rise up scratching and crawling from the damp ground. Dozens of them come shambling from every direction until they encircle the party like the concentric rings in a decaying tree stump. The stench of moldering flesh fills the air. The creatures do not attack yet.

I could have driven them safely to campus. Even with the snow on the ground I would have been back to Moira's room in twenty minutes with coffee and fresh pastries from Walter's, and Farley would be sitting here right now in his Viking helmet.

My fist is clenched so tight that the d20 has indented my palm. If I have to be honest with myself, the answer is no. I would not do anything different. I would not risk losing all of this—Moira and the boys, the tepee and the will-o'-the-wisps—even if it meant having Farley back.

At this point, I can have Cropaz send in the cavalry to save everyone's bacon or I can wipe out the entire party and be done for good with this stupid game and these so-called friends.

"Let's stop here," I say. "We'll pick this up next Wednesday."

Their death sentences have been commuted for another week.

"It is a work night," Gregor says.

"At least you don't have a thirty-six-mile commute."

I am not a good person. I understand that. It's a fact I can live with.

The guys collect their things and leave much too slowly. The dining room is a pigsty. I turn off some of the lights and pour the remaining half of my beer down the drain. On the deck, the summer air is muggy but tolerable. A citronella candle burns on the railing next to where Moira has hung her bikini bottoms to dry. I pull a chair next to hers and she reaches for my hand.

We still own those *Cello Suites* CDs. They skip now, but we keep them around.

The End of the End of the World
Stephen O'Connor

WHEN DAWN WAS NINE, she would lie on her bed and think of infinity while crickets filled the night with tiny cries. First her mind would go to the moon, then Mars, then to the edge of the Milky Way. From there, she would cross unimaginable emptiness, passing the Magellanic Clouds, the Andromeda Galaxy, and then galaxies so remote they were little more than theoretical possibilities. Soon the known universe was nothing but a trail of glowing dust shrinking behind her back, while the unknown expanded all around her, filling itself with ever more galaxies, clouds, black holes, and ever vaster emptinesses, so vast that the Milky Way, the planet Earth, New Jersey, her town, her split-level home, and even she herself, lying on her bed in a cotton nightie, diminished to entities of such profound insignificance they trembled on the edge of nonbeing—and in that instant she would lapse into a peacefulness so complete she could not distinguish it from joy.

The first time Dawn sees the bearlike young man with hair like a petrified dust cloud, he is standing outside the observatory with a glossy green-black glob resting on his hand. Feeling her gaze, he looks up and smiles. "A salamander," he says, and swings his hand around gently so that she might see.

When Todd was nine, space was something like a jungle gym into which, aided by rocket ships and wormholes, he could climb from planet to planet, star to star, galaxy to galaxy, until he reached the edge of the curved universe, where, by a miracle that only he might accomplish, he could slip through whatever it was that marked the boundary between existence and all else and enter a realm where no law of nature made sense and even mathematics had to be completely reimagined.

*

"Doesn't that kill them?" Dawn asks the bearlike young man. He is still smiling, and she decides he is excessively stupid.

"What?" he says.

"There's something on our skin," she says. "It destroys their pro-tective layer of mucus."

"Oh." The smile fades. "Really?"

"Of course," she says, but all at once it occurs to her that she might be thinking about fish. Or moths.

As the young man looks down at his hand, the salamander oozes over the tips of his pressed-together fingers, hits the rust-red gravel path, and, slapping the ground with its starburst feet, wriggle-walks into the high grass, where it is soon only an intermittent hiss and a twitching of green blades.

The young man smiles again, but then he looks worried. "Uh," he says. His smile comes back, but it's the neurotic twin of his original smile. He thrusts the hand from which the salamander has just oozed in Dawn's direction. "I'm," he says, "Todd Sbagliaro."

She sidles around the hand, in the direction of the observatory door. "Pleased to meet you."

Dawn is forty-three and Todd is thirty-eight. It's the stuffed-sausage rondure of his neck and cheeks that makes him look two decades younger than his true age. Also he has more than the usual allotment of human facial expressions. In between those connectable to things he is actually saying or doing, his eyebrows wriggle or tilt, and his mouth forms sneers, astonished *O*s, or dreamy smiles, all of which make it seem as if he is having spirited interactions in two or more dimensions simultaneously. Dawn, on the other hand, suffers from an expression deficit, and the majority of the expressions she does make are most commonly seen on gargoyles. She's six feet tall, sapling skinny, and habitually walks around with her forearms raised and her hands dangling. She has frequently been compared to a pray-ing mantis.

Seven months previously, Dawn and Todd each received an e-mail from the Wendall Institute for Interstellar Investigation offering them a three-month summer fellowship at the institute's "state-of-the-art observatory and astrobiological think tank" in Wendall, Montana. This year's fellows, "prominent scholars in the fields of radio and infrared telemetry, exoplanet habitability, hypothetical neurology, interstellar communication, and the sociology of advanced civilizations," would be investigating "The Problem of the Quiet Universe."

The e-mail did not expand upon the precise nature of the "problem," nor was the linked page at wiii.org any more illuminating. But photographs on other pages of the website showed mule deer grazing in a field of radio telescopes, a silver observatory gleaming atop a crag of red volcanic rock, and a gaggle of stubble-cheeked men in enormous cowboy hats playing guitars in front of a wall of bison, bear, and pronghorn trophy heads.

In addition to free access to research facilities, fellows were provided with room and board, expeditions to "natural and historic attractions," and a stipend of $50,000. Dawn was a professor of astronomy at Texas Tech, but had just been denied tenure. Todd's thesis on the physics of orphan-planet formation was ten years overdue and he worked as a salesclerk at Amoeba Records in Berkeley, California. Neither he nor Dawn hesitated more than half a minute before accepting the invitation.

When Dawn arrived at the airport, a white van with W.I.I.I. inscribed in two-foot-high evergreen letters on both flanks was waiting for her. The driver looked fifteen, but was wearing a white blouse with a gold brooch at the collar, a slim-fitting gray skirt, sheer stockings, and four-inch heels. She worked in the hospitality industry, she told Dawn, and only drove for the institute to save money for college. She wanted to major in hospitality. "That's the only kind of work there is around here," she said.

The receptionist in W.I.I.I.'s administrative office was tall and athletic, with Windex-blue hair. She was wearing cargo pants and a T-shirt with a hole just above and to the right of her belly button— apparently a cigarette accident. She touched Dawn on the shoulders and upper arms as if they were old friends. She smiled as if they shared a salacious secret. Her name was Jen. "We are so honored to have you here, Dr. Finnkeisse," Jen said as they walked across the grounds toward the Fellows' Residence. "Dan can't wait to meet you!" That smile came back and she stroked Dawn's upper arm.

Dan was Dan Wendall, the founder and benefactor not just of W.I.I.I., but of the town of Wendall. He was an oil and uranium tycoon and had more money than half the countries in the world combined. "His interest in the Earth naturally led to his interest in the sky," Jen explained. Two hundred and fourteen people lived in Wendall, and two hundred and two of them were Dan's top executives, their families, his wife, six children, and himself.

Dawn's room looked like a room in a motel that aspired to be a room in a bed-and-breakfast: doilies, glass-knobbed dresser, Shaker-style headboard, marble-top sink in an alcove composed entirely of mirrors. "Make yourself at home," said Jen. "Dinner is at seven o'clock." When she left, the room turned dim and lonely.

Atop Dawn's dresser was a photocopied list of the current W.I.I.I. fellows, three of them among the outside experts her department had approached when she went up for tenure. All three probably knew that she had been turned down. They might even have written the very letters that sabotaged her case. She lay on the bed and covered her face with her hands.

After a while, the vault-like silence inside her room made it impossible to breathe. She went for a walk.

The dining hall looks like the restaurant at Mount Rushmore—or at least how that restaurant looked in *North by Northwest*. Dawn has never been to Mount Rushmore, and she doesn't remember the movie well. But she does remember that the restaurant had two-story-high windows facing the stone presidents. This dining hall has two-story-high windows facing miles of ultragreen grass, a black sprinkling of Angus cattle, and a range of hills shaped like shark fins, each with two or three rust-red boulders on its flanks. There is room for a hundred people at the hall's redwood tables, but only one seat in the whole room is occupied—by the bearlike young man with the smoke-like hair whom she encountered on her walk. His back is to her. He is facing the view. Dawn contemplates taking a seat at another table, but then realizes that if she sits opposite this strange young man there will be less chance of her winding up face-to-face with one of the outside experts. "Hi," she says, sliding her plate between the silverware across from Todd.

There are things about sex that Todd just doesn't understand. Do women actually like to cover their bodies with strapped-together pieces of black leather and have their wrists chained to the bedposts? Do they really find their own breasts so sexy that they can't help fondling them every time they wake up? There is a way that perfectly ordinary men make the transition from standing beside a woman at a bus stop to lying naked with her under the covers of a bed—what is it? Of course he has seen countless movies and read countless books in which a series of deft insults traded with wry smiles leads directly to a full-body clinch under the pouring rain—but how is it possible to come up with so many deft insults in a row? Or even just one? And why is it that insults open the door to physical union and not frank declarations of love?

Todd can actually imagine proclaiming love to a woman, or looking into her eyes and asking if she would be interested in kissing him. Many, many times he has sat beside a woman in a classroom, or stood next to one at a record rack and wanted to cover her small, smooth hand with his big, hairy one—but why is it that every single time such a thought enters his mind, his ears go hot, the room begins to whirl, and a queasiness twists up from his stomach into his sinuses? Why is it impossible for him to speak even the word "hello" in the presence of a beautiful woman? Why do the very desires that propel the entire human race into one another's arms cause him to writhe in a silent, sweating mass of shame?

"Where *is* everybody?" says Dawn.

"Excuse me?" says Todd. They have eaten in silence for the last six and a half minutes. The sun has gone from beer gold to brick-dust orange. Fin-shaped shadows are rising along the slopes of the shark-fin hills.

"There's nobody here," says Dawn.

Todd looks over his shoulder, turns back, and shrugs. "Jen said some people would be delayed." He impales the last elbow of mac 'n' cheese on his fork and puts it into his mouth.

"Looks like *everybody's* delayed," says Dawn. "I don't see how that's possible. There must be sixty people on that list they left in our rooms, and they're all supposed to be here today."

"Fifty-seven."

"What?" Dawn's brow furrows vertically. She pushes her face forward and squints. Her hair is black and stringy, but she looks a bit like Joni Mitchell. Same cheekbones; that wide mouth and broad upper lip. As Todd begins to construct an image of the body underneath her fleece vest and T-shirt, he has to look away.

"Fifty-seven," he says. "On the list."

"Oh."

When Todd looks back, one side of Dawn's mouth is smiling and her opposite eyebrow has formed a skeptical check mark. She shakes her head and leans back in her chair. "Anyhow," she says, "it seems totally bizarre to me that fifty-five out of fifty-seven people should fail to show up on the day a conference starts. I've never heard of anything like that."

"Maybe it's like 'The End of the End of the World,' " he says.

Again her brow furrows, her face juts forward, she squints. But this time she doesn't say anything.

"You know," he says, "that Bradbury story—about the village that's so remote it never gets the news the world has ended, and so people just go on with their normal lives."

She lets out a loud, flat "Hah," smiles, and shakes her head.

Todd's face goes watermelon red and his ears start to burn. He wonders if she thinks he made a joke.

A half dozen teenagers in white aprons and muffin-shaped chef hats stand behind the brushed-steel serving table where three hundred pounds of uneaten pot roast, Cajun chicken, mac 'n' cheese, and assorted other dishes steam under orange heat lamps. One of the teenagers—the girl who picked Dawn up at the airport—waves her spatula and says, "Hope everything was to your satisfaction." The rest just stand there looking as if they are waiting for their grandmothers to finish taking an embarrassing photograph.

"Thanks," says Todd.

Dawn plunges her fists into the pockets of her fleece vest, lowers her head, and hurries past the teenagers, trailing the faint odor of liver and marmalade.

"This is crazy!" she says when Todd emerges from the dining hall.

They are standing on a concrete deck, looking out over a swollen creek that winds toward and then past them, its surface gently roiling, gelatinous and silver green in the failing light. Overhead, tiny points of yellow and pink appear in a sky that modulates from iridescent teal to indigo purple.

"What are we even doing here?!" she says.

Todd shrugs.

"This is a catastrophe!" she says.

"We just have to wait and see."

"Wait and see what?"

"It'll be different when the others get here."

She has been gazing at the creek, but now she reels around to look at him, her face in the dimness an agglutination of powdery grays and blacks. "Do you really think anybody is coming?"

"How could they not?" he says. "I mean, look at this place. They wouldn't hire all these people if they didn't expect a crowd."

"Why not?" she says. "The world is full of fuckups."

Todd shrugs. Then he sighs.

"I don't have time for this bullshit!" says Dawn. "I've got work to do."

Her hands plunge back into her fleece pockets and she lowers her head as if she is walking into a fierce wind. Her sandals make cha-cha sounds as she diminishes across the broad deck. She descends the three steps to the path back to the Fellows' Residence, and grows less and less distinct as she strides off into the gloaming.

A familiar loneliness gently settles in Todd's heart. He looks up at the sky, which has expanded and grown raven blue. Smaller points of yellow and pink—and also green—appear between the first ones, which grow brighter and brighter. Gradually the sky shifts from a light-speckled dome to an ever-receding loftiness in which stars hang like radiant dust motes. This is exactly the sort of night Todd loves most, and he decides to stretch out on one of the benches along the deck's creek side and spend an hour just looking up and feeling that gentle suction of the universe's vastness pulling along the length of his body.

But then the dining-hall doors open and the teenagers spill out into the night, chattering happily, lighting up cigarettes and joints. In an instant, Todd too has descended the steps and is walking along the path, which is illuminated as it traverses an acre of lawn by a double row of elfin streetlamps.

"Help yourself," says the handwritten sign taped to the brushed-steel serving table. To the left of the sign are three open boxes of cereal, some bowls, plates, cups, a carton of milk, and a coffeemaker the size of a small trash can. To the right, under the table's heat lamps, is a basin of oatmeal, the surface of which has gone pigeon brown, and a basin of scrambled eggs that have gone school-bus orange. Both heat lamps are off.

Todd pours himself a bowl of Sugar Pops and fills a cup with black coffee.

Dawn is sitting in the exact seat where he sat last night. She is holding a cup to her mouth with both hands and contemplating the cow-dotted hills. Todd carries his tray in her direction, suffers a crisis of confidence, turns a pirouette, and then blushes and places his tray at the nearest setting, which happens to be three seats down from Dawn. As he pulls back his chair, he hears her speak, but he can't make out her words.

"Excuse me?" he says.

"Do I look like I have bad breath?" Her voice is angry, but she is smiling.

"Uh . . ." He blushes again, this time so forcefully he hears a thumping in his ears. "I just didn't . . . you know . . . disturb you."

"Suit yourself." She turns toward the window and, once again, covers the lower half of her face with the cup.

Feeling that he has offended her, Todd walks around the table to the seat she occupied the night before. No sooner does he sit down than he thinks that she might not have actually wanted him to join her. But it's too late to move again, so he just contemplates his milk-slick yellow cereal, unable to eat. When, at last, he dares to look in Dawn's direction, he finds that she is staring right at him.

"Did you hear all that noise last night?" she says.

"Noise?"

"Yeah. Engines. People shouting. Sometime in the middle of the night. Two a.m., three a.m."

He searches his memory and then, just to be sure, he searches it again. "No."

"It went on for like an hour, first out in the parking lot. Then there were all these thumps in the corridor. And whispers. I figured it was the other fellows moving in, but . . ." She holds out an upturned hand to either side, looks around the empty room, shrugs.

"Maybe they're still sleeping," says Todd.

"Hunh."

"I mean if they got in so late."

"Maybe," she says.

"I bet we'll see them at the convocation."

"I guess," she says.

"Some of them, at least."

The schedule in their cell phones reads: "Convocation, Dan Wendall Auditorium, 9:00 a.m." Todd and Dawn are standing in front of a row of aluminum doors, surmounted by a row of foot-high aluminum letters: DAN WENDALL AUDITORIUM. Their cell phones both say: 8:58. They try every door, but each is locked so firmly it seems welded to its frame. Now their phones say: 9:04. From the concrete plaza in front of the auditorium they can survey the entire W.I.I.I. campus. A dozen mule deer tread hesitantly to the creek edge and then, independently, randomly, they lower their heads, raise them, then lower them again, like a cervine version of Whack-a-Mole. A small white dog tied to the empty bike rack behind the administrative offices keeps running off, only to be yanked so forcefully by its extended leash that it flips backward into the air and crumples to the grass. A dusk-colored sandhill crane flies just over the gleaming silver observatory on slowly wafting wings.

Nature everywhere; no people.

Todd and Dawn can look out for miles to that point where the blue-gray clouds touch the gray-green earth: not a single human being, not even a car—moving or parked. Their cell phones say: 9:13. They turn in circles with their hands on their heads. Their fists against the doors make no more sound than if they were pounding on stone. The edges of their keys make tiny clicks.

Jen, the blue-haired receptionist, is leaning against the front of her desk. She has very big teeth and is smiling. She gives Dawn's upper arm a quick rub as if she is polishing it. She winks at Todd. "Postponed," she says. "Didn't anybody tell you?" Her cheeks bunch like tiny peaches. Slivers of light beam off her eyeballs. She seems exceedingly happy. "You've got a free day!" she says. "We're waiting for the others to arrive," she says. "Have fun! We'll let you know ASAP." She gives Dawn's shoulder another polish. Todd gets another wink. "Bye-bye," Jen says.

They are two miles down a dirt road. On one side, six black Angus bulls behind three strands of barbed wire flick their dusty tails and make noises like small-scale geological catastrophes. The bulls stare at Dawn and Todd with eyes the size and color of eight balls. On the other side of the road, at a distance of a quarter mile, a single pronghorn stands motionlessly on an ultragreen hillside, also staring.

Dawn puffs out her cheeks, shakes her head, and turns a laughing expression toward the sky. "That's so impossibly naive!" she says.

"It's just simple mathematics," says Todd. "How can mathematics be naive?"

They are discussing Fermi's paradox—to wit: there are seventy sextillion stars in the visible universe, and thus several billion planets upon which life could form, and millions upon which, during the nearly fourteen billion years since the Big Bang, life must have achieved such technological sophistication that the electromagnetic noise of its machinery ought to be blaring out into the ether, and, lastly, there must be hundreds of thousands of civilizations capable of sending vehicles into space and colonizing other planets, thousands of which might, in turn, colonize others, which would mean that by this point every habitable planet in the universe, including the Earth, ought to have been at least visited—so where is everybody? Why is there zero evidence that we have company in the cosmos? Or at least no evidence capable of convincing anyone other than blubber-hipped eleven-year-olds and gray-haired hippies with copper pyramids on their heads?

"It's not the mathematics," says Dawn. "It's the assumption that all these other planets are populated by angels. It's the staggering disregard for the fact that life forms only develop intelligence so that they can dominate and destroy their evolutionary rivals. And, what is more, any civilization capable of sending vehicles into space will also have the ability to destroy its own planet several times over, just as we do. What is the statistical probability that the human race will survive this century? And don't even think about the next millennium! So why should we assume that the inhabitants of other planets are any less greedy, aggressive, incompetent, and perverse than we are? It's not the mathematics. On the contrary: the mathematics is exactly right. Millions of planets must have given rise to life capable of developing concentration camps and neutron bombs, and simple math tells us that most of those planets must long since have been reduced to smoking cinders."

There are things about sex that Dawn doesn't understand. Why is it that the men who start out acting as if their brains are entirely in their dicks are always the ones who end up weeping in the bathroom because you don't love them? How come stepfathers universally believe their marriage vows give them the right to pull down their stepdaughters' panties? Why is breakup sex always the best sex? Why is it that seven and a half years after she threw out her lying, cheating, certifiably insane German professor boyfriend, blocked all his e-mail addresses and phones, unfriended him on Facebook, bad-mouthed him to everyone she knew, including his ex-wife, and spent thirteen thousand unreimbursable dollars talking about him in therapy—why is it that she still can't walk past the bench where they first kissed without groaning and covering her face with her hands? Why, so many years later, can she still hear his love whispers inside her head? Why does she get drunk almost every night and go to his website to scroll through photographs of him standing in front of blackboards or behind podiums the world over, his eyes sparked with enthusiasm, his mouth in that lopsided warp that always makes her think of a baby's first laugh?

As Dawn and Todd come back down the dirt road and cross the highway onto Dan Wendall Drive, a fire engine–red pickup truck vrooms toward them trailing a corona of golden dust. At first it seems a luna moth is fluttering wildly behind the windshield, but then they see that it's a woman's hand—Jen's, in fact—waving at them. As the truck comes closer, the vroom starts to rumble inside their chests. Jen's waving hand swings away from the windshield toward the passenger window. Her face conveys extreme merriment, and she seems to be mouthing an emphatic message—though neither can make it out.

First the wind of the truck's passage blows the hair off their foreheads, then it sucks their hair sideways into the golden wake. Jen turns onto the highway and the little white dog leaps again and again against the cab's rear window, which is already smeary from its nose, tongue, and paws. The tires screech and the truck rockets down the road, dwindling within seconds to a humming red dot.

The dishes of the dozen silver radio telescopes in the field behind the observatory are tilted toward the ultragreen grass, conveying the impression that the telescopes have traveled an immense distance and are utterly exhausted, more spiritually than physically. Todd and Dawn approach the observatory's glass doors, which hiss open, then hiss shut behind them, replacing the peaceful din of cicadas and birdcalls with the hum of solid-state machinery. But the steel door to the staircase leading up to the observatory's dome is welded shut—actually welded: small metal plates span the gap between the door and its frame, each of them nubby and flame rainbowed at its edge, radiating darts of carbon dust.

"What the fuck?" says Dawn.

Todd shakes his head. "Whoa."

They walk down the hall to a door labeled RADIO TELESCOPE COM-MAND STATION. Same deal: nubby edges, rainbows, etc.

"Jesus fucking Christ!" says Dawn.

Todd keeps twisting the doorknob and yanking.

"I was just fucking in here yesterday!" says Dawn.

Todd lets go of the knob and kicks the door. "The whole reason I came here," he says, "was to use the radio telescope. That's the whole fucking reason!" He smiles and looks down at the ground, wondering if Dawn has noticed that he used the word "fucking."

"Who the fuck do they think we are?!" she says.

The dining hall is silent, empty, and the dim green of the ocean bottom. "Hello?" calls Dawn, and is answered only by the echo of her voice. The brushed-steel serving table is cold. The food basins have a greasy sheen at their bottoms, but nothing else.

"What's with this place?" says Dawn.

"Let's check out the kitchen," says Todd.

The kitchen is filled with a darkness that is like a pressure upon their eyeballs. Todd stretches his hand into it, hears a distant click, and the darkness evaporates, revealing a shelf of brilliant muffin hats, each with a pristine white apron dangling from a hook beneath. No teenagers in sight, however, only rows of steel tables stretching in all directions under long banks of LED lights emitting steel-colored illumination. Not a surface marred by an abandoned dish towel, ladle, or knife. Every pot is hanging from its rack, the cans on the shelves arranged by color and in spectrum order. Nothing but the muffled drum tap of water droplets on a metal sink bottom to indicate that Todd and Dawn are not the first human beings ever to enter this resplendent space.

The walk-in refrigerator does, however, contain three hundred pounds of cooked food, and there is a trunk-size microwave next to the yacht-size stove.

Dawn has trout amandine and Todd has mac 'n' cheese.

The clinks of their cutlery bounce back at them off the two-story windows and the fieldstone walls.

*

The night is gigantic. Dawn and Todd are lying head-to-head on neighboring benches looking up at the stars. At the bottom of the bluff, the swollen creek rustles amid the high grass on the engulfed banks. "What did you want to use them for?" she says.

"What?"

"The radio telescopes."

"Oh . . . nothing."

"Come on!" says Dawn.

"What?"

"Just say it."

"It's nothing . . . *really* . . . it's stupid."

"Say it!"

"Oh . . ." He heaves a deep sigh. "Well, I wanted to send a message."

"A message?"

"To the M13 star cluster."

"The M13!"

"I told you it was stupid."

"Why do you want to do that?" says Dawn. "That's twenty-five thousand light-years away! You'd be subatomic dust by the time you got a response."

"I don't know. It just seems so cool—the idea that millennia after I am gone, someone, somewhere in the universe might know I was here."

"What would you send?"

An owl hoots. Distant cow bells thunk dully, then go silent.

"Maybe just a series of prime numbers," says Todd. "Or a schematic of the solar system."

"I'd send a song."

"A song?"

"Sure," says Dawn. "It would have a repeating but complex pattern, so obviously the product of an intelligent species. Maybe it would give some alien a moment of pleasure."

"What song?"

"I don't know."

" 'Twinkle, Twinkle, Little Star'?"

" 'Moondance'!" says Dawn. "I'd sing it myself!"

"Or 'Moon River'?"

" 'Stairway to Heaven'!"

"I'd send 'Silent Night,' " says Todd.

"Huh."

"All is calm, all is bright . . ."

91

"That's a lullaby. You'd put the universe to sleep."

"I think it's beautiful."

"Oh, God!" says Dawn. "I need a fucking drink." She sits up. "Do you think there's a car here we could hijack and go into town?"

"There's a bar in the basement."

"What?"

"In the basement. A bar. The dining-hall basement."

The amiable sorrow of *Hotel California* burbles beyond an open door at the end of a pipe-lined corridor. Inside, amber light filters up through rows of liquor bottles and beams down in moody pools all across the room—the only inhabitants of which are thirty-seven taxidermied animal heads, looking out from the walls with that vacancy of eye that comes between the suspicion that one is chok-ing and the clutching of hands to throat.

"Hunh," says Dawn.

"It was the same yesterday," says Todd.

She hunches her shoulders, smiles, and holds out both palms in surrender to a delightful form of helplessness. Then she goes behind the bar and pours two shots of Knob Creek.

"I don't drink," says Todd.

"Nonsense," says Dawn.

A dozen small wooden tables crowd the space between the bar and an ankle-high platform on the far wall, which must be where the men in the giant cowboy hats played their guitars. Dawn brings the two full shot glasses to a table under a buffalo head, then goes back to the bar and grabs the bottle.

Taking her seat, she holds up her glass and waits for Todd to sit opposite her. When he lifts his glass, she winks and taps it with her own. "Clink!" she says, then empties her glass in a gulp.

Todd touches his glass to his lower lip and allows a single drop of bourbon to send a perfumed burning across his tongue. His eyes water. He winces and puts the glass down on the table.

Dawn talks.

She pours herself another shot, and talks some more.

Songs come and go. "A Horse with No Name." "Band on the Run." "Crocodile Rock." So do more shots.

Dawn's face flushes and her blue eyes begin to look turquoise.

After a while Todd asks, "If he treated you that badly, why do you still care about him?"

92

Dawn jerks her head to one side as if she has been hit. "Don't you know anything about love?"

"I just . . . ," he says. "I mean . . ." He shrugs, opens his mouth, but no words come out.

"Look," she says, "let's face it: most sex is just masturbating on somebody else's body—right?" She swallows a shot. "And in between you have to sit around pretending to be interested while this fucking narcissist babbles on and on about himself. You know what I mean? So you get—what?—maybe five good fucks out of any relationship. Ten, if you're lucky. Then it's time to move on." She makes a smile that is a variety of wince. "But every now and then you meet someone—someone who's . . . I don't know: *different.* And then sex is like this expression of your total delight in that person. Right? And that person's total delight in you. And actually, it doesn't matter what you're doing: taking a walk in the park, shopping at the Stop 'n' Go. It's all just like this nonstop fucking delight. Like you never lived before. But then, of course, one day: wham! It's over." She downs another shot. "And after that . . . Well, after that, life's just shit. Right? I mean what's the fucking point. You see what I'm saying?"

Todd takes his hands off the table and folds them in his lap.

"Oh, no!" says Dawn.

"What?"

"Oh, my God!"

"What?" says Todd.

"You don't know *what* I'm talking about, do you?"

He just looks at her like another taxidermied animal head.

A bleary leer comes onto Dawn's face. "I bet you've never even been kissed!"

Todd sighs deeply and crumples his lips. The corners of his eyes glisten.

"You poor baby!" She leans across the table, which lurches. As Todd flings out his arm to stop the sliding glasses and bottle, she presses her closed lips just beside his and makes a big smacking noise.

"There!" she says, sitting back down. "Now you've been kissed!"

Todd's face has gone shiny and red. He is staring into the eyes of a goat with a cigarette in its mouth.

"You've got lovely long lashes," says Dawn. "You wouldn't be half bad looking if you got a haircut and lost thirty pounds."

Still staring at the goat, Todd grabs his glass, throws back his head, and pours the fiery, perfumed fluid down his throat.

*

As Dawn hurries Todd along the path lit by elfin streetlamps, she clutches his arm with both hands, and stops every now and then to smile at him in the manner of a woman on the verge of losing consciousness.

Todd himself feels on the verge of losing consciousness, not because he has drunk too much (in fact, he only had that one shot of bourbon; well, maybe two), but because his head is spinning with too many incomprehensible memories: Dawn grabbing his hand across the table and saying, "Come with me!" Her tongue in his ear. Her low moan against his cheek. The electric detonations of pleasure effected by her fingers between his legs. Each of these events increased the probability of an ever-diminishing range of other events, until now, as the rectangular obscurity of the Fellows' Residence looms ever larger against the night sky, the probability of one heretofore inconceivable event rises to the level of certainty.

The pathway ends. The glass doors hiss. Dawn laughs as she leads Todd through the fluorescent dusk of the lobby to the elevators. She hits the up button and flings herself against him, twisting her wet mouth on his. Todd does his best to reciprocate, but can't rid himself of the notion that this is merely another of those dreams in which he is onstage before an audience of thousands, holding an instrument he has no idea how to play.

All at once Dawn puts her hands on his chest and shoves herself away.

"I'm sorry," she says. "I just can't do this."

She wipes her mouth on the back of her wrist. When she lowers her arm, her expression is flaccid and aghast.

The elevator dings.

The door opens, closes.

"It's not your fault," she says. "It's me."

"That's all right." Todd's head is lowered, his brow crumpled as if he has discovered a small, dead animal on the floor.

"No, really," she says. "I'd really like to, but—"

She smiles sadly and shrugs.

"That's all right," he says.

"Wait a second!" Her eyes brighten and her mouth opens as if she is about to laugh. "I have a much better idea!" She grabs Todd's hand and pulls him back across the lobby. "Why didn't I think of this before!"

The doors hiss. The night is loud with insect song and the sound of flowing water.

Dawn is naked, and Todd is holding his shirt in his left hand, not sure what to do with it. In his right hand he holds his cell phone, flashlight on. He is shivering.

"Come on!" Dawn cries. "It's perfect!"

She is up to her ankles in the grass-pierced water on the edge of the swollen creek, her clothes scattered along the shore on either side of her. Todd watches her T-shirt, sucked off a clump of water-piercing grass, slip along the roiling current just in front of her shins and vanish into the earthbound gloom beneath the crystalline sky.

"I don't know," he says dubiously.

"Hurry up!" she says. "The water's incredible!"

She takes an unsteady step forward and looks over her shoulder, gesturing for Todd to follow.

He flings his shirt onto the grass, slips his phone into his pocket, and applies both hands to his belt.

There is a shriek and a splashing wumph, as if a log has toppled into the creek.

No Dawn.

No grayish smear near the shore. No clump of darkness on the glinting current.

"Oh!" she cries, from some distance downstream, then again, from much farther down: "Oh!" And then, from ever-increasing distances: "Oh! . . . Oh no! . . . Oh my God! . . . Help!"

Todd hears the bubble and roar of the water, but can't see anything. He has flung himself into the creek with the intention of rescuing Dawn (though he does not, in fact, know how to swim) and his head would seem to be a yard beneath the surface, a situation he attempts to correct by thrashing his arms and doing something like a run with his sneaker-shod feet. After long moments of murk and resonant bubbling, the sounds go brittle, a new coolness strikes his cheeks, and he can make out the starry sky swirling overhead. He only has time to gulp a mouthful of air, however, before his shins collide with something hard, he is flipped forward and is once more beneath the surface, upside down this time, water drilling into his sinuses. He flails, kicks, twists, and punches, but can't tell whether he is going

95

up or down. Gravity no longer exerts any detectable influence upon his body.

Stars. Airborne sounds. His head coasting along a seething surface. He coughs and gasps.

"Help!" Dawn cries from somewhere downstream. "Ai!" she cries, "Oh!," and "Oh, my God!"

Each cry is louder and more distinct than the one before, until she seems barely an arm's length in front of him, then just at his side, and then he has passed her and she is receding quickly. He looks over and glimpses her angular back and right arm, pale gray against the dark riverbank. She has stopped shouting. She is clutching at something—a root? a branch?—and is pulling herself out of the water while he hurtles helplessly past.

First his shoulder strikes the muddy bottom, then his back, then his belly and leg. Then there is an extended instant during which his disassembled body parts whirl in a horizontal cyclone, and finally he is nose down on a stinking incline, clawing into vegetable muck to keep from being sucked back into the current.

Now he is standing in waist-high grass, rills filtering through his crotch, down his legs and into his sneakers. He figures he is only some thirty yards past where Dawn clambered ashore. He calls her name, but hears only the sawing of grass blade against grass blade, and the fluttery clatter of the water. He calls again—louder, then louder still. Nothing. A universe filled with inconsequential sound.

He starts to walk, his feet making suction noises inside his sneakers—and then he stops, having realized that he has a problem: this is the wrong side of the creek. If he wants to return to W.I.I.I., he will have to fling himself back into the frigid current. A shudder grinds through his guts. His teeth rattle. A wind sweeps down out of the vast sky and coats his shoulders with ice.

He is walking again, his feet plunging into invisible declivities and stumbling up sudden rises, grass stalks raking his shoelaces. He keeps thinking he sees Dawn just ahead, a smoke-colored wisp in the moonless gloom, but over and over she becomes a plastic bag on a barbed-wire fence, a drifting phosphene, a wind-rocked bush.

A black lace of trees looms on the far side of the creek, and through its interstices he can make out a trail of yellowish glints (the elfin streetlamps) and sparks of bluish red (the exit signs inside the abandoned dining hall). He edges sideways down the steep bank until he can feel the current eddying along the outside of his left sneaker. Here is where he was certain he would find Dawn, hunched and clutching her shoulders against the cold. Nothing but black water. Waist-high, pewter-colored grass. A sky exploding with stars. He calls her name, then a second time, then over and over—until the recurring silence becomes more than he can bear.

Drenched again, flashlightless, and blind (his cell phone having drowned in his pocket), Todd kneels at the place where he believes Dawn first stepped into the water, and runs his hands through grass and weeds. Unsuccess follows unsuccess, and he knee-walks forward, his fingers encountering branches and sticks, a beer bottle, a plastic shovel, and then something soft: Dawn's fleece vest. And just beside it: her underpants, then her jeans, and, finally, the downy cotton of his flannel shirt.

As he wrestles his wet arms into the sleeves, he wonders if the night is cold enough for Dawn to have succumbed to hypothermia. Has she slumped unconscious into the wind-stirred grass? Did she even make it out of the water after he drifted past? Perhaps her muddy fingers slipped off that root or branch. Perhaps the current was simply too strong.

The wallpaper photo on Dawn's cell phone is of a green-eyed black cat with plastic reindeer antlers clipped to its head. Todd swipes the bottom of the screen, taps the phone icon, and dials 911. He tells the woman who answers that a friend went swimming in a creek and he is worried that she has drowned. "It's been an hour," he tells the woman. "I keep calling her name, but she doesn't answer." When the woman asks for his location, he tells her that he is at the Wendall Institute for Interstellar Investigation. When she says she doesn't know what he is talking about, he repeats the name one word at a time.

"Never heard of it," she says. She's never heard of the town of Wendall either. "What's your street address?" she asks.

"I don't know," he says.

"How can you not know your address?"

"I already told you: I'm at the *Wendall* Institute. I was driven here in a van. I didn't pay attention to the street." Todd's voice is trembling. It is all he can do to keep from shouting.

"Well, if you want assistance, you're going to have to give me an address."

"Listen," he says, willing his voice to sound reasonable and firm. "A woman may be dying this very minute. Can't you just google the Wendall Institute and find the address yourself?"

"Hold on a minute." The line goes staticky.

After a couple of seconds, Todd hears a bleep and a sound like a whip snap. Then silence. The phone's screen has gone black. He holds the ON button down for more than a minute. Nothing happens.

Todd doesn't know whether to stay where he is or go back to the institute and try to find a working landline. Maybe it would be better to walk down the highway to an inhabited house—though the nearest could be miles away. He decides to wait, at least for a while.

He can no longer bear to call out Dawn's name, so he walks to the water's edge and only listens. Brilliant Vega is straight overhead, just where the ragged trail of the Milky Way edges into the ordinary night sky, and to its right: the constellation of Hercules, where, between the stars denoting the hero's pelvis and ribs, Todd can just make out what appears to be a faint yellowish star, but which is, in fact, the M13 star cluster.

The M13 is only visible to the naked eye on the darkest and clearest nights. Having spent his entire life in LA and Berkeley, this is only the second time he has seen the star cluster outside of a photograph. The first was when his Boy Scout troop went camping in the desert. His mother had insisted he join the troop so that he might make friends, but in the end, his solitary summer as a scout consisted primarily of false fart accusations, jokes about his Elmer Fudd laugh, and a dead lizard in his hiking boot.

That night in the desert, while his troop sat around a fire singing "99 Bottles of Beer," Todd walked off to pee, and then continued walking until he was far enough away that the fire's glow no longer interfered with his view of the stars. He had never seen a sky so dazzlingly crowded before, and, as he rocked back his head, the very first glimmer his eye picked out was the M13. He was so excited that he nearly ran back to tell everyone, but he knew they would only mock him, so he lay down on a patch of still-warm sand, and tried to see the stars clearly enough to tell which were near and which were so far away their twinkle had been traveling since the Big Bang.

He was still lying there when "99 Bottles of Beer" finally finished. After an interval of shouts, groans, laughter, and the scout master's imperious "Come on!" the troop began to sing "Silent Night"—a song Todd found so beautiful that, once more, he almost returned to the campfire.

Sometime later, he awoke to find that the singing had stopped and that the Milky Way had swung some forty-five degrees across the sky. He sat up and looked back toward the fire, now only a dawn-like glow against the rocks that the boys had ringed around it. The tents were zipped up, silent gray pyramids in the starlight. No one had called out to him at bedtime, let alone come looking for him. Perhaps no one had even noticed he was missing. Or cared.

For a moment he couldn't breathe, as if the Earth had become a vacant rock adrift in a vacuum. But then he lay back down and looked up. There was so much beauty in that glittering sky. So much freedom.

From Amitier
Gilles Tiberghien

—Translated from French by Cole Swensen

PETER SLOTERDIJK, QUOTING THE POET Jean Paul, observed that "books are huge letters written to friends." This is especially true of books of philosophy, and, more generally, of the activity of philosophy itself, which always postulates the existence, implicit or actual, known or imagined, of a friend to whom one's thoughts are addressed. And as it's such a solitary activity, it's perhaps even essential to its nature that it be based on friendship, that friendship be one of its conditions of operation. "It's an important question," writes Gilles Deleuze in his introduction to *What Is Philosophy?*, "because the friend as he appears in philosophy is no longer an extrinsic figure, an example, or an empirical circumstance; rather, his presence is intrinsic to thought, is a condition of thought itself, a living category, a lived transcendental."

That said, if in antiquity, as Deleuze and Félix Guattari claim, the friend became "a conceptual being," that phenomenon was connected to Greek society itself, to the anthropological status of the friend, and to the moral and political consequences of friendship, which determined the nature of that society. For instance, if speaking of equality between friends, as Aristotle did, is going to have a true resonance for us, we have to remember that this equality was originally founded on the deep discrimination that characterized the ancient world and marked a difference in nature not only between men and women but also between different men—those who were free and those who were slaves.

The friendship of the ancients was governed by discourse, *logos*, and was considered a virtue, which is to say, it was characterized by a "disposition to act" according to rule and in ways appropriate to men who are prudent, just, and capable of evaluating their actions and those of others. The whole of Greek philosophy, and its political philosophy in particular, presumes a potential community of thought, a *koiné* founded on the use of reason to master desire and thus arrive at the good; therefore, it was necessarily communal, shared by everyone for the profit of all and with happiness as its goal.

For the moderns, on the other hand, from Machiavelli and Hobbes on, reason would no longer be the foundation of politics. Whether based on the fear of death (Hobbes) or on compassion (Rousseau), the cement of social bonds was no longer seen as rational, which meant that society could no longer promise moderation and justice in the name of reason as its ruling factor. On the contrary, society came to be seen as the crucible for passions that it simultaneously willfully provoked and attempted to channel. The moderns, then, no longer considered friendship a virtue, and friendship had to adapt to this new state of affairs. Given this context, and despite Aristotle's statements, no one who came after could share even his best friend's happiness without also envying it. Moral feelings were no longer protected from the passions, which is how the theme of love came to be interlaced with that of friendship.

Considering the wide range of meanings that the term friendship has had from antiquity to the present, and that the Greek term *philia* evolved into the Latin *amicitia*, and that one or the other is translated today into various languages as *amitié, friendship,* and *Freundschaft,* Jean-Claude Fraisse concludes that "these complexities expose the pretensions behind any claim to reconcile the ancients and the moderns through the notion of *philosophia perennis,* and they demand the rejection of any method that is not exclusively historical."[1] Though not to scorn history or contexts of thought that have determined certain philosophical terms, particularly that of friendship, it seems to me that we have everything to gain by rethinking these terms in light of our own intellectual, social, and political contexts, so that we can fine-tune them to better address today's realities and needs.

This may well be the result of the relatively recent disappearance of a specific worldview rooted in values dominant for centuries; its disappearance has made us reexamine the human condition. In his preface to the works of Seneca, Paul Veyne writes, "We retain the right to base our dreams on the thoughts of the ancients, which we reuse as the men of the Renaissance reused the columns of pagan temples to build their churches." He goes on to demonstrate that the ancient concept of the self can still resonate with a modern sensibility: "Paradoxically, what was but a detail of Stoic doctrine—the autonomy of the self and the possibility of the self's working on

---

[1] Jean-Claude Fraisse, *Philia. La Notion d'amitié dans la philosophie antique* (Paris, Vrin, 1974), 20.

the self—has become for us a mode of survival, despite the disappearance of everything that Stoicism affirmed: nature, God, and the unity of the self."[2]

To return to the question of terminological precision, its importance has been emphasized since Plato's *Lysis*, which made it clear that the term *philia* is ambiguous and depends upon whether a particular friendship is active, passive, or reciprocal. The Greek term *philia* covered much more than the contemporary term *friendship* does and was not far from what we mean today by love. "If friendship is taken to mean all types of affection, it was, in Greek use, the strongest and the most developed affection. It eclipsed love; it had deeper roots than family feeling; it was sung of by the poets. [. . .] In the ancient world, friendship was what courtly love was in the chivalric and Christian world," wrote L. Dugas.[3] This explains the difficulty we sometimes have when we read Greek texts that refer to sentiments that, like instruments out of tune or tuned to a different key, don't correspond to what we mean today by the same words. In the ancient world, the word *philia* itself had already passed through a series of semantic slips. In Homer's time, it had belonged to the vocabulary of law and indicated a type of possession, but in time it had evolved to mean a type of affective relationship founded on reciprocal esteem. As Pierre Macherey notes, "The word Homer always used to indicate the affective relationship between two people that we call friendship today was not *philos*, but *hetarios*, a companion, he from whom one is inseparable."[4] The Greek *philia* is most fully developed in the texts of Aristotle, Cicero, Seneca, and the Epicureans.

In the preface to their anthology *The Wisdom of Friendship*, Jacques Follon and James McEvoy note that the Greek *New Testament* used the Greek terms for love very selectively and slanted them heavily toward the new (Christian) doctrine. In it, *eran* and its noun *eros* are systematically sidelined, and *stergueini*, which means familial affection, is almost never used.[5] *Philein*, because it is too

---

[2]Paul Veyne, "Introduction" to Seneca, *Entretiens et Lettres à Lucilius* (Paris, Robert Laffont, coll. "Bouquins," 1993), VI.

[3]L. Dugas, *L'Amitié antique* (Paris, Félix Alcan, 1914), 1–2.

[4]Pierre Macherey, "Le 'Lysis' de Platon: dilemme de l'amité et de l'amour" in *L'Amitié, dans son harmonie, dans ses dissonances*, under the direction of Sophie Jankélévitch (Paris, Autrement, 1995), 64–65.

[5]See also Plutarch, *Dialogues on Love* 767 b-c, which, as Michel Foucault points out, "plays on the words *sterguein*, to love, and *stegein*, to harbor, to shelter in your home." *Le Souci de soi (Histoire de la Sexualité*, III) (Paris, Gallimard, coll. "Bibliothèque des Histoires," 1984), 237.

theoretically loaded and is overly marked by ancient pagan doctrines, "is only applied to the relationship that Jesus had with Peter, Lazarus, and "the disciple whom he loved." From then on, *agapan* and *agape* "were used to speak of love because, having been previously marginalized terms, they were 'available.' [. . .] Our authors claim that, as a result, the word 'love' in all occidental languages (influenced by the expressions 'the love of God' and 'the love of one's neighbor') has taken priority, and the word 'friendship' has been relegated to a second place. Thus the incontestable primacy enjoyed by the word *philia* in the Classical and Hellenistic periods gave way to the term *agape*, just as the Latin term *amicitia* had to cede its place to *amor* and *caritas*."[6]

Since then, the notion of charity as the universal love of one's neighbor has gained an advance on other forms of love, limiting friendship to a privileged relationship between two or more individuals in an essentially private experience. The possibility of inscribing this experience of friendship in the public sphere was a question that had already been debated by the ancients, but in a context in which conflicts of interest also belonged to the public sphere, opposing virtue to glory or power, without either's arising from the private sphere alone (on the contrary, in fact, as domestic economy and the affairs of the home have nothing to do with friendship, even if, in some circumstances, Aristotle found relations of friendship at the heart of the family).

Friendship was theorized in the pagan world. Aristotle, more than anyone else, gave the concept the features that we still recognize today, such as an equality (of virtue) and an active reciprocity within a shared intimacy. However, this model was soon opposed by the concept of universal love as developed by the Christian church, in which humanity was the most valued aspect of the individual. The Christian community is founded on charity, not on friendship, and unlike friendship, charity does not require reciprocity. The relationship that brings friends together is undertaken consciously and willfully, which is entirely different from the open-ended category of *all neighbors* whom the church demands we love as we do ourselves.

Even today, there are echoes of this heritage that make friendship a troubled and generally neglected subject in philosophy. Sympathy, which Rousseau considered to be the basis of our relationship to

---

[6]*Sagesses de l'amitié, anthology des textes philosophiques anciens*, chosen and presented by Jacques Follon and James McEvoy (Paris, Cerf/Fribourg, Éditions universitaires de Fribourg, coll. "Vestigia," 1997), 25–26.

others, was distrusted by antiquity, which thought that its affective nature was beyond us and that it fell outside the control of reason. For the Greeks, discourse was clearly the essence of friendship, while we today often think of it as vain chatter, and, philosophically, it's stigmatized as an inauthentic mode of being in the world. As Hannah Arendt said of the ancient world, "with dialogue, friendship's political importance—and its humanity—are revealed . . . For the world is not human because it was made by people, and it will not become human because the human voice resounds within it; it will only become human when and if it becomes the object of dialogue."[7]

All this implies that friendship is not as obvious as is generally assumed. To have friends seems like the most natural thing in the world and the most culturally shared, and yet, in its primary sense, friendship implies a set of practices and values that is and remains for us a thing of the past—to borrow a famous phrase from Hegel. The social and intellectual conditions of its practice are different now, at least in the Western world, where individualism has taken precedence over every other value, and yet, to a large degree, we continue to live as if this were not the case. It's as if we still need to believe in friendship, even though we live less and less with our friends— and this was an essential condition of friendship for the Greeks: a shared life. This is the root of the importance of the community of friends that more generally relied on the political community—which the community of friends had, in turn, made possible.

One loves one's friends, but not with the same love one has for the beloved, be it husband, wife, or child. One loves, but what kind of love is it? We don't have a word to express it, to specify it. We've lost the diversity of terms that constituted the wealth of the Greek vocabulary, which not only could speak of friendship, but could also differentiate between various modes, while also taking into account social structures and practices that are, for the most part, not relevant today. Above all, we no longer have a verb to indicate friendship as an action, an ongoing activity; we have to make use of another vocabulary, which exposes the relatively confused ideas that we currently hold. With the loss of the word, have we not also lost what it means?

And yet, friendship is perhaps not so much lost as it is in need of being reinvented to fit a world that needs it more—and exactly to the degree that that world makes its reality problematic and makes it

[7]Hannah Arendt, "De l'humanité dans de sombres temps," *Vies politiques*, trad. B. Cassin et P. Lévy (Paris, Gallimard, coll. "Les Essais," 1974), 34.

difficult to realize on a daily basis, in the sense that it has transformed human communities into institutions ("the European Community"), agglomerations (such as the collectivities of the same name also sometimes misleadingly called "cites"), or religious or ideological schools of thought.[8] How can we truly live with our friends today? Various projects bring us together at times, but equally often drive us apart, allowing us, no doubt, to develop other friendships, but not to maintain them; they last only as long as we're working together, and evaporate as soon as the work is done because we lack other points of connection, other shared values that form the basis of social practice.

So I find myself looking for a verb that will be to friendship what the verb *to love* is to love, one that will express that it is not a state, but an activity, a dynamic and continual engagement. *Amitier*—to enfriend. As one might say "to engage"—with no time limit embedded in the term and a pledge of active presence implied.

* * *

Maurice Blanchot, thinking of Dionys Mascolo, considers friendship's beginnings: "There's no 'at first sight' with friendship; instead, it occurs little by little, the slow work of time. You've become friends before you're even aware of it."[9] Though that's not how I would put it; it seems to me that when one becomes a friend, one is necessarily aware of it. Friendship doesn't happen without some degree of self-awareness. The things we say and do both to and with our friends are the words and the actions of a friend. They wouldn't be if our intentions weren't friendly, and how could our intentions be friendly if they were unaware of themselves? And yet a friendship must be born, which roots it in time, though it's only after the fact that its birth is perceptible.

On the other hand, one can be misled by "protestations of friendship" that use the term for something actually alien to its principles,

---

[8]For more on this, see Jean-Luc Nancy, who, in his book *La Communauté affrontée* (Paris, Galilée, coll. "La Philosophie en effect," 2001), returns to the idea of community that he developed in *La Communauté désoeuvrée* (Paris, Bourgois, coll. "Détroits," 1986, new edition, 1999). In particular, he notes how much the idea of *Gemeinschaft*, for instance, is immediately associated with Hitler's regime in Germany and recalls the Nazi *Volksgemeinschaft*.
[9]Maurice Blanchot, *Pour l'amitié* (Paris, Fourbis, 1996), 9.

but that's a defensive position that usually soon reveals its true nature and the background thoughts on which it's founded. The true friend doesn't worry about what could be; he affirms without reservation that which is. He's not trying to mend a past whose shadow he fears; he engages a future from which he has everything to hope. Our earliest friendships, those of childhood and adolescence, are this sort. Then as time passes, we come to know others, less emotional and more professional, political, or literary, and perhaps more reasonable and temperate in their foundation. And, some would say, without illusions. And yet all friendships are nourished by projects, hopes, and promises—and therefore also by illusions. A friendship that doesn't expose itself to possible deception is no more than a partnership, an association. To be connected to another person by a contract does not involve a friendship, though one might develop as a side effect. To paraphrase Stendhal, friendship, like beauty, is a promise of happiness, and there is always the risk that this promise might not be kept. The promise is not for anything specific; rather, it's the link of friendship itself that is the promise.

Based on his analysis of *philia*, Aristotle tried to show that friendship is essential to our happiness precisely because it is an act, or a disposition (*hexis*), and not a state. Being kind is not enough because "he who is kind stops at good wishes, while a real friend also brings those wishes to fruition. Kindness is, in effect, the beginning of friendship: all friends are kind, but all kind people are not friends."[10]

In other words, friendship does not rest solely with intention, but requires the actualization of those intentions. Moreover, his preference for action over state of being means that, for Aristotle, to like someone is superior to being liked. The connection might not be immediately apparent, but will be if we think of the sense of fulfillment we feel when an expressed feeling is reciprocated as opposed to when it is not. To be liked might touch us—though it might also leave us indifferent, or even irritated—but it doesn't really change us overall. And yet, returning to Aristotle, what distinguishes liking a person (*philia*) from liking a thing (*philésis*) is that the former always asks to be returned; it supposes a reciprocal action. If mean-spirited people are incapable of friendship, it's because they prefer things to people, or they treat people as things, not as themselves and not *absolutely*, but as part of an arithmetic of joys and sorrows—in other words, relative to themselves and as other things. The mean-spirited

---

[10]Aristotle, *Eudemian Ethics*, VII, 7, 1241a 12, 1241a 15.

expect no more from people than they do from things. Solitary, with no sense of community—which also means no elementary sense of justice—they cannot know friends. It's a case that doesn't come up often, for, as Plato points out in *The Republic*, even a band of thieves who associate in order to commit unjust actions can't completely transgress the rules of justice, which is the only thing that can maintain agreement and friendship.[11]

So, while in principle *philia* presumes a reciprocity of feeling, in practice, there's simply something inherent in friendship that wants to share the feeling with another. And yet the desire is not enough in itself; it also must be realized in a "common life," which for a friend is an end in itself; it's the act for which the desire was only an impetus. "For," as Aristotle rightly says, "there is no friend without an effort and no friend for a single day; it takes time."[12]

Commenting on this passage, Derrida emphasizes the notion of time and the insistence on effort or shared experience: "To get to the act behind the *hexis*, to continually renew or reaffirm the viability of a friendship, presumes a reinvention, a reengagement of its freedom."[13] This does not devalue the childhood friendships that stay with us our entire lives, for the time he's talking about is the time required for a friendship to develop, not how long it lasts nor how much time is shared—people are not necessarily better friends for having been friends longer.

Friendships in youth, though, do have a very particular status. They are involved in the beginning of our lives. They're "full of promise," being the intensified sensation of all friendship. Such a friendship is a founding moment, one of oaths that bind, of projects that call, and of promises that tie us to others. This doesn't mean that it's a purely virtual relationship—quite the opposite; the founding gesture of the friendship is always occurring again, always reactualizing itself. Evoking the Aristotelian definition of nature, it could be viewed as *the act of what is in force to the degree that it is in force*, except that "it is much more beautiful to say 'virtue' than 'nature.'"[14]

And childhood friendships aren't flickering, tentative friendships; on the contrary, they affirm, with an overflowing force, a new link that seems as solid as its discovery is recent and charged with the enthusiasm of an approach to an unknown shore. Once the attraction

---

[11]Plato, *The Republic*, Book 1, 351c.

[12]Aristotle, *Eudemian Ethics*, 1238a 1, 1238a 3.

[13]Jacques Derrida, *The Politics of Friendship*.

[14]Aristotle, *Eudemian Ethics*, op. cit., 1238a 13, 1238a 14.

of novelty has passed, if the friendship lasts, something of its capacity for wonder will remain the age at which the link was forged, and its value will be recognized by comparing it with other links forged that were forged afterward without replacing it.

This kind of friendship corresponds to the Aristotelian category of things principally founded upon pleasure, "for young people live in the empire of passion, and are engaged, above all, with what pleases them and with the pleasure of the moment."[15] For, when the object of pleasure changes, friendship changes too, which happens often because "the pleasures of this age are subject to abrupt variations."[16] These are the friendships of our youth, those that go back to the time that we were creating ourselves, in that time between childhood and adulthood.

The concept of adolescence in the modern sense is fairly recent, dating back to the second half of the eighteenth century. From that period on, it has been considered a stage of life separate from childhood, an intermediary stage that some consider the product of a new system of the transmission of knowledge.[17] Be that as it may, Rousseau, for whom "adolescence is the age of neither vengeance nor hate," but rather that of "commiseration" and "generosity," thought that "the first feeling that a carefully raised young man is open to is not love, but friendship"[18] because people are first sensitive to people like themselves before being affected by the opposite sex—which raises the question of friendship between the sexes.

Adolescence is a period of innocence, when our feelings are so strong that the pleasures and, above all, the pains of the other are our own. The logical outcome of Rousseau's principles and social vision suggests that *self-love*, that sensation that leads people to self-preservation, as long as it's held in check by compassion, spontaneously engenders friendship. When an adolescent enters the world, this self-love is transformed into the sense of *self-esteem*, which leads us to put ourselves before others.[19] As soon as this shift occurs, friendship is lost whenever self-consideration becomes the guide. Reason, on the one hand,

---

[15]Aristotle, *Nicomachean Ethics*, viii, 3 1156a 19-b 6.

[16]Aristotle, *Nicomachean Ethics*, viii, 3 1156a 19-b 6.

[17]See Philippe Ariès, *L'Enfant et la vie familiale sous l'Ancien Régime* (Paris, Seuil, coll. "L'Univers historique," 1973). Anne Vincent-Buffault, *L'Exercise de l'amitié. Pour une histoire des pratiques amicales aux XVIIIe e XIXe siècles* (Paris, Seuil, coll. "La Couleur de la vie," 1995).

[18]Jean-Jacques Rousseau, *Emile* . . . It's at this age that one is able to share pleasure and suffering, to experience "compassion," which, in "taking us out of ourselves" allows us to experience the suffering of others.

[19]Rousseau, *Discourse on the Origin and Foundations of Inequality*.

is exclusively calculating, while on the other, it has no power over emotion. This means that the one cannot be conquered, elided, or led astray by the other. Besides the fact that Rousseau is describing friendship in the modern sense, founded first on feeling[20]—and without considering what it means for his own philosophy—it's worth noting that this is the same account that people today evoke, at least implicitly, when they claim to be skeptical, whether slightly or extremely, of feelings of friendship.

The friendships of youth are sometimes exalted in order to compare them to friendships between adults, casting the latter in an unfavorable light. The idealization of friendship in some nineteenth-century novels, as well as the implication that the feeling is no longer possible in our modern world, is largely responsible for friendship's reputation for being chimerical and utopic. The time of promise corresponds to *"l'age des possibles."*[21] It's this stage of life that inspired the *Bildungsroman*, or the coming-of-age novel; according to the romantics, *Wilhelm Meister* was the epitome of the genre. The guiding concept of such works and of the bonds of the friendships they depict is that of a consciousness developing a sense of self through being tested by the world, usually by a series of encounters that also gives the work its narrative structure. One strain of romanticism tended to privilege *internal friendships* over the more "heroic" version—also estimable in their eyes—of external friendship, which "always demands that one win new brothers," as Schlegel put it in *Lucinde*. He thought of internal friendship as "entirely spiritual"; it does not need action in order to be tested. It's a universal feeling that binds us to others, and "he who feels humanity and the world in his deepest self cannot, without difficulty, seek a universality, a universal spirit where there is not one."[22] Curiously, here we again find the progression that leads from the ancient concept of *philia* (which, again in Schlegel's words, "always uses virtue to tighten the ancient knot") to the vision of Christian love, which "in its humility, knows how to honor the divinity of the other."[23]

Hegel was not wrong in thinking that romanticism was the fulfillment of Christian art, and therefore also the fullest representation

---

[20]As Allan Bloom has showed, stating that "Rousseau radicalizes the modern conception according to which man is essentially a being of feeling rather than a rational animal." *Love and Friendship* (New York: Simon & Schuster, 1993).

[21]To borrow the title of a beautiful film by Pascale Ferran.

[22]Friedrich Schlegel, *Lucinde*.

[23]Ibid.

of Christian love—even if he considered his contemporary romantics already beyond the sphere of art. Rooting the promise of love and the constancy of friendship in loyalty, he writes that "friendship in this sense develops principally in youth. That is its moment in human life." But, he adds, clearly each man must make his way in the world to a social position, make a name for himself, and start a family. Thus, friendship, which begins in "a fusion of feeling, will, and action," is later dominated by more or less common material interests, which often give rise to discord. Even if one can still speak of friendship or intimacy in middle age, "it is no longer the friendship of youth, in which one of the two friends never decides anything without consulting the other and would never do anything that would make the other unhappy."[24]

This view is characteristic of a "bourgeois" vision of the world, of a way of life subordinated to the demands of production and profitability, a "realist" vision that fits what we mean today by the word friendship, but that is, in fact, a contradiction split between the aspiration to an ideal companionship and a pragmatism calculated to replace a dream, creating a social context for amicable relationships while simultaneously draining them of their substance. Thus friendship as Montaigne conceived it, for example, would be no more than a sweet dream, a luxury enjoyed only by poets and the young—and by the ancients, who could attain it because they were focused more on spiritual than economic prosperity. From this perspective, Greek society would be to civilization what adolescence is to the evolution of the contemporary individual.

What other kinds of friendships are possible? That's the key question. For, in fact, for the most part, what binds us to a friend is not at all concrete, and is more often a word than a contract, and it's impossible to foresee all the conditions that may arise. What guarantees do we have that another's word will be kept? Hannah Arendt considered a promise to be a way of diffusing an unpredictability rooted in a constitutional uncertainty—what will I be tomorrow?—and on "the impossibility of foreseeing the consequences of an act among a community of equals."[25] For her, a mutual promise assures the cohesion of a group when its members are dispersed. A promise maintains the ties of friendship that distance could otherwise erode. Friendship is also—just like love—something that is wanted, and a promise

---

[24]G. W. F. Hegel, *Aesthetics.*
[25]Hannah Arendt, *The Condition of Modern Man.*

participates in this willingness; it is, according to Nietzsche's construction, "a continuity within wanting," "a veritable memory of the will."[26]

This means that the man who has overcome this uncertainty, who "is like no one but himself," the man who is "master of his own will, independent and persistent, the man who *can promise*" to use Nietzsche's terms, has acquired a true self-understanding and self-reliance and so exercises a certain power over circumstances and time. He has his own internal judge, and finds the source of his values within himself. He is, in other words, a person who has attained virtue, or the "human excellence" theorized by the Greeks, and who attracts the kind of admiration that fosters the ties of friendship.

In light of this, I don't see how Blanchot could have written: "Friendship is not a gift, not a promise, and not categorical generosity. As an incommensurable relationship between one person and another, it is the outside connected to its rupture and inaccessibility."[27] It's not that I don't agree with the second clause, it's that I don't agree that it excludes the first, except perhaps by reducing a promise to a word that determines the circumstances and engagements that bind friends. Blanchot is most likely using it in the generic sense, but at a deeper level, the promise is the motion that makes all friendly or loving relations dynamic. The "promised" is the product of a fundamental promise that could also be called a *hope*—a meaning that we still find in the phrase "the promise of," which means the hope of—the hope that opens up the future in and for a loving or friendly community. Friends are always hoping for something that will fundamentally link them, and it's not anything specific; for example, one does not hope that the other will change in some particular way or do some particular thing; rather, what friends hope for is hope itself, the very thing we live on, and friendship is the promise of an endless hope that allows friends to undertake together what they cannot do alone. And that requires us to never give up those youthful moments in which we think we're going to accomplish today what, in fact, life will endlessly defer. You have to know, and without cynicism, how to occupy this very gap and how to keep a certain distance—which is, no doubt, what distinguishes childhood friendships from those of maturity. It's in this sense that friendship is not a state but an activity, not an *ergon* but an *energeia*. Things that could be done without

---

[26]F. Nietzsche, *Genealogy of Morals*, Vol. 2.
[27]Maurice Blanchot, *The Writing of the Disaster*.

111

friendship, but that we never actually do, become, thanks to friendship, effectively and intellectually desirable, even imperative, to the point that we can't imagine why we haven't done them before—they seem that obvious.

This promise has a name: it is joy. It's not just the pleasure of being together that fires the mind and provokes spontaneous laughter, the desire to joke about nothing and everything. It is, even more deeply, the tendency to go always a bit further, to surpass ourselves in the direction of what we do better together and can only accomplish together, the one with the other and each one for himself. What we give each other mutually, we consider as excess, *without premeditation*, as they say in cases of involuntary homicide. Except that, in this case, it's a matter of life, not of death. To someone who complains that they haven't done all for us that they could have, we say, "It's the thought that counts." But in this case, the gift surpasses the thought; it is pure promise, the promise to overflow our friendship toward a higher friendship, the paradoxical promise to attempt together what we could only do alone, one for the other: "Ah! seest thou not, O brother, that thus we part only to meet again on a higher platform, and only be more each other's, because we are more our own? A friend is Janus-faced: he looks to the past and the future. He is the child of all my foregoing hours, the prophet of those to come, and the harbinger of a greater friend."[28]

---

[28]Ralph Waldo Emerson, "Friendship," *Essays: First Series*, 1847.

All of Us
Michelle Herman

ALL OF US WERE MIDDLE-AGED. All of us were tired. All of us had children, many of them grown or almost grown. Two of us were single mothers of still-young adopted children and thus were especially tired, as was the one of us who'd given birth to twins the year before (at forty-five, after three rounds of IVF)—she was *spectacularly* tired, even though the father of the twins, who was nine years younger, was in residence, sleeping on the far side of their California King, the twins nestled between them.

But there wasn't one of us who *wasn't* tired: none of us had had a good night's sleep in at least fifteen years. *Fifteen?* one of us said. *Try twenty-one.* (She was the one of us whose eldest daughter had just dropped out of Cornell and moved back home.) One of us—who had a thirteen-year-old daughter she'd adopted out of foster care the year before—wondered aloud then if she'd ever get a good night's sleep again, and one of us (she was the mother of twin ten-month-olds with her much younger husband) said, *God, seriously, I was just asking myself the same thing.* Two of us—one whose twenty-seven-year-old daughter was teaching in China, and one whose son was seventeen and newly driving *and* who'd recently become a stepmother (her new husband, in a reversal of the paradigm, had left his young wife for her, a woman of his own age) to two children under four, of whom her husband shared joint custody with his abandoned young ex-wife—said, at exactly the same time, *No, not a chance.*

Three of us, in fact, were now stepmothers. One of us was a step-*grand*mother—her second husband's daughter had just had a daughter of her own: the baby was five years and two months younger than our friend's only child. *We all call him Uncle Henry now,* she had said last week when some of us were out to dinner and she passed around a photograph of her five-year-old son holding his baby niece.

At first, when John said it—just teasing, you know?—I was sure Henry would hate it. Remember last year when we told him he was going to be in his sister's wedding? And he started crying and he wouldn't stop? He kept saying, "I can't, I don't want to, I'm just a little kid," and it took hours before I figured out that he thought it meant he was getting married? But somehow this *is all right with him. He wants to bring the baby in for show-and-tell. He says he's going to ask everybody in his kindergarten class to call him Uncle Henry.*

Is that cute or is that awful? one of us, whose children were both in college, asked. *Honestly, I just can't tell.*

He's yanking your chain, one of us said. She was a psychotherapist; her children were teenagers. The rest of us laughed. *Is that your professional opinion?* one of us asked her.

No, really, said the one of us who was a step-grandmother (and the mother of five-year-old Henry, wife of John, stepmother of Minerva). *I think he's enjoying it. And he seems terribly amused that his half sister now refers to me as Grandma. "Let's see if Grandma can figure out what you're crying about," she'll say to the baby.*

All of us groaned. None of us felt old enough—we *weren't* old enough—to be grandmothers. One of us had just had twin babies! Two of us had started new careers within the last few years. We were forty-four through fifty-one years old. We were just getting used to middle age. Old age was next, still far away. *One thing at a time,* we told each other. But we knew it didn't always work that way. Maybe it hardly ever did.

*

All of us had been friends for a long time—ten, twelve, fifteen, twenty years. Two of us went back further still, to college (the two who'd gone to college here, in this town, where all of us would end up living), and came into our circle as a pair. Among the rest of us, there

114

was some uncertainty about who'd met whom first, who had been the last to join us, and (for that matter) when it was that we'd begun to think of us as *us*, a circle we eventually closed, allowing no one else to be admitted. None of us could recall when or how this had—by unspoken agreement—occurred either.

We'd met, all of us except the two who'd met in college and then claimed this town as home (or, perhaps, vice versa: were claimed by the town, which all of us found charming), when our careers and marriages—for all but four of us were married then—were just starting out. Very few of us had children. None of us who taught, either at the university or (as one of us did) at the high school, had yet been granted tenure. None of us had yet survived a life-threatening disease.

But that was when we were all in our early to midthirties. By middle age, three of us had been sick, one near death, and were now well. Three of us were sober alcoholics. Three of us now were unmarried. Four of us were in our second marriages; one of us was in a third. Only one of us had never married—although one of us had been divorced for so long that by her middle forties (she had married at twenty-two and divorced by twenty-six) she insisted that she could hardly remember what being married had been like. (Still, she said, she remembered well enough to know that she never wanted to be married again.)

One of us had married for the second time so long ago she swore she had retained no memory of her first marriage. *None at all?* the rest of us asked. *Not even of the fights? Not even that*, she said. *Not even why you left?*

Not even his name, she said, and all of us supposed that was a joke.

*

All of us, even those of us who still dressed the way we had at sixteen, who still wore our hair long (one of us had waist-length hair), relied on expensive beauty regimens. Two of us used Botox. All but four of us colored our hair (only two of us had let our hair go gray; the other two had not yet started to *go* gray). None of us had gone as far as plastic surgery, but some of us talked (idly, it was sworn) about it. (*Perhaps*, one of us said, *if we lived on one of the coasts?* The rest of us laughed, but a number of us wondered if this might be true.)

All but one of us had "issues"—only one of us did not invoke the word ironically, with scare quotes—about our weight. One of us had been thin all her life but tried not to be impatient when we spoke of low-carb versus counting calories, or when one of us complained of always being hungry or of being perfectly successful at Weight Watchers or Jenny Craig until 9:00 PM, when she would work her way through the refrigerator and the pantry before bed. Two of us had once been anorexic, one of us bulimic. One of us insisted she was overweight but wasn't and had never been, at least not since we'd known her (had she ever? could it be? she was so thin!), and when *she* spoke of the diet she was on—she was always trying a new one, something none of us had heard of until she turned up at lunch or dinner worrying over the restaurant's intransigent menu—all of us (except the one of us who'd never in her life been on a diet) would become irritable, but we did our best to hide it. When, for example, she told all of us we *had* to try the Suzanne Somers diet—which, she explained, allowed fruit twenty minutes before carbohydrates or an hour before protein and fat, and forbade meals at which protein or fat coexisted with a carbohydrate—we tried not to roll our eyes.

In general, we tried not to roll our eyes over each other. We tried to excuse each other's foibles, eccentricities, mistakes, and habits. We tried not to judge. But when one of us begged off on plans she had already made with us—as one of us often did—it was only with great effort that we did not speak of it, except to say, *Not coming after all then?* The one of us who often canceled was the only one of us who would not make plans to join us for dinner or a concert or a movie unless she knew her husband would be otherwise engaged—and if, at the last minute, it turned out that he would not be, she would break her date with us. (One of us, the playwright, did sometimes call her and her husband—who, when at a gathering together, stood side by side throughout—"the Bobbsey Twins," but only in the presence of the two of us who we all knew could be relied upon not to repeat such a thing to all the rest of us.)

*

All of us were Democrats. All but one of us were irreligious. One of us had been a preacher's kid. Three of us had been raised Catholic. Four of us were Jewish. One of us, raised Methodist, had converted to Judaism upon marriage, in her twenties, and was by middle age "more Jewish than" her husband (so her husband joked, she said— she herself did not make jokes about this): she volunteered at the synagogue to which they belonged. She washed the bodies of the dead: she was one of the Chevra Kadisha—the holy society. She did not keep kosher but she observed all holidays, including minor ones. All of us and all of our families were invited to come to dinner each autumn under the sukkah she reassembled every year, and for Purim, when our children were young enough to be interested, she would hold hamantaschen-making parties in her kitchen.

One of us—she'd gone to Catholic school; her mother's youngest brother was a priest—had also converted to Judaism when she married but abandoned the conversion (*as easily as stepping out of a pair of shoes that fit too loosely,* one of us who was Jewish by birth but entirely unobservant—as three of us were—remarked, sotto voce, at a Christmas party at the ex-convert's house) when the marriage ended. After she married for the second time, the children celebrated Christmas and Easter with their mother, a playwright, and her new husband, a psychologist, and Hanukkah and Passover with their father (he was a newspaper reporter) and his Jewish-by-birth TV-news-producer girlfriend (whom we knew, for although she wasn't one of us, she sang in a choir to which two of us belonged and played violin in the community orchestra with another of us, who played the flute, and eventually we had all been introduced to her at concerts, in the lobby afterward).

All of us had grievances about the people we were married to, or whom those of us who dated had relationships with and were eventually disappointed by (because they turned out to be unavailable or because they were too available, because they would not marry again "under any circumstances" or because they were too eager to [re]marry, especially if they seemed desperate for help with the children of whom they had partial custody).

All of us were sympathetic to one another's troubles—or at least all of us made sympathetic noises, and if we didn't sympathize, we kept that to ourselves.

*

Nine of us were married to men, three of us married—or all but married—to women. One of us had once been married to a man and was now all but married to a woman. None of us had ever stayed at home full-time, year-round. None of us had ever had a nanny (it was not the sort of town in which one had a nanny), but we had all had babysitters—students at the college, mostly (those of us with children nearly the same age had often shared our sitters, or passed them around)—and sometimes foreign exchange students who lived in for a semester or a year and helped out. Most of us had made use of the university's day care and early preschool.

Only two of us had ever *wished* to be at home full-time. (Those of us who taught were at home full-time every summer and for winter and spring breaks, *which is plenty*, all of us who taught said. One of us didn't mean it.)

Almost half of us had Ferberized our children—let them "cry it out," trained them, early on, to sleep in their own cribs in their own rooms—and the rest of us had variously shared our own beds with our children or made frequent exhausted trips to our crying babies' rooms each night for months or years, or else had moved out of our bedrooms and into our children's, sleeping on a twin bed bought just for this purpose and installed there, for months or years.

Four of us had had abortions. One of us had had multiple abortions while she was still in high school, long before we knew her. Four of us had tried for a long time to get pregnant, and three of the four had. Two with IVF.

*

One of us hated her husband but would never leave him, she told all the rest of us—that was how much she dreaded being alone. (This was not speculation on our part: she said it herself, though only after several glasses of wine, when she also confessed that from time to time she entertained a fantasy about her husband's death. People are so solicitous of widows, she said wistfully. She looked around at us. *Aren't they?* she asked. But none of us were widows yet. We didn't know.)

One of us, who had been single when we'd all first met, had moved two thousand miles away when she'd married her husband, and at first she'd kept in touch, calling one or another of us at least once a week, sending letters and postcards, remembering all of our birthdays. But as the years had passed, we heard from her less and less frequently, and by now we hardly heard from her at all. (And even so, we still thought of her as one of us.)

One of us fell in love with her ob-gyn soon after she turned forty-four—and he fell in love back, although the two of them did not do anything (or much of anything) about it. They exchanged hundreds, perhaps thousands, of e-mails, and had long talks on the phone when they could manage it; they met for whispered, nervous conversations (was there anywhere in town that truly was private, she asked us rhetorically—where someone who knew one of them wouldn't spot them out together and wonder what *that* was all about?) and twice, when they were sure no one was looking, hand-holding and kisses.

The kisses she told all of us about only after the affair was over—but it wasn't an *affair*, all of us said (except the one who'd moved away, who didn't know anything about it—who didn't know anything about what any of us were up to anymore). There was no proper name for it, we all agreed (except for one of us, who at first suggested that what had transpired was what was called an *emotional affair*—and the

119

rest of us, sensitive to language, sensitive to sentimentality, scoffed, and the one who'd said it, the only one of us who did not use scare quotes around "issues," the only one of us who read the sort of magazines that featured articles about "emotional affairs," backed down, agreeing with the rest of us).

One of us had been beaten—just once, but once was enough—by her first husband. One of us had not slept with the husband she'd had from the start—by now they had been married for eleven years—for at least the last six years, she said, and possibly it had been even longer. *You don't know?* one of us asked. She shrugged. *I didn't start counting right away.*

One of us, married just as long, swore that she and her husband had sex twice a week.

Most of us, however, did not speak of our sex lives at all, except sometimes to talk about what we had been like when we were teenagers or girls in our twenties. How wild we had been! we said. Or else: how sheltered. How cautious—or how reckless. How foolish. None of us claimed to have been wise. Were we wise now? Wis*er*, at least?

All of us wondered.

*

We would get together for dinner or for lunch, two or three of us or a small group of us or all of us at once (except the one who'd moved away, and—if her husband wasn't otherwise engaged—the one of us who was referred to as a Bobbsey Twin from time to time by one of us), and we would complain or brag about our children and we would complain about the people we were married to or dating. We'd complain about our jobs, our weight, our hair, our lives, mostly (but not always) good-naturedly, and we would tell stories and repeat good jokes we'd heard. We talked about what we'd been reading and what movies we had seen with husbands, wives, partners, or dates; we talked about the news and about trips we'd taken recently to New York City or Chicago or LA or Washington, DC, about the plays we'd seen, the art museums we had visited, the restaurants we'd eaten in.

We talked about our parents—those of us who still had parents. Two of us were orphans. Two of us had lost one parent, one of us when she was still a child. She was the one of us who hated her husband, who daydreamed about his death but would not divorce him. She was the one of us who was an orchestral cellist.

*

We were musicians, painters, poets, playwrights, and professors. One of us was a museum curator, one a psychotherapist. One of us had opened an art gallery the year before with the woman she'd just married; one of us had left a longtime job as an administrator in the School of Humanities and Arts at the university and was now enrolled in cooking school (she was the one who spoke of "issues" unironically). The one of us who taught high school taught English and advised the drama club, was the faculty adviser for the student newspaper and literary magazine, and coached a poetry performance team. (She also wrote short stories, but only two of us knew that about her.) The one who fell in love with her ob-gyn was a painter. The one who had adopted the child she had been foster parenting was the one who had been married once, so long ago that she could not remember married life—she was the museum curator.

One of us sang early music and gave piano and voice lessons privately. One of us was an astronomer—she was the outlier among us, the only one, we teased, who had a head for math. We would hand her the check to work out when we all went out to dinner.

(In truth, the one of us who sang professionally and gave music lessons was better at arithmetic than the astronomer was. None of us except her knew it.)

121

One of us was a professor of comparative studies (she was the one of us whose daughter was in China, the one of us who had not slept with her husband for the last six years). She had served on a faculty committee with the astronomer ten years ago at the university and then soon after had run into her at the opera house downtown, during intermission. The professor of comparative studies, like the astronomer (who was the only one of us who had never married—who had never even lived with anyone), had gone to the opera by herself, and the two went out for drinks afterward and enjoyed a lengthy conversation. Our circle was still incomplete then; the astronomer was quickly adopted into it.

Had the astronomer been the last addition? None of us were sure. Both the museum curator and the gallery owner (who'd worked for over twenty years in other people's galleries and dabbled in photography and sculpture), who'd come into our circle through the painter—who herself had come to us, we were almost certain, through the art history professor—had become our friends around the same time. The rest of us, we were also almost sure, had all already known each other. But it was so hard to remember—we had all been so much younger then. *Practically children*, we liked to say, and then we'd laugh. *We didn't know anything then*, we said. *We were so innocent!*

And optimistic, one of us said.

Yes, and optimistic, all of us agreed, although not all of us remembered it that way.

*

We had all been friends for a long time when the painter fell in love with her ob-gyn somewhere between her first (and only) office visit and their third exchange of e-mails after it. She told us everything about what had happened between them except for the kisses—*I was ashamed to tell you that*, she told us later—but none of us held it against her. Not the kisses, and not the secret. We all had secrets, even though we all behaved as if we didn't.

122

*

All of us were smart, reasonably well informed (all but one of us read or at least skimmed the daily *New York Times*, three of us watched the nightly news on television, all of us listened or said we listened to NPR in our cars), and passionate about particular causes (education reform, public transportation, the environment, health care, homelessness). Ten of us had graduate degrees. One of us, in addition to the poet among us, wrote poetry (this was not a secret; even her students and her two grown children—she was the art history professor and enthusiastic convert to Judaism, whose daughter had dropped out of Cornell—knew all about it), and one of us *read* poetry (which surprised the rest of us, and in particular the poet and the art history professor who wrote poems in her spare time). The one who read poetry was the astronomer, who said that poetry was the only sort of thing worth reading, other than the journals that she was obliged to read and *The New York Times*. One of us, who wrote popular novels, was insulted by this (she told some of us, and we told her she was being silly—even the poet among us told her she was being silly, though secretly she was insulted too, as the astronomer did not read contemporary poetry, only famous long-dead poets).

One of us—the one of us who had until two years before been in administration at the university and who had a teenage son from her first marriage and two young stepchildren thanks to her third husband (who'd left his young wife for her)—read only magazines and cookbooks now and didn't mind (or didn't seem to mind) when we teased her about this. One of us had a weakness for thick Hollywood biographies, and one of us read mysteries and literary thrillers (the poet among us insisted that the latter was an oxymoron). One—the novelist—could not bear, she said, to read other people's novels, and read only memoirs. The poet read novels. The cellist read the letters of the famous long dead. The playwright read plays and European history. (It was impossible for any of us to recommend anything to read to any of the rest of us, or to give each other books as gifts—and yet, stubbornly, we did both anyway.)

Michelle Herman

The one of us who was an English teacher at the high school was the only one of us who read short stories for pleasure, and one Friday night when nearly all of us had gathered at the home of the astronomer, she spoke of a story she had read in which the protagonist, a man of thirty-five, reflected that he was at "the age of grief."

The poet said, *I think I know that story,* and the psychotherapist said that she thought she knew it too. The cellist said, *Wait—what? Thirty-five is the age of grief? What does that mean for us?*

It means that the writer of the story is still in her thirties, said the poet, and all of us laughed. But after a moment one of us—the astronomer, in whose living room we all sat with our wine or Diet Coke or seltzer—said, *Still. Maybe it's true anyway.*

Then what would *that mean for us?* one of us—the one of us who sang early music, whose husband was a decade younger than she was, who had just last year had twins—asked. She made the question sound as if it were a joke.

It would mean that we are in the age of postgrief, one of us—the painter—said. And the poet, who had just been left abruptly by the woman she'd been living with for fourteen years, said, *Oh, let's hope so.*

*

The painter was the youngest of us. She had a four-year-old son, but the ob-gyn she fell in love with was not the doctor who'd delivered him. That doctor had been female, and she had delivered all our children, except those who'd been adopted and the newest ones, the twins. None of us could remember now which one of us had seen her first and recommended her to all the rest of us. But it had been two years now since she'd given up her practice, so suddenly that none of us had even managed to get a referral from her (the one of us who'd had the twins last year, who sang songs written over a thousand years ago, was already seeing a fertility specialist by then, who had referred

124

her to an obstetrician with particular experience with those with "elderly primigravida" in their forties).

We hadn't even realized how dependent we were on the doctor we had all been seeing for so many years (two of us got our Zoloft prescriptions from her, and all of us had told her things we hadn't even told each other) until she was gone. *She didn't even say goodbye!* we said. (One of us had heard that she'd left town to tend to her dying mother; another had heard that she had *fled* town, leaving not only her practice but also her husband for a woman whose child she'd delivered; one of us had heard that she was, in fact, still *in* town, but in hiding—that she was being treated for advanced breast cancer and was not about to spend the time she had left taking care of us and all the other women in her busy practice—*including her lover*? one of us, the playwright, who it seemed could not resist saying this sort of thing, could not keep herself from asking, and the rest of us hushed her.)

The playwright had been the first to see the new ob-gyn—he had been recommended by a sometime colleague in the university's theater department, where our playwright friend would teach a class occasionally—and she had found him genial but generally unimpressive (of course, we had all been so devoted to our former gynecologist, it was going to be hard for anyone to live up to our standards). Three of us had scheduled annual exam appointments with other ob-gyns who'd been recommended by a colleague or a client, but in the meantime the painter, overdue for her checkup, kept the appointment she'd already made with the doctor recommended by the set-design professor to our playwright friend who'd found him wanting, and then she fell in love with him.

The rest of us never met him, and what she told us made it difficult to form a picture of him: he was kind, he *listened* to her, he asked a lot of questions she liked answering, he acted as if everything she said—as if *she*—mattered. He was sweet. He was so *nice*.

And that's enough? some of us asked. (Not that every one of us wasn't thinking the same thing. The rest of us were just polite enough to

125

wonder silently.) Our friend the painter was quiet for a moment. But finally she said, *Haven't any of you ever fallen for somebody because he was kind to you?* All of us said no, we hadn't. But most of us, in that very instant, suddenly remembered a crush on a divorce lawyer, a particularly sympathetic-to-our-side marriage counselor, a gentle periodontist. A yoga teacher. The always-friendly mailman.

None of us had ever let it go beyond a crush, however. (Briefly, we all asked ourselves if a partial explanation for this would include our having so effectively concealed how much we appreciated the divorce attorney/mailman's kindness—for if our friend, with her small, demanding son and the pressure to complete her new series of paintings in time for a scheduled show in New York City, and her brooding, handsome, trumpet-playing husband, had fallen in love because of kindness, surely *he*, the ob-gyn, had fallen in love back because of her appreciation of his kindness.) But there was this too: none of us who were married, we were certain, would have let our marriages be threatened by mere kindness—only passion. And those of us who had been married but now weren't had no recollection of so desperate a need for kindness that it bloomed into a crush, and the one of us who'd never married had no experience of it—we had no idea what she was talking about.

*

But it didn't matter. The romance (such as it was) was doomed to fail. Our friend had known this from the start; she supposed that her beloved had known too. She was an artist of some note, married to a jazz musician also of some note—and even so the two of them, along with their precocious, high-strung son, were always on the brink of a financial crisis; she dressed like a Gypsy, wore her hair down to her waist, drove a twenty-year-old pickup truck, and was a supporter of numerous left-wing causes. She had nursed her son until the week before his fourth birthday, when he had weaned himself. And the ob-gyn was a Republican; he wore suits and ties; he owned more expensive cars than he and his wife, an anesthesiologist, could possibly drive—a *collection* of cars, he called them. He had once spoken of a patient as a "breast-feeding fanatic" because she refused to supplement her nursing with bottles of formula as had been suggested by her pediatrician, she'd reported at an office visit. *Honestly, can you*

126

believe that! he had asked our friend. *The baby isn't gaining weight and she refuses to give him a bottle!*

Even if they had been single, childless—free—there would have been no future in it. So she pointed out to us when it was over, and we nodded, gravely.

But of course they weren't free. Both of them were married; both had still-young children (*he* had three under thirteen). He even declared himself to be *happily* married—he went so far as to insist that he was *deeply in love with* his wife. The painter snorted when she told us this—she couldn't help it—and one of us (the playwright, who could always be counted on for sarcasm) obligingly responded, *Sure, it stands to reason then that he would trade a million e-mails and elaborately arrange four secret meetings with another woman* (we did not yet know about the kisses). But this was the wrong thing to say, for the unhappy painter now took pains to point out that what her beloved *actually* said was that he was deeply in love with his wife *too*—that the emphasis on "too" was notable—and that he had said this very sadly. We did not say anything at all then. We were quick studies, all of us.

But what difference did it make, we thought, if he had said it *sadly*? What difference did it make, in fact, if he *was* "deeply in love" with both his wife and our friend—who might not have been particularly "happy" in her marriage (or in general—but who among us was?), but still had not considered that she might divorce her husband and run off with the ob-gyn? (Although after it was over, the playwright was unable to resist remarking: *Still, if she had, just think! This town would have gotten a reputation as a place where gynecologists run off with their patients.*)

The truth was, we felt sorry for the painter. During the ten months that she had been in love, or had imagined that she was—had told herself she was—even those of us who envied her also felt sorry for her. Only the novelist, who had no memory of her brief, early, child-less marriage (so she swore) and could not be counted on to keep a

127

dinner date with us—she was the one of us who was now a step-grandmother as well as the mother of five-year-old Uncle Henry, who had cried over his half sister's wedding—would invoke the phrase "in love" when she spoke of her feelings for her present husband. The rest of us had not been in love for a long time—not even the one of us who was in her third marriage, who read women's magazines and was learning how to be a chef, with her new husband's blessing; not even the three of us who dated, had romances, dragged ourselves through periodic breakups. Some of us debated whether there was any difference between *being* and *only imagining oneself* in love. How could there be, one of us asked, when being in love *was* an act of imagination? (It could have been almost any one of us who asked.)

Either way—being or imagining—it sounded exhausting. And we were already so exhausted.

Still—it was a complicated sort of feeling sorry for the painter that we all felt while she was in the midst of it.

*

And then it was over, and our pity for her was uncomplicated. We petted her and brought her little presents—chocolates, books we thought she might like (we were wrong), bottles of wine. The cellist and the high-school English teacher both made mix CDs for her; the art history professor and the aspiring chef brought baked goods (a sponge cake and a pie) they had made themselves. We put our arms around her when she cried. We helped to keep her son distracted, hoping to keep him from noticing his mother's grief.

And when, soon after this, the one who'd moved away so long ago called one of us (then called most of the rest of us, one after another—for it seemed that there was no one she could talk to in the place where she had lived now for so many years) to say that she had just found out her husband had been having an affair, we were full of pity for her too. And she too wept, and while we couldn't put our arms around her from two thousand miles away, we made comforting sounds, we told her we had never liked him (though in truth we hadn't really known him; we hardly remembered him), we told her we loved *her*.

But what should she *do*? she asked us, each in turn. Should she forgive him—stay? Or throw him out? Or leave him in the house and take the children? Should she force him to go to counseling? He didn't want to go to counseling. He didn't want to choose between her and the other woman *but he knows he has to*, she told all of us, one at a time. And then there was the matter of the children. *My children mean more to me than anything*, she told us he had said. But obviously that could not be true. Not *more than anything*, we said—to her, and to each other. We didn't say it in the presence of the painter.

Take them and go, one of us—the only one of us who had taken her own child and gone when she'd ended her first marriage, who was now in her third—advised. The museum curator, married once so many years ago that she could not remember it, agreed. Three of us, including the painter, urged forgiveness. The rest of us, to various degrees, equivocated. One of us reported to the rest of us that she had asked, *Do you still love him?* And that our old friend had been infuriated by the question, had said, *How am I supposed to know? I don't even know what that's supposed to mean.*

*

She had been a translator and editor and something of a writer herself, but unlike the rest of us, she had given up all work but motherhood—*and taking care of him*, she added bitterly—when she'd had the first of her children. Her husband's work paid very well (we could not remember what that work was, only that it had brought him out west, had taken her away from us—but it was too late to ask about it now; it would make it seem as if we hadn't been paying attention). She had not worried about money since the start of her marriage. But now she was very worried, she reported. Was *that* why she wasn't leaving? one of us who thought she should leave asked the rest of us. *No*, one of us said—it was the art history professor or the cellist. *Nobody would stay just for the money.*

And then we debated that—just as we'd debated *in love* versus one *imagining oneself in love.* All of us enjoyed this sort of conversation—or perhaps "enjoyed" was not the right word. "Indulged in" was better. All of us indulged in this sort of conversation. We could discuss such things, wondering aloud about them, arguing about them, trading our positions on them endlessly. It was only doing something that was difficult.

And yet—after some months had passed—our old friend and her husband did do something. He moved into the guest room and they went to counseling together. She would come home from each session and call one of us—or several of us, one after another—and report on everything that had transpired. When her husband confessed that he was still seeing the other woman—that he'd never stopped seeing her—we were on the phone with her for hours.

And he blames me, she told us, one by one. *He says he never felt nurtured. That's what he told our therapist! He had the nerve to say I'd never* nurtured *him. But here's the thing—that's not my style. You know me.* Now we were confused, each of us, one by one. *Did* we know her? After all this time?

Still, we said. *That's no excuse for what he did.*

That's not the point, she said.

It wasn't? we asked. What was the point then?

The point, she said furiously—and for a moment each of us, all of us, imagined what it might have felt like to have been her husband—*the point is that he never* told *me that he needed nurturing. Is it fair to hold it against me that I didn't give him something that he never even let me know he needed?*

No, it wasn't fair, we said, staunch friends even at this distance, even after so much time. We were confused, our pity suddenly turned complicated, and all of us—even those of us who weren't married—wondered all at once about what might seem obvious to us but wasn't to the ones we loved, and who loved us.

But still we said it. *Not fair!* we all cried. *Not fair at all!*

*

Finally, our old friend and her husband were divorced. And some time after that, she married again, as did her ex-. The counseling hadn't worked, she said, but she told us about how they had "come to terms," and how the children, afterward, had seemed no worse for wear, how both she and her first husband were much better off than they had been before. The phone calls came less and less frequently and then eventually stopped. By the time all of us received our invitations to her eldest daughter's wedding, a whole decade had gone by.

By this time four more of us will have divorced, including the painter—but not including the comp studies professor who'd long ago stopped sleeping with her husband. The Bobbsey Twins divorce. The former administrator, now a chef and the co-owner of a gastropub with a fellow student from the cooking school, divorces her third husband. *Never again*, she says, but we do not believer her.

One of us is widowed now. Not the one who had daydreamed about it, the cellist—she is still married to the same husband. Four more of us have lost our parents. Four of us are now orphans.

Many of our children finish growing up, leave home, begin their own lives. Five of us are grandparents. The one of us who'd moved away, whose eldest daughter is now married (three of us flew out west for the wedding), adopts a baby with her second husband, although she is fifty-six. A private adoption. She calls just one of us—one of the three who'd come to her daughter's wedding—to report this news

131

and asks if she would spread the word as she sees fit. A few weeks later, all of us receive engraved announcements.

The playwright doesn't say a word, which surprises all of us.

The poet, who has just suffered through a terrible divorce from the woman she was married to for only a year, and who has now joined the ranks of the sober among us—now there are six—suggests, over dinner, that we may have reached the age of *post*-postgrief.

All of us laugh. *Hear, hear,* says the painter. *Here's to being beyond being beyond grief,* one of us—it's hard to tell which one, as we are all still laughing—says.

None of us believe it. Even so, all of us raise a glass—some wine, some water. The age of grief is never-ending, we all know that. All of us are grieving, always, for one thing or another, or one person or another, or ourselves.

Trailer

Robert Clark

THE LAST TIME WE SPOKE was July 17, 2010. My phone bill says I called him at 1:23 in the afternoon at a number near Asheville, North Carolina, and the call lasted for one minute; I must have left a message or else we spoke for just a moment. He called me back at 2:30—this was 2:30 my time, so it was 5:30 for him; and I picture the heat of the day having just crested, the shadows pooling on the east side of his crappy trailer—and we spoke for ninety minutes. That was not long for us; sometimes we'd go on for two and a half hours. Still, in hindsight, ninety minutes seems a long time: I think now, hadn't he gotten hungry; didn't he need to piss or take an insulin shot? But he would rather talk; talk at all costs regardless of the wants of body or soul. Like me, he cared only for words.

I called him back the next afternoon at 2:28, again for just a minute; again I left a message; we never spoke again. Doubtless the message concerned nothing much of consequence, maybe something I said I'd follow up on or maybe I merely wanted to talk. Maybe I wanted more of what I'd had the day before: gossip, commiseration, flattery. But he hadn't picked up: he was outside walking among the other crappy trailers, chatting with the cat lady who lived in the double-wide opposite him, or perhaps he'd gotten a ride into Asheville for an appointment with the psychiatrist who orchestrated his battery of medications: Depakote, Lamictal, Neurontin, Risperdal, and Seroquel, separately or in concert depending on the pitch of his mood, thrumming or stagnant or shattered but, in any case, haunted. Or he might merely be lying on his couch, not answering, too sapped and bled out to lift the receiver. Knowing that likelihood, I tried not to take it personally; at times he was hardly a person to himself at all.

Together, though, we were above all else mutual narcissists. When we looked in the mirror we saw, of course, ourselves, but also each other: divorced middle-aged men; once "promising" authors who'd run out of gas; men in trouble with women; depressives and maniacs in and out of various therapies and drug regimens; men bewitched by certain nostalgias embodied in music, landscape, and especially

133

books; but most of all men who wrote or wanted to get themselves writing again and couldn't.

I would like to claim this amounted to a great friendship, that we supported and protected and encouraged one another even if we could never quite save each other. Certainly I couldn't save him. I didn't even know he was dead until eighteen months after the fact. But that is in the nature of writers. The book you are writing—or failing to write—is indistinguishable from yourself; is always the main and pretty much only thing. It precludes the extreme sorts of compassion friendship can require: inconvenience, even sacrifice, or loyalty. As Fitzgerald said of his friend Hemingway, "Ernest would always give a helping hand to a man on a ledge a little higher up." Hemingway, to be sure, was a championship bully and interpersonal larcenist. But I myself promised Jeff (that was his name) for four years straight that I would come visit him. Yet I never did, even as he was fired from the menial jobs that were his lot, was checked in and out of psychiatric wards, dashed his heart against one woman or another, lost his credit, his car, and his home, all the while laying down miles of ink, albeit in notebooks rather than actual manuscripts; sketches, outlines, and proposals rather than stories; words rather than writing. I did finally go to Asheville and to the trailer just outside of town two years after he'd died, but only when I thought I might get a piece of writing for myself out of it.

I intend for that to sound frank and unsparing—I mean for it to mean that for you, the reader—but the truth, the emotional, felt truth, is elsewhere, somewhere altogether less dramatic and perhaps less meaningful, at least in the way I intend. Which is not to say I'm being untruthful or insincere, or even that I'm valuing style over substance, in creating an impression. I am merely trying to make things interesting.

So let me stipulate that I feel bad that Jeff is dead and that I wish I had done any number of things differently while he was alive; that if I am not quite ashamed of myself, I have many regrets; that if I am not exactly guilty of anything I am not innocent either. And if I cannot say what or why that condition is, I would like to try to describe how it was and how it is or, rather, remains.

But Jeff described that approach just as well, unbeknownst to me and on that same day we'd talked for the last time. He wrote in his journal, "Do not need to understand it to write about it—*how* is the interesting question, not why. As long as you can say *how* it was, what it was *like*." I know this because I persuaded Jeff's mother to

134

let me see all the papers and notebooks he left behind, and that was in his entry for July 17. From my own archive of e-mails I also know we talked that day about agents and editors: later that evening I contacted my agent with the address of the editor of Jeff's first and only book; the editor had moved to a new publishing house and Jeff must have thought he might be a good prospect for the novel I was then trying to place. I in turn prompted Jeff to buy some books (Julia Blackburn's *The Three of Us*, Simon Gray's *The Smoking Diaries*), not that it required much effort to persuade him to do so. Over one manic weekend during an efflorescence of his bipolar disease, he'd ordered $1,500 worth of books and CDs from Amazon. Amazon took them back (I think he'd volunteered to send an explanatory note from his psychiatrist), but even in his most levelheaded moments he could not forgo buying books or making lists of ones he wanted or loading up his online shopping basket with another dozen titles. Jeff believed in "models," in the template, or at least inspiration he hoped to find in someone else's book for his own books. And if it wasn't in one book, maybe it would be in the next one, or perhaps the one after that; would be the lucky bet in his Amazon queue, the daily double, and he could see his way beyond the notebook and into the tale, the work, the thing itself. My approach was different: I wanted my books to be self-generating—I feared contamination or didn't want to be in anyone's debt—and in any case I was never as broke as Jeff nearly always was. I could support my own habit and at times I enabled his. In his journal entry for July 17, he'd noted the titles of the books I'd recommended and I know from his own e-mail archive (to which his mother also gave me access) that he ordered one of them that same evening.

It pleases me that he thought enough of me and our conversations to not only jot down the books I liked, but (I also see in his journals) to take down some of the advice I offered. For example, after that list of books he wrote "being preoccupied with the scaffolding rather than the substance" and I know I said this because it is something I still say to writing students today; that often the conceits or opening lines and paragraphs or epigraphs that seem so essential at the start are things the writer needs to clear her throat, to launch herself into the work, and, having served their purpose, can then be jettisoned. And now I read the journal page again and I also realize that it was not Jeff but I who must have said "*how* is the interesting question"; that the remark is written directly above the list of books, among the things I said that day.

So I said it and Jeff rendered it again in his scrolled and pitching, precise and headlong cursive italic. He'd have been in the trailer, on his couch or at his desk, the cats (one tabby, one piebald) dozing, the tolling of the crickets outside taut and sheer. He would have had music on (maybe the Byrds singing Dylan's "My Back Pages") and that would have mellowed the heat, defused the piercing light through the window even as evening fell, and he would have been consoled by it; and maybe by putting down the words that had passed between us, the veil of Seroquel and all the rest lifted for a moment.

Nothing, though, came unstuck. The journal pages from the weeks that followed tell how Jeff tacked between a novel (called *Bend*) and a memoir of his childhood (*This Boy, That Town, These Mountains*) and now and again a third thing would heave into view, a sequel to his one great success, *Where the Roots Reach for Water*. That book had been a memoir of his lifelong depression and the relief he got by giving up SSRIs, finding faith, and marrying a compassionate and understanding woman. But after publication, after the reviews and awards, the faith ebbed, the marriage withered, and it turned out depression was really a misdiagnosis. He was bipolar, and profoundly so. Medications and hospitalizations saved his life, or at least stopped him from ending it himself. By the summer of 2010, he'd attained a kind of equilibrium and he began to imagine he could write about that. He thought he'd call the book *Balance*; he'd sketch and outline hard for a few days, but then turn back to the novel or the childhood memoir or merge two projects: why not deploy the first chapter of *Bend* as a prelude to *Balance*? Or he'd think about writing poetry. He was friends with a poet who'd won a Pulitzer Prize and Jeff would e-mail him and more or less ask, "How do you write poems?" and the poet would reply, cordially but with gentle evasion; he wouldn't or couldn't say.

My own advice didn't get him anywhere and hadn't, truth be told, gotten me very far either: my desk and notebooks were a mirror image of Jeff's; seventy-five pages of a stalled-out novel, two first drafts of personal essays that I fancied might metamorphose into a book, and a previous novel I couldn't sell or even place with an agent. At the time we talked, I thought mine was a different case from his, not so far gone. My circumstances would change (be restored to what they'd been during my own instant of success) any day by way of a phone call or e-mail from New York. Now, three years on, I see there was no difference between us; that there still isn't—the phone call or e-mail hasn't come—except that I am alive to grasp the fact of it.

That recognition hasn't taught me much. I still offer advice and lately I've been suggesting to my students that they attempt what I call a "thought experiment." Suppose, I like to say, everything were different, not just the circumstances but the categories; suppose the problem were entirely elsewhere, no longer where or what you thought; and now you call it by a different name, address it as something new and startling, and both it and you are transfigured.

So: suppose Jeff and I were not quite so defeated by our incapacity to form the words we needed, or perhaps we'd come to think it wasn't words we wanted at all. Because one more phrase will make no difference in the galaxy of sentences that constellated our worlds, even if that phrase was precisely, stunningly congruent with how this or another thing seems to us. And maybe that thing never required us— never asked us—to write about it anyway, but only to be loved, attended to, loved not for what or why it is, but how it is. All that and more could be accomplished in utter silence. Jeff and I could rest then; he could have rested, not craved so much and frustrated himself so much, and survived (which is to say simply remained just here, just now, wherever near Asheville that is) and his presence attended to, perhaps by me. That, beyond all the books I might ever write, would be plenty to desire.

Here's the last thing he wrote after we'd talked on July 17:

> What I have reached is nowhere near redemption or rebirth, it is acceptance. And having arrived here, I realize this is where I've gone wanting for nearly fifty years.

He would have written that sitting on his couch just before or after he clicked the Amazon order button (I think he would have liked the book, if he ever read it; there was always more than he could ever get to). And it was on that couch that the cat lady from the next trailer over saw him through his window two months later, apparently asleep. She knocked on the door repeatedly and, when there was no response, banged on it hard—"I beat on it as hard as I could," she told me when I came to Asheville—and then she called 911. The EMT came and the sheriff and then the coroner. The next day someone from the county arrived to secure the trailer and his personal effects. "His cats were locked in there," she'd tell me. "I'd managed to put some food inside for them earlier and I told the county people I'd adopt them but they said they had to go to the pound: that was the rules. And I begged and begged, but they took them away—those poor babies. Jeff loved those babies. Seems to me that was the very cruelest part of all."

I thought about that last thing she'd said and dismissed it: what was it compared to Jeff's being dead, or a book, his or mine; the one I might just then begin? But then I write a little in my journal, envying his italic hand. I conduct a thought experiment, and think, yes, why not; why shouldn't it be that way, the pitiful how of it, exactly so?

Plane Light, Plane Bright
Jonathan Carroll

"HE WAS NEVER LUCKY with the stars, so he switched to planes."

They were sitting at the bar of the 25 Hour hotel in Zurich. Outside it was raining. She was drinking whiskey and a few minutes before had asked him to tell her a story. A rainy night story. A two-whiskey story. He loved doing that. He loved talking with her anytime, but *this* story . . . well, this one was special. He knew she'd be hooked by it because she liked weird things. It was time to tell it to her anyway to see what she thought. Because it *was* about them after all. . . .

"I don't know what you mean."

"He has that dog, Tasha?"

"I love that dog. It's a Vizsla, isn't it?"

"I don't know—I'm not big on dogs so I'm not the one to ask. Anyway, the animal's an energy *bomb* so Marco always takes her to the park near his house at night for a good long run to tire her out. He sits on a bench while the dog *voops* around doing her biz. In the past whenever the sky was clear he'd make a wish on the first star he saw. It's a kid's thing but he said he's been wishing on stars all his life. None of them ever came true, so eventually he switched from stars to planes."

"What do you mean? He wishes on *airplanes*?"

"Yup. His park is on one of the flight paths to the airport so planes are always flying over it day and night. Besides wishing on stars, he had another superstition: if any night he saw six planes fly overhead while he was sitting there, he'd have luck the next day."

She sipped her whiskey and put her other hand on top of his. Her fingers were long and thin. She wore deep red, almost carmine, nail polish. He loved the fact she always wore finger and toenail polish. It made her look even more like a 1930s or '40s movie star—Rita Hayworth or Veronica Lake. He was so glad she was in his life again. He was so glad she was back.

"I'm coming home. I will help you heal.
You will help me grow. We will grow together."

139

The note she wrote to him saying she was returning. He kept it in his wallet.

"And did *that* work?"

"Yes, in a way. According to Marco it did. But *all* of this is according to him so you can take it with a grain of salt if you like. Anyway, when stars failed to grant him any wishes, that's when he switched to airplanes. You know that old rhyme *'Star light, star bright, first star I see tonight. I wish I may, I wish I might, first star I see tonight.'* Well, he changed the words and replaced 'star' with 'plane.' So now it went *'Plane light, plane bright . . .'* "

"And it worked?"

Instead of speaking, the man slowly nodded yes but the expression on his face gave nothing away.

She waited a few moments for him to continue. When he didn't, she smirked and took her hand off his. "No. You're goofing with me."

"I goof you not. *We're* here, aren't we?" He didn't mean to say that second sentence yet, but it just came out on its own. The beans were spilled.

She lifted an eyebrow. "What does *that* mean? Are we part of this story?"

"We *are* this story."

They'd had a stormy relationship. No, that's an understatement—they'd had a TYPHOON relationship. A five-act Italian opera with innumerable melodramatic comings and goings, tears, pointed fingers and accusing voices, bombastic breakups and whispered or typed or written in careful cursive carmine ink, 'I can't live without you.' They were both the boat and the hurricane sea they were trying to get across. He was married to someone, she was married to someone and then they weren't but not at the same time. They got together, they broke apart, they fought, they made up. It was endless. It was necessary, sort of. Mr. and Mrs. *Sturm und Drang.*

Yet the constant bass line of the relationship, the one steady thrum throughout the whole connection, was their souls couldn't keep their hands off each other, even when others were in their lives, thousands of miles separating them, weeks and months passing without a single word exchanged. Part of them—often different parts, granted—could not imagine a life without the other and this was the psychic glue that bound them.

She narrowed her eyes, not believing him for a second but eager to hear what came next.

"At first none of the wishes came true. He wished for this, he wished for that—nothing. But then his dog got sick—some kind of rare blood disease that moved in fast and took no prisoners. Marco *adores* that animal and was gutted by the news. It was especially bad when he would take her to the park and see her still race around for a while but then get tired and have to lie down because the sickness was starting to devour her.

"So one night on seeing his first plane he just wished it would go away. That's exactly what he said, only that—"I wish her sickness would go away."

She crossed her arms, unconvinced. "And it did?"

He nodded. "It did."

She looked at him hard—like he was trying to sell her something fascinating but fake. "Are you telling me the truth? *Really?*"

"Really. The veterinarian said she should have been dead in a month. That was last summer."

The expression on her face slipped from skepticism to something like awe. "That's the absolute, hand-up truth? You swear to God?"

Amused, he nodded. "When was the last time you said 'swear to God' to someone, when you were seven?"

"Don't change the subject. Get on with the story." She moved the whiskey glass around in small furious circles on the bar, her mind whizzing around what she'd heard, her eyes going back and forth between the glass and his face. She still didn't really believe him, but the child she once was wanted to very badly.

"It frightened him. It scared him that it might be true and not just a coincidence—that he was able to make dreams, *his* dreams, come true. So he tried it again but only on a small scale."

"Like how?"

"Like one time he counted the change in his pocket, put it back, and wished that it would double."

"And—"

"And nothing—it stayed the same."

"So the dog healing *was* a coincidence—"

"Nope, because the *next* thing he wished for happened exactly as he wanted."

"What was that?"

"Let me tell you about his third wish instead." Next he did a strange thing. His hands were resting on the bar. Lifting them, he pointed both index fingers at her, then at himself. At her again, then at himself. At her again . . .

She stopped moving the glass in circles. "What? What are you saying?"

He kept doing the pointing thing but stayed silent.

"Stop that! What are you *saying*?"

"I'm *saying* that, according to Marco, you and I getting back together was his next wish. And look at us—here we are. We were his third wish."

"No!"

"Yup."

"He said he *wished* us back together?"

"Yes. And here we are." He put his hands back down on the bar and looked at them. He wouldn't raise his eyes to hers.

"You already said that. When did he tell you this? When did he make the wish?"

"On October 7."

"How do you know it was that date exactly?"

"Because he *told* me; he was very specific." Now he looked at her but his eyes were odd. They said something else was coming, something she didn't necessarily want to hear. "Do you remember that you left on October 7, and exactly a year later to the *day* he told me you were coming back."

"Why didn't you tell me any of this before?" She was annoyed at him for withholding all of this from her until now.

He shrugged, dismissing the idea. "Because I knew you'd react exactly this way. You think any kind of magical or religious stuff is bullshit, so what was the point? It's like talking to an atheist about God."

In an instant there it was again after all this time, just as he had expected—*the* look. The sullen, icy expression on her face that said she was only seconds away from lashing out, snapping off a clever nasty gibe that was half response, half castration. How many times in the past had he been the target of her verbal venom? How many times had his soul recoiled or in righteous anger punched back just as hard at her toxic remarks; these inevitable preludes to one of their fights that left them both skinned or staggering, all love for each other gone at the moment.

He closed his eyes, ready for her blast. Nothing ever changes, does it?

"Do you believe him?"

Eyes still closed, he was surprised both by the gentleness of her voice and her question.

"Yes, yes, I do."

"Why? Because you're superstitious?"

"No. But I'm afraid to tell you the reason."

She pulled on her ear, willing him to open his eyes so she could look at them and gauge him. *"Afraid—why?"*

"Because I know how you're going to react."

"Don't be so all-knowing—just tell me, please."

Instead of speaking, he reached into a jacket pocket for a small well-worn leather notebook she'd given him for his birthday years before. She smiled seeing it in his hand. From another pocket he pulled out the plum-colored Parker 51 fountain pen that was the other part of her gift. Uncapping the pen, he wrote two words on a piece of paper, ripped it from the notebook, and handed it to her.

She looked at the paper, dropped her head to her chest, blinked and blinked and blinked. Her mouth tightened until her lips almost disappeared into each other. She folded the paper in half and in half again until it was too tight to fold anymore. By the time she'd stopped, her right hand was shaking. "Why didn't you *tell* me?"

He stood and, to her surprise, walked away. She jumped up and hurried after him. *"Why? Why didn't you tell me?"*

People all across the room looked at them.

Blank faced, he slipped the book and pen back into the same pocket. "Because it was too late. That's what the doctors said—it was too late. You had left me. You were down there together with your pilot. What was the point of contacting you? You said you were happy with him. I knew you'd come back if I told you about this, but I didn't, OK? I didn't want pity and I didn't want to interrupt your life. Silence was the last gift I could give you."

"Gift! Fuck you! Just *fuck* you!" With two hands she shoved him out of her way, stamped out of the bar and across the lobby to the elevators. He knew not to follow her.

Half an hour later he gently opened the door to their room on the fourth floor. She wasn't there but that didn't surprise him. He took off his clothes and went into the bathroom to shower. Naked, he stood and looked at himself in the mirror. He had lost a great deal of weight since they'd last seen each other but she hadn't said anything about it, although tonight would have been the first time she'd seen him naked in a little over a year.

On the counter was her bag of toiletries. Next to it the large electric gizmo she used to heat her hair curlers. All of it was so familiar to him. All of it had lived in his apartment for a while that last summer together before she left and disappeared into silence. The summer when he always knew she was nearby in another room and not hours or long flights away.

That morning when they'd met at the Zurich airport, her plane from Johannesburg had arrived only shortly after his and she'd struggled with her suitcase to get to their meeting point on time. When he saw her come through the arrivals gate her long chestnut hair was sun streaked and all over the place. She was looking down at her bag, which was wobbling because a wheel on it had gone psycho and was half moving, half twizzling round and round like a bratty kid turning in mad circles then dragging his feet while exasperated Mom pulled him along by the hand.

He couldn't see her eyebrows until she was up close and at that moment when he should have looked closely at them he was too overwhelmed by her actually being there right in front of him after more than a year. All he could do, all he *wanted* to do then was take her in his arms and embrace her, inhale her, *devour* her; the eyebrows and all the rest they would talk about eventually.

Hours later, stepping closer to the hotel bathroom mirror, he looked at his pubic hair. Much of it was now a very noticeable cinnamon red where once it had all been a uniform dark brown. He reached down and ran his fingers through it, still astonished this was actually happening. Even more astonishing was the fact that he was still alive to see it.

The day the doctor told him the grim results of his tests, he'd called his best friend, Marco Sachs, and asked if they could have a drink together. He needed to tell *someone*; needed to have someone who cared near him to unload this terrible fact on and talk about it.

Of course, once upon a time he would have called *her* immediately. But by the time that awful day of reckoning came, she was already months gone. Once both believed their relationship was as solid as a stone in their hands, but when it turned into snow yet again she fled. He knew there was nothing Marco could do to help but be a compassionate friend, hold his hand, and hopefully say something comforting, *anything* that might lighten for even an hour the impossible weight of his horrible new reality.

But Marco showed zero surprise when he told him. "I know about it. But you don't have to worry—you're all right now, even though I could tell you've been sick for a long time. Go back to the hospital in a week and get all the tests done again. You're fine; you're not sick anymore. They gave you the results of the old tests; those are wrong now."

"What are you talking about, Marco? I just came from the doctor— it's over. He said I have maybe six months max."

"Well, he's wrong. I swear that you're OK. *Get the tests done.* Get them done *today* if you want. I'll walk you over to the hospital." Marco smiled reassuringly and put a hand on his shoulder. "One hundred percent, pal. You're 100 percent healthy. Trust me."

And he was. But only after he got the new test results back days later had Marco Sachs told him about the wishes.

They were in the same restaurant where he'd gone to announce his doom to his friend, only this time it was to celebrate his resurrection. The drinks were on him, of course, and they'd had two or three before the subject of the wishes came up.

In the middle of his explanation Marco said, "The irony is they don't work for me—only for the things I love, like you and Tasha. Every time I've wished for something for *me*, it doesn't happen. But making both of you healthy again? No problem."

Someone knocked on the room door. He slipped into the bathrobe supplied by the hotel and opened the door. She stood out in the hall with both hands on her hips, a look of steely anger still on her face.

"I forgot—you had the only key." She brushed past him and walked into the room. He had to suppress a smile because he could feel her fury buzzing around and off her like a hive of angry bees, all of it clearly directed at him. She sat down on the smallish bed, both arms rigid at her sides as if she were about to spring up again at any moment. "You're all right now? You're cured?"

"Yes, completely."

She shook her head in disbelief. "How can that be? Do you know what the recovery rate from that is? I just looked it up here." She took a smartphone from her purse and stuck it out at him like a gun. "Seventy-nine percent of all people who have it die within six months. And the long-term survival rate is tiny. But you're saying you're absolutely *cured*?"

"I am—100 percent all right, 100 percent healthy again."

She raised a hand and put it on top of her head. It almost looked like she was trying to hold all of her thoughts in. "How is that *possible*?"

He went over and sat down on the bed but far enough away from her so that she wouldn't feel crowded.

"Marco made one of his wishes for me."

She turned slowly toward him. In that moment he remembered to look at her eyebrows. And there it was—the exact same colored red-orangey hair that grew on him was threaded throughout the darker hair on both of her brows. Marco had said that's how it would start—on her, the eyebrows; on him, his bush. And when it became really noticeable, the change for both of them would accelerate. Seeing this striking color streaked throughout her eyebrows and even some showing up in the hair on her head, he knew it had begun for her too.

When Marco came back from the toilet at the restaurant that day, he looked at his old friend a long time and finally spit it out. "I did something else you may *not* like when you know all the details. But please understand I did it only because I wanted you to be happy."

How could he not be happy? He had just been given a reprieve by this magical friend from an all-but-certain death sentence. "What are you talking about?"

Marco sat down hard in his chair. "I made another wish for you—I wished that Raleigh would come back. And she *is*—"

His breath caught in his throat. "*She's coming back?* You wished that too?"

Marco raised a hand to stop him, to shut him up. Then he took a drink, although there was almost nothing left in his glass. "Yes, but wait—I gotta explain some things to you first before you get all excited and start celebrating. These wishes? I told you before that they only work for others, never for me. But when I do make one, it not only comes true but I also see the *outcome* of it as soon as I make the wish. I see what the result of it will be in the future."

"Yeah, and?" Weeks ago he would have told Marco he was nuts or some such dismissal, but now having seen and experienced firsthand that his pal was telling the truth about the wishes, he waited excitedly. Plus she was coming back! How could he not be bursting?

"When I wished for Tasha to get better I saw that she *would*, but only for another four more years. Then she'll die and there'll be nothing I can do for her. But that's good in a way because I can cherish the time we have left together while preparing the best I can to live without her. When I wished for *you* to get better, I saw that as a man, you'll live to be eighty-four."

"What do you mean, *as a man?*"

Sachs picked up his empty glass and drained it as if there were still something inside.

"Marco? What do you mean by that?"

"I wished for Raleigh to come back to you and she will. Soon. I wished her to come back and that you two would be together again for good. And you will if you want, but there's one big problem."

"What problem?" His heart began to sink. She was coming back because Marco wished it. Marco's wishes came true. His now-healthy body was solid proof to him of that. What problem could there be?

"When I made that wish for you two, I saw some things; things you're not going to want to hear."

"Like what?" Unconsciously he straightened his back until it almost hurt.

Sachs tapped the table several times with one knuckle. He was figuring out how best to say this. Was there any way to say it right? Maybe just tell the truth and deal with the reaction. "I told you when I make a wish, I can see how it's going to turn out in the future. Well, when I did it for you and Raleigh, I saw something you're not going to like."

"You said that. What is it?" He tried to keep the edge out of his voice but failed.

"You two will never be able to succeed romantically. You can be friends forever and that'll be fine, but not as a couple. Never. It's not possible."

"Why not?"

"Because you're human. As humans, you're only ever fated to be friends, best friends, acquaintances, business partners—anything but lovers. You can be friends with her forever, but never as a couple. You'll always have the same problems. It's fixed but I don't know why. You have to believe me. Of course you can try—move in together, get married—you can try all you want to make it work that way with her but it never will.

"I love you, you're my best friend, and I only want the best for you. So I'm telling you all this straight-out to try and save you any more heartache later. You two have been through enough of those ups and downs already." At that point Sachs was so wrought up with emotion for his friend and his doomed hope that he said the rest almost without thinking. "Never as humans—only as foxes."

"*What? Foxes?* What did you say?"

Marco signaled the waiter for another drink. "Do you believe in reincarnation?"

"No."

"Well, *do*, because it's true. That's another thing I've learned from these wishes. Don't ask me to explain—just take my word for it. You and Raleigh have been bonded to each other throughout history in life after life. As animals, insects, even *plants*; in this incarnation you happen to be people, but it's not the first time you were human together. You guys have been a whole menagerie of different beings but were always connected and I guess always will be until whatever comes after . . . life here.

"I don't know why. Karma maybe? Or certain things need to be worked out between you two here before you can move on to the next level? I dunno. But the only time you've ever been a successful *couple*, if I can call it that, was when you were foxes. *Vulpes vulpes*—red foxes."

A burst of laughter. "*Foxes?* Raleigh and I were foxes?"

"Yes and it was the only time in all of your incarnations together that you succeeded as a pair. You can laugh as much as you want, but it's the truth. And you more than anyone have experienced what happens when I make a wish. If I tell you this is part of that process, you better believe it's true."

Now she saw something on his face that made her frown and lean hard forward to get a better look at him. "Your eyes! They're a different *color*! You had blue eyes—you *have* blue eyes. Now they're *brown*?" She pulled back, still frowning. "How is that possible? People's eyes don't change color."

For the first time that day, he lied to her. "It was probably all the medicine. They gave me a lot of very strong stuff when I was in the hospital. Who knows what else it did to my insides."

She shook her head, not believing a word he'd said. "I've never heard of a person's *eyes* changing color because of some medicine they took. How could any chemical do that to you?"

He shrugged and fake smiled.

"Doesn't it freak you out? When you look in the mirror and see that your eyes are a completely different color after forty years? Doesn't it *bother* you?"

To avoid the question, he needed to take her mind off his eyes.

"No, but you know what *does* bother me, Raleigh? Machines. When you're sick they put you into different *machines*. Have you ever had an MRI, or a CAT scan, or how 'bout a bone densitometer? That's a mouthful, huh? *Bone densitometer.*"

Thrown off by this abrupt change of subject, she shook her head slowly. What was he getting at? Why was he talking about machines and not his eyes?

"They're all scary as shit. Not only because of what they'll say about how sick you are, but because they need to be *this* close to you to work properly"—he fast flicked his hand out palm up toward her face, stopping two inches from her nose. She flinched. "That's right—*this* close. You're lying on your back naked under a sheet, inside a *clicking clacking clanking* machine for what feels like hours. With the MRI they slide you completely *into* this long, narrow cylinder that's like a torpedo tube on a submarine. But before they do that, they put a giant clamp-like thing over your chest that keeps any part of your upper body from moving. For close to an hour you cannot move or the image is spoiled. You just have to lie there dead still and keep your claustrophobic, panicking self from going completely batshit crazy. But that's just the *machines*. Next are the medicines—oh, the medicines are a whole other kind of torture—"

Lie number two—he'd never had to take any. Magic Marco had eliminated any need for them with his "plane light, plane bright."

"What are you saying?" She was now completely off-balance. What she'd seen and learned in the last hour had knocked her off her moorings about him, his health, their relationship . . . everything.

"I'm saying what really *bothered* me, for want of a better word, was being sick alone without you."

She almost shouted, "But I told you I would have come back if I'd known!"

He shouted back, "*I didn't want that!*" and slapped his leg. "I didn't want you to come back out of *pity*. Out of a feeling of duty to what we once *were*. I wanted you back after you finally realized there was nothing better out there in the world than this, than us.

"But you *didn't* feel that way, especially after you got together with your pilot. So if you *had* come back when I was sick, you'd have only been biding your time till you could leave again and go back to him." He spat out an angry grunt and made two fists. "Better for me to be alone in those machines than having you out in the hall pitying me and waiting for text messages from him." Overwhelmed by the memories of those very bad days, he stood up and walked to the window.

He loved her; God, how he loved her. But at that moment he almost hated her. He needed her like air in his lungs. He didn't trust her an inch. That's why he'd asked Sachs three days ago, three days before she was to return, to make another wish for him.

"*What?*"

"You heard me. Can you do it, Marco?"

"Of course I can do it, but that's not the point. You're out of your mind—you don't want this."

"Yes, I do."

"But how about Raleigh, would *she?* How do you know it's what she would want? Don't you think you should ask her first?"

The two men stared at each other across the table and their silence was a very dark thing between them for the first time in all the years they had known each other. Marco Sachs could not believe his friend's request. That's not true—he *could* believe it because more than anyone, he knew the turbulent history of this couple. But still—

"No."

"No what?"

"No, I don't think I should ask her. I'm asking you—can you do it? *Will* you do it?"

Sachs felt like his opinion had been split right down the middle with a sharp ax. On first hearing the request, half of him thought it was a mad, selfish, and utterly reckless thing of his friend to want, plus who knew what the consequences would be. On the other side, part of him thought it was the most beautiful demonstration of absolute love and commitment he'd ever heard.

He had to say it, to get it out. "If Raleigh hated it, it would be like you were taking her as a slave. Really—it would be like some kind of slavery to do that to her if she was against it."

"But that's the beauty, Marco—*she'll never know.* Make your wish with all the right conditions and fail-safes so by the time of the change, we'll have completely different brains. Words or ideas like slavery won't be part of our, what did you call it before—our *vulpes vulpes* minds or vocabulary. We'll only be two foxes again madly in love, like old times. If that's the only way we can really be together, then, yes, that's exactly what I want."

*

That first night in the hotel after several more hours of talking, they went to bed quietly but not peacefully. They did not make love but minutes after they got into bed she slid over and, pushing her back up against him, took one of his arms and pulled it over her chest.

"Let's go to sleep and talk more about this in the morning. I'm exhausted and my mind is too full now to think clearly. I feel like you've come back from the dead even though I didn't know until today that you'd died. Or that *we* have."

He nodded and pulled her in a little tighter. He wondered when she would want to make love again. He wondered what she had been like in bed with the pilot. He wondered . . .

About two hours later he was awoken out of a deep sleep when she cried out and sat straight up in bed. As the fog of sleep cleared from his mind, he could hear her panting. She had been having a nightmare and it must have been a bad one because the panting went on and she didn't lie back down again.

He knew all these signs from the old days when they lived together and she'd had nightmares fairly frequently. He asked gently, "Do you want to talk about it?"

She put her face in her hands and rubbed it vigorously. "It was so *real*! I haven't had a dream that real in years. I could feel the grass and the dirt under my feet, smell things and taste them. I tasted warm blood—warm, hot, coppery blood . . . *blecch*!

"I dreamt I was chasing this little mouse or rat. I couldn't tell exactly what it was except it was small and gray and maybe even a baby. We were zigzagging back and forth through this big, open meadow. I was on all fours and absolutely flying along. I must have been an animal too because I was running so fast. When I caught up, I snatched it in my jaws and just chomped right down on its tiny body. Something crunched and I could feel it squirming in my jaws. It screamed this really high-pitched, horrible, dying sound. That's when I woke up."

He said nothing.

Gaijin
Sallie Tisdale

BY THE TIME I MEET Takeshi at the train station in Kanazawa, I am as at ease in Japan as most visitors can be a few days after landing. The *gaijin*, the outsider, blurred with travel, leaves the overnight flight to trek through an enormous airport to a train like no other, leading to a city like no other. I stand balanced among people who maintain a single inch of space between them as though by force field; people staring, reading and sleeping, propped up in corners and leaning on poles. A rail-thin young man with dyed red hair and pale skin wears a T-shirt that says WHY DO MEN DREAM TROUTING THERE. Businessmen doze standing upright, their briefcases against their chests. Schoolgirls in navy-blue uniforms and white knee socks chatter to each other beside a young man reading an erotic manga; on the cover is a schoolgirl in a navy-blue uniform and white knee socks.

What the Japanese call a town is a city to me; what they call a city is Tokyo: thirteen million people and puppies for rent by the hour because no one has room for a pet. Tokyo never stops talking: loudspeakers repeating safety announcements and commercials projected on the sides of buildings; the *wee-woop, wee-woop* of green traffic lights; hawkers in suits and white gloves on the sidewalks calling out their wares; the hoot and whistle of ringtones; a low, distant temple bell; the squeal of brakes; the tinkle of bicycle bells; workers singing out from stores. The streets stream with office workers in strictly timed waves as trains arrive, two minutes apart, with a low, hard whoosh. Guards with megaphones direct pedestrians across the crowded streets at several angles, past cars called More and Bongo and Mysterious Utility Wizard. The air is sticky and hot and smells of fish, sewer, exhaust, and perfume. The streets are a vast pachinko parlor fever dream, and they never end.

I am here to do research for the Japanese portion of a book of stories about female Zen masters; I've been here before and I speak a little of the language—just enough to find my way and handle most of the courtesies of daily life in a land built half on courtesy and half on struggle. I manage to find my way to a tiny single room at a business hotel—a narrow bed with a little sink and toy shower. I seem to be the only woman and the only Westerner there, and I hear doors slamming, men shouting and laughing, the sound of heavy feet running up and down the halls.

I go out for supper and try to eat a whole fried egg with chopsticks, because my other choices were curry doughnuts or eggplant and basil pizza. I love the dense flavors of Japan, but I'm not quite ready for them yet, for the aloe vera–flavored yogurt and squash chewing gum and slimy fermented seaweed—for the intensity packed into a single bite that seems a reflection of how they pack their psychic depths and complex lives into small, tidy rooms and dark suits. After the egg, I ask the young man wearing a T-shirt that says BEADED WRITER for an order of *banilla ice-u cream-u*, and it arrives on a bed of cornflakes with whipped cream on top.

I buy a few cookies at a grocery store and use the toilet, a dreamy pink room with buttons beside the toilet labeled "please to wash bottom" and "press to play back flushing sound to muffle toilet sound" and "Powerful Deodorizer increased absorption strength for removing odors" and I wonder why *that* isn't on a T-shirt.

Back at the hotel, I drift in the sleep of lost time zones and have a strange threatening dream of people baked into casseroles with only their heads showing, revolving in a display case.

I met Takeshi in San Francisco, where we were both visitors. He was a young Buddhist priest fresh from the training temple, sent to the United States to polish his English—already good, but with a thick accent. I was visiting the Zen temple where he was staying. There was no good reason for us to become friends, but we had a shared urge to exploit each other, to be a person one knew on the other shore. The confusing fog of status between us—an older woman and a younger man, foreigners, a lay teacher and a priest—was not much of a concern. In Japan, he had the upper hand except for the difference in age, an odd gap somewhere past older sister. But I am American, the mother of two grown sons, and comfortable with the peculiar dance of Buddhist rank and how much of it mattered in the soft social world of the States. Shortly after we met, he told me that he had no memory of his life before the age of eighteen because he had had a blood clot from "too much running." Maybe that helped too; maybe his amnesia included the early social programming that made him uncomfortable with such things as friendship outside the lines.

Sallie Tisdale

He was not free of all his conditioning. He is the eldest son of a temple priest, and the pressure to follow the father's path in such a family has no equal in America outside the military and the police. In some families, it doesn't matter if you believe in Buddhism any more than it matters if you like the army; the path is laid out the moment you are born. But the finishing-school trip to America and the city on the water had tainted him. He loved it so, and longed to stay. I've been told by other Japanese friends that it takes only one visit to the US to become less than wholly Japanese—to feel forever a little awkward in the homeland. To be changed by those soft social boundaries.

Takeshi and I hung out for a few days, went out for meals, talked about a lot of things. He helped me with my poor Japanese and I helped him with his much better English. We wandered the streets of San Francisco, admiring the light; he was particularly entranced with the bakeries. We made plans to meet in Japan some months later. Before we said goodbye, he told me (a little ashamed and a little sad) that he wished for more than a longer stay in America. He wished for another life, to be another.

"Not go back to be a priest," he said, not go back to his father's role in a little temple attached to his parents' house where he and the unknown wife he was expected to find would live for the rest of his life.

After a day of recovery, much of it spent dozing on the thin hotel bed, I find my way onto the Shinkansen bullet train. The bullet train is as comfortable as a living room and bento girls walk up and down the aisle bearing hot tea and tidy meals. The emerald rice fields and factory towns, the massive apartment blocks and marshes of tall grass pass in a blink.

Takeshi is waiting on the platform, younger and shorter than I remember. He is dressed in the neat pressed *samue*, the clothes that mark him as a priest and that he wears almost all the time when he is not in formal robes. He looks pleased to see me, almost giddy. His—and his parents'—house is connected to a small complex of temple buildings, a narrow, cramped two-story box. He shows me to my double tatami room with a thin futon and buckwheat pillow, and then to the bath, where every guest will want to go—sink and changing area in one room, shower and tub in the other, automatic toilet in yet another.

154

I bathe and we eat a long, long dinner with his mother and grand-mother, kneeling on tatami for hours. His grandmother's spine is deformed; the postwar years of hunger twisted an entire generation. She is barely four feet tall and bent almost ninety degrees at the waist. She is also, I begin to suspect, demented, giggling, touching my sleeve, murmuring to herself. I have brought gifts, and give her a large fancy bar of soap. She tries to eat it.

His mother presses more sake on me and I refuse, but Takeshi advises me to drink—to, as another Japanese friend told me, "Get it over with." I go to bed a bit drunk, cold, and feeling immensely clumsy in the little room with its precise and simple furnishing.

The next day, we drive for hours into the Noto Peninsula to visit a few important temples and spend the night at an *onsen*, a hot springs resort, in the traditional town of Wajima. My simple Japanese won't do for research, and I know that a male priest will open doors for me that I could never open as a woman alone. In his turn, he is testing the way. He hopes to lead small tours up to Wajima, a center of traditional lacquerware—a way to make extra money and, he tells me frankly, get away from home and the temple and the endless, numbing duties of the priest.

He gets lost several times. "Oh!" he says calmly. "Wrong road." We double back, and he makes a note. We talk about San Francisco, his memories of the city burnished like a dream, and his so-limited future destiny. Egrets bob in the fields of deep-green rice, water glint-ing silver between the shoots. This is hilly country, a wilder land, green and empty, with fog twisting between dark hinoki cedars.

We reach Yokoji, once a vital center of Soto Zen Buddhism in Japan, and now cared for as a historical site. This was also a center for women's practice, and to my delight there is another priest visiting who knows all about the women's history here. He guides us around the property without hurry, showing me where the women's build-ings used to be in a moist, shady dell, telling stories of the distant and the recent past. Takeshi stands one step behind me in the translator's corner, speaking quietly for us both before we finally say goodbye.

We stop for bitter foamy green tea and adzuki-bean biscuits in a tea shop; Diana Ross is singing "Love Child." The young woman who bows deeply when she brings the tea is wearing a T-shirt that reads A POSITIVE SOCIAL CONTAGION.

I ask Takeshi, not for the first time, to justify the policy that still keeps women out of most of the training temples. After all, they were welcomed at Yokoji, alongside the men—centuries ago. Then

155

they were not. I had wanted to do such a thing; I had wanted it greatly; I had made the start of an effort to leave my life for a time and do
what he had done. What he had not wanted to do and did anyway, I
had wanted to do very much and could not.

"So many difficulties," he says. "Men and women practicing together, no. Must be separate. And that is against the Dharma. And so
better for no women."

I correct his English. "Better for *you*," I say, "that there are no
women."

He is pleased with this construction. "Yes!" he agrees. And that,
he seems to think, is that.

A typhoon is coming, he tells me after talking briefly with the tea-
shop attendant. The rain is slashing at us sideways as we dash to the
car, distant thunder pounding. We drive on, past pine trees and sea-
grass and stands of bamboo bending in the slate-gray storm. We
round the curve of the peninsula and are beside the sea all at once,
the entire distant horizon black.

Takeshi is unworried about the storm, and we stop as planned at
Sojiji-soin, a training monastery much like the one he attended. A
crowd of young men in *samue* meet us cheerfully at the gate, a few
greeting Takeshi by name. They are younger than my sons, compact
and homogenous, seeming glad of the disruption in their day and
each taking a turn to shake hands with the American woman. It is a
beautiful place, dim and moist in the rain, thick with story and time.
In such a place, the group moves as a body—sits and eats and sleeps
as a body, turned in one direction. One doesn't love it or hate it; one
just does it. Most of these young men are simply the eldest sons of
temple priests.

We reach Wajima in a torrent. "What do you want to do?" I ask.

"Drink beer!" he says. He stops at a store and returns with beer,
whiskey, and grilled-shrimp-and-pepper-flavored Pringles.

We check into the *onsen*, a great curve of hotel next to a rocky,
wave-spattered shore. He directs me to the baths, tells me to enjoy a
soak, and to meet him in the dining room—"in your *yukata*," he
adds, the plain kimono available in my room. I am the only woman
in the huge women's bath, where a deep tiled tub is filled with clear,
steaming water next to a wall of glass looking out at the sea. There
is a precise etiquette for the bath and I'm glad to be alone; I've stumbled through the steps several times in front of silent, observant
women. The bath is delicious and the green water reflects the strange
light: harsh beams of white sun breaking through the sooty storm

here and there, the frothy waves splattering the black rocks below.

It is strange to go to the dining room in what feels to me like a bathrobe and slippers that are far too small. But all the guests scattered here and there are wearing *yukata* as well, as are the men in the bar watching a samurai soap opera, as is Takeshi, who is already there, waiting. He orders and soon large lacquer trays arrive, with many compartments filled with small servings of all kinds of food.

Takeshi spears a prawn, chews, looks around. He is enjoying this little trip away from home. I think he is enjoying the fact that people aren't sure what to make of us together here. He has had one taste of other, and it was enough. I've had more than one—how else does a round American woman of a certain age end up practicing a foreign religion? I could calculate the probability, but what is probable in a human life? There have been times when I thought it would be better not to taste at all, because a new taste lingers. It reminds us, always, of what might have been, what might be otherwise, if one had chosen otherwise—if even a single step had been different. We are all *gaijin*, strangers to our own lives at times, waiting for that train.

We go back to his room and sit on the tatami by the window, where thick white clouds slide across the sea in front of the implacable storm. He pours me a little whiskey and leans back with an enormous bottle of beer and we watch the typhoon breathe and slowly fade. We don't talk. He looks terribly sad, sitting cross-legged on a thin futon, staring out to sea.

I love it here. I love Japan, the odd collision of known and strange. I love the way they sometimes do small and ordinary things so well: a giant bee in a fragrant flower beside a trickle of water from a bamboo tube where nothing need be at all. I love Zen and the practice, the temples and the silence; I love what I chose. Takeshi sits and drinks and watches and finally falls asleep, the *yukata* still neatly tied and his big bare feet crossed on the tatami.

The next morning I wake up early and sit by the big windows, watching the rough shore, aware that I am coming down with a cold, my chest hot and tight. There is a fine misting rain over the thick green hills. We are going to the market and another temple full of young men a lot like my friend and not much like me. I feel a little wretched and full of joy; I love it here, and I don't have to stay.

For Sandra
Robert Duncan

—With an Afterword by Margaret Fisher

The Invention of a little booklet cahier (RD) for Sandra her birthday 1982

poems in prose & verse

1

THE warbler draws, I
write, drawing the words,
what do the birds say
sweeter than the water
of the friendship, amitié
that would guide my
hand, I too, even as Kitaj's
little song beneath his
breath
to sing

2

Talking of cities, Rome,
Venice, London, New York,
Paris where we are, San
Francisco where we will yet
to be — how lovely vistas
and residences come to us,
walks and rests. As if just
for our souls' sake, for our
spirits these concerts, these
museums, these façades,
these rumors of great hours
were presented. WE WERE
meant, all our lives, to be
here where we together are
wherever
in this change of weather

3

What else could ever be a
gift but this little suite of
poems given me in addressing
you as a form of gift —
Of my hand, this script, this
souvenir   we will remember.

        Let the sun
attend some morning
light alone it seems can say
in transforming our rooms and
rues, "bathing" our intent.
    It is a ruse of this verse
to need the universe
to give   a sense of what
it means   I in turn form
for a gift, for a membrance
    of being born —

4

It must be simple and so
light. It must go
with only words to touch
such centers in the soul
a smile might spread

and like a drawing
be immediate, searching
and yet beyond account
speak for me

I did not know what else
to you   love's mystery
could come thru
in riming a response
in the beat   The heart

means to be felt
entirely   gift .

5

So there must always be lovely
women in me calling forth this
delight in being, this consolation
in reverie. Dark as the dream
be, and harsh as the measures
of what proclaims itself Reality—
always clear, always sweet
this cup of water Rachel at the
fountain offers me. Always
cool and medicine complete,
her voice, her touch, her
momentary lingering regard
    softly softly   wood dove
I hear the last echoes in the
well.   How soft, how close
the star above.

Robert Duncan

~(✕)~

one copy only made of this
little suite that would be
sweet for Sandra Fisher
her birthday gift May 6
1982 at 61 rue Galande

Robert Duncan

POEMS IN PROSE & VERSE

1.

The warbler draws, I
   write, drawing the words,
what do the birds say
sweeter than the water
of the friendship, amitié
   that would guide my
hand, I too, even as Kitaj's
   little song beneath his
          breath
  to sing

2.

Talking of cities, Rome,
Venice, London, New York,
Paris where we are, San
Francisco where we will yet
to be—how lovely vistas
and residences come to us,
walks and rests. As if just
for our souls' sake, for our
spirits these concerts, these
museums, these façades,
these rumors of great hours
were presented. We were
meant, all our lives, to be
here where we together are
wherever
in this change of weather

3.

What else could ever be a
gift but this little suite of
poems given me in addressing
you as a form of gift—
Of my hand, this script, this
souvenir   we will remember.
        Let the sun
attend some morning
light alone it seems can say
in transforming our rooms and
rues, "bathing" our intent.
    It is a ruse of this verse
to need the universe
to give   a sense of what
it means   I in turn form
for a gift, for a membrance
    of being born—

163

4.

It must be simple and so
light. It must go
with only words to touch
such centers in the soul
a smile might spread
and like a drawing
be immediate, searching
and yet beyond account
speak for me
I did not know what else
to you   Love's mystery
could come thru
in riming a response
in the beat   the heart
means to be felt
entirely   gift .

5.

So there must always be lovely
women in me calling forth this
delight in being, this consolation
in reverie. Dark as the dream
be, and harsh as the measures
of what proclaims itself Reality—
always clear, always sweet
this cup of water Rachel at the
fountain offers me. Always
cool and medicine complete,
her voice, her touch, her
momentary lingering regard
   softly softly   wood dove
I hear the last echoes in the
well.   How soft, how close
the star above.

one copy only made of this
little suite that would be
sweet for Sandra Fisher
her birthday gift May 6
1982 at 61 rue Galande

—Robert Duncan

Afterword

Margaret Fisher

SANDRA FISHER AND ROBERT DUNCAN

ROBERT DUNCAN WROTE FIVE "Poems in prose & verse" to Sandra Fisher for her thirty-fifth birthday. The poems memorialize an event that transpired between them in Paris. Because the poems allude to an aspect of their friendship that we cannot know, the principals having passed away, this introduction will set the scene: a seduction scene, "sweeter than the water / of the friendship . . ." (poem 1).

In the spring of 1982, Robert joined his good friends the American painters Sandra Fisher and R. B. Kitaj for a month of work in Paris. They expected to set up shop in a building near the rue de l'Odéon and the Boulevard Saint-Germain, where, according to Sandra, Balthus (Balthasar Klossowski de Rola) had lived when he painted his quixotic canvas *The Street*. In the end, Sandra and Kitaj rented apartments in a different building, but Balthus remained ever present in their thoughts, letters, and conversations during their yearlong Paris sabbatical. They had recently made a pilgrimage to the Villa Medici in Rome to see interiors memorialized in paint by Balthus—fireplace, windows, baseboards, floor and wall designs—against which he had placed such vibrant and shocking nude figures as to implicate his viewer in a fantasy world of seduction. Since January the two painters had taken to posing their own models in the first-floor apartment by the heat of the fireplace. The memory of Balthus's Roman light tempered the cold, damp months in Paris that passed under the shadow of the ancient church of Saint-Julien-le-Pauvre. Sandra wrote to me in the coded language of nineteenth-century romanticism:

165

> From my earlier fears of the cold winter here, Paris has
> become the most romantic place possible! The fireplace at
> rue Rollin has become the center of my life. Of course, I have
> twice as much work preparing for a model than I do in London.
> Also, am painting a small head of M____, the copyist I met in
> the Louvre. He's extremely handsome, with a blue serpent
> tattooed on his forehead! Since he doesn't speak English, my
> French is improving enormously!

Robert's arrival mid-April, followed by mine soon after, lowered
the temperature for a time. We were no match for fires stoked by
long hours of drawing and painting the nude figure, undoubtedly
fueled by fantasies of Balthus and his marble fireplace. Or so I
thought, until I came upon Robert's poem among Sandra's papers. "It
is a ruse of this verse / to need the universe / to give a sense of what /
it means" (poem 3). That was written for Sandra, who knew what
Robert was getting at. The outside reader needs something of Sandra
too, for access to Robert's meaning. Her unmatched beauty and keen
intellect, augmented by erudition, consummate social accomplishment, restless ambition, expressed sensuality, and a predilection for
fantasy and seduction combined to produce a potent cocktail. Many
men never recovered from her effect on them, nor wanted to. Robert
appears to recover his equilibrium with a "souvenir" in a new genre,
"a little booklet cahier," meant to deflect Sandra's charms, savor the
moment, and catalog, in poem five, the contradictory forces that
inform his identity.

My older sister made her reputation on the male nude, sometimes
caught in flagrante delicto, in the act, and always as the natural
object of her desire. It is the subject for which she will best be remembered. Eighteen years after her death, Germaine Greer—feminist author, art critic, and provocateur—counted Sandra among the
best six painters of the male nude: Pontormo, Rubens, Degas,
Munch, Schiele, and Fisher. Sandra often said she wanted to bring
the heat of close studio quarters into the painting, the excitement
engendered between painter and model, and wanted to get that into
the painting. Sandra's American contemporaries had used the nude
to rail against the socioeconomic conditions of their time. Like
Balthus, Sandra's nudes evidence no discontent, no displacement,
crime, malaise, ennui, social inequality, or political bias. But unlike
Balthus, who refused to link his paintings to his biography, Sandra
made no secret of the pleasure she took in the anticipated scandal of

her subject or in the seduction of her models. Her models, for their part, often enjoyed the lasting friendship that followed upon her charm and seduction.

Lawrence Ferlinghetti had earlier stopped by the Paris apartment, the fire in him stoked anew by a passion to draw the nude figure. He attended classes at the San Francisco Art Institute, where the models held short poses. "Ugh!" Sandra wrote in reaction to this. "Who thinks that students have the genius and experience of Matisse at 70! What one needs at the beginning is to have a long, good look!!"

Sandra's long look often turned into a prolonged afternoon or an amorous weekend affair out of town, the former with Kitaj's encouragement; the latter sparking one crisis after another between them despite their professed and preferred open relationship. While Robert's visit provided an excuse for a much needed time-out, it appears Sandra appealed to him to explore his manhood with her, inspiring the fifth poem in which he writes of the "lovely / women in me." The final lines, "softly softly wood dove / I hear the last echoes in the / well" (poem 5), conjure, in this context, the nymph Echo and her prey, Narcissus.

Sandra's pulse had always quickened when Robert visited. She had recently moved to Kitaj's Kensington flat when Robert arrived as a houseguest in 1973. She raved that Robert was the most brilliant person she had ever met; his breakfast conversation exhausted her before she had her first coffee. She described him in a letter: "He wears his grandmother's brooch at his neck instead of a tie and the long hair falling from his 54-year-old hairline is pulled back in a clip. His voice is the loudest, squeakiest and highest-pitched of any one else's in the room. If you don't know his work, try *Roots and Branches* first." During a subsequent visit in 1977, Sandra drew Robert nude in her Sydney Street studio.

In our setting, Paris, 1982, it was Kitaj who would draw Robert, clothed, the drawing destined for the cover of Robert's next book of poems, *Ground Work II*. And Robert would write the introduction to Marco Livingstone's forthcoming monograph on Kitaj.

Sandra and Kitaj rented the apartment above their own for Robert—two rooms and a curtained bed in the foyer for me. Robert's line "What do the birds say / sweeter than the water / of the friendship, amitié . . ." (poem 1) describes perfectly the garrulous ease of the arrangement, like birds at the bath. I wrote home, "Duncan and I come and go, we all eat lunch and supper together, take naps at the same time and read voraciously indoors (the weather is terrible). We have learned to be excited and mutually stimulating, as well as to be calm and quiet in each other's presence. Robert poses for RB and Sand in the afternoons & 'earns his supper.' They want me to do the same." For those afternoon sessions, Robert either wrote or read aloud from his poems while keeping a steady tempo with one hand, as if conducting music.

The Paris month proved to be pivotal to our diverse futures, an account of which is beyond my scope here. Robert had a sixth sense about this: "We were / meant, all our lives, to be / here where we together are / wherever / in this change of weather" (poem 2). I interpret "change of weather" to mean the inner changes that took place. Of Paris, Robert wrote, "these / museums, these façades, / these rumors of great hours / were presented" (poem 2). Unlike the nurturing atmosphere of the apartment, the life and history of the city did not touch the clockwork of their souls.

One external incident gave a glimpse of those inner gears, each learning something new of the other. The American poet Anne Atik and her husband, French-Israeli painter Avigdor Arikha, invited our group for dinner. Discussion hovered around the painters Domenichino and Poussin, on their application of the color red, and whether to describe their shadows as warm and cool, or as light and dark. Avigdor, a Poussin scholar, became increasingly impatient with us. The others were good-natured explainers and knew how to deflect his bite, as I did not. I suffered a withering attack. Robert gallantly came to my defense. It was an emotionally complicated, fulfilling, and unforgettable act of friendship that was also independent of friendship. The evening's tensions, gaffes, heroics, and rivalries exposed new strains within our characters we had not yet tested against the friendships that had formed. We left early and walked in the mist along deserted Parisian streets, half drunk on Avigdor's good wine. Passing a wall where couples kissed passionately in the street, I whined, "I haven't been kissed so since I left California." Robert kissed me full-on, on the lips. Sandra was shocked, not that he had kissed me, but that he had not kissed her.

Photo of Sandra Fisher, mid-1980s.

Robert Duncan by Sandra Fisher (detail).
Color pencil on paper. Signed "for Jess with
love from Robert and Sand June 1977."
Robert Duncan Papers, The Poetry Collection
of the University Libraries, University at Buffalo,
State University of New York © 2016 Max Kitaj,
reproduced with permission.

169

Hansel, Gretel, Grendel
Jedediah Berry and Emily Houk

THE BOY WALKS WITH MUD on his sneakers, kicking at skunk cabbage, slapping mosquitoes. On his T-shirt are gallows birds, fanged demons in wizard-whorl, skullheaded soldiers. He has come to the forest to scavenge parts for his monster.

The girl's territories are the narrow places between bog and strip mall, parking lot and train tracks. With her hood up, she is invisible. With her arms out and her palms upturned, she can feel the wind talking.

The boy marches two clicks from the abyss, deaf to his own footsteps for the thrashing in his headphones: *evil spirit, in moorland living, endured the dole in his dark abode.* He collects trash-can lids, rubber tires, milk crates, tinsel from dead trees, burlap. These the bones and organs, nerves and flesh of his project, the only thing hungrier than he is.

The boy sees teenagers in the burnt orchard by the river, cigarettes cindering orange in the gloam. Eddie and Rick, their names are, brothers with yellow hair, and haughty Marco, and quiet Larry, who likes to hurt things smaller than he. Their chief is Dan, and Dan gets signals from the fire department on the radio strapped to his belt.

The boy will be thirteen soon, but he swears he will never be a teenager.

The girl keeps a bone in her pocket. She touches it when she wants reassurance. It's the bone she gave to her brother once. She found it sitting on his windowsill, collecting dust. He probably doesn't know that she took it back.

Brother and sister have this in common: they drop things wherever they go, often without realizing it. Trails of small white stones, torn

170

bits of paper, candy wrappers, scraps of bread. A means to find the way back home—or whatever.

The girl worries that one day she'll accidentally drop the bone. That it will lead her someplace she doesn't want to see again.

From her perch on the water tower, she hears the hum of the electric lines, the cries of river gulls, the grinding splutter of engine brakes from semis descending the hill into town. She sees teenagers moving in packs between convenience stores and hatchbacks, parking lots and thickets. The teenagers chomp shoplifted chips and chocolate bars. They make out in backseats and under bushes. When the girl blinks three times, she can see that the teenagers don't have shadows.

Down by the creek, the boy scores true treasure, a big green wheelbarrow. It squelches as he draws its bulk from the mud. The bottom's rusted out but the wheel's still good. He trucks it rumbling over root and stone to his secret clove near the landfill.

The monster makes from the boy's offerings more of itself. The wheelbarrow is the top of its head, some nylon rope the tendons of its arms.

The boy lights a candle, sticks it to a rock beside a dozen charred wicks. He sits staring into the flame and nods his head to the music, *death-shadow dark, hater of men.*

The monster remains still. When the boy goes home, he follows the trail of wood chips he doesn't remember leaving.

"They're doing housework," the girl warns him at the door, and the boy groans. Housework means their father testing every electric cord in the house with his ammeter. It means the third wife cutting words from the dictionary and pasting them with their definitions to things around the house: *aloe* to the aloe plant and *faucet* to the kitchen faucet, but also *stoic* to her favorite mug, *doubt* to the curtains, *trade gap* to their father's chair.

Their father turns the lights off and on, off and on. He says, "Does it seem dimmer in here than it used to be?"

The girl watches her brother help himself to more mashed potatoes, more gravy. He's been out in the woods all day, and she can smell the sour-milk smell of him. She thinks about the food going into her

171

brother and being absorbed by his body. The more he eats, the more she can disappear. She wants her skeleton closer to the air. She wants to touch the wind with her bones.

After dinner, the girl fetches the boy a bowl of ice cream. "Describe it to me," she says.

He takes a bite and says, "It's ice cream."

"Describe it to me like I don't know what ice cream is," she says.

He shrugs and says, "The cold hurts my teeth."

She adds another scoop to his bowl.

The boy is not friendless, but his friends have all been taken: by summer camp, by a stepfather to a mountain lodge, by a job on a tugboat. The boy makes charts in preparation for their return, rolls polyhedra to test the results. Six on Divine Intervention: Key to the Haunted Realm. Fourteen on Cave Encounter: An Unnatural Spring. Eleven on Family Curse: Forgetfulness.

The stereo he found in the woods. One of the speakers crackles, and burning smells ooze from the receiver. In the heat he conjures stats for demons and assassin-bears, for the Living Hand of the Iron God. He hopes his monster isn't jealous. He maps forbidden caverns, another sheet for every level down. He goes deep enough to pause summer.

Alone at night, the monster is sinew and gristle and ache of stone, a memory just out of reach, faint as a flicker of candle flame. Nightflight, sulfurous.

It tries to speak but its growl is gone. Tries to prowl but it has no feet. Rusting scrap for ribs, vines binding, earthwarmth mixing with the coldscent of metal and tang of trash. Lovely, lovely smells.

Down by the river, amidst the crooked black trees of the burnt orchard, the teenagers are having a party. By the fire they smoke their cigarettes and drink beer from cans, faces hot, butts cold. In pairs the teenagers go into thickets to make out, and when they return, teenagers look at teenagers with knowing looks. Dan, chief of the clan, ponders the chatter of firemen over the radio while sharpening his knife, which is very long. Like the teenagers gathered by the fire, the blade of his knife casts no shadow.

*

The girl wakes to a bright buzzing crackle. From her bedroom window she watches a glow above the sidewalk go from white to blue to smoking orange—then an eye-scorching *pop* followed by darkness, a break in the skin of the world.

The power is out all morning. "Transformer blew," her father tells her, and later he's part of the crew that lifts the new gray drum into place.

But that word sticks with her—*transformer*—and so does the scar of the light's bright lashing. From its depths seeps a warm, whispering bath of funky juju. Every word it speaks is its name, and its names are infinite.

In the basement, the girl sorts through a shoebox of paper dolls. As a kid she cut figures from magazines—a woman running in her bathing suit, a smoking cowboy, kids holding bottles of soda. She made clothes for them: raincoat, parka, top hat, bloomers, all with folding tabs. The dolls look strange together, disproportionate each to each, a weird race of giants and dwarves.

Now she craves their flatness. Turned sideways, the idols go unseen. They are masters of disguise, hosts to any power.

The girl feels the ghosts of cats slink close. To them the dolls are an emptiness, inviting as cardboard boxes. The girl tempts one nearer, and the doll of a boy with a picnic basket shudders at its edges as the ghost slips inside.

The monster's thoughts are shouts in an empty cavern. That it has two arms is a point of confusion. It remembers torches, loud men with yellow beards. It remembers a hand on its cheek, brow pressed to its brow, skin thick with the musk of the fen. *Mother.*

Now this little man, juicy attendant, hunts monster parts and binds them. A creator and a healer, but he isn't good at what he does. He doesn't seem to know that he hums music only he can hear.

The monster still can't move. It is a haunted statue, a static hunger, a vault of want.

*

173

In September, the boy's friends return. The boy doesn't tell his friends about the monster, but he shows them the new charts and maps. Strangely, no one wants to play in the campaign.

They have, the boy thinks, spoken to one another *in advance*. There is, he suspects, *a conspiracy afoot*. Rob goes to the movies with Linda, Luis with Jennifer, leaving the boy alone with his un-uttered incantations.

He remembers the one time his sister played. She'd had in her inventory an enchanted lantern. Liars standing in its light would cast two shadows.

The boy dreams grisly deaths, dice rolling ones again and again. He returns to his monster, feeds the unused charts through its nail-lined jaws.

The girl does her homework in the cemetery. English on the roof of a crypt, algebra by the pond under the willow.

The third wife waves to her from the path. "Hello!" she calls. "I've been thinking—"

The girl pulls her hood up, and the third wife blinks. She clutches her jacket to her throat.

"Funny," the third wife says, "I could have sworn."

The boy emerges from the woods behind the gas station. Teenagers are here, drinking from a bottle wrapped in brown paper. Before the boy can put his headphones back on, Eddie says, "Hey."

"Hey," the boy says.

"Hey," says Eddie's brother Rick.

"Hey," says Marco, gold curls shining.

Quiet Larry says nothing, only nods to Dan, who shows the boy his knife, and gives him a lord-to-vassal look.

"I heard you're going to be a teenager soon," Dan says.

The third wife goes with her survey team down to the river. They're siting the location for new power-line towers. She watches a sailboat nearly get crushed by a barge and thinks, *Why do we bother building anything?*

Her theodolite is labeled with the word *theodolite* and its definition. She turns the telescope so she can peer into the burnt orchard

174

to the north. She used to go to parties down there, back when she was a teenager. The third wife is glad she's not a teenager anymore. It was, she thinks, like being in a horror movie for seven years. The third wife has never seen a horror movie.

She wonders if the orchard burned in her lifetime. She wonders what started the fire. Maybe the trees just grew that way, she thinks. Maybe the fruit they bore was fire.

The girl overhears her father and the third wife discussing ghosts.

"Electrical disturbances, basically," her father says.

"I saw one in the cemetery last week," the third wife says.

"Our thoughts are bundles of electrical charges," her father says. "When we die, the thoughts can get out and wander on their own."

"The ghost looked so much like your daughter," the third wife says.

"Must have been my grandmother. She was a weirdo too."

The girl screams, and two lightbulbs explode in the kitchen.

Her father shrugs. "See?" he says. "Electricity."

In the abandoned zoo at the edge of town, the boy goes walking with the teenagers. Dan's radio squelches and he switches it off.

"There's so much to explain," Dan says to the boy. "So much about being a teenager that you still have to learn."

The boy wishes he were here with his sister, just the two of them. She would tell him about the ghosts of animals in their cages.

"You know that place down by the river?" Dan says. "The burnt orchard?"

"Scorchard," says Eddie, and his brother Rick says, "Torchard."

A squirrel runs down out of a tree. It sees the teenagers and panics. Quiet Larry corners it against a wall and aims his BB gun at its head. A sharp huff and the squirrel's head explodes.

"Anyway," Dan says, "you should come with us to this party on Saturday."

Their father is out on a job, driving his pickup but barely watching the road, eyeing the power lines through his open window.

His job is to tend to the giant that sleeps in the lines. To keep it from waking and throwing off its encumbrances. Siphoned through substations and transformers, the giant's breath feeds a million small machines. The machines expect so much that the father feels an ache in his chest when he thinks about it.

He thinks of his third wife, in league with the earth itself, her magnetism the pull that wakes him. He thinks of his second wife, the sparks that flew between her and his children, their words burning him in the crossfire. His first wife, when he remembers to think of her, is a fluttering light at the back of his children's eyes.

Squatting by a substation, chewing on a stalk of grass, he hears the alternating current of the giant's breath, in and out. He rides the waves of its sleep, the better to keep it sleeping. He hears, from the deep places of its dream, a rumble like thunder underground.

In the garage, the boy finds his father's spare truck battery. He lugs it down to the clove, hooks it up to the monster's head with jumper cables. He lights a candle and puts on his headphones: *Of Cain awoke all that woful breed, etins and elves and evil-spirits.* The boy sleeps. He dreams of a path of white stones. When he puts one of the stones in his mouth, it dissolves like bread.

The tape clicks off at the end of side B, and the boy startles awake. The monster is gone.

Heatlight leaves an afterimage in the monster's eyes, blue and white and gold. Standing takes time, the weight of detritus falling, shifting into place like stones grinding together. Bonemeal, hunger, one step, two.

The monster feels a flash of satisfaction with its new feet, slats of sturdy iron. Minded of mankind, it pursues their sharp scent through the twilight. But there's something else, a hollowness. Once there was a cavern, alive with home and sorrowrage. Once there was laughter in its heart, and something between its teeth. Moss, edge of iron, taste of silt. The monster does not know what it needs.

Then the forest falls away, and it sees the giants. They march into the distance, skeletal, bound by drooping tethers. They are even more hollow than the monster.

The boy sees his sister on the bridge over the creek. "I hardly see you anymore," he says.

"I see you all the time," she says.

"You're barely a flicker," he says.

"I'm only burning away the weak parts," she says.

They hear a splash and look down to see ripples in the water where a fish must have hit the top of the world and gone back down again.

The monster comes and goes from its lair. Sometimes the boy finds it and walks with it. The monster doesn't talk, but the boy can hear the buzzing of its thoughts like a thousand wasps in its wheelbarrow head.

It lumbers through the woods under the train trestle. Two teenagers are making out in an abandoned car. The monster tears the roof off and eats the teenagers one at a time, jaws moving thoughtfully. The teenagers are too cool to scream.

The boy thinks it might have been Luis and Jennifer. When did *they* become teenagers?

Cutting through the woods on her way home from school, the girl finds footprints on the muddy bank of the creek. A giant bear? No, the paws of the beast left corrugated markings. She cracks her knuckles, follows the tracks as far as the landfill. She notices a set of smaller prints beside the larger ones. She cracks her knuckles again.

The boy digs through the third wife's tools until he finds a compass and some good pencils. Then he digs under a stack of comic books for his pad of map paper, rows and columns of interlocking hexes, cool blue ink on heavy paper.

He sketches real topographies for once, the wilds between the landfill and the river. Dotted lines for the paths he knows, a wavy one for the creek, an X for the burnt orchard. Certain big trees he draws in miniature, the rest are masses of wavy lines with vertical bars for trunks.

He cranks the volume on his stereo. *Men may say not where the haunts of these Hell-Runes be.*

He has to guess at the width of the swamps, but he knows exactly where to put his greatest secret. *SECRET CLOVE, NO TRESPASSING.* Below the words, he draws the monster's face, its fanged grin a malediction. Finally he adds the key, 1 hex = 1/4 mile, a serpent's snout pointing north.

*

The girl follows stones that her brother left, a trail into the ravine, along the edge of the swamp and around the landfill. She finds the monster. A distant shout prickles the back of her neck, tells her to hide. Instead she runs her hand over the monster's body. Rebar, wheelbarrow, milk crates, tires. Bittersweet and ivy.

She whispers to the monster the way she whispers to the ghosts of cats. The monster moves, minutely. It looks at its left arm, then sags again.

There's a big hole in its chest, some loose paint cans in there. She plugs the hole with a tire, puts her hands on her hips. "You're still missing something," she says.

She leaves the monster at dusk. She sees movement at the edge of her vision, a trick of the light. The narrow places that comprise her fiefdom feel narrower than usual. It's getting dark, but she'd know her brother in any light. His headphones give him the silhouette of a bear, and she can hear his music even from a distance.

When he sees her, he jumps, then takes his headphones off and says, "You should be home."

"You should be home," she says.

"It's getting late," he says.

"Let's race shopping carts," she says.

"Seriously?"

Up the ravine they go, sister first, grubby sneakers slipping on rocks. They know the path better than they know the halls of their house. The lone light behind the grocery store is like a lantern, its beams harsh in the crisp night air. They haven't done this for a long time. They test the wheels of shopping carts and pick the best. The best aren't very good.

"Ready?" she asks.

"Ready as rain." That's just something he says.

The girl gives her brother the bone. It looks tiny in his thick fingers.

"I thought I'd lost it," he says.

She's lightening her load, preparing to fly. And it does feel like flying, the two of them together, between the trees and down to the bottom of the earth. She hears someone whooping and laughing, and it's her.

178

*

The boy calls Dan and says, "I don't think I'm going to be able to make it to the party."

Silence from the other end of the line.

The boy says, "I've got this project."

Silence again.

"You there, Dan?"

"I'm here," Dan says. "Are you there?"

"I'm here," the boy says.

"I'm here, you're here," Dan says. "It's almost like the party has already started."

The boy thinks Dan isn't alone. There's another presence, like low static but not from their connection, breathing with their breaths.

Dan says, "I heard your sister is going to be a teenager soon. Maybe we should invite her instead."

The boy isn't sure which is supposed to be the greater threat: him left out or his sister left alone with those wolves.

"So we'll see you there?" Dan says.

The boy nods, then remembers that he needs to say something. But before he can speak, Dan says, "Good," and hangs up.

The boy takes four cans of beer from the fridge and stuffs them into his backpack. His father's working the late shift. He imagines him scaling one of the power-line towers out by the cement plant, gazing with a giant's view of town. He wonders if what his father sees squares with the map he made. He wonders if their house is visible from up there.

Outside, the third wife is raking leaves. The boy hears her pause, maybe to say something. He walks more quickly down the sidewalk.

The girl's invisibility must be wearing off, because the third wife catches her in the kitchen and says, "I thought maybe we could do something together tonight, just us girls?"

The girl looks desperately around the room. Amidst the clutter on the counter are two horror movies that she rented in the summer, never watched, never returned. She snatches them up and says, "Let's watch these."

The third wife's face wilts as she reads the titles, *Trail of the Fiend*

179

and *Covered with Blood 2: Haunts of Darkness*. The girl knows that the third wife has never seen a horror movie, and she thinks she's won. But the third wife smiles and says, "I'll make popcorn."

A fire burns in the burnt orchard. With his headphones around his neck, the boy can hear the scrape of slow metal on stone. Teenagers stand facing the flames, quieter than usual. Rick is the first to spot him. He tugs the brim of his baseball cap, and his brother Eddie looks up. A half dozen others look or don't look.

"Hey," says Eddie, and the boy says, "Hey."

"Hey," says Rick.

"Hey," says one of the teenagers the boy doesn't know. *Hey, hey, hey.*

Quiet Larry stays quiet. Dan's radio adds its static to the hiss and pop of the fire. The boy hits stop on his tape deck.

A horror movie flashes on the television. The girl sneaks glances at the third wife. She waits for her to cringe from the gore on the screen, but the third wife just leans forward in the blue light, like someone who is about to be told a secret. Her hand travels back and forth between the popcorn bowl and her mouth. Sometimes the third wife smiles and laughs, like she's in on something.

A fire burns in the burnt orchard. The teenagers are mostly boy teenagers, but there are also a few girl teenagers. Rick and Eddie lift a wood pallet and set it on the fire. Sparks fly up toward the moon, a bright sickle behind thin clouds. The teenagers pass around a bottle of whiskey.

The boy remembers the beer and takes it out of his backpack. No one looks interested. Pasted to one of the cans is the word *beer* and its definition, clipped from the dictionary. He sets the cans on the ground.

Larry stares at Dan like he expects him to do something, and Dan looks nervous. Thinking of the squirrel that Larry shot, the boy wonders who's really in charge.

*

A horror movie flashes on the television. The telephone rings, and the girl jumps. The third wife doesn't notice, doesn't turn away from *Trail of the Fiend*.

"I'll get it," the girl says, and she goes into the kitchen.

It's Marco. She can't think of why Marco would be calling. He isn't friends with her brother, is he?

"Hey," Marco says.

"Hey," she says.

He wants to know if she has plans. He wants her to come to a party, down at the orchard. "There should be beer," he says.

"You think I care about beer?" she asks, genuinely curious.

There's a pause. "I guess I don't know what you care about. But you're invited."

The girl twists the cord around her fingers until she's wearing a plastic mitt of spirals.

A fire burns in the burnt orchard. Marco shows up, his curly hair shining in the firelight. He gives Dan an unsecret wink. Then he sees the beer and pulls a can from its plastic loop.

The boy watches a barge move slowly upriver, riding low in the water, fully freighted. The others have quiet conversations in groups of two or three. He wonders what they're waiting for. He opens a can of the beer and sips. He sips again and nods.

In the horror movie flashing on the television, a woman walks alone through a barn. Something moves behind the walls, but the woman doesn't see.

The girl reaches into her pocket for the bone, but of course it isn't there. She fakes a yawn and says, "I think I'm gonna hit the hay."

The third wife looks up. "Aren't you curious about how it ends?"

"These movies all have the same ending," the girl says.

The third wife looks startled. "Well don't tell me what it is," she says.

The girl goes upstairs and pulls her hood up. She eases the window open and climbs out onto the porch roof. By the time her feet hit the grass, she's invisible again.

*

The fire in the burnt orchard burns lower. The beer is getting warm in its can, but the boy keeps sipping. When he sees his sister arrive, he feels like he might throw up. She gives him a funny look, but the boy can only stare.

Marco prances over and puts one arm around the girl's shoulders. She shoves him away and he prances back, hooting. The others laugh.

Dan says, "All right," and the laughter stops.

Larry is watching Dan carefully. Dan's radio squelches. He switches it off and takes out his knife. "So which of you wants to go first?" he says.

The boy takes the knife. He sets the tip of the blade near the heel of his left shoe, against the edge of his shadow.

"Don't," his sister says, and the teenagers look at her.

The boy tries to make the cut, but his shadow squirms. He feels it like an ache in a muscle he didn't know he had. He presses harder. The beer rolls warmly in his stomach, and his arm feels weak.

"I can't do it," he says.

"Should we do it for you?" asks Larry. It's the first thing the boy has heard him say tonight. He sounds eager.

"I'll do it," the boy's sister says. She walks over to him and holds out her hand. The boy gives her the knife. She kneels, bringing the blade close.

"Ready?" she says.

"Ready as rain," he says.

The girl throws the knife toward the river. It flies in a high flashing arc and disappears into the cattails.

"Run," the girl says, and they run.

They have a head start, but the teenagers are faster, because teenagers have longer strides and no shadows to slow them down. Dan tackles the boy and the boy feels the air go out of him. Eddie grabs the girl's arm and swings her around; the girl gets free, but then Eddie's brother Rick tackles her.

The boy's backpack has spilled open. On the ground is his map of the forest. Larry picks it up and says, "Interesting."

182

*

A teenager goes looking for the shadowless knife. A teenager shines a flashlight at the map of the forest. A teenager lights a cigarette and smokes it, exhaling smoke through his nostrils. A teenager finds the shadowless knife. A teenager goes back for the whiskey. A teenager keeps the boy pinned to the ground. A teenager holds the girl's arm too tight. A teenager points a flashlight at the sky to see how far the beam will reach. A teenager points to a spot on the map of the forest and says, "There."

They follow the paths the boy marked, the winding ways along the creek and over the bridge. The forest looks ragged and hungry. The boy says, "This isn't a good idea."

Dan says, "Keeping secrets from us is, like, the opposite of how this is supposed to work."

Eddie looks a little sad about the whole thing. His brother Rick punches him in the shoulder.

In the boy's secret clove, teenagers shine their flashlights into the trees and over the ground. They shine their flashlights on the rock covered with melted candle wax. On the ground the teenagers find a few cracked bones, the bones of teenagers.

"Like a goddamn summoning ritual," one of the teenagers says.

They find some scrap metal, some twine, a lot of broken sticks. There is a hole in the forest where the monster should be.

"Where is it?" Larry says.

"I don't know," the boy says, and he doesn't.

Larry holds the knife to the girl's shadow. "Where is it?" he says.

"I don't know," the boy says.

Larry starts cutting, and the girl's shadow squirms.

"Larry," Dan says.

Larry gives Dan a look, and Dan looks at the ground.

"Where is it?" Larry says.

"I don't know," the boy says, but this time he does.

The monster's shadow is like a cold breath on the back of Larry's neck. He turns and screams. The monster picks him up in one hand,

and Larry screams again. Quiet Larry's screams aren't quiet. He drops the knife. The monster chews Larry carefully, starting at the top.

The other teenagers run, and the monster runs after them. The boy and the girl run after the monster.

"Great party," the girl says to the boy. The boy can't tell whether or not his sister is joking.

The forest is hungry, but not as hungry as the monster. It swipes trees aside to get at teenagers. Most of the teenagers go quietly when they go into the monster's mouth, and other teenagers respect them for this.

The windows of houses up on the ridge flash blue with light from televisions. In a clearing at the bottom of the slope, Dan, Eddie, and Marco stop running. They're the only teenagers left. They turn to face the monster, ready to make their final stand.

The monster crashes into the clearing and takes a deep breath of electrical moonlight. It blinks with eyelids the boy gave it, fake leather torn from a school-bus seat.

A tall someone appears on the slope. It's the third wife. She walks down into the clearing and stands between the teenagers and the monster. She sees the girl and says, "There you are! I followed your trail—"

Of popcorn, the girl realizes, feeling the warm slick of butter inside her pocket. She must have stockpiled it there and dropped pieces on her way.

But the third wife has stopped talking. She sees the monster and tilts her head. She seems to think carefully about what she's seeing.

The monster picks the third wife up in one hand. She doesn't scream, but the girl does.

"Oh," says the boy.

"It's all right," the third wife calls down to them. "They all have the same ending."

The girl runs to the monster and presses her palm against its leg. She feels its hunger, undiminished. She feels how narrow it is despite its girth, captive to an inner thinness. The monster is, she thinks, a monster of her own dominion. She climbs up its leg and pulls the tire out of its chest. The space is just right for her to curl up inside.

"Here we are," she says.

The monster feels pain for the first time since it woke here. The pain is in its chest, along with a new warmth. It would fall to its knees if its knees were better at bending. Instead it wavers, exposed in the clearing while the tiny men watch. So fleshy. So easy to pull apart. But this clearing is nothing like the wilds of its youth. The monster is far from home.

It lifts the small creature to its mouth. With its other hand, it grabs that arm and holds it steady. Then it wrenches the arm free from its body, cracking sinews of rope and wire, iron frame bursting. It sets the arm on the ground and the hand opens.

In its chest, jammed between rusting metal and twisting vines, the girl sighs.

The third wife, whose name is Laurie, gets up and brushes herself off. She seems grateful but also a little disappointed. She curtsies.

The teenagers run, and the monster goes after them. Not for eating, just for something to chase.

They burst from the woods shouting, stumble through a playground and over a backyard, dash across a county route and into a parking lot. Drivers don't understand what they're seeing.

The girlmonster sticks Marco in a tree and leaves him there. Quietstalking, it sets Eddie on top of his own house, because it ate his brother Rick and feels a little bad about that. Dan it locks inside a cage at the abandoned zoo.

On his radio, Dan hears the firemen talking as they search for him. He cries when one of them says that he'll make a good fireman someday.

This body is not the narrowness she's accustomed to, but it is a fine thing to tower so, here in the heart of her brother's electrified hunger.

Her brother, her friend. He built this thing and she completed it. A horror, but it's theirs and it's them. Buried inside those clanking velocities, she thinks it might even be beautiful.

Back in the clove, the girl tumbles out of the monster's chest and onto the marshy ground. She's covered in grease. Her brother comes to her, the third wife behind him like a shadow. He lets out a long breath and presses his forehead to hers.

The monster lies down in the usual place, joints groaning. A moment later, it's asleep.

The girl's body feels different, muscles and bones and skin working in concert. A monster's body, full of fire. She could use it to hunt down anything, even herself.

Sister and brother return the next day, but the monster's hollow is empty, and the following day is the same. The boy fingers the bone in his pocket. The girl zips up her hoodie, purple and new. The third wife gave it to her. She hasn't yet identified its powers.

Her brother gives her a small corroded spring. It must have fallen from the monster when it tore off its own arm. She puts the spring in her pocket.

The boy claims territory in the dining room. For his birthday, his sister gave him a new set of dice. He scatters them over the table, a hoard of bright gems. Dan is here, and Eddie, and Linda. They check their inventories and study the maps, readying characters for the new campaign.

When the third wife comes home, she sets her hard hat on the shelf next to the father's hard hat. The father is in the kitchen, making pizza and polishing his ammeter.

"Looking for ghosts?" she says.

"Only the ones looking for us," he says.

The sister is on the outskirts of town, perched in a tree with one hand in her pocket. She looks toward the river. The monster saunters down the power-line corridor, as it often does at dusk.

Jackals

Diane Josefowicz

ISN'T THAT LYNDON JOHNSON?

Spine arched, head thrown back, Lorraine was gesturing toward the clutch of ex-presidents who'd been figured like saints on a bank of stained-glass windows. Her bracelets glinted; the choker at her neck suggested other possibilities. Lorraine was an ostentatious fake and, as usual, Paul wanted to wallop her. But they'd been married so long he'd grown used to such urges and the mechanics of their suppression. Everyone else—they were six that evening, including himself and Lorraine—offered bland smiles. They too had resigned themselves to Lorraine.

I'll be *damned*, she continued, squinting at the windows across the bar, oblivious to Paul's irritation, to the condescension of the group. It *is* Lyndon Johnson.

Yes, someone said, in a dull, down-regulating tone. Right there next to him is Tricky Dick.

Paul tilted his head, hoping a shift in his literal perspective would effect a similar shift on the level of metaphor, permitting him to see his wife differently. Perhaps reality was no more solid than the view through a kaleidoscope, bits of colored glass that could be rearranged with a twist of the mechanism. Twist: surely Lorraine was too old to play the dimwit. Twist: surely they'd been married too long for that. And yet, there it was: the coquettishness, which hadn't suited her when she was younger and didn't suit her now. But you couldn't change the raw materials; light comes through glass in only one way. That's what he'd been told in counseling. He'd bridled at the advice, but then he was just like that, a man who bridled at advice. Bridling didn't make the advice less apt. It didn't change the reality: she wasn't part of their group. She hadn't gone to school with them; she didn't get their jokes. Maybe he shouldn't have dragged her along.

But then how long had it been since they'd gathered like this? Thirty years? Thirty-five? Paul couldn't bring himself to do the math. Calculation taxed him more than reminiscence as he turned the far corner on middle age. They'd met as first-year psychiatric residents,

187

anxious to shine—and they had, briefly. But time had dulled them all. Jack Stolz had developed the drinking problem they'd all foreseen; Rory Beck had lost all his hair, and much of his vitality, to chemo; and Paul winced when he noticed Kath, with whom he still shared an office, talking around nouns she kept forgetting. Even King Smalls, who had been such a dynamo, organizing double dates and tailgate parties when the rest of them could scarcely stand from exhaustion, had retired to Florida. How could aging, a natural process, produce so much that felt unnatural? Still it was good to meet, especially here, where time had stopped with Watergate: the chairs and tables were the same, as were the too-bright light fixtures that lent the place the familiar if unlovely air of a hospital cafeteria, and then there were the ex-presidents, caught forever in the glass wall of shame.

Rory had extracted a passel of school photographs from his wallet and the pictures were making the rounds. The grandkids were endearing, with cowlicks and gap-toothed smiles, their attention seemingly caught by something exciting happening just over the viewer's right shoulder. Perhaps it was the prospect of adulthood. It always looked so compelling at that age, Paul remembered. He smiled wider with each photo, aware of making an effort. The others also seemed uncomfortable, their praise coughed up, obligatory. Paul's face ached from all the politesse.

I can't believe, Kath was saying, how much this place has changed. The milk stout isn't even on the menu anymore.

Behind her, a large-screen television was tuned to some athletic contest. Paul could see green fields, and men running across them, and, now and then, a flicker as the signal weakened.

There's a lot that's not on the menu anymore, King was saying. Eggs, steak, butter.

Rory lamented: ice cream! They all winced and then simultaneously burst out laughing. Togetherness had its pleasures. It felt good to share a concern, even if it was only about cholesterol.

Even we aren't on the menu anymore, Kath said.

Her remark brought the usual silence thumping down. Why always this modesty around the topic of sex? Lorraine sniffed, and Paul braced himself against another wave of irritation. He would have to try not to find some trivial pretext on which to berate her afterward, in the hotel room.

Kath excused herself with a wave of her clutch.

Speaking of sex, Stolz began, shifting into the chair that Kath had vacated.

Or not speaking, Lorraine murmured.

Everyone ignored her—freely, since, with Kath gone, there was less need to keep up appearances with the opposite sex. Paul felt marginally better: their sexism, at least, remained lively. Though they'd finished school during a period of expanding egalitarianism, he considered them all men of the college in the old style—well, except for Kath, who was not a man at all, of course. She'd been part of the first coed housing experiment, when the boys made a point of pissing against her door. The egalitarian movement had assimilated everything, even the pools of piss, and look what had happened: the college didn't produce men anymore, just wave after wave of undifferentiated graduates. You had to be an imbecile not to feel the loss.

Paul's thoughts had only grown less shareable, that was another problem with aging.

Have I got a story for you, Stolz said.

Over Stolz's shoulder, a penalty flag unfurled against the green.

You know what the dementia did to Stanley, Stolz said. His wife had to put him in a home.

Stanley was their teacher, the one they'd all sucked up to, elbowing one another aside in their compulsion to impress. Stolz leaned forward, warming to his story. What a putz. Resentment surged through Paul.

I went to see him, Stolz said. He greeted me same as ever. He was wearing his smoking jacket, looked like he was just on his way to the office. Can you imagine. He sits me down. He looks me in the eye. He says, The women here.

The women! exclaimed King.

Always the women, Rory echoed.

All crazy! Stolz was shouting. Crazy!

Paul said, Yeah?

I mean, Stolz emended, that's what he says to *me*. He says, There's this woman, this—

Old lady?

Lorraine touched the tip of her nose, their secret signal: shut up.

I didn't want to actually *use* those words, Stolz backtracked.

Quietly King asked, Where's Kath?

I mean, she's an old *widow*—

Gesticulating, Stolz knocked his glass to the floor.

A flurry of napkins descended, and a round-cheeked girl whom Paul thought too pretty for her nerd glasses swept the shards into a dustpan, the crack of her ass just visible above her belt.

That *is* him, isn't it, Lorraine asked, plucking his sleeve. Isn't that LBJ?

Paul didn't respond. It was important to let reality hit people. Stolz, for one, needed a wake-up call. He was obviously impaired.

The waitress returned with a refill.

On the house, she said, handing it to Stolz.

What's this, a sippy cup?

That might actually be appropriate, Paul said.

The waitress made excuses: it had been such a busy night they'd run out of pint glasses and had to switch to Solos. She eyed Stolz and he stared back mildly—Paul recognized the trick— until she looked away.

Lorraine prompted: You were saying, Jack? About the widow?

Lorraine would grease the rails of his own oblivion with the same competent charm—for which, it occurred to Paul, he might well be grateful.

Wet lipped, Stolz was winding up to his punch line: So she'd come into the room, the widow. She was talking a blue streak, the way they do. Stanley listened for a while. And guess what he said?

Just back from the bathroom and trailing perfume, Kath asked: What?

We have to stop.

A shrink's line. Their laughter was polite, indulgent. The curmudgeon would never change, that was the point. They liked to believe that they were similarly faithful to themselves. That their lives expressed an essence that, whatever it might have been, was unquestionably theirs.

Stolz, meanwhile, was staring into his beer. A qualified victory had never been enough for him. Paul remembered a lesson from Stanley: people are like stuck compasses, they don't shift more than five degrees to either side. It was important to keep expectations realistic.

The waitress dropped the check, which was fine by Paul, who had already resigned himself to an early night. Even in residency, their outings often did end this way, with one dumb move that scattered the group. After a scramble for coats, they tumbled onto the street. *Yahtzee!* Lorraine murmured behind her raised hand. The darkness pitched around them and they slipped the mooring their assembly had provided, bidding each other good night.

*

190

On Monday, Kath found Paul's door open by a finger's width and the whole office charged with a strange atmosphere. Fraught. Some days, her patients told her, it's better to stay in bed, and she saw the rightness of that view even as she tried to convince them otherwise. Depression had a pedagogy. For one thing, it taught self-preservation. Nothing bad could happen to you if you didn't leave your bed. That self-preservation was more necessary in some contexts than others— well, teaching that was *her* bailiwick.

Most days she felt up to it. Not today. She slipped off her clogs— she preferred to work in socks—and padded to the kitchen, where she located her mug, its interior glaze addled with cracks from the stream of hot drinks that lubricated her day. She ran hot water from the dispenser into her cup, dunked a tea bag, and, having girded herself with this ritual, went to look in on Paul.

He didn't answer her knock. She considered calling out but then retreated to the kitchen, trying not to feel slighted by his lack of response. A tiny practice like theirs depended on the willingness of each partner to understand the other, to provide quick bursts of support. All she'd done was the professional thing, making sure to check in with him when he seemed to be having a rough time. She didn't deserve the cold shoulder, but then, if Paul was difficult, well, he was just being Paul. She opened a cabinet and became so absorbed in rummaging for a snack that she didn't hear Paul enter the kitchen.

There was a thing, he said, causing her to jump. Sorry.

That's all right.

Like a child taught to watch his step, he'd learned the trick of moving noiselessly. She found a bag of pretzels and slid it toward him, the rigid plastic bag crackling. She wanted him to know she wasn't mad about him creeping up on her, pouncing.

So there was a thing?

The other night at the bar. When you left to use the bathroom.

Oh?

He told her what Stolz had said about Stanley and the older woman who'd accosted him at the home and, in doing so, brought Stanley back to himself, to Stolz, to the world.

That's how Paul made it sound: like the old woman had accosted Stanley.

Oh, that Stanley, she mused, trying to buy time. It was hard to square Paul's sour narrative with what she remembered of that night, its density of shared experience, especially toward the end. Her next words bolted from her: The grand old man can't also be a dirty one, can he?

Who said anything about *that*?

Sorry, she said, meaning it. How could she have failed to corral that thought? He didn't reply, and she felt even worse. She watched him leave. She knew this aspect of Paul well enough. Beneath the posturing was a core orientation, a way of being in the world that was as much his own as his fingerprints, yet she knew that this quickness to take offense was more obvious to others than it would ever be to himself. To himself he was just *right*. She'd puzzled over it many times: who was Paul in that self-righteous moment and who did she, Kath, become for him? But even after all the cogitating she had to admit that she had no idea. At bottom lurked an energy she associated with sex. They listened for a living. But for him it was different, Kath thought. For him listening felt like a shock to the body's integrity, like diving into the ocean, enduring that assault on all the senses, one's perception suddenly reduced to green, cold, salt, wet— oh, and the smell, that faintly menstrual rot. He had to stand firm against that, perhaps.

Or else what she felt must be wrong, an echo of her own damage, nothing to do with him at all.

Maybe he was just blurting.

She had an adolescent patient whose eyes were like her husband's. On bad days, she sat with this young woman and failed to listen, distracted by private wonderings: what other children might her husband have? What lies secured her happiness?

She caught Paul in the corridor on his way to lunch. The downstairs door slammed: her next patient was arriving.

What did your wife say about Stolz's story?

Paul shrugged, avoiding her eyes.

You didn't ask?

What does it matter? She's not like us.

In her office, Kath checked her teeth in the small compact she kept in the pocket of her work coat. Pressing her tongue against her lower incisors, she felt for the gunk where she knew it built up. She'd have to see the dentist soon.

Not like us, she thought. What a thing to say.

But then again, what *couldn't* you say after thirty years of marriage?

*

Kath knew she was too wound up to drive. The trip was a mistake, the day too bright, the business ahead—just grocery shopping, which shouldn't have bothered her—overwhelming. Behind her eyes a pressure had built, the tension of psychic material badly repressed. All she wanted was to sit in a darkened room and hold her head. Still the groceries had to be collected. Besides, she pep-talked herself, wasn't she used to doing things on her own, through any sort of madness?

She drove carefully, avoiding potholes.

It was only after she'd parked that she discovered she'd forgotten her list. She donned sunglasses and fussed with her wallet, arranging bills and receipts, waiting for a solution to occur to her. None did. She'd have to work from memory. The pressure behind her eyes intensified.

The store was crowded. She kept her sunglasses on, knowing she looked crazy. So what. She hefted bunches of bananas, heavy yellow-fingered hands. She wished she was wearing headphones.

It was useful to divide problems into types. There were abstract problems, like trying to draw a line between one country and another, and concrete ones, like ordering a milk stout. Similarly, there were thinking problems and feeling problems. Today's problem *felt* like a *thinking* problem, which made it something of a conundrum. She couldn't stop *thinking* about Paul's story and this inability *felt* bad. Unless it was the story itself that was the cause of the bad feeling, and her rumination was just a symptom. A story could infect you like a virus. Perhaps Stolz's story had made Paul sick in just that way, and Paul needed to relieve himself of whatever the story had produced in him, some unbearable state of mind. She knew from her long association with Paul that the compulsion to tell these stories was partly competitive: Paul had heard the story during those minutes she'd spent in the bathroom. He needed to remind her that he'd been on the scene when she'd been elsewhere. No doubt Paul had once suffered from a parent who tantalized, who kept the door open on scenes better left unspied upon. Perhaps—though she resisted this thought—he had excitedly imagined her in the bathroom, primping; in fact, she had spent some minutes staring into the mirror and wondering how she could get through the evening without slapping someone. Lorraine's cackle had set her off, Kath remembered. But she couldn't reconstruct the details. All she recalled was that Lorraine had made an unfunny joke, something about the dead presidents at the back of the bar.

Kath turned, too quickly, and in her haste jostled a woman nearby who was wearing a lot of makeup over her tan. Apologizing, Kath darted away, down the vitamin aisle. It was getting hard to breathe. Maybe she was losing her mind, misplacing it the way she might her keys or her phone. She had to *contain* Stolz's story, even as it congealed inside her like hot jam in a jar.

The aisle wasn't quite deserted: a girl sitting at a card table was carefully filling plastic cups with bright yellow juice.

Sea buckthorn juice, the girl said. Try some.

Kath selected a cup, sniffed its contents.

It tastes better than it smells, the girl assured her. She was fresh-faced with smooth, plump skin of astonishing clarity. She looked familiar. Kath couldn't place her.

It's full of antioxidants. Genghis Khan made his soldiers drink it.

The stuff slid down Kath's throat, cold, bitter, but not, for all that, undrinkable. The plastic cup felt oily against her lips.

What do you think?

It tastes character building.

The girl laughed. She had good teeth, well spaced and regular.

The juice was expensive. Kath took a bottle anyway. She was stirred up. A dumb expenditure wouldn't kill her.

She was in the parking lot when the insight came: she'd always felt a bit left out among that lot, the residents. Paul had stimulated her envy by retelling that story in the office as if she'd not even been *at* the pub. Admittedly, she'd ceded the field by visiting the bathroom, but surely that was no reason to punish her. In other words, it was standard Paul behavior. He was a monster at bridge, snide about small errors. She hated to play opposite him, knowing she'd have to hear all about every hand she might have played differently. Was an inference to be drawn?

Something was *wrong* with Stolz's story.

Juice pushing's just a sideline. So's waitressing at the ex-presidents' bar. Dorinda does her real work here at the nursing home. She doesn't get paid, not yet. She's just a volunteer. But she knows it's the work she's meant to do because she struggles just to show up. The work puts an important strain on her, her teacher says. Her body arrives at the job before she does and it will sometimes be fifteen or twenty minutes before she feels herself click into place, a tumbler turning somewhere within. Sometimes she doesn't arrive at all, and on those days,

194

she can't make her body and her mind line up. The tumbler doesn't turn; the pins don't get a chance to click. Her teacher says: That's how you know.

She clings to her teacher's faith. That he only teaches yoga doesn't matter. It's his presence in her life that makes the difference. At the nursing home she feels like she's stuck in a vat of vanilla pudding: vanilla walls, vanilla sheets, vanilla protein drink for the patients who can't be trusted to chew, which is to say, most of them. It's dull work, vanilla work, pushing the cart down the vanilla-colored hall and back again, doling out one cup at a time, waiting for the patient to drink its contents, taking the empty cup, marking the sheet: who swallowed, who didn't. The television blares in most rooms. Slack faces watch, eyes tracking slow. Dorinda believes people don't understand this kind of living—the lessened pitch, all colors greatly faded. Vanillaed. Occasionally while with a patient she catches a flash of the person who'd once fully inhabited that flesh, and knew what it meant to have a memory, to have had the experience of having seen someone before. Since she herself needs so much more experience, she's inclined to patience. She'll apply to medical school someday. She doesn't have the grades but grades aren't everything. She wants to specialize in geriatrics or suicidology. She's interested in forms of life just this side of dying. Try putting that in a personal statement.

She stops outside the old doctor's room, 4B. He's in the armchair, wrapped in his fancy jacket, slippers on his feet. The room has an echoing quality that makes it peaceful when television is off, which it usually is. He doesn't like television. He likes staring out the window.

Doctor.

His face contorts as he struggles to recall her name. Finally he says: Dorinda.

She responds with a puppy's wide-mouthed smile. She can't help it. What she feels for him is hard to explain.

You wouldn't know it to look at me, would you, the doctor says, as if he'd heard her thought.

She's been told he's a psychiatrist. Aren't they supposed to be intuitive?

Wouldn't know what? Now he's asking the questions.

She hands him the cup. He swallows, grimacing. He's obedient.

That's awful, he tells her.

I know, she says.

You know.

195

He says it gently, so she feels the blade. Which she does, every time—even that one time, when the gangly middle-aged dude with the beer gut and the whiskey breath had come to visit and she was on her guard with both of them. She's supposed to be on her guard at all times. But she isn't. She likes this patient's feisty quality, how he mocks and flirts, insulting her so she can't feel like she knows everything. She doesn't know everything. Maybe she doesn't know anything.

That's why I'm going to medical school, she adds. To know.

We have to *stop*, he tells her. That's what he said to Whiskey Breath too. *We have to stop.*

Another staffer might call him agitated. But his statement has a lively quality, consistent with his smoking jacket and wry flirtatiousness. It doesn't have the dully repetitive quality of a perseveration. He's trying to hit the right note, she thinks. It must be like trying to make a shot in tennis. You keep at it until you hear the ball against the sweet spot and then you know.

See you tomorrow, she says as she takes her leave. Looking back from the doorway, she sees that he's already gone, staring out the window again at the empty service road.

When she returns with the cart, the station nurse asks wearily: Did something happen?

In 4B, she says.

A charmer, that one. Was he aggressive?

Dorinda takes the cups, one by one, and throws them in the trash, leaving the doctor's cup for last, the vanilla dregs still in it. She looks behind. No one is watching. She lifts the cup to her mouth.

Stanley remembers so little now. But he still remembers the excitement of early July, when the university vouchsafed to him another litter of first-year residents. Always they were eager to please him and not anywhere near as eager to exercise restraint with their patients. Oh, how they resented the outpatient ward, where they interviewed mere neurotics whose problems, they more or less secretly felt, could be resolved through the application of a little willpower. They saw those patients as inferior to the more exotic pathologies inhabiting the locked wards on the upper floors, where they, those greenhorns, preferred to be.

They needed time on the locked wards themselves, he caught himself thinking. Then they would see how far their ideas about will and power would get them. They would be improved by such done time.

But there was no wishing for that. Sadism went around like the flu. He'd figured out how to use that energy: he'd created a whole pedagogy and even—*quelle horreur*—won a teaching award. How they'd bristle at the tasks he assigned: Yes, by all means, take a history, but submit it to me in the form of a sonnet. *A sonnet?* He'd smile and nod, all innocence. Talk about will and power. He'd edit the results, make the students read aloud. He'd interrupt: That's where the line should break. Does it? Break? Just there? They'd blush, stutter. Now and then he'd get a weeper. The sting of humiliation was meant to take some of the starch out of them, so they wouldn't sting, or starch, a patient. That was the idea, to protect. Wounding them in this small way would make them more sensitive to the wounds of others.

Or so he hoped. How easily he fooled them all, not least himself. He was getting it back now, though. Take that fool Jack Stolz, who still had to mock him, projecting death wishes ("You have to stop") and threats ("chemical restraint"). But wasn't restraint always the watchword? Soon the nurse will arrive with her syringe full of euphemism. He won't fight. No sarcasm, no stink-eye. He'd just float; for once he'd remember how evenly to suspend his attention; he'd try to imagine what life was like for that candy striper. Not the way he might have imagined her once, not the old luscious fantasy, but as she might actually want to be imagined. Although he can do very little for anyone in his present, diminished state, he can still dream. And while he can, he will.

They gathered again for Stanley's service—a memorial, since he'd been cremated—at a church that, despite its age and historic significance, displayed exactly zero ex-presidents in its windows. There was no beer, either—although Stolz, swaying in the pulpit as he delivered his eulogy, seemed to have made do, nipping from a flask he slipped in and out of a pocket while everyone pretended not to notice. Paul was sitting with Lorraine, folding and refolding the paper on which he'd scrawled notes for the dull eulogy he'd just delivered. He suspected Stanley had planned the whole affair in the days after his diagnosis, before the dementia could interfere with his desire to control everything. The event had an overly rigid quality, even with Stolz nattering drunkenly on. How little control he seemed to have over his long arms and legs. Thank heaven it would be over soon. Rory would give a speech, Kath would read what Stanley's wife had prepared, they'd attend the catered luncheon for as long as Stolz could stand upright, and then they'd adjourn to the ex-presidents' bar. In fact, Paul was looking forward to it.

Seated in a pew across the central aisle, Kath was slightly masked, her face obscured by a large-brimmed straw hat that matched her suit, tropical wool in a bruised purple that was almost black, a color he felt as a rebuke. He'd offended her somehow, in recent weeks. Perhaps they'd make it up tonight. King hadn't made it; bad weather tied him up in Tampa. Rory wasn't showing well and perhaps should not have come either: he looked like he'd been stuffed into his shirt, already the armpits were dark, and he kept running a finger under his tie—a pointless gesture, as he could no more loosen his necktie than he could loosen his grip on his own identity. Identity: in the end it was nothing more than the armored bunker in which they had all entombed themselves, gladly for the most part. Or so it seemed to Paul.

The last benediction given, Stanley's family filed out ahead of the congregation, which had risen as a body. The first and second wives, with their children and stepchildren, spurted up the center aisle, making no eye contact, exchanging no greetings, as if they too were ready to move on to some more special and bearable after-party, some ex-presidents' pub of their own. Following them, Stolz managed to trip over his own feet and go sprawling down the aisle before popping up again—thank heaven—like a tweed-coated jack-in-the-box. Paul stepped out next, offering an arm to Lorraine as she picked her way down the pew. She scowled, pulling her shawl around her, and surprised them both by stumbling into his arms. *Christ*, she muttered and huffed off. He trailed behind, breathing urgently by numbers. Was it so necessary to have a hissy fit now, in front of his colleagues? As if to prove the point Stanley was forever making about relationships—how no sooner had the bride and groom sworn to love, honor, and protect than the one would move too fast or too slow for the other on the way up the aisle, and the stranger within would show its talon and snarl, as one of Paul's patients, a poet, had once put it.

He found Lorraine outside the coatroom. He could tell from her gestures and tightened expression that she was speaking angrily about the gathering, insulting his friends, no doubt. But he couldn't hear anything above the band, which had started up a gospel number. The Dixieland horns mocked the solemnity of the architecture. The effect was sheer Stanley, too clever by half. Yet something *had* changed: what should have irritated today only caused Paul to brim with tenderness. What a teacher Stanley was, what a magician! And what a miracle Lorraine seemed to him then, still standing patiently by, sticking with him despite his faults. Bending to her ear, he whispered, What did you call them, my love?

Oh, when the saints—

The Cardinal

Brandon Hobson

WHEN I WAS A TEENAGER, I knew a boy named Monfiori who lived
in the neighborhood. He was pale skinned and thin with wiry hair.
Everyone at school hated him, but for a while he was my only friend.
He ate cockroaches for a dollar and huffed paint behind the wood-
shop building. He smoked cigarettes in my bedroom despite my
weak lungs and my coughing. My mother was worried people would
think I was a troublemaker for being friends with him.

"We're like hemophiliac brothers," Monfiori said. "They tell us
don't bleed, don't bleed, but we're dying anyway. They don't know
anything."

Sometimes he played jazz on a toy trumpet. *Variations on Monk
in C*, his own creation, this arrangement—or so he claimed. "Psyche-
delic funk," he called it. We drank cheap vodka in his basement and
I played drums on upside-down buckets. I liked being at his house because I could drink and smoke over there without anyone knowing.

"My mom has jazz records," I told him. "She listens to them on
nights she wants to be left alone."

"She'll be alone soon enough when you die," he said.

Monfiori said we were both dying. "Might as well poison ourselves," he said. "At least that way we'll die in our sleep." He'd
already gotten two blood transfusions. He had bruises and moles all
over his body. He was the ugliest boy in our school, and maybe the
meanest.

One time in his basement we smoked a joint and he told me he
was going to set the school on fire. "We'll watch the whole place go
up in flames," he said. "I'll send smoke signals to the Indians. Fuck
the police and everyone else."

Monfiori and I had to do twenty hours of community service for
stealing guitar strings from the music store downtown. We were
going to use them to tie the spokes and chain of his brother's bicycle
so that he would crash. They caught us later in his backyard. We had
to go to juvenile court.

"My son's not a bad kid," my mother kept telling everyone.

*

That winter I fell ill with a stomach virus and my asthma flared up. The breathing machine they put me on was loud enough to hear all through the house. At night the dogs next door kept me awake with their barking. They belonged to our neighbors, who were an old couple, immigrants from Poland. Their names were Milosz and Gertrude. They brought me soup and crackers and a dessert called *faworki*, which they said was known as angel wings.

"They're for good luck," Gertrude told me. "It's a Polish specialty."

My mother and Gertrude became close. They talked about bread and sausages and red wine. Milosz made paper airplanes for me. From my bed, in my sickness, I watched him pull up a chair. He folded a piece of paper into an airplane and tossed it across the room.

"I had a son once," Milosz told me. "My wife and I lost him. He was about your age."

He stared into the floor. He seemed to be searching for the right words. We could hear my mother and Gertrude laughing in the next room.

"His name was Aleksander," he said. "He liked to play the piano."

I could see the lines in his forehead, the loose skin of his jowls.

"My son, my son," he said.

He folded another piece of paper. I watched his fingers move, all bone and skin. He concentrated on each fold, creasing it, holding it up to the light to make sure he got it right. He folded the paper into a bird and handed it to me.

"You can name it anything you want," he said.

"Aleksander," I said.

I held the paper bird. I noticed Milosz's hands were trembling.

"Aleksander it is," he said. He stared into the floor.

When I think back, I know I was a very lonely child. My mother called me imaginative. Those days I was sick I would often see a male cardinal appear on the branch outside my window. One morning I opened the window and he flew in. He was such a beautiful bird. He flew wildly around my room. He glided from desk to bedpost, from bookshelf to lampshade. His wings were red like velvet. He was proud but silent. He seemed to be attentive to some inner presence, as if he had a clear point to make as he strutted across the window-sill. Once, he spread his wings proudly for me. This was his own show, a brief abandonment of the natural world, his own strange fantasy. The last time I saw him, that winter day I was ill, he flew in and shook the frost from his body. I let him eat sugar from my hand. In the pale gray light of my bedroom, in one final, cool gesture of farewell, he cocked his head to look at me, then flew out the window.

For several weeks Milosz continued to bring me paper birds made from colored construction paper. I hung them with string from my ceiling so that they twirled constantly. There were red birds, blue birds, yellow birds, purple birds. Monfiori didn't like them. "Can we set them on fire?" he asked.

"No."

"Aren't you too old for this? Look at this place."

He challenged my integrity. He dared me to cut myself and bleed. I challenged back and he laughed it off. One Friday I stayed the night at his house. We drank his mother's vodka until late. I fell asleep on the floor in his basement and woke up at some point in the middle of the night, feeling sick. I found him sitting in the corner of the room, watching me.

"What is it?" I asked.

He mumbled something.

"What's wrong with you?" I said.

"We're both dying," he said. "We'll die together."

I was sick the whole next day. In my room, Milosz sipped wine and told me stories about a boy who kept birds to fend off devils. "The birds protected him," he said. "They changed colors and held healing powers, like tiny gods or angels. They showed courage. They taught the boy to believe in himself."

Milosz wheezed and coughed. I coughed too. His glass of red wine seemed to glow in the dim room. The paper birds twirled above our heads.

One night I woke to something knocking at my window. I sat up in bed, pulled back the curtain, but saw nothing. Outside, the wind was blowing. It was a tree branch, I told myself, and went back to sleep.

Later I dreamed of the cardinal at my window. The cardinal spread his wings, glowing red in the night.

*

Weeks passed and Monfiori left as quickly as he entered my life. I saw him for the last time later that winter. We sat in his basement drinking cheap vodka and smoking cigarettes. I watched him wrestle his little brother to the floor and punch him in the chest until the boy started crying and ran out of the room.

"You need to stop being mean," I told him.

"I'm not," he said. "We're dying, so what does it matter?"

He turned on the strobe light. We stayed up late in the night listening to some sort of death metal, all screams and guitar. I remember slamming my body into the wall. I remember lying on the floor and pulling a blanket over me.

I'm convinced he tried to poison me in my sleep. The next morning they found me unresponsive. I don't remember being carried out of the house, the ambulance ride, or anything else. I woke up in a hospital bed on the third floor of Southwest Central Hospital, where they watched me for several days. There, my mother kept telling the nurses I wasn't a bad kid. They fed me tapioca pudding. They helped me out of bed and tried to talk to me, but I wanted to be left alone. I watched cartoons and old movies on TV.

"He's a quiet kid," one of the nurses told my mother. "He never talks."

When I returned home, the first people who came to see me were Milosz and Gertrude. They brought me angel wings. We drank tea and listened to old records on the antique record player. I mostly kept to myself in my bedroom.

My mother said Monfiori tried to hang himself and they took him away. He wouldn't be coming back for a while.

"That boy is nothing like my son," my mother told Milosz and Gertrude. "He was trouble, it's so sad," she said.

They all agreed I was nothing like him.

"My son's very happy," my mother kept saying.

First known photograph of Lincoln, 1846.
Courtesy of the Library of Congress.

Your Friend Forever, A. Lincoln:
The Enduring Friendship of Abraham Lincoln and Joshua Speed

Charles B. Strozier

> *. . . he allways thanked Josh for his Mary.*
>
> —Abner Y. Ellis

ON FEBRUARY 25, 1842, ABRAHAM LINCOLN wrote a letter to his devoted friend, Joshua Speed, who had written him the day before reporting on Speed's marriage to Fanny Henning:

> I received yours of the 12th. written the day you went down to William's place, some days since; but delayed answering it, till I should receive the promised one, of the 16th., which came last night. I opened the latter, with intense anxiety and trepidation—so much, that although it turned out better than I expected, I have hardly yet, at the distance of ten hours, become calm.

Speed had gotten married on February 15, and clearly had promised Lincoln he would write, as soon as he possibly could after consummating his marriage, to report on its outcome. Speed, it seems, had barely tumbled out of his wedding bed on the morning of February 16 before writing. In fact, even though "it turned out better than [Speed] expected," Lincoln the next day was still not calm "at the distance of ten hours." That is a long time for a man, then thirty-three years of age, to be experiencing such anxiety from the news of how his twenty-seven-year-old friend's wedding night turned out.

Abraham Lincoln made Speed (whose side of the correspondence is unfortunately lost) his vicarious substitute in the courtship of Fanny. Through Speed he could work through his tormented fears of intimacy. While making Speed's marriage his own indirect realization, his relief is palpable. "I tell you, Speed, our *forebodings,* for which you and I are rather peculiar, are all the worst sort of nonsense." He then recounts the dreaded passing of days for him in his letter of February 25 as he awaited news of the wedding

205

with an obsessive-compulsive intensity punctuated by gratuitous underlinings.

> I fancied, from the time I received your letter of *saturday,* that the one of *wednesday* was never to come; and yet it *did* come, and what is more, it is perfectly clear, both from [its] *tone* and *handwriting,* that you were much *happier,* or, if you think the term preferable, *less miserable,* when you wrote *it,* than when you wrote the last one before. You had so obviously improved, at the verry time I so much feared, you would have grown worse.

But a shadow remains.

> You say that "something indescribably horrible and alarming still haunts you.["] You will not say *that* three months from now, I will venture. When your nerves once get steady now, the whole trouble will be over forever. Nor should you become impatient at their being even verry slow, in becoming steady. Again; you say you much fear that that Elysium of which you have dreamed so much, is never to be realized. Well, if it shall not, I dare swear, it will not be the fault of her who is now your wife. I now have no doubt that it is the peculiar misfortune of both you and me, to dream dreams of Elysium far exceeding all that any thing earthly can realize.

The perplexing line in the letter ("You say that 'something indescribably horrible and alarming still haunts you'") suggests Speed felt great relief at his ability to carry out sexual intercourse with Fanny but remained troubled that the sky did not suddenly clear and the heavens part. Lincoln at first seems not to be particularly worried about Speed's feelings that something "indescribably horrible" still haunted him, writing with confidence, "You will not say *that* three months from now." But he cannot entirely dismiss Speed's fears that his "dreams of Elysium" would never be realized. His argument addressing these concerns here is somewhat elliptical. On the one hand, he is confident that Speed's fears will fade in due time based on the most welcome news that the marriage consummation went well. As long as that is over, things have to improve, and Speed's anxiety will gradually dissipate. It would seem the message from Speed was: "Things went well, but I still feel bad." Lincoln's encouragement of Speed, on the other hand, reflects some ambivalence for Speed's continued doubts that, given his identification with his friend, poses the danger of circling back onto himself. Lincoln gently chastises

Speed and tells him his unhappiness lingers from his nervous temperament and "will not be the fault of her who is now your wife." But perhaps feeling bad for this subtle criticism he immediately returns to his identification with Speed and affirms their common experience with emotional problems.

In that imagined joy lies a contradiction. Speed's marriage means he will never again be available in the same total way for Lincoln. He is now joined with Fanny, forever apart. Lincoln had been more empathically attuned to Speed than anyone else in his life and nothing matches in intimacy that kind of connection with another. To lose it leaves one feeling lost and alone, abandoned, despairing. Speed's marriage, for all the joy it brings Lincoln, is simultaneously a moment of dreaded loss and even a kind of symbolic death. In his triumphant experience of love, Speed categorically abandons his friend, though Lincoln tries mightily to relish Speed's new love.

Lincoln continues in his February 25 letter:

> Far short of your dreams as you may be, no woman could do more to realize them, than that same black eyed Fanny. If you could but contemplate her through my immagination, it would appear ridiculous to you, that any one should for a moment think of being unhappy with her. My old Father used to have a saying that "If you make a bad bargain, *hug* it the tighter"; and it occurs to me, that if the bargain you have just closed can possibly be called a bad one, it is certainly the most *pleasant one* for applying that maxim to, which my fancy can, by any effort, picture.

This story from his father about hugging a bad bargain, seemingly told as something of a joke, comes across as inappropriate, even odd. He does not feel at all that Speed has made a bad bargain in marrying Fanny Henning. On the contrary, he feels Fanny is lovely and a perfect match for his friend. What he tries to address is Speed's continued doubts, which he gently mocks while at the same time identifying with them. The befuddled argument is all part of Lincoln's confusions in dealing with his complex feelings about Speed and Fanny. He wants Speed to be happy in his marriage. At the same time, he hates losing Speed to Fanny and wants to keep him for himself, something he plays out with the subterfuge of enclosing a separate letter to Fanny:

> I write another letter enclosing this, which you can show her, if she desires it. I do this, because, she would think strangely

perhaps should you tell her that you receive no letters from me; or, telling her you do, should refuse to let her see them.

I close this, entertaining the confident hope, that every successive letter I shall have from you, (which I here pray may not be few, nor far between,) may show you possessing a more steady hand, and cheerful heart, than the last preceding it. As ever, your friend LINCOLN

On April 15, 1837, Abraham Lincoln rode into Springfield from New Salem on a borrowed horse, with "no earthly goods but a pair of saddle-bags, two or three law books, and some clothing which he had in the saddle-bags," as Speed later wrote to William Herndon (who tirelessly gathered material about his former law partner after 1865). Lincoln first "took an office," which meant arranging to set up quarters with his new law partner, John Todd Stuart, and found a cabinetmaker willing to build him a bedstead. He then walked to Speed's store on the west side of the square, tossed his saddlebags on the counter, and asked how much it would cost to buy materials for a bed. Speed calculated the price of the mattress, the blankets, and other needed materials as Lincoln browsed the store, noting the cost of each item. As he walked around, Lincoln told Speed he had just been admitted to the bar and was joining John Todd Stuart as his partner. He also told Speed of his plan to turn a small room adjacent to Stuart's office into a sleeping room and that he had in fact already hired a local carpenter to build the bedstead. Speed calculated it would cost him seventeen dollars (though in another account Speed said the figure was thirty dollars). He offered to grant him credit for the cost of the materials, which at first Lincoln refused, and he nearly left the store, as he was still heavily indebted from his failed store partnership in New Salem and had only some seven dollars in his pocket. But Lincoln finally replied, "It is probably cheap enough, but I want to say that cheap as it is I have not the money to pay. But if you will credit me until Christmas, and my experiment here as a lawyer is a success, I will pay you then. If I fail in that I will probably never be able to pay you at all." Speed was struck by Lincoln's sad tone: "I never saw so gloomy, and melancholy a face." He told Lincoln that since the "contraction of so small debt" affected him so deeply, he would offer another plan. "I have a very large room, and a very large double-bed in it; which you are perfectly welcome to share with me if you choose." Lincoln asked where the room was, and after Speed told him, without saying a word, he walked upstairs and deposited his meager belongings. He came downstairs and, with his face "beaming with pleasure and smiles," announced, "Well Speed I'm moved."

Abraham Lincoln at twenty-eight years of age in 1837 was still rough around the edges but also on the way up in the world. As befit a figure well known in the state legislature, his pants no longer hung well above his boots; he even had a black suit and had begun to sport what became his distinctive top hat. He was a fully certified lawyer now and the junior partner of an old acquaintance and fellow Whig legislator, Springfield's leading lawyer, John Todd Stuart.

Lincoln wore his thick black hair parted on the right, bracketing his large ears and accentuating his long face. His strong mouth often broke into a smile when he told jokes, which was frequently, and dimples appeared in his cheeks, especially on the right side. His sparkling gray eyes were round and deep and suggested mystery and a haunting tension. They evoked a perennial sadness that few friends or colleagues fully understood. A decade after arriving in Springfield, Lincoln once referred to "my old, withered, dry eyes" that "are full of tears yet," and in the 1850s, well before the war, he said his "own poor eyes" might not last to see the end of slavery. The eyes suggest a kind of premature insight that carried its burdens and took its toll. Profundity was a part of Lincoln's earliest style.

Lincoln, Joshua Speed said once, when he first saw him, was "ungainly" and, at another time, "a long, gawky, ugly, shapeless, man." Lincoln, Speed continued, was six feet, four inches tall, "a little stooped in the shoulders," with "long arms and legs, large feet and hands, a high forehead," and a head that was "over the average size" (which had the subtextual meaning in the nineteenth century that its owner possessed unusual intelligence). Speed's physical description of Lincoln sets up his observation that "He never lost the mobility of his nature, nor the kindness of his heart." Speed also noticed Lincoln's gray eyes and the wrinkles in his face and forehead, which deepened with age, the way channels dig into streams. Lincoln was a "very sad man," but when he warmed up "all sadness vanished, his face was radiant and glowing, and almost gave expression to his thoughts before his tongue could utter them." Speed often pondered what it was that "threw such charm around him" and concluded "it was his perfect naturalness. He could act no part but his own. He copied no one either in manner or style."

Joshua Speed, who turned twenty-three in November 1837, was a strikingly handsome young man. He was the scion of a distinguished

Kentucky family and had been born in 1814 on a large and prosperous plantation just outside Louisville. His father, John Speed, owned as many as sixty-two slaves in 1829. Joshua, however, disliked his father and set off for Springfield in 1834 to make his own way as a merchant. He spoke in a southern drawl and wore his curling dark hair long, nearly reaching his earlobes and just above his collar in the back, lending him the appearance of the contemporary romantic English poet Lord Byron. Speed's thick eyebrows framed wide blue eyes that were set apart evenly in his long but proportioned face. His nose reached nearly to thick lips that in turn framed a sharply defined, angular chin. He was smoothly shaven. He was of average height and thus dwarfed by his friend Lincoln. Robert Kincaid describes Speed as "friendly, handsome, blue-eyed, medium-sized." In the earliest surviving image of Speed, a small oval painting typical of the time, he looks confidently out from the canvas, a man ready to run a store and invest wisely. He seems intelligent, friendly, warm, and gentle. "He took a lively interest in public affairs," his nephew wrote later, and "his personal friends and associates were in all parties." His friendships, however, were "never affected by political or religious views differing from his own."

Speed was prepared psychologically to idealize Lincoln. He was younger, more uncertain about himself, more vulnerable, softer. Lincoln was physically impressive and bore himself with the assurance of the fine athlete he was, his height exaggerated by his tall hat. Speed speaks with awe of Lincoln's involvement in the "manly sports" in New Salem in which he either engaged or helped judge. Lincoln's physical presence and athleticism drew Speed into his orbit. One expression of Speed's instant attraction was that he spontaneously refused to charge Lincoln rent. It is commonly assumed now by scholars that the transaction nevertheless carried an implicit financial obligation and that there was an unspoken agreement that Lincoln would handle Speed's legal matters for free. While that may have been true later (though also open to question), this interpretation ignores the fact that Speed himself makes no mention of such an arrangement in his account of welcoming Lincoln into his home and bed. Speed is otherwise quite detailed about the sequence of events leading up to and involving Lincoln in these years. In fact, Speed seemed instinctively motivated at the outset *not* to complicate his relationship with Lincoln by tethering it to financial obligations and placing it on a formal, business basis. He wanted their relationship to mature into a real friendship.

Lincoln's self-presentation was as someone older than his age, in contrast to Speed, who appeared younger, thus lengthening psychologically the five actual years that separated them. Speed was not unaware of this dimension of their friendship. In describing Lincoln in New Salem, he notes Lincoln earned the sobriquet "Honest Abe," but once in Springfield, "as he grew older," Lincoln came to be called, affectionately, "Honest Old Abe" as early as his midthirties. The introduction to Speed's *Reminiscences*, written by his nephew John Gilmer Speed, adds that Speed "regarded life with a serious business-like gravity, which led him to seek the companionship of young men of like disposition, or of persons older than himself."

Speed seemed to bask in Lincoln's easy assumption of superiority in his own self-presentation, which was joined to a ceaseless ambition. Lincoln reached for the stars. Orville Browning said of Lincoln in this period that he was "always a most ambitious man." Herndon agreed. His ambition, said Herndon, was a "little engine that knew no rest." The "sober truth" is that Lincoln was "inordinately ambitious," which became manifest "in the year 1840 *exactly*." Herndon's dating of the beginning of something so much a part of one's character as ambition may be overly precise, but it reflects his keen awareness of Lincoln's early sense of his own potential greatness. There was at this point in Lincoln's life a gap between his ambition to be a well-known lawyer and leading Whig politician (his dream was probably to be a senator in the mold of his hero, Henry Clay) and his actual existence as a small-town lawyer at the far edge of a large country. In a typically ironic and self-deprecatory line in an 1838 letter that speaks to his keen awareness of this chasm at this point in his life between actuality and ambition, Lincoln refers to "all my fancied greatness." Those closest to him saw the potential greatness but didn't feel it was all that fancied.

Given the difference in their social status before the mid-1830s, Lincoln was actually more worldly than Speed. By 1837 he had lived in three states; taken two flatboat trips to New Orleans; had all kinds of personal and business experiences in New Salem; served two stints in the Black Hawk War, in which he chased Indians to the border of Wisconsin; and had become a leading Whig in state politics and lived in Vandalia. Speed, to the manor born, knew luxury but little more than life at Farmington (the plantation where he was born and raised) and two years of service in a store in Louisville before coming to Springfield in 1834. His life had been privileged but circumscribed.

Lincoln also stood apart from Speed in his intellectuality. Speed had a more formal education, including his incomplete stint at St. Joseph's College. He probably studied some Latin, perhaps a bit of Greek, and was exposed to readings in the humanities, mathematics, some limited science, and religion. But he was not intellectually inclined. In his many letters to his father and brother, along with the large number of letters he wrote Herndon after the war, Speed is clear, direct, and articulate but never makes literary allusions that suggest deep learning. He is passionate about the major political issues of the day and would play an important role for Lincoln in the early stages of the war, but nothing he writes is original or even provocative. He was shrewd but not profound, honest, moral, and engaging without possessing the qualities of mind that would set him apart from other respectable young men in Springfield.

Though mostly an autodidact, Lincoln read more widely and deeply than his friend. Lincoln was unchurched but had absorbed the Bible into the very fabric of his soul, especially the book of Matthew, references to which are everywhere in his writings, though he also evoked directly or indirectly any number of Old Testament stories in his writings and speeches throughout his life, including Genesis, Psalms, Isaiah, and Ecclesiastes, for example, as well as subtle references to less well-known books like Samuel and Hebrews. One of Lincoln's uses of the Bible was to make covert allusions to it in his speeches (as opposed to his more direct quotations, as in the "Discoveries and Inventions" speech or "House Divided"). One very good example of a covert allusion occurs in the Lyceum speech in 1838. His point about mob rule is that it comes from within and is not imposed by an outside tyrant. "If destruction be our lot," he says, "we must ourselves be its author and finisher." The covert reference here is to Hebrews 12:2: "Looking unto Jesus, the author and finisher of our faith." That kind of reference surely resonated with his audience without Lincoln having to play a religious card. "Lincoln got the preacher's points," Robert Bray astutely puts it, "without acting the preacher."

He also knew most of the great soliloquies in Shakespeare by heart and warmed to long discussions of the plays themselves, especially the tragedies, and the intricacies of plot and character development. He came to know some contemporary poets through Speed, especially Lord Byron (Speed said later, "I don't think he [Lincoln] had ever read much of Byron previous to my acquaintance with him"), but Lincoln never read anything as deeply as Shakespeare. He knew the law well, including what was then the fundamental legal text in the Anglo-American world, Sir William Blackstone's *Commentaries on the Laws of England.* And no one reveled in the daily paper more than Abraham Lincoln. He read it with the passion of a writer and politician. He was a powerful and effective speaker in that era before microphones and teleprompters. He knew how to project his high-pitched but resonant voice to an audience that might be in a church hall, a meeting room of an inn, or outside at a fairground. He was a master of mood. He often joked with folksy charm to large and small groups of mostly uneducated people, putting them at ease but also never talking down to them about the complicated and contentious political issues of the day. He honed all of these skills on a daily basis in his law practice and frequently gave political speeches and at times major speeches on topics of interest to him.

No one was more appreciative of Lincoln's intellect than Joshua Speed. "No truth was too small to escape his observation," Speed wrote, "and no problem too intricate to escape a solution,—if it was capable of being solved. Thought, hard, patient, laborious thought; these were the tributaries that made the bold, strong, irresistible current of his life." Describing a speech Lincoln gave in 1840, Speed stressed his "wonderful faculty" to deliver long and complicated speeches without notes. He remembered everything. "He might be writing an important document, be interrupted in the midst of a sentence, turn his attention to other matters entirely foreign to the subject on which he was engaged, and take up his pen and begin where he left off without reading the previous part of the sentence. He could grasp, exhaust, and quit any subject with more facility than any man I have ever seen or heard of." His mind, Speed felt, "was like polished steel." If you made a mark on it, "it was never erased. His memory of events, of facts, dates, faces, and names, surprised everyone."

On the face of it there was nothing unusual in Speed sharing his bed with Lincoln. The living and sleeping arrangements Lincoln and Speed worked out were quite typical of this period and place in American history. Inns at that time, with few rooms, simply separated the men from the women and were often only slightly larger than residential cabins. To make some money, an owner might even enlarge his loft, which could only be reached by a ladder. The shared room would then have a fireplace where food and liquor could be served. Everyone crowded into all available space—for warmth as much as anything else. Both before and after Lincoln met Speed it was a common experience for Lincoln to share a bed with other males. Richard Lawrence Miller has put together a list of all the

213

males Lincoln slept with before he arrived in Springfield: a hired hand in 1830 with whom Lincoln was working; McGrady Rutledge, Stephen Perkins, Daniel Burner, Slicky Bill Greene, and Abner Lewis during his years living in New Salem; John Stuart in Vandalia during the legislative session of 1834–1835; and after Speed left Springfield, Milton Hay for a time, as well as William Herndon and Leonard Swett when they were out on the circuit together, though that could mean sleeping in more communal quarters with several men huddled under shared blankets to keep warm, waking to drink what his colleague Henry C. Whitney called "tough" coffee.

Domestic architecture at the time, as well, forced a sharing of beds for the typical family, especially as one moved west from the major coastal cities on the Eastern Seaboard. Speed, for example, was raised on a wealthy Kentucky plantation, but by today's standards the house at Farmington is hardly imposing, and there were two adults and many children living in it. He certainly paired up with his male siblings to sleep, even though we don't know from available evidence which ones, where, or when. Later, in boarding school, Speed undoubtedly shared a room and perhaps a bed with a schoolmate.

On the frontier as Lincoln experienced it there was never any measure of private space. As a young boy, he slept on a cot in the same room with his parents and one older sister in a tight log cabin in Kentucky. When the family first moved to southern Indiana (Lincoln was seven), joined by some of Nancy Lincoln's relatives, the Sparrows, and an illegitimate cousin, Dennis Hanks (then eighteen), they lived for a year in the lean-to, fighting off the snow and cold, in a home not much of an improvement over camping outdoors. The next year Thomas Lincoln enclosed the cabin but never put in windows, and he had not yet finished the roof before winter. It was only after 1819, when Lincoln's new stepmother, Sarah Bush Johnston, a widow, arrived with three children from a previous marriage, that Thomas added a loft to the log cabin; the boys slept in that common space.

So there was nothing unusual in the culture or in the historical moment in the mere fact that Lincoln and Speed slept together. Custom and individual experience, however, are not always congruent. The experience of a sensitive or talented few may depart sharply from that of the many. Social history provides necessary context for biography but cannot fully explain individual psychological experience at any given time. Just because it was common in nineteenth-century America that men slept together does not mean it was of no significance that young Lincoln, at a critical point in his development, made the most important friendship of his life with another young man with whom he was to sleep for the next three and a half years; one very tall man, the other of ordinary size, in a double bed, probably stuffed with corn husks, hair, or feathers, each perhaps loosely draped in a bolt of linen (or, as noted by Whitney, sometimes Lincoln on the circuit wore a "short home made yellow flannel undershirt & had nothing else on"), tossing and turning in their dreamscapes. The question is, what does it mean?

In recent years, a number of historians have assumed that Lincoln and Speed had sex and were homosexual lovers. Larry Kramer, the playwright and AIDS activist, even once claimed a source of his found a secret diary of Joshua Speed, along with prurient letters, hidden under the floorboards of the old building that housed Speed's store, documents that detail his sexual relationship with Lincoln. Since Kramer has failed to produce the diary, most agree it is a hoax. Furthermore, the find would be quite remarkable since that building basically "underwent a bad fire in 1855," as reported in the local paper, and burned to the ground.

In fact, there is no direct or indirect evidence to prove that the Lincoln-Speed relationship was sexualized, or was known as sexualized, witnessed as such, or talked about as homosexual by any contemporary friend, neighbor, or citizen in nosy Springfield, then or later in the oral history. Writers as varied as Jonathan Ned Katz, Charles Shively, John Stauffer, and Clarence A. Tripp, among others, have fallen back on the tendentious argument that two young men sleeping together who were so closely bonded and who wrote such intimate letters to each other must have sexualized their relationship. One needs to consider such an argument rather closely. Its main flaw is that it imposes twentieth- and twenty-first-century assumptions on nineteenth-century customs and attitudes. We live in an era in which attitudes toward homosexuality have radically altered. While there is still resistance in some social sectors and in the backwaters to gay marriage, for example, and many young men who present as gay are unfortunately still bullied, for the most part Americans (especially those under forty or so) are increasingly at ease with all forms of homosexuality, feel gay marriage should be legalized everywhere (as the US Supreme Court recently held), gay adoption made legal, etc.

The social context of nineteenth-century friendship presents a picture so different from the present in so many particulars that it can be hard to fathom. It was a social reality then that homosexuality was wrong and should be condemned—though the term itself only came into use in the latter part of the nineteenth century in Germany and then gradually spread to the rest of the West. Sodomy was illegal. When it became manifest, sodomy, along with some instances of bestiality (or, as it was called, buggery), was severely punished. The condemnation of homosexuality, however, joined the culturally sanctioned belief that young men could, even should, be close and loving with each other—as long as the boundary against sexualization was rigidly maintained. Psychologically speaking, American culture at the time approved of expressive intimacy but punished homosexuality, and the boundary between sensuality and sexuality was clear. Expressions of love and affection between young men, often in florid literary terms, were encouraged, along with some restricted touching, but eroticism of any kind and especially sexuality that involved the genitals or orgasm were strictly forbidden. Very commonly, young middle-class men had intimate but not sexual male friendships in their twenties and into their thirties that bridged the world of childhood playmates with the families then created with female sexual partners. These specifically nineteenth-century male friendships served as vehicles for the uneasy transition from the comforts of childhood into a world of dreaded intimacy with idealized but remote, heavily garbed, and sexually guarded women. Loving and intimate male friendships during this specific phase of the life cycle were psychological by-products of the way nineteenth-century culture sharply divided the two worlds that men and women inhabited into gendered separateness.

In New Salem between 1832 and 1835, Lincoln respectfully courted the beautiful and remarkable Ann Rutledge. They were at first discreet because Ann had been betrothed to another man who left the village. But by about 1834 she gave up on her fiancé and began to talk about marriage with Lincoln. Ann was a woman of "Exquisite beauty," Slicky Bill Greene later wrote to Herndon, matched by an intellect that was "quick—Sharp—deep & philosophic as well as brilliant." She was "gentle & kind a heart as an angl [sic]—full of love—kindness—sympathy." And so on in the words of some fifteen respondents to Herndon. But suddenly in August of 1835 typhoid swept Central Illinois and Ann died a gruesome, painful death.

Lincoln was distraught, fell into a clinical depression, and became suicidal. By all accounts, it was the first time he had fallen in love, and his extended courtship bound him to this impressive young woman. The sheer number of his friends and neighbors who recalled how extreme his reaction was to Ann's death should be taken seriously. Lincoln told Mentor Graham he "felt like Committing Suicide often" after Ann died. A neighbor, Hardin Bale, later reported that Lincoln had to be "locked up by his friends" so that he would not commit suicide. Did they create something of a suicide watch through the first crucial few days after his betrothed's death? That seems to be what Bale is suggesting, since none of the twenty-five or so log cabins strung out along New Salem's single dirt path had actual locks. But the closeness of the quarters would have allowed Lincoln's friends to stay with him in his grief, perhaps take away any razors he owned, and try to talk him back from the edge. Lincoln told another friend and neighbor that he dared not carry a pocketknife after Ann's death. Some have disputed the suicidal meaning of this statement, but that is exactly why in psychiatric hospitals no sharp objects of any kind are allowed. You simply cut the veins in your wrist along a vertical line and you bleed to death.

Ann's sudden death was tragic for Lincoln, and, to use a term of great importance in contemporary psychoanalysis, it was also traumatic. Two factors contributed to Lincoln's traumatic reaction to her death. First, it came without warning and was extremely painful to witness. Typhoid is a bacterial disease that runs its course in three to four weeks and brings a rising temperature (to 104 degrees), diarrhea, intestinal hemorrhaging, encephalitis, delirium, and, if untreated, as of course it was in New Salem in the mid-1830s, often death.

But second, the extremity of Lincoln's reaction to the death of Ann Rutledge, especially the testimony of his suicidal inclinations at her loss, suggests he had a fragile self that was extremely vulnerable to loss. In this, Lincoln seemed *retraumatized* by Ann's death. His wild despair and depression, in other words, because they reached such extreme lengths, lead one to suspect that they evoked the earlier losses of his mother (when he was nine) and sister (when he was eighteen), losses that left him vulnerable to fragmentation as an adult when faced with events that directly or symbolically evoked the childhood trauma of his mother's death and to a lesser degree that of his sister. Lincoln knew intimately of the "death scenes of those we love," as he later wrote to Joshua Speed.

A dark despair of childhood origins lingered in young Lincoln. For the moment, his depression was relatively quiescent. He was in a state of what the psychoanalyst Erik Erikson called a moratorium, that moment in youth when a troubled, and often talented, young person holds at bay peremptory developmental demands, keeping them dormant and suppressed without being resolved, waiting for a kind of inner transformation that will permit the construction of a usable identity. Erikson stresses that someone in such a developmentally delayed state of tension slows things down, easily slips into "tortuous self-consciousness," and most of all recoils from intimacy. The danger in closeness with another is the potential loss of self. For Lincoln, the unconsummated love for Ann Rutledge and then her sudden, tragic death brought back in full force the earlier trauma of his mother's death. It left him feeling that those he most loved died.

Lincoln was only marginally less depressed when he arrived in Springfield on April 15, 1837. At first he and Joshua Speed were cautious with each other; Lincoln even failed to share with Speed the story of his relationship with Ann Rutledge. It took time for him to feel safe and trusting with Speed. That level of friendship seemed to develop after about two years and was clearly in place by 1839. Then nothing could break their bonds of affection. They worked during the day some two blocks apart but otherwise were seldom separated (at times Speed even went out on the circuit with Lincoln just to be by his side). They finished each other's sentences. After they awoke, each day began with a light breakfast. They were together again for their main meal at the genial home of court clerk and entrepreneur William Butler, and had supper back in the store.

In the evenings, especially in winter, when not reading or talking, a fascinating male salon gathered in the back of Speed's store by an expansive fireplace. The group consisted of the leading political and intellectual figures in town. Among those who came were the leading Whigs in the state (Edward D. Baker, Orville Browning, John J. Hardin, and others), Democratic figures (John Calhoun, Archer Herndon, Josiah Lamborn, and even Stephen Douglas, whom Lincoln later debated), politician-turned-judge Jesse B. Thomas, William Butler, and whoever else might fit cozily in back of the store and be able to contribute to the conversations. They came to talk about everything under the sun, share stories, but they mostly came because they knew Lincoln would be there. His humor, wisdom, and humanity were already legendary. In advance of the gatherings, Speed must have arranged the kindling, probably with Herndon (then his clerk in the store), and lit the wood in his fireplace, prepared coffee and cider, and perhaps added something sweet or savory for his guests. Speed never expected to take full part in the discussions, competing against some very smart and assertive men. Besides, that was not Speed's style. But he could—and did, as his list of memories reveals—enjoy watching and listening, seeing faces gleaming in the fires he made, hearing appreciative laughter in response to Lincoln's stories. Herndon also made no claim to have spoken at these caucuses. He was in any event a college dropout who gratefully sat at the feet of educated, well-read, and high-minded men speaking on "politics, religion, and all other subjects." Herndon felt greatly privileged to attend these sessions and spoke of being dazzled by these orators' "brilliant thoughts and youthful enthusiasm." There in the room, Herndon says, "public sentiment was made." The same dry-goods store in which Speed and Herndon measured and cut ribbon in daylight was a different and magical place by night.

The rough maleness of the gatherings in Speed's store found its counterpoint in the "Coterie" that assembled in the home of Ninian Wirt Edwards. Edwards was the son of the first governor of Illinois (and a graduate of Transylvania University in Kentucky, where he gave the graduation speech in Latin) and the husband of Elizabeth Edwards, the sister of Mary Todd. At their home on Quality Hill, sometimes dubbed Aristocracy Hill, just to the southwest of the square on Second and Jackson Streets, Elizabeth and Ninian greeted guests in French, hosted frequent parties with dancing and violins, and set a standard for social elegance unmatched in Springfield or, indeed, in any of the surrounding towns of central Illinois. The house itself was two stories and large enough to hold within it "a dozen prairie-farmer cabins," as Carl Sandburg colorfully put it in *Abraham Lincoln: The Prairie Years*. Elegant brocade embellished the eaves, along with ornamental railings, engraved doors, and a long driveway that deposited visitors at the front veranda. At the north end was the large parlor where the Edwardses hosted their parties and soirees (and where the Lincolns were married on November 4, 1842).

Mary Todd came to live with the Edwardses in June of 1839. She was a striking young woman at twenty-one years of age (and thus nine years younger than Lincoln) and the scion of another distinguished and slave-owning Kentucky family. Her earliest photograph from seven years later shows an attractive woman gazing expectantly at the camera. Full cheeks accentuate the softness of her face. Light brown hair pulled back from a high forehead frames wide eyes and a petite nose. The mouth is a straight line over a rounded chin. A long graceful neck plunges into folds of obscuring Victorian fabric. Short arms are propped uneasily, one against a chair, as she waits through the long exposure. Her long-fingered hands rest in her lap.

Mary Todd was never seen as beautiful, but one childhood friend accurately described her as "certainly very pretty with her clear blue eyes, lovely complexion," a bright and intelligent face, and a "perfect arm and hand." Ruth Painter Randall describes her as a "bright-faced, eager girl, impulsive, quick-tongued, warmhearted, affectionate, mercurial, interested in everything, joyous with life." James Conkling said Mary was the "very creature of excitement you know and never enjoys herself more than when in society and surrounded by a company of merry friends." Even Herndon, who despised Mary (and the feeling was mutual), described her as vivacious, infectiously enthusiastic, and delightfully witty. Ninian Edwards said she could "make a Bishop forget his prayers."

It is imaginable, though not documented, that Lincoln met Mary the summer of 1837 when she briefly visited her sister in Springfield, but he certainly became acquainted with her after she arrived in 1839. Interestingly, it was Speed who was the intermediary. "Through the influence of Joshua F. Speed, who was a warm friend of the Edwardses," Herndon wrote in his biography based on his personal knowledge of both Lincoln and Speed at the time, "Lincoln was led to call on Miss Todd." Elizabeth Edwards emphasized that once Lincoln was "led to call" on Mary he quickly became enthralled: "He was charmed with Mary's wit and fascinated with her quick sagacity—her will, her nature—and Culture—I have happened in the room where they were sitting often and often, and Mary led the conversation. Lincoln would listen and gaze on her as if drawn by some Superior power, irresistibly So."

It seems that within months Lincoln and Mary began to talk about marriage. Elizabeth Edwards, who with Ninian encouraged the courtship, says Lincoln "Commenced Seeing Mary" in the winter of 1839–1840. What does that mean? What it was *not* was a declaration to the world of their engagement. There was definitely not an exchange of a ring, as there might be today, and no announcement that would have attracted a lot of attention. But to have "Commenced seeing" each other, in the words of Mary's sister and confidante, means their relationship was in some state of courtship, and possibly an advanced one, by the early months of 1840. Whatever understanding existed between Lincoln and Mary, however, was relatively private, and few—other than Elizabeth Edwards and Joshua Speed—knew the details. Things actually progressed to the point that in the fall they planned their wedding for January 1, 1841.

Then, suddenly, in a move that has baffled historians ever since, Lincoln broke off his engagement with Mary sometime in late December 1840. Various explanations have been offered. One of the oldest is that Lincoln was intimidated by the social status of the Todds. Lincoln, however, was not one to be easily intimidated and, if anything, bore an air of natural superiority, even arrogance; he once quipped that God only needs one "d" but the Todds require two. Others have noted that Mary got fat in the summer and fall of 1840 and Lincoln turned from her in disgust. This blinkered interpretation rests on a misread of two contemporary letters. On September 21 James C. Conkling reports to his fiancée, Mercy Levering, that "if she [Mary] should visit Missouri [again] she will soon grow out of our recollection." The other source is Mary's letter in December, also to Mercy Levering, in which she mocks herself as a "ruddy *pineknot*" with an "exuberance of flesh." But Conkling's letter is hardly definitive and could be simply a joke about Mary, who was a dear friend and whom he knew Mercy loved. To read it as decisive proof that Mary had gotten so fat as to disgust Lincoln stretches its potential meaning. Furthermore, Mary's letter actually indicates, if anything, that she has *lost* weight, if one reads the whole passage. She is indeed the "same ruddy *pineknot*," she says, but now *not* with an "exuberance of flesh, as it once was my lot to contend with." Lincoln had long since fallen in love with a short woman who tended to be plump and who worried about her weight. That would not seem to have changed in the fall of 1840.

Of much greater importance, many have argued, was the presence of Matilda Edwards. This beautiful eighteen-year-old cousin of Ninian Edwards's left her father's home in Alton to go visit Springfield in November, just in time for the swirl of parties associated with the meeting of the legislature in special session in early December and in regular session in January. The adorable Matilda, with long, golden locks, even pinned up as a respectable woman would have worn them, turned the heads of many men and she reputedly received twenty-two offers of marriage. Matilda has come to occupy the central role in the reinterpretation of the broken engagement in recent years. The argument is forceful in its simplicity: Lincoln fell in love with Matilda soon after her arrival in Springfield, and that precipitated the

221

break with Mary. The evidence, however, is highly contradictory, though the main problem with the Matilda theory is the fact that she herself categorically refuted it. Elizabeth Edwards specifically says she asked Matilda after all the drama surrounding the broken engagement unfolded, "if Mr. Lincoln Ever Mentioned the subject of his love to her." Matilda's answer was, "On my word he never mentioned Such a Subject to me: he never even Stooped to pay me a Compliment." Unfortunately, Matilda died at twenty-nine in 1850, so Herndon could not track her down for an interview, but her statement to Elizabeth, a reliable witness present through all the drama and in direct contact with all the players, is without qualification. Furthermore, Matilda continued to live with Mary for almost another full year, and the two were friends. Mary, who held grudges, would never have tolerated a friendship with the attractive young Matilda in the very house in which both lived if she had felt that Lincoln had broken his engagement over his infatuation with her.

Lincoln's odd behavior in the late fall of 1840 actually only begins to make sense if we bring Joshua Speed into the narrative.

Lincoln was not fully conscious of any of the psychological subtext of the events surrounding his broken engagement with Mary Todd. Desire lurked in forbidden realms. He reached out to find love, but those efforts were thwarted by his much deeper connections to Joshua Speed. That tie had long given solace. He felt a safe haven in the confidence, trust, and security of friendship with Speed. It was a balm that banished the terrors of depression, and washed out the self-doubts he felt about love, sex, and intimacy. Lincoln wore his confusions on his sleeve. But Speed shared the same doubts. Despite how he portrayed himself to people like the Edwardses or Orville Browning or any number of others in town, Speed was candid with Herndon about his own engagement the summer after Lincoln's broken one: "Strange to say something of the same feeling which I regarded as so foolish in him—took possession of me—and kept me very unhappy from the time of my ingagement until I was married—"

Joshua Speed had a reputation as a handsome young man who was something of a flirt. Lincoln in a letter alluded to his friend's many courtships ("Ann Todd [Mary's sister, later married to Charles M. Smith], and at least twenty others of whom you can think"). Mary Todd talked about his "ever changing heart." Unlike his socially awkward and introspective friend, there was nothing "peculiar"

(Elizabeth Edwards's characterization of Lincoln) about Speed, whose even features and handsome face, modesty, intelligence, and solid business sense drew people to him. Speed, raised in luxury on a Southern plantation and having enjoyed the benefits of some formal boarding-school education, was at ease in social situations, able to mingle, make small talk, dance, and enjoy good company. Ninian and Elizabeth Edwards were both fond of him (he was their "warm friend," as Herndon puts it), and, as Ninian told Herndon, he was especially eager for Speed to marry Matilda Edwards after her arrival in November 1840.

Matilda could not have been unaware of Speed's advances (and Ninian's wishes for her to marry him), just as word of Lincoln's seeming love for Matilda, communicated to everybody except Matilda herself, must have reached her ears. These overlapping courtships, sexually unconsummated and full of ambiguity, had one very important meaning missed by all observers: they indirectly joined Lincoln and Speed. Both men, it seems, were heterosexual, but at this moment in their lives their most intense and meaningful emotional connection was with each other. That grounded them and bound them tightly together. They spent much of their time with each other and most nights tumbled side by side into that creaking bed. Each knew the other's deepest feelings, feelings otherwise kept private and apart from others. Each found reflection of self in the other, a kind of mirroring that silenced doubt and confusion. Even Herndon, who idealized Lincoln, liked Speed, and slept in the same room (but in a different bed) for two years, could only guess at the depth of their friendship and the intensity of their connection.

This context of courtship confusion also explains much about Lincoln's break with Mary. There is no reason to doubt he loved her as best he could at this stage of his life, which is to say he loved with great ambivalence. But at some point Lincoln and Mary were engaged, with their wedding planned for January 1, 1841. He broke it off—when, exactly, is not clear—without a good explanation, something that confused her and compounded her hurt. She retaliated with anger, sputtering about how the deceiver shall be deceived, whatever that meant to her in the moment, and he tried to convince himself that he had broken the engagement because he loved Matilda. At the time, he probably thought that was true, or he may simply have been allowing Mary to have this explanation, which at least lent the broken engagement a measure of rationality least wounding to sensitive Mary's self-esteem.

The event behind the events in the fall of 1840, however, was that Speed had decided in that late summer, probably around August, that he was going to leave Springfield and return to Louisville. His father had died the year before and all the members of the family were imploring him to return and help run the plantation and take care of other issues in the extended clan of which he was the recognized leader. The issue for Lincoln was not Mary Todd or Matilda Edwards, even though the noise of his confusion played out on a stage of courtship and broken engagement. What mattered to Lincoln was the imminent departure of Joshua Speed. That threatened the ground of his being. Lincoln went a little crazy in this winter of his discontent.

Lincoln and Speed had long found a recognition of self in the other and established the kind of empathic bond that gives meaning to life and wards off despair. Lincoln, about whom we know more, was especially vulnerable at this stage of his life. He met Speed when he was just coming off his suicidal depression after the death of Ann Rutledge and was still finding his way in his new professional identity. At first, it seems, he was cautious with his new friend. But in time and within the frame of their constant interactions Lincoln came to experience a deep trust in Speed, a trust that calmed Lincoln. He seemed to experience his friend as soothing, engaging, warm, supportive, and unchallenging.

Speed's imminent departure threw Lincoln into a panic. Speed began winding up his complicated finances in the late summer of 1840, calling in debts (in part by putting ads in the local paper) and making arrangements to sell his store and the goods within it to his clerk, Charles Hurst, who took possession on January 1, 1841 (the notice appeared in the paper on that day). Lincoln separated from his shared bed with Speed on the same day and moved into the Butler home. The intensity of his suicidal depression in January 1841 was truly surprising, both for him and for those who cared about him. Lincoln's friend Orville Browning, who happened then to be staying with the Butlers, where Lincoln moved on the first of January (because the legislature was in session), reported later in an interview with John Hay that Lincoln's "aberration of mind" and "derange[ment]" lasted a week or so. He was so affected, however, "as to talk incoherently, and to be dilirious to the extent of not knowing what he was doing." Browning in turn told Herndon that Lincoln that month was "Crazy as a *loon*." Jane D. Bell said in a contemporary letter that Lincoln "came within an inch of being a perfect lunatic for life."

Speed was one of only two people allowed to tend to Lincoln (though Elizabeth Butler, who had long darned his socks and made his meals, hovered nearby and reportedly urged Lincoln to recover). A. Y. Ellis, in business with Speed and close to Lincoln, wrote Herndon later that after Lincoln took to his bed, "no one was allowed to see him but his friend Josh Speed & his friend *the doctor* I think Henry." Speed said Lincoln went "Crazy," adding important details about Lincoln's suicidality. They "had to remove razors from his room—take away all Knives and other such dangerous things—&c—it was terrible." Speed wrote, "In the winter of 1841 a gloom came over him till his friends were alarmed for his life."

Nor was Lincoln unaware how mad he had become. In two revealing letters, written on January 20 and January 23 to his law partner John Stuart, then serving in Washington as a congressman, Lincoln acknowledged the shame he felt at his collapse ("I have, within the last few days, been making a most discreditable exhibition of myself in the way of hypochondriaism") and three days later bemoaned his "deplorable state" of mind, expressing what is best described as the negative grandiosity so typical of clinical depression: "I am now the most miserable man living. If what I feel were equally distributed to the whole human family, there would not be one cheerful face on the earth. Whether I shall ever be better I can not tell; I awfully forebode I shall not. To remain as I am is impossible; I must die or be better, it appears to me."

Lincoln gradually returned to his practice and his duties in the legislature, though always under the watchful eye of Speed and his other friends. Though no longer living together, it seems he and Speed remained nearly inseparable that spring, ate their meals with the Butlers, and resumed their close interactions. By late May or early June 1841, however, Speed could no longer delay his return home to Louisville—but only after extracting a promise that Lincoln would come visit him soon. In fact, that visit came in August. Lincoln was unsteady emotionally when he arrived in Kentucky on August 18, 1841. He was "moody and hypochondriac," as Speed later wrote Herndon, and "at times very melancholy," clearly manifesting a "deep depression" that especially pained Speed's mother, Lucy, a kindly and nurturing figure. But his sadness, his regret over hurting Mary, and his continuing despair over whether he would ever resolve the issues of intimacy in his life continued to lurk in his soul. Perhaps the relaxed atmosphere in the loving Speed family helped, as did the freedom from his law practice, which had been intense that spring and early summer. Most of all, however, Lincoln was now reunited with Joshua himself. Ninian Edwards later said that Lincoln "was taken to Kentucky—by Speed—or went to Speed's—was Kept there till he recovered finally." Having pressured his friend to visit for some months, Speed now created the safety in which Lincoln could honor his melancholy feelings. He was able to shed his mask.

Lincoln and Speed hung out together, took long walks, and generally relaxed. Then, somewhat surprisingly, and suddenly, Fanny Henning captured the heart of Joshua Speed, who quickly developed the same sense of confusion and hesitations over intimacy that Lincoln had experienced a year earlier. Lincoln himself described Fanny as "one of the sweetest girls in the world." There was nothing about her, he continued, "that I would have otherwise than as it is." His only concern is her "tendency to melancholy," though he adds immediately, "This, let it be observed, is a misfortune not a fault." So Fanny joined the magic circle of depressed friends. It was hardly something Lincoln held against her. He is clearly fond of Fanny and feels she is wonderful for his best friend. Her melancholy, which he must have immediately spotted, is her misfortune. The mistake, he advises Speed, would be to blame her for her depression. In contemporary terms, the advice is not to confuse the girl for the symptom.

The overlap of courtships and friendship now turned Lincoln into the strong one encouraging Speed onward in love. That seemed to be why Speed could not let his friend leave him alone in Kentucky, and so boarded the boat with Lincoln to return to Springfield on September 17. That fall the two friends were again inseparable, though we lack evidence where they stayed. The suspicion is they in fact returned to their bed above the store (which Hurst still was paying off to Speed), but certainly they were sharing their deepest feelings with each other. Speed was terrified whether he could go through with his marriage to Fanny, now scheduled for February 15, 1842. Lincoln took it upon himself to identify with Speed, his feelings and confusions, and vicariously to make his friend his stalking horse in the move to intimacy.

Speed rose to the occasion and decided to leave Springfield and return home on the first of January—an auspicious first anniversary of what Lincoln had called after his own broken engagement the previous year the "fatal first." Throughout the last days of December, Lincoln began drafting a long letter for Speed that he intended to press into Speed's hands on his departure. It is a curious scene: the two together, talking of their mutual fears as Speed prepares to return home to marry Fanny, while Lincoln drafts his long letter of encouragement, perhaps storing it, as he wrote it, in his top hat. That letter was meant as a kind of talisman for Speed. In it Lincoln embraces Speed's struggles as his own. "Feeling, as I know you do," begins the first sentence, while the second paragraph opens "Why I say it is reasonable that you will feel very badly." Lincoln sought to soothe his friend from a distance and in the process hold himself together. He allowed himself to become so fully identified with Speed that he could feel as his own his friend's anxieties about the approaching marriage with Fanny. Lincoln was in and of what Speed felt. For the moment, that deep connection kept them united symbolically, as Lincoln projected himself into his friend's experience and as Speed held on to the talisman he had been given to ward off the evil eye of hopelessness.

The turning point of Lincoln's emotional life was that letter he wrote Speed on February 25 with the knowledge of the successful consummation of the marriage. After that Lincoln was no longer tethered psychologically to Speed and their friendship quickly lost its emotional intensity. Speed developed his own life with his spouse, becoming in time one of the most successful businessmen in Louisville. Lincoln, freed now by his successful vicarious experience of intimacy, was able to try again with Mary Todd. Sometime that summer of 1842 he and Mary started courting in secret; after all the noise of the broken engagement, neither wanted to start up the local gossip machine. It was a thrilling time for both Mary Todd and Lincoln as they planned their wedding with only a very few friends in the know.

Lincoln, however, turned to Speed for one last note of encouragement before he could finally embrace Mary. On October 5 he wrote Speed about "that subject which you know to be of such infinite solicitude to me." Lincoln notes the "immense suffering" Speed endured from his engagement to his marriage and how Speed never tried to conceal it from Lincoln. Now, "You have been the husband of a lovely woman nearly eight months. That you are happier now than you were the day you married her I well know; for without, you would not be living," which is a curious and oblique reference to Speed's own possible suicide talk at some point in the buildup to his marriage. Lincoln has Speed's word for his happiness now, however, not to mention the "returning elasticity of spirits which is manifested in your letters." Just to be absolutely sure, however, Lincoln asks: "Are you now, in *feeling* as well as *judgement*, glad you are married as you are?" He knows that such a question from anybody else would be "impudent" and "not to be tolerated." But Lincoln trusts that Speed will "pardon it in me." He urges Speed to answer quickly, "as I feel impatient to know."

The reply must have been encouraging, for Lincoln and Mary Todd were married on November 4, 1842. A week later Lincoln added in a business letter to a friend: "Nothing new here, except my marrying, which to me, is matter of profound wonder."

Painting of Joshua Speed, 1842, artist unknown.
Collection of the Speed Art Museum, Louisville, Kentucky.

NOTE. This essay is based on material in my book of the same title from Columbia University Press. I would like to acknowledge my research assistant, Wayne Soini.

Glenn Gould Syndrome
Spencer Matheson

GLENN GOULD IS TAKING a break from recording his own transcription of the *Siegfried Idyll*. It is the middle of the night. He rides the elevator from the Eaton Auditorium on the 7th floor to the Eaton's Department Store on the 6th floor. Outside it has begun to snow. He stops in the Kitchen Appliances Department to test the heft of 5 different waffle irons in a self-conscious parody of the way he tests Steinways. Then he makes his way to the Furniture and Bedding Department, where he lies down on his favorite Sealy Posturepedic. He loves being here in the dark silence that everybody else sees loud with crowds. The residue of shoppers' hopes that all this stuff will make them happy makes him happy.

Even in summer, Gould wears an overcoat, sweater, scarf, thermal underwear, flat cap, and knit gloves with the fingertips cut off. Neither personal branding before that term was conceived, nor fear of cold before winter but something stranger: protective gear in a protocol of his own devising. Because at the end of a great love affair that will begin here, tonight, he developed what he conceived of as an allergy to women. He was in the habit of mummifying himself year-round before this, it's true. But who fully understands a thing when he starts doing it?

*

In the basement of the store, a woman emerges from behind an elaborate golf-club display. Her name is Golsheh. She's been hiding there since last light. Her hip is rock stiff. Her skirt is long, loose, paisley. She is a great dancer, fluent in classical, contemporary, and Persian folk traditions. Admittedly, even in Isfahan there was but a small community capable of appreciating the purity and elegance of her phrasing—smaller than the sort of circle you might find dedicated to public onanism in Ontario. But in Toronto, she hasn't danced for a crowd of more than 13 people—depressing immigrants in chunky loafers who rue rock sugar. She stopped dancing because with the

229

arthritis in her hip she could barely walk some evenings, and because her physician told her it might stop the miscarriages. It didn't. The less she's been able to express herself as a dancer, the more her father's depressive genes have begun expressing themselves.

So she had driven to a vacant lot on the edge of the lake, and taken her knife—her *peshkabz*—from her handbag, and held its tip to the bottom of her ear, ready to take her life. One final phrase to perform: elbow out and down, head up in opposition on the same line. Looking up, she had seen the headless CN Tower, soon to be the tallest building in the world. The space they were building into was about to cease being what it had always been: sky. The pointed tip was already making a slight incision in her soft skin.

That's when she remembered the sound of Gould playing Bach's 6th Partita. It was as though some spirit had poured a revitalizing potion into her ears. She felt its lightness and warmth descend into her body. And that was enough to bring her back from the brink. She let her hand fall into her lap. The impulse to end—alive only moments before—had been killed by the life Gould brought to the music of a long-dead German. She thought of him somewhere out there in the city, imagined a white line rising into the sky from where he was, imagined following the line to him. In Eastern Iran, there is an idea—*gowati*—that the psychologically ill can be healed by music.

*

The ancient knife is in her purse again tonight. Her father, who had died alone in Isfahan, had given it to her—bone hilt, hollow-ground blade—to protect her in the New World. The knife is in her purse because her husband who, being brutal, sees brutality everywhere, orders her to carry it with her for protection. Rising up from underground to find Glenn Gould in an empty department store was going to be a kind of performance, and she knew from experience that if it was to be a good performance, she needed witnesses, spectators, and, since she couldn't have those, she put the knife in her purse—its possibilities would prick at least some of the expectant tautness she needed into her. The knife is in her purse because she half hopes an Eaton's night watchman will find her and turn her over to the cops, who would have her prosecuted for plotting the death of a national icon, even if they probably considered him to be a weirdo faggot. In the prison visiting room, she'd be protected from Brian by an impregnable sheet of glass. The knife is in her purse to make us fear for

Gould though you can Command-F his Wikipedia page and find no "stab" or "Golsheh." He died at 50, as he had predicted.

Gould's prescience is one of the things she loves about him. Maybe because she fancies she possesses a little prescience herself. She left Isfahan because she sees the prime-numbered beast of 1979 coming. Right after 1978. She left home this afternoon because she senses she can either save Gould as he had saved her, or help make his fall a beautiful phrase. Then again, she's been wrong before. She had expected to be spotted hiding behind the golf bags. She had expected to be found by a good Canadian man with a snooty WASP name, a Spencer or an Elliott. But she had been found by a charming, violent, hairy man, and had married him cognizant only of the first and last adjectives. What appeared to be a probing and intelligent gaze was actually just a thyroid problem. How silly to have wasted time, hope, and jet fuel when so many men in Isfahan fit that description. Which is the thing about having been a phrase away from killing yourself, you've come so close to losing everything that losing anything now seems like nothing. Which realization makes you live, finally. Which is why she's decided not to wait to be found anymore, but to find. She wanted to meet the man she considered to be the greatest artist in the world? Then she would.

When she first learned English, she confused which with witch, and the former has remained pleasantly spooky to her. She possesses an Iranian admiration for language, and the dancer's fascination for literature, the art on the far shore of music. At the beginning of them, she had pressed Brian to pass on any advice as to how she could speak more properly. Funnily enough, the only grammatical instruction Brian ever remembered receiving in high school was to go on "which hunts," and to cut out that formal pronoun in favor of the more colloquial "that." Which makes her love her whiches all the more. Canadians colloquialize everything, to the point where the whole society resembles its food: tasteless white mush. Gould's against-the-grain penchant for big words and florid phrases was one more thing to love about him.

She goes from Sporting Goods into Men's Shoes and up from underground on the unmoving escalator in the middle of the art deco store, her ballerina pumps making no sound. Any man walking with her—and what man wouldn't dream of walking with her?—would have to turn to make sure she was still with him. Fatefully turn, to see her face one last time before she was drawn back into the underworld. Did I mention Golsheh's beauty? That her face was so exquisite the memory of it might be enough to bring a man back from the brink? She detects movement in her peripheral vision, turns to face it. Through the chained glass doors on the main floor, she sees the snow, beating around the sodium lamps like moths. She hears the silent street.

*

Gould pulls the duvet up under his chin. What an extraordinary building. Built 53 years ago, when it seemed like a good idea to have a 1,300-seat art deco auditorium atop a department store. And he had played his first-ever public concert here at the age of 13. A snowy December day in 1945. The darkest notes making their way down through the booming organ pipes and into the store, filling shoppers with foreboding, or the sense that something important had just happened, and they'd missed it. Today is the 3rd day of the 2nd month of 1973 and he is 41—all prime numbers. Old enough he needn't do things he doesn't want to do anymore: play concerts, eat food without ketchup on it, fly to New York to record. It's here—in this building full of stuff—that he'll encode the sound of his hands moving hammers and dampers. To be decoded and amplified through African diamonds into ephemeral waves out there in the world of unknowable silences, affecting people, or annoying them as they ride elevators. He likes elevators. Likes moving without having to move his body, rising into spaces that were uncircumscribed by walls when he was born.

He thinks about the empty, expectant seats above, the neat rows and stacks of stuff below: coffee tables oriental carpets TV trays amplifiers drills electric blankets that could become defective and incinerate sleepers styrofoam cups juicers wicker baskets blue bowls basketballs baby bottle teats breast pumps ballerina pumps thimbles scissors thread lighter fluid dental floss paperweights nail clippers hockey sticks doohickeys doilies peppermint pots Eiffel Tower statuettes tourniquets chess sets bookends headboards knickknacks night tables settees toupees tepees baseball gloves oven gloves tape to mend what is broken hammers to break what is whole plastic hall runners and carpet remnants geranium tulip poppy seeds gold chains crosses and Stars of David. The unknowable patterns in which waffle irons and 7 irons go out into the world, patterns Gould imagines, white pins on a Toronto map, shifting into new shapes 13, 23, 43 years from now. 43 is too much somehow, 2016 unimaginable. Gould imagines it, his body underground with most of the now new stuff in this store. How long will a waffle iron lie in the earth ere it rot? 800, 900 years? His pocky corpse might scarce hold the laying in.

How long would it take him to become a corpse, if someone were to draw a knife along the line of the College Street sodium streetlight lying across his belly? 41 seconds? The juice for those lights, and for the recording equipment upstairs, would be nuclear these days, wouldn't it? Developed by the SLOWPOKE-1 reactor, which was developed just up College Street. The atom still considered indivisible 41 years ago. Time's just too presto. He'd like to take it slower. People tell him to take his Lincoln slower down College Street, but he would not like to do that. *Siegfried Idyll* could be slowed a little. He'll try when he goes back upstairs.

That settled, he's free to turn his mind to more interesting matters. 199, 919, and 991 are all prime numbers he thinks, lying on the Sealy, un-sleeping. He's pleased with that: lying on the Sealy, un-sleeping. Great assonance. Excise the onance, as he was trying to excise onanism from his afternoons, and you get great ass, and your mind turns to the woman born of your rib in your dreams, the woman you love but haven't yet met, the woman whose face fades upon waking before being erased by the bright afternoon light. You hope you see her again that night, without that threatening figure beside her.

In the good versions of the dream, you take that woman to the cottage on the lake. You sit beside the fire with her in silence. Or you listen to Richter's Diabelli Variations, op. 120: factors coming out the yin yang. Mark of the devil. No, Gould would never record it. It'd be like asking for some affliction. Curse his contrapuntal mind: never a thought of heaven without the thought of hell.

This is where and how he primes himself to play. The stuff down here in the department store gives substance to his musical thinking. There is no need to sully it with thoughts of the piece itself or— God forbid—piano plunking. Better to save the ketchup calories and uppers he downs for use by neurons, not mutton-headed muscle. Speaking of which, his doctor keeps telling him he doesn't have enough muscles. That his vertebrae are keening dangerously forward, unrestrained, as in a void, his kyphosis that of a 90-year-old. His physician had actually recommended sit-ups, or Jazzercise—the mutton head. Gould opts for a near-nightly lie on the Sealy Posturepedic, a bed whose benefits are embedded in its very name, whose sound springs resist the great magnet in the heart of the earth, forever drawing him down.

*

In their prime, great dancers often conceive of life as a void—incapable of offering resistance to the body. Then they turn 43. And they sadly recall what they knew when they were 2: that life is like this department store—full of coffee tables and stuff you could bump into in the dark. Golsheh goes past oriental carpets and bean bags, and beefy black telephones, all of which will be used to apprise their owners-to-be that someone alive now is dead. 9 years hence electrical signals will be decoded and converted to the sound "Glenn Gould" in these receivers. Little does Golsheh know the part she will play.

She rises through Lifestyle Gifts and Lingerie, floats past the Ladies' Powder Room, through the Christmas Bazaar, Carpets and Curtains, and the Fur Storage Service, empty—she imagines—this time of year. All this *stuff* we've gotten along without for millennia—not perhaps without getting a little tetchy at times, but still—superfluous shit. Then again, to pare your life down to a knife wasn't so advisable either. Golsheh goes through Gardening and Home Supplies. Golsheh means rose garden. Actually Golshan does, but whatever; a rose by any other name, etc. Point is, when she dances, she dances, and when she sleeps, she sleeps, and when she wanders in a rose garden, if part of the time her thoughts turn to coffee tables and stuff, the rest of the time she reins them in, to herself, to her solitude, to the rose garden.

Golsheh goes through Health, Beauty and Fragrances, tiny droplets of today's testers suspended in the air: oriental roses, myrrh, pomegranate, musk. Hollow harkening to her life in the Old World. Perfume has always seemed a sad ploy to her—cover yourself up to make people love you. Musk is the secretion of the male deer, the word having immigrated into English from the Middle Persian word *musk* مشک, which came from the Sanskrit *mushka* मुष्क, meaning "scrotum," because of the similarity in shape of the sac on the abdomen of a male musk deer. Musk is the smell of a dancer in a trance.

There are darker notes here too, acidic and foreboding, like the smell of a blade, scents she's sure she can only detect because she's here alone, in the dark. Notes beyond words—ancient, dissonant, incomprehensible as Gould's beloved Precambrian shield, which she went to with the last Canadian she dated before Brian—a sensitive but sexless WASP, apparently without any primal instincts whatsoever. She should have held on to him, but she was not sexless, and, anyway, who knew what other adjectives she'd have discovered in time. Now Handbags. Now Babies and Children's Wear, OshKosh B'gosh overalls and baby shoes, the air powdery and poignant. The scent of something you'll never have. As poisonous as the smell of someone you've loved and lost. She'd be in a busy department store, on an escalator, and she'd smell her father's Eau Sauvage, and the little girl's excitement at seeing her daddy again after a long absence would prick her, and then she'd have to look up and see the New World, another man.

Moved, rising on the unmoving escalator, she imagines tripping, her face meeting the step's metal teeth—dancer thoughts. Not 23-year-old dancer thoughts, but 43-year-old dancer thoughts. She thinks about Gould's coming fall. How sad it would be to watch him descend. Better to kill him than to watch his addictions fug out his playing, let his already game tastebuds become unconditional fans of Fran's Diner. All that life! Why not gather some of it to herself, instead of letting it seep into the air to be inhaled by unworthy Canuck schmucks?

She's close now. 5th floor. Optical Services. Did I mention it was a beautiful time? Do you also remember the warmth of oranges and browns, the impressionistic grain of video recorded on magnetic tape, cozily lit by nuclear-powered tungsten? Like Golsheh and Gould, the prime minister did what he wanted. He wanted to dance a pirouette behind the queen's back? Then he would. He wanted to date the same white-masked black pianist Gould had dated? Then he would. He wanted to go against the grain of reigning disdain for WASPS in Montreal as a teenager? Then he would drive the English stake Elliott between Pierre and Trudeau, and leave it there, separating the French names.

*

Gould hears something. A ghost in the building 5 years before it is abandoned to ghosts? Or the constant hum of huge underground turbines flushing air—already flushed through thousands of shoppers—back through the building? Dirty, *dirty* air, he hears his mother saying. Bang a drum, scare some bejesus, 2 seconds later you have silence. And that's how all sound was for millions of years, since the dawn of hearing—rising and falling, living and dying. Then yesterday, we made machines, and now we're forever surrounded by forever sounds, same pitch, same volume, never nuancing. Worse, we figured out how to record, to make eternal even the dying sounds. Who's to say

235

what this does to us? Who's to say what seeing millions of beautiful women does to man, evolved only to see a handful in a lifetime?

His reptilian brain registers movement now, registers the movement as a threat, not incorrectly, as it turns out, just some years prematurely. This is it. The long, familiar hum of routine is about to be drowned out by a rising phrase in a minor key, a phrase that will die one day. He's about to fall in love. Something in him is about to go haywire. Am I exaggerating? What was Gould's playing, if not a form of exaggeration? As he said: What was the point of recording a Mozart sonata for the umpteenth time unless you were going to make listeners sit up from the first notes and say to themselves: This is an event.

He listens. With some difficulty, having no abdominal muscles to speak of, he sits up on his forearms. There he is, middle-aged, in the middle of the Furniture and Beds Department, in the middle of the night, in the middle of the bed, somewhat elevated. He looks across to the mouth of the escalators. In the middle ground, the strangest display he's seen here—electric blankets hanging from the ceiling, like stingrays, tail wires hanging almost to head height, inviting shoppers to hang themselves. A rueful parody from Golsheh's friend, the department manager, who had been a marine biologist in Tehran. With his usual prescience, he says to himself: This is an event. And what he imagines isn't far off: a deranged man with a knife, Beethoven-wild hair, and Bach-like sexual appetites (20 children!) who's come to stab him, and then diddle him. Gould was afraid of being diddled after death, but that is another story.

Come to think of it, it's entirely apropos to this story.

"Is somebody there?" he says, his voice disappearing into the mattresses and bedding all around.

"Mr. Gould?" comes the invisible woman's voice, materializing amidst all that stuff. "I'm so happy to have found you. I wasn't sure you'd really be here. At these x, y, and z coordinates. At this moment in time."

Deranged. Definitely deranged. But a woman. Perhaps he could overpower her. Probably not. Where is she anyway? The sound seems to be coming from somewhere near a pyramidal pillow display, 100 percent Hungarian goose down, for a pre-allergic world. Did I mention it was a beautiful time?

"Here, now, space, time. It's nice to know someone else thinks about such things. Most people these dark days seem only to think about their stuff." He doesn't know why he's taking this chatty approach; oh yes, he does. He wants everybody to love him, even the deranged; he's an artist.

"Space and time that is of a piece with your first-ever concert, played on the organ here in 1945." Golsheh has the Persian propensity for poetry, and a lyric voice.

He doesn't know how she could know about that; oh yes, he does. He broadcasts all this information about himself into the world. But he's still startled when people actually hear it. He wants to be heard in every home. He wants to be alone. He wants to live, not too long, like Mozart, but rather longer than Mozart nevertheless. He wants the 800 or 900 years the compression, equalization, and coding of recording seem to offer. As Golsheh would later tell him: he's a man, he doesn't know what he wants.

"It's funny you should say that," and he is genuinely struck. "I was just thinking, not 5 minutes ago, that it's as though all the times I've ever played here are lined up together, outside of the time that happens outside this building. Lying here, it's like 1945 was just this morning."

"To answer your question—"

"Did I ask you a question?"

"You are who you are, Mr. Gould, because you are not normal. And normal's no good, you're right. But a normal person would wonder why I am here, and I feel I owe it to you to answer that question." She hears the feathers in the duvet being crushed as Gould shifts in bed.

He's afraid her plan might not be entirely normal. "Agree about normality, my dear, of course. So no need really to—" To what? Where is she anyway? "Can you see me?" he asks, gripping the covers, which Golsheh's friend Meriam, the manager of the Furniture and Bedding Department, leaves out for Gould every evening before she goes home, along with a pillow and sheets for his exclusive use. Gould had written her a charming letter detailing his midnight penchant for her Posturepedic, and his germ phobia, and she had been only too happy to oblige the great man. When Meriam mentioned it to Golsheh, she knew at once that she would do what she is about to do.

She draws her forefinger across the knife handle. It seems to love the heat of her hand. "Only your outline. And you me?" She steps out from behind the pyramidal pillow display. She's tall. Her hair is big, and tightly coiled. Gold coils catch what light there is and draw it to her right wrist, hanging by her side, by her loose skirt, from another climate. The other hand is buried inside a large purse that could contain anything.

"Only your shadow."

His huge glasses flicker for a second. "What big eyes you have," she says.

"The better not to see you with. On second thought, at the risk of asking a normal, unmetaphysical question: How did you get in here?"

"I hid behind a stack of golf sticks in the basement when no one was looking. At 4:44 this afternoon. The store closed, I dozed, my feet went to sleep, no one found me. 4:44 is a deathly unpropitious number according to the Chinese. No matter. I am Persian."

"Ah, yes, I wondered. But your accent is so faint. And you didn't say: 'an eh-stack of golf eh-sticks.'"

"What big ears you have," she says, and she starts moving toward him, slowly. Something is about to happen. But if he's the wolf (a lot of arm hair has sprouted since he turned 41), it should be his prerogative to attack.

"Are you afraid?" she asks.

"Somewhat. Nothing extraordinary about that, though: I'm afraid of the city of Philadelphia." And of being diddled when I'm dead, he does not add. "And as to the question I didn't ask, but you wanted to answer: Why are you here?"

So she tells him, about the vacant lot, which, for reasons unclear to her, she could only think about in French: *terrain vague*. She tells him about looking up at the headless CN Tower, imagining a time beyond her final phrase, which he watches her shadow perform, standing over him, right beside the bed now: elbow out and down and head up in opposition on the same line—a contrapuntal movement. She tells him that the memory of him playing the 6th Partita had saved her. She hears how hard he is listening through the gloom, which is why she tells him so much.

The story triggers something in him. It's majestic. And improbable. On paper, he'd find it twee, unbelievable. But he wants to believe it. It confirms the redemptive power of art, which he'd never quite dared believe in himself. And there's something about her—the way she moves ever so slowly toward him in a loping limp, as though he were the great magnet in the heart of the earth. Have you ever noticed how the scent of people we fall in love with is already familiar to us when we meet for the first time? He does believe it. Says it to himself again to make sure—yes, he believes it.

Her leg rests against his, the duvet in between. There's a softness to its hardness. What light there is pools on the pads of her fingers as they reach toward him. Her other hand grips the knife handle. Now it's like the back of her neck is drawn upward with a rope, and the sides of her neck splay, like a cobra, about to strike—decidedly, nothing about her body makes sense. It's a beautiful phrase that makes him fall for her, hard.

The darkness on her face dissipates a little as it draws nearer. He can make out a substantial, slightly bent nose. Eyes like black holes. Her right hand rocks him gently backward, off his forearms, and onto the pillow, following him down, keeping a constant, frustrating distance between their faces. Now that he's on his back, looking up, she pulls the knife from the bag, and starts running it softly up the side of the coat, searching for the spot. For a moment he thinks maybe he feels a tiny coolness there, but he can't credit the sensation; anyway, there are other, more pleasurable ones to attend to. She gives off great heat.

She imagines unwrapping him—slicing through coat, sweater, shirt, skin. Down into the light at the heart of him. Her sweet breath on his lips, the moment lasts an eternity. She covers half the distance, and half again, and half again, as in a mathematical paradox, eternally condemned to covering increasingly minute distances without ever reaching him. The knife finds the place. Quickly, cleanly, she cuts. Their lips touch. The world shatters into so many stars, the world trembles and the world sways, the world breaks but the world stays. Her knife is back in her purse, and her hand is on his cheek, as though to tell him everything will be OK, and for once, his body understands.

Reborn, as in a dream, more serene than he has ever been, he takes the elevator back up one floor. Boldly, he makes what many consider to be his greatest recording—the *Siegfried Idyll*, written by Wagner for the birth of his son. Later used in the opera *Siegfried*, about a youth who knows no fear. Until he sees a beautiful woman, and wakes her from a magic sleep, with a kiss. At first light, northern cardinals starting to sing, the snow letting up, he descends the 7 floors to his Lincoln Continental, and when he reaches into his coat pocket for the key, he notices that the big, horn-shaped bone button that usually keeps his pocket closed is gone. Not only that, but there's a small, neat cut in the wool there, from what must have been a very sharp blade.

She had wanted some *thing* that had belonged to him. An object

239

to remind her it hadn't been a dream, that their bodies had actually come up against each other.

He decides to drive and think, digest the night. He likes driving in the snow. He imagines her tramping snowy sidewalks in her ballerina pumps. Her purse was big, but it's still hard to imagine a woman like her carrying galoshes. Golsheh galoshes. Every time he tries to recall her face, his memory defaults to the sound of her voice, its quiet and deep. Green swirls up off Lake Ontario, something he's seen, and knows must mean—something about what was here in the eternal prime, before all this. His cheek still hot where her hand had first touched him. A B-flat beep snaps him back into his lane—he'd been drifting lakeward, into the unplowed part of the 401, his favorite prime-numbered freeway.

The tempo of his driving scandalizes as much as the tempo of his playing, albeit with an earthier audience. Maybe his presto Lincoln piloting is about doing a Dean, before it is too late, and people start to forget they used to compare the two. Doing a Dean, I mean: crashing into some Donald Turnupseed type, some grad student, say, cruising College Street on his way to prime the SLOWPOKE-2 reactor, the fusion of the Gould and Dean legends, indivisible, except by the Jaws of Life, used widely outside car-racing circles like Dean's only 7 years from now. In the particle collider others in his building call a parking garage, Gould frequently smashes into concrete columns, rehearsing for his big bang. J. G. Ballard's *Crash*, which recreates the Dean crash, is published this year. 23 years later, Cronenberg will make it into a movie, set in Toronto.

And so they begin. February 3, 1973. At the prime hour of a prime-numbered day, in a prime-numbered month, in a prime-numbered year, they become a couple—the prime prime. Divisible only by him or her. What else could divide them? Her husband could. Brian carried a knife too. A hunter's blade that could sever the ties that bound them. Her husband the ogre who had stolen her away, up Don Mills hills, down Don Valley valleys. Her husband of the dead gaze. How did she live with this, when she wanted to live?

*

It is difficult in 1973 not to know who Glenn Gould is but, reassuringly, Brian seems to have managed it. He likes racquetball, and maraschino cherries, and writing "wash me" on dirty cars, and he belongs to that disconcerting minority of people who are unaffected by music of any kind. Golsheh likes to think that if Brian doesn't know Gould exists, there can be no affair to discover, no body for Brian's knife to come up against.

Gould is a ghost when Brian's in town. But—*alhamdulilah*—he is often in Detroit, trying to penetrate Chrysler with the carburetor primer he designed, and then Gould whisks Golsheh up to Uptergrove—his family's cottage on Lake Simcoe—the sweet, ciggy smell of Brian still fresh on her. Beery bitterness and sea-breeze car freshener. She says the name Uptergrove turns her on. He likes it when she is turned on, but for some reason doesn't like her saying this. Why not? He thinks about it while playing Mozart, when it is easy to think of other things. Somehow it seems to discount his childhood memory of sitting on his mother's dimpled knees, Mozart-picking on the Chickering. There is something disturbing in seeing Golsheh straight-back sitting on the same acid-green armchair Grandma Gold (not a typo) and his mother had slumped on, Golsheh's grace and length superimposed on his mother's lumpen limbs, her forward-keening (toward glory for her son) torso wrapped—not tightly enough—in glaucous sausage skin. The double-exposed scenes he'd seen.

In the middle of them, there is a summer evening in Uptergrove, birds and air muted. The silence of a winter evening, everything covered in snow. The world braced for something. Above them blue sky. To the west, a bank of black clouds. Out of the silence, children's voices, plain playful at first. As they draw closer, they grow darker, like the sky. The skies fall—on the children first. Their blue shirts turn black. They grow from dots into human figures with limbs. They are close now, at the gate, begging for shelter. Gould lets them in. Golsheh goes into the bedroom, adds blouse above skirt, waits, head in hands on the edge of the bed. He can't recall as vulnerable a sight as her limping away from him, and locking the door behind her. He thinks he hears her sobbing in there. It is absurd. He has broadcast any number of meaningless facts about himself, but not a soul can know the most important one: that Golsheh exists, and he loves her. And so we get a mostly blank year on the timeline of Gould's otherwise manic life. Having no witnesses makes them feel a little like they've never been.

Those afternoons in Uptergrove: windows open to the light coming across the lake like white folds in shadowed cloth. He plays in his bathrobe and she dances, wearing only a long skirt. When the nuclear warheads fall (as Gould is sure they have every time he hears large furniture being dragged across the floor above him), he and

Golsheh can make their living playing piano and dancing for the mutant kings of the New World—every place looking like Gould's beloved Precambrian shield. Music—Schoenberg—for melted keyboards, played on melted keyboards, and the roots of her ancient vocabulary of movement meaning something again. And with all the burnt hands, applause would no longer exist—paradise. A heaven filled with the scent of Fartein Valen. How postmodern music would resonate postapocalypse! The holocaust that would break our obsession with moronic pentatonic ditties. Hope that a whole new generation might be raised on atonal music. Kids fishing 3-headed pike off stone bridges, happily humming 12-tone rows instead of "Twinkle, Twinkle, Little Star."

Gould's furrier father began using the name Gould instead of Gold in 1939 in order to disguise what he assumed people would (wrongly) assume to be Jewish roots. Prissy, prejudiced WASPS with money, people like the Eatons might be more inclined to drop dollars on a Gould sable than they would on a Gold sable. The province of Quebec's tagline is: "*Je me souviens.*" Has been for as long as I can remember. What are Quebecers supposed to remember? What WASPS with names like Matheson and Gould (who considered himself "the last of the Puritans") did to them, which, all 20th-century things considered, wasn't much. In 1973 my parents were hesitating between the names Elliott and Spencer. I'm as old as I write this as Gould was that year. If they'd opted for the former then I wouldn't have a homonym, also Canadian, alas, who published an unspeakably bad story in *The Rusty Toque,* and who Googlers must (wrongly!) assume to be me.

The actor Elliott Gould was born Elliott Goldstein, his father was also in the garment industry, and like Pierre Elliott Trudeau, he wooed Barbra Streisand—Glenn Gould's only pop-music hero, besides Petula Clark. Elliott and Barbra married, but Streisand couldn't be persuaded to change her name. Elliott's natural expression is that of someone who has just seen a ghost. An expression that, engraved over the years, has come to make him look like a ghost. Perhaps this seeming spook-seeing was just fatigue, the black holes around his eyes the consequence of the energy it must have taken for such a hunched, pale, and patently strange-looking man to make a name for himself in sunny Hollywood. Probably there were Goldstein ghosts. Only one subject for literature since 1945. The only place Gould ever played a concert in his comforting overcoat was in sunny Israel. Where he played the *Goldberg Variations,* a piece containing the name Gold—still legally Gould's the day he died. Before Gould broke the old way of playing Bach with that first recording of the *Goldbergs* in 1955, they were better known by another name: *Aria with Different Variations.*

Accelerando. Ma non troppo.

1977. Only 2 more years until Iran fires the first volley against modernity. The opening piece of violence in a shape-shifting war that will mar the century to come. Both Gould and Golsheh like to read novels in which couples are buffeted, then torn apart by great historical forces. Being buffeted by nothing and no one, they become annoyed with each other. Both are unable to chart the waters of their anger to their source, the overhanging vegetation being too thick, as it was in southern Ontario, when the Europeans arrived. Gould's obsession with the North grows—blank white landscapes, the same in every direction, lethally cold.

Both dress their primal rage up with some other idea, covering it in layers and layers of ideological clothing, believing it disguised. Getting it ready to go onto the stage of their relationship, the auditorium empty. She reproaches him for leaving the stage, liveness, life itself. In favor of disembodied simulacra of sound. Vanity, she says— the false promise of a technological eternity. She reproaches him for desecrating Bach with commerce, stamping the crass Columbia Records logo onto something sacred. They've been together for some time; she knows how to hurt him. She returns to a daily dance practice and she reproaches him for becoming ever more riddled with the Western malady of search for momentary satisfaction in ever-new sensations. He reproaches her for reproaching him so much. She faces the pain in her hip, and he tries to buoy himself in a never-ending succession of stimulations with painkillers, uppers, muscle relaxants, antianxiety meds, and sleeping pills. She turns to God. He reproaches her for believing in God only because she was in a cold, empty country that didn't. He says she's only a contrarian, that if she'd stayed in Isfahan she'd be a rabid atheist. They've been together for some time: he knows how to hurt her. She believes in the immutability of the physical, of the body. He believes in thought, in ideas. She limps, he leans toward her, as though praying, please let's stop this. But he's as unable to stop as she is. She forms a small troupe, and choreographs a piece—the jumping-off point is the simple phrase she almost performed on her neck. He envies her moving up out of the lowly standing of performer, as he wished he could. Being an artist saves her. His art had saved her. Being an artist is killing him. He only ever eats fried foods and ketchup. She grows taller, closer to the sky. Her olive skin whitens. His white skin turns green. They love each other. They can't stand each other. She leaves him.

Maraschino cherries are going out of fashion. Nobody sees the point of the 7th floor decorative auditorium topping anymore. Sound no longer has a place above stuff. They board it up, leave it to dust motes and ghosts, until September 2001. The store floors—basement through 6—are converted to offices. All the new stuff needs new space, so it is moved into the bunker-like Eaton Centre, which has no windows on the world, nothing to remind those inside that time is passing, just the nuclear-generated lamps of eternal acquisition.

Where once there were black telephones coffee tables oriental carpets TV trays amplifiers drills electric blankets that could become defective and incinerate sleepers styrofoam cups juicers wicker baskets blue bowls basketballs baby bottle teats breast pumps ballerina pumps thimbles scissors thread lighter fluid dental floss paperweights nail clippers hockey sticks doohickeys doilies peppermint pots Eiffel Tower statuettes tourniquets chess sets bookends headboards knickknacks night tables settees toupees tepees baseball gloves oven gloves tape to mend what is broken hammers to break what is whole plastic hall runners and carpet remnants geranium tulip poppy seeds gold chains crosses and Stars of David Sealy Posturepedics—now there are smoky offices. Where shoppers once wandered, bright with the promise of stuff, office workers now schlep dim eyed down dim corridors with bathroom keys on waffle iron–sized keychains, as though to void oneself was to void oneself of short-term memory. Secretaries smoke cigs, gulp diuretic Folgers instant coffee in styrofoam cups, log time, wishing it would go faster, wishing themselves after work, at dance classes, or Jazzercise, resuscitating their broken desk-job bodies. Where there was a Sealy Posturepedic, now there are work-space dividers stopping pulp and paper salesmen from seeing, but not hearing each other: "Well how are ya, Hal? How's the weather down in Brampton today?" Wishing themselves with *Frampton Comes Alive!* and some pot at night. The bosses in the corner offices buy the stuff that makes time go faster: magnetic tapes giving way to floppy disks that demagnetize, giving way to hard drives full of stuff that seemed important then, their 1s and 0s seeping into landfills now. None of it annihilated by hijacked planes, but almost all of it gone forever nevertheless: the work, the stuff, the people. Only one subject for writing since 2001.

Thomas Bernhard published a goodly novel about Gould the year after he died, then translated it into English 11 years later. About

Gould's genius making 2 almost geniuses allergic to the piano, and life itself. One kills himself.

To too meticulously describe a condition that has yet to affect the general populace is not believable. But remember that only a century ago, even the term allergy was unknown. Modernity unceasingly creates new conditions for ever more allergies. For Gould, the prime sufferer of what might (wrongly!) be mistaken for a misogynistic condition, it begins, like so many spirals begin, as sadness. Golsheh is gone. Acute, unfulfilled desire for her becomes something else.

The first symptoms present as lightheadedness while playing Hamlet with the Lower Rosedale Shakespearean Society, when Gould reaches across his coffee table to touch the arm of the woman playing Ophelia, though she's already dead at this point in the play, an arm so Golsheh-like, so Golsheh-lithe:

How long will a man lie i' the earth ere he rot?

FIRST CLOWN. I' faith, if he be not rotten before he die—as we
    have many pocky corpses now-a-days, that will scarce
    hold the laying in—he will last you some eight year
    or nine year: a tanner will last you nine year.

Then he is doubled over while sharing an elevator with a woman wearing a silk scarf, white camel-hair coat, and a broad hat that casts a shadow over all except her bright red lips. He almost wretches looking at the women's underwear section of the Eaton's catalog. Not to mention driving into a Dundas telephone pole after seeing Wonder Woman on a billboard. He's always been good at associative thinking—he sees what is happening. He takes measures. Barricades himself in his apartment, and in funky-stuffy all-male recording studios, where he hopes he will be safe from the deadly memories beautiful women might incite.

Gould is wrong about some things, right about others: chunks of Mozart being chumpy, Lincoln Continental seats being comfortable, and being under Mount Pleasant ground at the age of 50. He considers waiting until the prime of 53 but his back hurts, and anyway no one had ever noticed his other births and deaths—that he'd played his first public concert at 13, recorded the (32-part) *Goldbergs* at 23, or retired from live performance at 31.

So in the fall of 1982 he gets up, viscera a moment after bones, farts softly, makes some Maxwell House instant coffee, pops a couple uppers, sits down, downs an Arrowroot, and rereads the letter he wrote to Golsheh in the middle of the night, propped up in bed. He asks her to come to him. They have not seen each other since she left him, 5 years ago. Satisfied, he picks up the phone and calls down to the concierge of the Inn on the Park: "I have a letter for you, Tara," he says. "Please flomp tomple it to its destinated flooby doober." Tara doesn't exactly speak Gould-ish, but she has the vocabulary of an intelligent dog and, anyway, a concierge is safe to assume that a guest does not want her to spell-check (though this mightn't have been a bad idea in Gould's case) a letter, but to do what concierges are, 99.1 percent of the time, asked to do with letters: mail them. He puts his hand on C7, his painful seventh vertebra. He hears a C7 chord spiral out of the *Siegfried Idyll*, the piece he'd fearlessly recorded for piano just after meeting Golsheh, and conducted for orchestra 2 months before this, in what was to be his final recording. A new melody tries to fly and crashes. His sense of accomplishment forever dinted by not having become the composer he so wanted to be. He had been too afraid. To press keys was one thing, to draw music out of the void was another.

Comes the appointed night. 3 o'clock in the morning. Gould lies on his bed, waiting for her. It strikes him, in an expression it would be anachronistic to attribute to him, that in a few moments, he'll be "living the dream," the dream of dying, his beloved at his side. Even if, in the dream, most people don't usually die *because* their beloved is at their side.

No one notices her as she crosses the lobby of the Inn on the Park on the diagonal, heading for the stairs instead of the elevator. She hates elevators. Walls all around, descending underground, like a coffin. She rises to him on her own 2 legs—her limbs more and more mantis-like. Limbs Gould had loved. Were they? Human tissues regenerate every 7 years at the outside, they say. She is mostly a new person already. Gould gave her the courage to leave Brian, and leaving Brian gave her the courage to be with someone good. Some part of her yearns for Gould still.

He's left the door open a crack. She peers in, the darkness from the corridor spilling into his apartment. He's in bed, looking at the ceiling, looking funereal snazzy in his navy suit, red carnation in buttonhole. There's a blue bowl on the table, a yellow box of Arrowroots, an envelope from Herbert Kutscha, Kempten, Federal Republic of Germany, on his doormat. She steps on it; he'll be happy to have a trace of her when she's gone. In her pocket, she fingers the button she took from him in 1973, that close-distant night on the 6th floor of a department store moved underground, when they had started loving each other.

His reptilian brain registers movement on the periphery of his vision, correctly and contentedly registers the movement as a threat. She slips through the door and glides to the edge of the bed. Even lying on his back, he is hunched forward, his body riven by its singular devotion to the piano. His humpback had always been disturbing to her, but here, tonight, in the half-light, she sees the beauty of it. She notices the formerly white socks, which look like they've been dipped in coffee and dried on a radiator, several times. On the toe, the old Air Canada logo. He couldn't have flown for years.

The space where this happened is air now, crisscrossed by drones, birds, and maybe even meteorite pebbles that had, in larger form, ricocheted off the spacecraft *Voyager*, which contains the compressed sound of Gould playing the prelude from Book 1 of *The Well-Tempered Clavier* in an isolation booth. The Inn on the Park was brought down, the blank space overdubbed with the stubby Toyota on the Park. Gould being a Lincoln man would have found Toyota suspensions too tight, too upright. Then again he loved the tightness of the Sealy Posturepedic.

"No overcoat?" she says. "No gloves?"

He shakes his head, as though to suggest they needn't speak anymore, and they won't. She pulls her purple scarf—it has 100 tiny mirrors sewn into it—from her neck, elbow high and out and down, head up on the same line, her hand sweeping wide and close to his face. It's a long moment he seems to have seen before. A curtain closing, hiding her away as it reflects him back to himself. Then it's pulled open, and he sees her loosened hair, her pale neck, her dear face, again. A beautiful phrase.

He holds his hand out. Time is still thick. He fears there isn't enough left of what they'd had, that she won't touch him. It's dark outside. There's a new light in her eyes. She is with somebody, maybe even somebody good, he sees. Good. She puts her hand in his. It is like being branded. He knew it would hurt. He didn't know it would hurt this much. He pulls her toward him, and she follows. It would be wrong to say she knew she was killing him. And it would be wrong to say she didn't realize something was happening.

She lifts her fine hand, and he sees the knuckle bones have risen, pitched tents under her skin. The arthritis makes it look like she's clenching some invisible object. A knife, he thinks. She is actually holding something. It's the button. The talisman she doesn't need anymore. She touches his cheek now. Lightning enters his body where her skin meets his. He imagines tiny blood vessels blooming there. Many men, not just those in the kind of solitary confinement prisoners and late-period Gould experience, say they'd die to be touched by a beautiful woman. Only Gould has actually done it. Her hand drops to rest on his collarbone, the pain dangerously close to his heart. Ogre's hands encircle his neck.

With her other hand, she describes an elegant arc whose end point is the other collarbone. Her left hand slides up and over his shoulder and blooms behind his back, dropping the button onto his pillow. He hears the small sound, a blip, barely alive before it dies. Now he'll have a thing to remember her by, she thinks, to remind him I wasn't just a dream.

Gould's heaviness, the draw he's always felt from the great magnet in the heart of the earth, finally—finally—gives way to a light, exquisite emotion. He feels he could fly away. Slowly, solemnly, as though she knows exactly what she is doing, she bows her head toward his. They drink each other's breath. They remember. He can see the starbursts of tiny black stains on her irises, which he remembers he used to think of as the scars of some ancient sadness. He had forgotten her eyes. How had he forgotten her eyes?

The moment lasts an eternity. She covers half the distance, and half again, and half again, as in a mathematical paradox, as though eternally condemned to covering increasingly minute distances without ever reaching him. And then, when their lips finally touch, the world shatters into so many stars, the world trembles and the world sways, the world breaks, but the world stays, and when she opens her eyes, there they are, the sky over his fallen face the pale blue of fresh day. She gets up and leaves, closing the door softly, not wanting to wake him. He has had his stroke. The encounter wasn't quite enough to kill him immediately, as he had hoped. He will live his last 7 days in darkness, seeing nothing, only hearing.

There is 1 witness. The Inn on the Park night watchman notices her striding under the rising moon, birdsong beginning in the waxy-leafed trees lining the driveway. She will mark his mind in a way that will puzzle him for years. There is her beauty, of course, but it's more than that. There is something about her lightness, and some sense—it hardly made sense—that he had seen a woman who had accomplished something. And eventually, without ever having shared it with anyone, the thought of her will grow quieter and quieter, until it gives way entirely to silence.

Head Full:
Prelude to a Friendship
Paul Lisicky

We were walking beneath thick trees, laughing too hard, and we both felt it at the same time. It passed from eye to eye, quick, gone. The awareness felt like the click on a cap of medicine. We were here, now. And though we'd only been taking long walks for two weeks, it was already getting harder to imagine when we hadn't been trying to crack each other up. I hadn't even known I'd been a corpse. I'd been in dead time, waiting to be undead. What follows is an outtake from my book, The Narrow Door: A Memoir of Friendship, *which wants to think about my twenty-six years with the novelist Denise Gess. I think of this as a prelude to the action in the book: those late, last minutes before an unexpected best friendship got under way.*

I'D HEARD HER NAME BEFORE I saw her face. It came from the mouth of my first creative writing teacher, a lithe, athletic woman whose impeccable appearance summoned up a bygone Hollywood: part Janet Leigh, part Tippi Hedren. She said Denise Gess as if it was a name I should know, or was going to know very soon. There might have been a current of resentment in this news. After all, my teacher was a gifted, dedicated writer. She'd been a student of Donald Barthelme. She had already written several novels, none of which had been published, and every time a book of hers cycled through the rounds, she altered her name a little, adding a syllable or clipping off a name, as if she were starting all over again. She led me to think that Denise Gess, a student in the graduate program in English she was encouraging me to apply to, was a name I should know. Denise's first novel, *Good Deeds*, was already getting rave reviews months before it even came out.

*

249

For me "Denise Gess" inevitably summoned up Judith Guest, the author of *Ordinary People*, a novel that had been popular back then. Or maybe not so much the novel, but the movie, starring Mary Tyler Moore in a devastating, eviscerated performance. I was scared of this performance, maybe because I couldn't find Mary Richards, the vulnerable character she played on TV, anywhere in her face, wrists, ears. This role seemed to swallow her whole. Where was her big, happy head, her tiny body, her dancer's legs, the personality of a sixteen-year-old girl attached to the body of a woman, so determined to be perfect? Where was her funny voice with the endearing slide in the vowels? Always about to burst into tears even when she was smiling, soldiering on? This *Ordinary People* Mary leeched all the playfulness out of her eyes, which might have been why I associated the name Denise Gess with something curated, moneyed, and clean. It couldn't have been further from my own last name, which I didn't say aloud so I didn't have to take in the confusion in anyone's face. I just introduced myself as Paul, as if that was all you ever needed to know.

She was already at the seminar table of my romantic poetry class when I first walked in. It didn't occur to me to sit anywhere close to her. Instead, I took a chair at the opposite end of the room so I couldn't be subject to any conversation. I opened my textbook, aimed my face down at Blake's *Songs of Innocence and Experience*. I tried to imagine a compelling point about how the two sets of poems fit together: maybe there was something to say about how "A Little Boy Lost" dialogued with "A Poison Tree." For the next five minutes I tried coming up with a scrutable perspective to slow the dense, high panic in my chest. I thought of a bat, a chirping brown bat, knocking on my collarbone from inside.

And yet I couldn't stop stealing looks at this Gess. People were walking in, taking their chairs, tossing down their backpacks, but the room was a lot more alive in her corner. It was as if a dog whistle were being blown and only I could hear it. She sat in her chair as a dancer would, right leg folded and tucked under the left, dressed in black, black scoop-neck top, black linen slacks, flat black shoes, an immense flat cordovan purse on the tabletop in front of her. Everyone else sat relatively still, obedience shaping their postures, while she slid around in her chair, fingertips extended in dual directions, her body both talking and listening at once. Most of the other students, all women, cultivated an air of practicality about them. They were softer; they required scarves around their necks, the plushness of their skin. Denise, on the other hand, was near to the bone, as if it didn't matter to her that her heart, liver, lungs, breasts, and sexual parts were closer to brute danger.

The professor had an air of benevolence about him. He smiled in the manner of a parish priest, as if he were about to lift his arms, raise them high above his head to say, "Let us pray," after which we were to bow our heads. He opened his book, asked us to open our own books, and started to speak at length about Blake. His sentences were so sculpted that it was hard not to wonder whether he'd spoken those same words, in the same order, for the last dozen years. Once he got going, the kindness seemed to come less from inside him than outside the room. He rarely looked any of us in the eye, even though he certainly wanted us to feel seen. Maybe it was nerves. Or perhaps too painful to take in the fact that he was teaching Rutgers faces rather than Princeton faces. The Princeton faces would have focused on him; they would have looked right through him to their sunlit futures. The Rutgers faces were likely more complicated. We all wanted multiple things, things we couldn't put a name to. How do you look at people who want to leave their husbands, or find their husbands, or shoot heroin up into their fingers, or fuck on the garage floor rather than in a bed, or move away from the state of New Jersey, without yet having an inkling of any of that?

The afternoon sun saturated the fabric of the rolled-down blind. What was I doing here? I had never been a fan of school: most of my creative work was animated by a desire to bypass it, as well as all the dreads I'd associated with it, the pressure of conformity, competition—years and years of sour stomachs, anxiety enough to compromise the immune system. And now here I was pinned to those hard chairs again, the most banal kind of resignation, although the idea of graduate school certainly sounded credible to my parents and their friends. I should have been designing houses. I should have been playing my guitar in a too-tight coffeehouse, risking the crowd's indifference. As for writing? I knew I could write a story, a funny story. But a lot of people could write funny stories.

*

There was no doubt Denise always knew she was a writer. I'd never known anyone with so little doubt about her capacity to handle the task set out before her. It was not a task she believed she needed to earn, all the more intriguing given that she didn't come from a literary family; her father was a mailman, her mother sold cards in a Hallmark shop. If Denise did have doubts about her vocation, she kept them hidden, as one would the airplane-size vodka bottles behind the stacks of dishes in the china closet. In the weeks ahead she developed a theory about Blake's line breaks. The professor agreed with her up to a point; there was a shove in his reply, which invited Denise to push back. She was never afraid of pushing back. Her face went gold. It smoldered every time she called the professor by his first name, Bob, as if she and Bob were equals, had always been so. Or not equals. Maybe she knew that when her book came out and her face was on the cover of *The New York Times Sunday Book Review*, Bob would be standing in line at a bookstore, waiting for her to sign it. Then later he'd try to teach the book and get it all wrong, and she would have to walk into the room, ready to interrogate his simple assessment.

To see them banter was a little like watching sex, or some version of it.

I looked around at the women around the table. They couldn't take their eyes off Denise: the hands always in motion, the bracelets ringing on her thin olive arms. The expressive eyes that believed literature could take care of you, could make you feel known to yourself, less alone. She was onto something, whether they wanted to take it in or not. They'd gleaned that a devotion to literature insisted on a pact with the body. You covered it. You made sure it wasn't noticed. Denise, on the other hand, was *body*. She didn't hold that body against you. She didn't use it as a threat. She invited you along, as if you could be as vital as she was if you were willing to come along. But what was I to do with her instruction in an English Department in which the professor who taught James never once mentioned same-sex desire in relationship to that work? If only he'd been bold enough to speculate about Marcher's withdrawal from May Bartram, or just questioned the root of the relationship between Mallet and Roderick Hudson: "You came and put me into such ridiculous good humor," says Roderick to his mentor. So many contradictions around those tables, it was no wonder I spent half those years blinking, looking for the correct stanza, in a fugue state. Occasionally when I couldn't process the contradictions, I drifted up toward the ceiling and pictured Denise's face up on a screen, the big screen, playing a vulnerable but tough woman who fell in love with all the wrong men, surviving everyone who tried to fuck her, destroy her.

To push out the walls of the seminar room. Not at all to be at the center of that room, but what? There was a village inside me, but I didn't have a clue as to how to get that village out. The enclosure I'd built around that village was exhausting me. Words: more treacherous, and potentially full of trouble than any of the tools of music, where you could hide between the notes, enfold yourself between pauses and breaks like a bat inside a crack in a wall. You could be a great dancer and hide, a great sculptor and hide, an architect, a city planner, an oboist, an actor, and I'd chosen a field that required you to stand naked in front of your reader. Words did not give you safety. Words were magnificently scary in what they exacted of you. I both wanted to run away and slide into the great furry arms of them, be mauled and screwed senseless if that was what they required.

My writing place was in the far end of the basement, a few feet from the huge metal box of the heater. I felt drawn to the purr of the motor, the way it kicked on and off every five minutes, as if it were sucking fresh air into the house, then blowing it out into the yard, atop the barberry. I'd made a cage for myself down there, at my father's drafting table. I figured my writing would possibly be better if it were conducted in the most unappealing conditions possible. I made sure I didn't shift too much on the high metal stool. I only went upstairs to pee at least fifteen minutes after I felt the urge. Perhaps in part I was trying to appease my father, who believed that hard work justified a human life. It didn't so much matter what the product was, but how you pushed, bullied yourself. It could not look like I was playing—or having fun. I made myself a little med school there, but with pens and paper instead of scalpels and forceps. I felt far away from the outdoors, from everything that mattered to me: plants and animals and music and sex and God.

The door opened. "Paul?" my mother called from the top of the steps.

I stared at the words on the page. Where was syntax? No cause and effect. It unsettled me to see how easy it was to deface a piece of paper.

My mother called my name again.

I could have cried, I'm writing, but that would have translated to: *selfish*. I knew she was deliberately distracting me from my concentration even as I knew she wanted me to succeed at my writing. Achievement was as important to her as it was to my father. If I were to be published in a magazine, my mother would have shown up at the newsstand at 7:00 a.m., carried all dozen copies to the cash register, then, on the way home, slid them individually into the mailboxes of all the women from the church choir she had a wish to feel superior to.

Out in the garage, I lifted the grocery bags from the car, burning in the face. It wasn't like I was actually writing anyway. Possibly I was even grateful to be summoned out of the cage.

I slugged cans into the pantry shelf. Her back, shy; her shoulders tight as she ran a hard stream of water at the sink. I couldn't stay upset with her for long, for she was my other half, right? There was no way I'd ever be otherwise, as she'd named me after her twin brother, Paul, who had died when they were seventeen. She talked about Paul all the time and never let me forget how funny he was, how smart, how sweet, how beloved, how curious—I'd never measure up to the myth of him. But connections are always deeper than names, and I suspected I'd learned how to watch over her long before I'd been able to form sentences. Her rolled eyes, her glances, the movements of her fingers, which were always sore these days, none more bent than her wedding-ring finger—I was always attuned to her like a guide dog, as if it had always been my duty to check in on her emotional temperature, especially when she and my father had been fighting noisily into the night. And whenever my watching was too acute—when she caught me doing it, though she wanted me to—she pushed me away, for there was something not right about a child being too close to his mother, particularly if that child was a boy: everybody knew what that meant. At such moments, it was hard not to believe she was the saddest human alive, even though she'd always appeared to be happy. You're always smiling, said a woman in the supermarket when I was five. And I remember looking up at my mother's mouth, the swipe of coral lipstick at the tips of her white teeth, and thinking, she's right. How lucky I was to have a happy mother. Happy was the mark of love, happy the sign of being chosen—we all wanted to be known as happy, right? And I held on to all the possible meanings of my mother's happiness as the two of us stepped over the grate by the automatic doors. So many objects fallen through the grate, into the soot and lint, never to be scooped up again—dimes, a makeup compact, blue plastic gum-machine rings, coupons, receipts, two S&H Green Stamps, ballpoint-pen caps. Unhappiness beneath the soles of our shoes while the two of us walked forward, across the parking lot, the sun heating our heads.

If you were to tell me that someone was to come along to replace my twin, I'd have said: impossible. And if that same person was to say her name would be Denise Gess, I'd have said it once more. A sky-rocket, a shelter, a skylark: what would Denise have wanted with me? No, absolutely not. I did not have time for a real best friend. Besides, I already had a head full. Not to mention a house balanced across my shoulders, even if I was lurching now, right leg so far ahead I was practically on the ground.

Two Poems
John Ashbery

PLAYING IN DARKNESS

The men on top of the hill
launched a new dirt lobby
meant to outstrip the precious,
that is, previous, tentative
by a better than three-to-one margin.

And slightly without you
horrified spectators esteem the rain input.
You would have too crude shelter
of boards circling a central meaning place.

Arrhythmia! You pant. Not by a long
chalk, crotch shot
on a bowling team, English-worthy kebabs.
Let Fido confide, or cough up. I can't
vouch for the clientele, in lockdown mode.
They don't want you there, aporia.

Mrs. Mulligan down the hall broached the topic
long after everyone had gone home
into the night.

John Ashbery

DESERT MOMENTS

We watched his regular camera
until it became nervous.
There were other horns inside for us,
things the pasta brought, never to be paced over.

My gosh! The President of the United States!
Years and years went by like that.
It was impossible to keep track of them.
I'm all about truth, and meaning. In the end
they said they were delighted with what they found.

Circuits are busy. Of course, we're not going to sit here
and wait. I have met you in the small shops,
a large cookie presence. It was "robust."
Save me the czardas

at Puke University.
I'm glad he goes in there.
That was the president, you clucks.
Why is it taking so long?

We might come closer (the eldritch mother's refrain
over twenty-three years ago).
Oh, that's what that is.
Then suddenly it's forty years later,
and I was like, "Holy shit!
I'm just happy to be alive!"

It's almost like you've done something
totally preppy. Your hands are a little dirty,
though.
Yrs and oblige,
Holofernes J. Crinkleaf.

"Dear Smitten . . ."

The Soft Disconnect
J. W. McCormack

LIKE A BUG IN A BOOK that gamely improvises a bridge from each plummeting page, the evildoer called and we two friends, being two poor examples of the *sinner* class, answered.

My partner and other-through-all-ages is Lunch, so-called for a congenital hoggishness that extends itself gut-wise into general behavior, and I am called Breakfast for reasons that are similarly apposite with wit to physical virtue. The hammy hand and the rakish black pudding are we—but I cannot help but think we might have fared better had we another meal between us.

When I close my eyes and set my stainless-steel memory to *emulsify*, I see the curd-stains on the bedspread that had become tendriled about my dear partner's egg-white whey-flesh, this being the only attire that Lunch had managed to obtain on his way to silence the ringing culprit of his spoilt day-slumber. The next image is of my partner quieting the phone's receiver with one bulgy knuckle and, emitting the breath-flavor known as *mustard sausage*, avouching my participation in a caper.

I will speak for us both, though we are the same: we are mountebanks, we fancy ourselves recalcitrants and revolutionaries. But the world calls us criminals. Jug jobs for dosh and finn—what the class of men known as *lay* call bank robberies—were Lunch's buttered bread, the eggs in my oatmeal, but what the berk on the other line was hatching made our usual bust and screw look like dinner (a meal we both abhor). A *soft disconnect*. Oh yes, boys.

Back in the nog-days, when Lunch and I were pursuing our degrees in the Malefactory Arts, the university halls were eternally abuzz with rumors (begun by the tenured rogues, stool pigeons, and other base *canards* who were our professors, then passed on to the knavish student body) of a means by which to black-out the city—say, perhaps, by scrupulous application of sharpened shears where the wires meet—and by this botching of the cables achieve what every true scalawag dreams of: an entire society rendered criminal. The butcher boy robbing the printer's devil under the blinded eye of the magistrate, only to trundle homeward and discover that the glazier has had his way with the sum total of his vulgar possession. A perfect wheel, where mutual treachery would make for a fluid distribution of wealth, a never-ending variety of lifestyle.

Oh, what dreamers we were in those days! You should have seen Lunch; he used to strut like a dauphin down aisles of garbure, hefting his girth with the same grace with which he'd polish off his first pork casserole of the day or inveigle the shills on the sidewalk to keep their eye on the pea as he transferred it between inverted cans marked Potted Meat. A member of the *Gargantua* class with the bacon-strangled heart of a champion; I knew my opposite number at first sight. But look at my poor Lunch now: inhaling hoagies in the getaway car, our array of drills and lock picks pastrami-moist, sausage-sized fingers chafing against the trigger. You'd need a map to find his inner thigh, boys—a map as exquisitely detailed, if you'll forgive the belchy transition, as the one to the electric heart of the city that our employers slid under the front slot of our grubby basement flat once we agreed to enroll in the scheme.

I should've smelled sour milk right off. Their reference was our school-days chaplain, Father Thierry Delmonico, a onetime asphyxiator of clerics who'd proved the figure of speech, of the type known as *paradox*, beginning "he who fucks nuns will later join the church" by joining the priesthood in his old age, a straightened Saul whom I gathered meant to christen us two apostles to do the work properly known as *dirty* in his stead. On our way to the rendezvous, I identified our accomplices as members of the *bungler* class. But the real liability was dear old Lunch, devouring a bouquet of corn dogs as I sucked my oatmeal through a straw, sweating mayonnaise as we made our descent into the sewers—I should've seen the jar of olive oil cached in his shirttail, should've calibrated the outcome of his sweet ass, his sucrose posterior, in proximity to all that electricity— but instead I silenced the little voice in me, like the ghost of so many embryonic chickens, chanting, *You've gotten so sloppy, you're gonna get us both caught!*

The proposed boondoggle was a nicked page from the *Vademecum* of Carlos Calisaya, a profligate philosopher of the *genius* class whose aphorism *The dialectical origin of social oppression is the padlocked door* anticipates a conclusion of the variety known as *foregone*, namely that equality proceeds from breaking and entering. I'd thumbed my way through my undergraduate copy till its page numbers were anointed with cream cheese, the annotations pockmarked with poppy seeds, and vellum so packed with gluten that I needed a knife to peel apart the leaves before countering good old Lunch's notoriously bunco proofs and *reductios* (back when a love of sophistry overcrowded Ragù Bolognese in my friend and partner's ponderous innards). The soft disconnect itself was mere extrapolation—on the part of a consortium of Graduate footpads, crimps-in-training, and Bachelors of Hooliganism—from Calisaya's famous dictum *Daylight is the plectrum of the Primogeniture.*

Our employer proved to be the rapacious skinner William "Smooth-bill" Brodie. He arrived at our rendezvous at the Municipal Aviary decked out—apropos of a low profile—in soap-locks and chav duds, sporting an infinitely waxable handlebar. He asked if we fancied a smoke and, before Lunch or I could get an aff or neg out our argle-blasters, whisked a match from the brim of his bowler hat and planted its accolades on a meerschaum that supplied his initials for the benefit of the short-on-memory. Brodie was a swell of the *jackdaw* class, ran euchre and whist games at the Bone Flute, original as sin and, like all originals, ruled by a unitary passion. His mania was bird-watching and so the yolk of the scheme was delivered by way of the entendre specified as *double*, with us lifting our binoculars to the cagey trees where the flock was going all flappertoy and wackadoo in the evolutionary endeavors of mating (alternating prey or passage as dictated by primal inclination and the selection known as *natural*).

"The world turns on a worm, see? Word from the owl is, couple of sparrows get the worm in their beak, could be the pigeons migrate. No one likes a squab, boys, but if the bluebirds wear out their wings on finches and crakes, could be the cuckoo gets the nest. That's when the woodpecker widens the hole. Next thing you know, feathers start to fly around and no one's a dove no more, got me? Every rook and raven on the wire wants a hollow tree, boys. All you got to figure is whether you is a sparrow or whether you is a canary."

And then, in deference to the science of omen and augury, a speckled exemplar of the origin of all currency—that is, an egg—toppled out its wreath and into my potato-peelers. I commenced a curiosity as to whether I'd seen the last of shabby adversity. Maybe it was time for a couple respectabilized mugs of the larcenous gentility like me and Lunch to slip the roux-and-ragpick that'd been our mutual lot so far and make good on the racket known as *higher education* by cashing theory and thesis for the maximal citywide pandemonium.

And so, by suchlike delusions of the *grandeur* class, I found myself trailing dear old Lunch's Vesuvian rumple-stump through the city's cloacae. Scraping my shins on sewer pipes of the fit classified as *Procrustean* while I, with utterances hindered by the flashlight clutched in my jabber-box, provided navigation from our map's noodly circumscription of tunnels to the earthly navel all funnels and faucets lead to.

Measure by flatulent measure, the unmentionable macadam of the nether regions revealed its nadir. I rolled up my map and took hold of Lunch's suspenders just in time to be ejected by the pressure qualified as *pneumatic* out the heating vent and into the energizing nexus of every light fixture, phone cord, and security rig in the whole metropolitan gut-storm. May the coffee in my veins turn to lard if I tell a lie, boys, that place was a glorious blueprint gone gunmetal gray with dials and wires crisscrossing like the precarious dream of a construction worker fast asleep on a bed of girders. And in the center, a massive buzzing squid, a towering generator of the *phallic* shtick, whose mission was the same as ours: transposition and conversion of powers. My lovely Lunch subdued the security guards by forcible exposure to his reeking sweat bags and the attendant fleet of janitors and electricians underwent a metamorphosis of rubber noses and adhesive whiskers until we were yap to yobbo with the accomplices assigned by Brodie's outfit. There was Kid Glove John Longacre, Whisky Johnny, Big Jon Jissom, John Lee Leftside, Johnny "Mock Turtle" McManus: the Johns. Not so bungling after all.

Everything was cream and George Washington pie as I and my old confidant began our work. The Johns jiggered the cameras, monitored the red arrows at the center of each gauge for sudden moves, and did their best to decipher the readouts spewing in a neat soufflé from underneath the circuit board. All this time, my pal Lunch was scaling the generator by way of his unfurled girdle, which he had wrapped around either side so he could hoist himself up like a lineman, with me riding shoulder-top to the old sock and sipping a cup of tea I'd prepared from the scalding water that dripped in increments from the open spigots and the bags I customarily carry in my pockets.

Our ears brushed wires. Each hummed with the ghost of two million televisions and radios, even as the pipes issued a symphony of shower taps and storm drains. Placing my teacup on the flat of my porkpie, I flipped over the map Brodie's boys had slid under my door and consulted the diagram on the other side.

A gingerly snip of a certain cord of linguine-like manifestation and the Johns reported that every stoplight and neon-beer logo on Bottle Street had abruptly fizzled out. A plucked angel-hair and the five-card shysters and showgirls of the Theater District were deprived of their red-lights, the names of screen idols demoted to the obscurity of their patrons inside the darkened marquees; a clipped spaghetti sucked the electricity from three-quarters of the Tenth Ward and two of the Six Points; and a rerouted cable of the *fettuccine* class eclipsed the Financial District, opening automatic doors and stifling bank alarms. *Carlos Calisaya*, I thought, *I've done you right proud* and quoted from memory that ineluctable maxim from the Fagin of philosophers: *crime is the only moral ideology because only crime sees reality with rods and cones untainted by spotlit subjectivity.*

One by one, the windows of the gridlocked waffle above us began to flicker out, the underworld having made good on the proposition defined as *analytic* and literalized its sobriquet, casting a shadow from under the very rock to which the slavery of wages known as *society* confined us. Trains, clocks, and the damning jangle of cash registers: the indifferent dough-cranks of routine ground to a halt over our heads—I only wish I could blame that unleavened rumbling for my failure to detect my good Lunch's first gastric tremors. But the red flags of the coming disaster had been there since my old friend and partner's unceremonious belly flop into the private sector. They had been the cellophane twisted round the toothpicks plunged through each compulsively devoured BLT, the raised welts on the cornmeal coating shelves upon shelves of pickle jars, the red-pepper flakes covering the moonish mounds of coleslaw one found festering in the brim of my buddy's fedoras. And, finally, they were the fungoid and plankton toppings previously concealed in an undisclosed cache, now dressing the pizza pie Lunch, unbeknownst to the rest of us, had been engaged in preparing throughout all our iniquitous labor. Only as his sauce-dipped digits reached for the olive oil ensconced in his quivering flesh taco did we realize how his appetite—and, since I cannot keep from blaming myself, my own ignorance of the dawning midnight snacking hour—had betrayed us.

The bottle swirled the air as it plummeted, as if tasting the distance from Lunch's outstretched thumbs to the control board. The impact sent an ominous crackle through the instruments and put a shard through John Lee Leftside's right hand—but I kept my crumpet, boys, and fished the flour (an ideal coolant) out of my beloved Lunch's elephantine breast pocket, passing it overhand to the scrambling Johns even as I fought for equilibrium atop my bucking behemoth, my too-much-changed friend and partner. Lunch's girdle had become distended in all his swiveling and now snapped like a slab of bacon, leaving me no choice but to abandon ship and dangle with one hand from the piping while drinking the dregs of my tea with the other, captive witness to the airborne ballet now working itself out before me.

Lunch, in lieu of the terra known as *firma*, plunged one hairy drumstick into the high-voltage spiderweb still strung overhead, the concerted knotty mass of which sagged like a small intestine before my partner made a spectacular midair pirouette and forced a trembling, tofu-pale thigh into the generator's remaining cilium. From there, he twisted deeper into a progression of coils that shortly had him subdivided into dozens of bulging slivers. Soon my bulgy comrade was cocooned within the entrails of the metropolis's central switchboard. The Johns jumped up from their dials and charts to relay what the stalks of light shooting crazily on and off through the open-ended plumbing rigs confirmed: Lunch was now physically hardwired to the city mainframe, the progress of its power lines indentured to his every twitch and hiccup.

As for myself, stranded amid the drainpipes like a fish of the *hooked* persuasion, I happened to peer into a gaping faucet and what should I see but the unmistakable *louche* decor of a house of the repute qualified as *ill*—Vera's Primas, to be exact, and there was the proficient Vera Lyons herself, disciplining her latest magdalen over one knee on the scarlet divan.

Habitual voyeurism is a preference second only to cereal. Life was temporarily worth living once again. But this tableau had one gargoyle too many. Creeping in through the wainscoting, as-of-yet unobserved by the panoply of pouting soubrettes, I spied the obstreperous gospel grinder Father Delmonico, no doubt waiting for the blackout to reconcile the ormolu and lapis lazuli with the color of his Cossack before sharpening his Psalter on the belles of the barrelhouse, in flagrant violation of that proverb of the *axiomatic* class, "All that is easy is not free."

I'd been used, my friends, hard-boiled by a poacher of the *Tartuffe* class. As the *Vademecum* tells us: *The shill and flimflam man answers to an honesty of his own, while Hell hath nothing but torment in store for the chouse-at-heart who wears Heaven's sandwich-sign.* Vowing to balance this banquet once and for all, I reached into my shoulder holster for my usual syrup (the cavalier's condiment) and greased myself up one-handed. And then—would

263

you believe it?—I shimmied up the pipe like a regurgitated short-stack and emerged from the boudoir's bidet, narrowly evading the exposed derriere of one of Vera's scrimmers. Caught by his collar just as he was preparing to ravish a Delilah, Father Delmonico—rather than admit he'd been apprehended with his fingers in the jam jar (so to speak)—lapsed into improvised panegyrics before the assembled tradeswomen and moonlighting hot-corn girls, asserting that *he* was the victim of *their* uplifted skirts (and not the verse of that particular vice). All I had to do was think of all the sins I wasted in confession. And then I threw the fridge at him, boys.

We dueled baguette to holy wafer, we raised rhubarb and hugger mugger, we smothered our knuckles in grits and corn flakes before erupting into fisticuffs as the girls danced a scandalous bolero. We took turns trying to strangle each other with sausage links while the piano played a tarantella. I admit I had my back to the wall after Delmonico brought a demijohn of vino down over my head and prepared to transubstantiate me with the broken bottle—but just then, the lights went out. Attaboy, Lunch! With the bagnio rallied behind me, I unforked the dimmed chandelier from its chain and brought it down on the Pharisee's blinded melon. The flicking of the crucial switch was too timely to be accidental—and, in appreciation, I spread a generous helping of cucumber on rye and flushed my old friend's daily bread down the toilet, where, with any luck, it would find his open gullet. Then, figuring every peck deserves a slosh, I emptied a bottle of absinthe down the sink.

From the fire escape, I took stock of the flash-lit day dawning in the middle of the night and beheld a criminal's carnival where the ovoid doors of busted bank vaults rolled down the streets like hubcaps. Tenners rode the wind in the manner of kites and the air was scented with gelignite and other elements of the *explosive* class. A rumpus seized the city, albeit selectively. A bank robbery enacted by Tom Faraday's goon squad in Whitehall under cover of darkness ran afoul of suddenly glaring lamplight in Bughouse Square, forcing the assembled army of moll-buzzers and chinchilla coats to stow their swag in fire hydrants before the leatherheads could round them up. Across town, the Boothouse Boys hit the dirt known as *pay*, looting a jewelry store stripped of sirens only to have the lights come up just as they ran afoul of "Humpty" Van Dyke and his infamous Sewer Rat gang crossing over from Barrow Town, igniting an impromptu gang fight. Even Bill "Smoothbill" Brodie's gang of Sparrows got their feathers plucked after their escape route swerved into an abrupt limelight, signaling them out against the otherwise enshadowed thoroughfare.

The city's population of fluorescents danced like a disco floor. It was not mere chance that dictated each aurora, but the unmistakable stamp of the largest life I knew. In that pandemic light show I glimpsed the spirit of my friend. Yes, Lunch—now delivered from his former corpulence and incarnated in the very flow of things—was his old self again, a bloated Bogart with a direct feed into the electric unconscious, marvelously bringing to pass the formerly shanghaied promise of his school days by way of the skelter known as *helter*.

Faced with a wayward throng of cracks and screeves, orphans and urchins, pimps and buttoners, all outlaws after my own heart crowding the curbstone—well, what could I do, boys, but join in? I borrowed from Vera accoutrements of the *petticoat* class and, with those colored skirts as my royal standards, I waved the motley mobsmen, still clutching their outsized suitcases stuffed with bills, through the blitz. I knew every raisin in my partner's mental muffin and thus, leaping from ledge to ledge, sliding down drainage pipes and clinging to caryatids, it was easy as quiche to keep two steps ahead of the next flare-up.

Oh, we were a team again. His was the griddle and mine the batter as we collaborated on a double-deck caper of the *revolution* class that reversed the fortunes of the marginalized, put government tender in the greasy palms of the misfit, the physically disfigured and socially suicided, and unhooked even so fundamental a hierarchy as day and night. They were chanting my name down in the vacant lot, toasting the jentacular saint of Mayhem with pillaged stereos and torches.

But I was just a man, boys, and so, having slid down the railings, carried on their shoulders to the center of the lot, I cleared my snotchute and prepared to address the masses. I was going to begin (as a hush settled across the asphalt) by quoting at length from Calisaya's *Vademecum*—*If fear and finance are the clothes with which society hides its nudity, then night is a striptease*—and go on to say that no connection is *soft*, all connection is *deep*. Radioactive. Because we are all playing the part of parsley on the earthly plate, each of us an outlet for the airways. Blips lost in a system from which no book or brickbat can permanently unplug us. But dear old Lunch was the real hero, even here, in a city of villains.

265

But before I could commence my speechifying, a sequence of flashlights sputtered to the position qualified as *operational*, revealing that my audience had fled. In their place was a wall of bobbies, gendarmes, and flatfeet, and all aiming their heaters in the direction of my icebox. Things followed in the course properly allotted as *due*, with the Black Maria coming to cart me off to the hoosegow. When it opened its doors, I beheld the woeful personages of the Johns, chainlinked like a string of daisies—but I say it could've been worse, boys.

Lunch did his best to keep me cheery, twinkling inside the neon and halogen, glimmering under the manholes in anticipation of the inevitable overload and causing the passing television sets to show the same channel so I could follow the story. When they asked for my plea and the public defender wondered aloud who was to blame, I couldn't find a grain of fault with my impalpable friend partner. No, Your Honor, it wasn't society or the company I kept, it wasn't me childhood nor a lack of opportunity, it was—(well, what you think, boys? I blamed my diet).

And as for Lunch, my coconspirator and all-purpose corn flake, my soul's laxative, cheese of my cottage, he is part of all of us. He is the inlet and the outlet, the ac/dc, the electric toothbrush. He is the city's umbilical and extension cord, and all our power stations are answerable to him. I watch him flicker here and there, I see sparks now and then, I know it is the last of my friend and partner, that he is the city's digestion. And, come to that, spare a thought for me, as I choke down the prison's rank toaster fodder, as I serve out my sentence for daring to dream that we could all sup from the same pail. Seeing me in this state, you may well ask: Do I feel that my friend sold out, now that he is not only part of the system but its very center? No, boys, I will say this much about my old friend Lunch. He never sold out to get where he is. He stole it.

Passages
Isabella Hammad

AHMAD FARIS AL-SHIDYAQ TRANSLATES the Orientalist Lamartine as follows:

> The Arabs smoked tobacco from their long pipes in silence, watching the smoke rising like graceful blue columns until it dispersed into the air in a way beguiling to the observer, the air at the time being transparent, gentle.

I was in the no-smoking room of a café near Clock Square. The room was like a little conservatory—sloping ceiling, glass doors overlooking a vegetable garden. Weeks without rain, the imams were praying the *salaat al-istiqa'* for the farmers. I noticed two men sitting on the far couch. One was gray and haggard (just released from prison, I would shortly be informed; "Come to the protest this weekend, give me your number?" *Remember: don't get on their records, do not be seen at any marches, stay inside on Fridays*). The other had a scarred face, he was thin, and his eyes were pale blue.

"Are you international?" he asked. And then, "Are you a student?"

"No," I said. "I'm just reading Ilan Pappé," and I showed him the spine of the book, with a Library of Birzeit sticker near the bottom.

"Oh yeah, such a great guy," said a blonde, turning and leaning over the back of her chair. American or Canadian, a tattoo on her arm—*May I live Simply so that Others may Simply Live*—ah, I thought; they all know each other, I'm the only stranger in the room, that's why.

And Ahmad Faris al-Shidyaq discusses Chateaubriand as follows:

> [Chateaubriand] writes that he saw an American Indian woman with a thin cow and said to her, bewailing its state, "Why is this cow so thin?" and the woman answered to him, "She eats little," and again he provides these words in English, to wit, *She eats very little*. In yet another place he

267

writes that he observed fragments of clouds, some in the shape of animals and others in that of a mountain or a tree or similar things.

Knowing this, you will appreciate that, in objecting to my talking of things that are of no interest to you but are to me, you are simply being stubborn.

With feigned casualness, I accepted the invitation to dinner. Another blonde joined us outside the café, a Dutch girl, lost and wan. "I'm a backpacker," she said with a shrug. The freed man couldn't join—he had to return home to his wife.

"See you next weekend," he said to me, and I nodded.

In his novel in four volumes, *Leg over Leg*, otherwise known as

The Turtle in the Tree
concerning
The Fāriyāq
What Manner of Creature Might He Be
otherwise entitled
Days, Months, and Years
spent in
Critical Examination
of
The Arabs
and
Their Non-Arab Peers
by
The Humble Dependent on His Lord the Provider
Fāris ibn Yūsuf al-Shidyāq

published in four volumes in the year 1855 (Gregorian), Al-Shidyaq writes:

Do I hear someone objecting here and asking: "What is the point of this banal tale?"

We walked down the slope to the border between Al-Masyoon and Ein-Menjed. Rami with the scars bought a white plucked chicken from the butcher, the neck like a nailless thumb, and Alexia bought eggplants for soaking up the oil, and I bought yogurt to clean our mouths.

His name was everywhere before I even saw him. Salah, Sallih, Sully, Slah. It was his apartment we had returned to, where we chopped the onion and fried the black-skinned slices of eggplant until they were rigid with oil and crisped some cauliflower brown and dripping—Rami had learned to cook in prison, he said—and the man whose name was everywhere was away that evening at a talk within forty-eight borders (Israel, in other words). He would be back later, they said, you'll meet him. Sal, Sale, Sole. Rami turned the maqluba and said that if you carry your anger in your heart, you are still in prison. *They* do not suffer if you are angry! Only we suffer if we are angry. Anger is a prison we carry around with us. The ultimate freedom is in forgiveness.

Finally, at nearly a quarter to one, the master of the two-bedroom apartment permanently registered on Couchsurfing.com—*I need this, this life, you know?* he would say in explanation some days later, rubbing his fingers together as if he were touching *this life*—came in through the front door, laconic and slouching, teeth and eyeballs nicotine yellow, a woman behind. Laughing, they were laughing: Sal's permit had expired at midnight, so he pretended to talk on the phone in the backseat while the young English woman—Jewish, North London—drove through the checkpoint playing Israeli music. The two of them still reeling with the thrill, she gasped, "I can't believe I did that! I've never done anything against the law before!" She had big dangly earrings. She used to work in Cape Town, she would tell me later. That she'd had an affair there, with a married man.

Immediately Sal did not like me. Because, it seemed, of where I came from. All of us smoking on the balcony—Ah, you are from Nablus? pointing at me with the cigarette. High people. Very . . . sophisticated.

Rami started telling us about the way they passed messages in the prisons. How they were always being moved from prison to prison to stop them from organizing, how they organized anyway through their coding system, how the guards all knew, it was one big game, how they, the prisoners, put paper inside plastic and melted it into a seal "like this" (a folding gesture) until they could swallow the message whole without digesting it. *Yanni*, we are more organized in the prison than out of it! How sometimes the guards forced you to eat laxatives to shit it out fast, how, if you succeeded, you passed the plastic-covered notes with your lips to visitors—Salih said he did it once with his mother; she was so nervous giving the message, she leaned into the booth and kissed him on the mouth.

When we went back inside, Sal plugged his iPad into the socket. He turned on a YouTube video of Leonard Cohen playing "So Long, Marianne."

"I am older than I look," he said to me, leaning on the kitchen counter and running a hand through his mass of black curly hair. Then he laughed, with disdain, and asked me my age. I found him childlike in his forthrightness. My answer was a lie, just two or three years off. I would find out later he had lied also, and made himself younger for me.

His scorn was the same each time I saw him after that, and always because of where I came from. We are not high people like you, he would say, or something along those lines.

One day he changed.

"I want to use you," he said.

It was late morning, windy and bright, and we had alighted in Jerusalem from the Qalandia bus.

"You could be useful to us. You know, another type of Palestinian, another story. You are white. And you have that accent."

I am allegedly descended from Ibn Battuta. Otherwise known as: Abu 'Abd Allah Muhammad ibn 'Abd Allah Il-lawati A-Tanji ibn Battuta. A Sunni Berber, a great traveler through Dar al-Islam. In the year 1355 by the Gregorian calendar, Ibn Battuta visited Nablus, a Palestinian valley town in Greater Syria, where, among other things, he had sex with a local woman. That woman gave birth to a boy. She named him Kamal, "Perfection," and there starts the family tree between the olive branches and the dusty earth skin.

Nablus is like Sidon but more so

writes Battuta in his *Rihla*, otherwise known as "A Gift to Those Who Contemplate the Wonders of Cities and the Marvels of Traveling."

*and the melons are of excellent quality. It is a Little
Damascus, full of trees and streams, and full of olives.*

Sal came from the village of Hizma. To most people the name
Hizma now refers to one of the checkpoints to Jerusalem by which
a red-roofed settlement stretches out over the plain. Sal's father
had been an olive farmer. He died, said Sal, of a heart attack the
day the wall rose over his grove and they could not complete
the harvest.

He liked to speak to me in Classical Arabic. It was what I understood
best; I hadn't mastered the dialect. O Lady, O Moon, he would say,
ya qam-ra-tun jameel-a-tun, Ya Fattah.

Ahmad Faris al-Shidyaq tries to explain the oddities of words in the
Classical Arabic language that are similar in meaning and also similar in lexical association:

> Thus, <u>among the characteristic associations of the letter *ḥ*</u>,
> for example, are amplitude and expansiveness, as in the
> words *ibtiḥaḥ* ("affluence and abundance"), *badāḥ* ("broad
> tract of land"), *barāḥ* ("broad uncultivated tract of land"),
> *abṭaḥ* ("wide watercourse"), *iblindāḥ* ("widening out (of a
> place)"), *jaḥḥ* ("leveling out (of a thing)"), *raḥraḥ* ("wide and
> spread out").

In my defense, I never did say he could use me.

Soon after that trip to Jerusalem, we started walking together in the
evenings. At first Rami joined us, and then when Rami went back to
Bethlehem to deal with his divorce it was just me and Sal. Every
night we walked, and for hours; I walked myself to sleep, until I
could barely take another step. Just through the neighborhoods, in
circles. In Ramallah, as in other Palestinian cities, nothing is per-
pendicular. Walking, you are always confronted with hills: the land
comes up at you.

Look at this beautiful view of the sea, said Sal, gesturing from where we sat on our pile of rubble out at the piles of garbage ahead, trenched between the earth-colored high-rises. Half of them empty, ugly shells, black sky visible through the gaps in the concrete. It was a joke: every few days we put our trash in the Dumpster on the road, and then some guy came and tipped it between the buildings. What was the difference? I heard once there was trouble in al-Bireh, the trash was spilling in, there was no space—what was needed, perhaps, was to erect a wall. A wall between us and *it*.

murtadaḥ ("scope, freedom"), *rawḥ* ("breeze"), *tarakkuḥ* ("spaciousness"), *tasṭīḥ* ("roof laying"), *masfūḥ* ("spreading (of water)"), *masmaḥ* ("ample room") as in the saying "Keep thou to the truth, for it is ample room, i.e., space," *sāḥah* ("courtyard"), *insiyāḥ* ("bigness of belly"), *shudḥah* ("roominess"), *sharḥ* ("laying open").

"How come I tell you these things?" said Sal. We were sitting on the roof of the American Colony Hotel, having a beer. He had just given a talk to a group of Australian Jews about forgiveness, and I had spent my day with a historian in the Old City.

So there was this guy, a *really cute* guy, with a great *ass*, who was new in his cell.

"Where was he from?" I asked.

Sal's eyes widened. "Oh my gad," laughing, surprised, "he was from Nablus!" He slapped the table. "I can't believe it. *Wallah*, but he was soo cute, *wallah*, you won't believe. And it happened, *shway shway* yanni. I'm not gay, you know that, right?" And he laughed and ran a finger through his hair, and twizzled a curl at the base of his skull. His fingernails so yellow. "And then we slept in the same bed—you know we have these beds with two levels—"

"Bunk beds."

"—yes, and he was on the bottom and I was on the top. And then one night, he came up to my bed and—*yanni* we hid each other with the blanket, and we had a paper and he drew a picture . . . and . . . you know, like this." Laughter.

"And? What happened then?" I coaxed him.

He lit a cigarette. " *'An jad*, it's so weird, I never tell anybody this before. *Wallah*, you are so strange. How do I tell you this? It's like you . . . I don't know how it is. Anyway, well, so we drew these pictures, and *yanni* of course we touch each other in the bed," laughing, "and then . . . one day during the lunch hour—you know it's easy to touch each other and no one will notice in the night, but you can't fuck, *yanni*—so . . . one day during the lunch hour we went back inside—we had arranged, I said I had like a headache or something, and, in simple, we . . . you know, we fucked! But it was so—oh my gad it was like so much pressure, because the guard, of course—and if anybody saw us"—sharp intake of breath—"*Waw*, but it was really so hot." He laughed. "And I was . . . you know . . . I was the . . . you know it was his ass. And then afterward he wanted to . . . to me, you know, to be—we call it *luti*, I don't know how you say in English—but I couldn't. I just couldn't."

"Why?"

"*Yanni*, it's not me, I'm not gay." He sucked on his cigarette and smiled at me. Then he reached for my hand. "I can't believe I told you this. And you don't judge me. You are like no Palestinian girl I ever met."

Among <u>characteristic associations of the letter *d*</u> are softness, smoothness, and tenderness, as in the words *burakhdāh* ("a smooth, limp woman"), *tayd* ("kindness"), *tha'ad* ("soft, tender plants"), *tha'd* ("soft dates"), *mutham 'idd* ("clear-faced (of a boy)"), *muthamghidd* ("fatty (of a kid)"), *thawhad* ("fat and well formed (of an adolescent boy)"), *thahmad* ("large and fat"), *khabandāh* ("fat and full (of a woman)"), *khawd* ("young and well formed (of a girl)").

A sunny morning in Jaffa. The night before we had been at a party in Tel Aviv, a Hanukkah Thanksgiving with a group of left-wing American Jews (and still I was asked that age-old question, eternally on every mind: Can I ask? Do they—do they teach terrorism in the schools? *No*, sir, they don't teach hate, sir, they teach *life*, sir. And there's no need to teach hate) and were about to get the bus back to Jerusalem.

"What is this?" he asked me.

I hesitated. "It's an oral contraceptive," I said.

"What is that?"

"An oral contraceptive—you really don't know what that is?"

"Baby, I spent half my life in prison."

"Oh, you're kind of old looking for twenty."

"Quarter, whatever. What is an—oral . . . what?"

273

"It's hormones, it stops women from getting pregnant. You have to take it every day, even if you're not having sex."

"What? *Waw*, you take it *every day*? Sheesh. I'm glad I'm not a woman from—from England."

"Yes, I bet you are."

"And what's that?"

"That is Fluoxetine."

He twisted his open hand palm up, that voiceless, questioning gesture understood the Arab world over to mean what? how? why? what's going on? what's wrong with you?

"Have you heard of Prozac?"

"No. What is it?"

"Oh, Sal, let's talk about it another time. We need to get the bus."

"And what's this again?" He was teasing now, pointing at my eye.

"A contact lens."

"I remember. Contact lens. Will you show me?"

"No."

> *rakhwaddah* ("soft (of a woman)"), *rahādah* ("softness and pliancy"), *'ubrud* ("white and soft (of a girl)"), *furhud* ("plump and handsome (of an adolescent boy)"), *umlūd* ("soft and pliable"), *fulhūd* ("fat and comely (of a youth)"), *qurhud* ("smooth, fleshy, and soft"), *qishdah* ("clotted cream"), *ma'd* ("large and fat"), *murd* ("boys with downy upper lips but no beards"), *maghd* ("smooth and fleshy"), *malad* ("youthfulness, softness, and wobbliness"), and so on to the end of the rubric. To these may be added, under the heading of figurative usages, such words as *raghd* ("generous and kindly"), *sarhadah* ("ease of living"), *majd* ("glory, generosity"), and so on.

I decided to introduce Salih to my Israeli friend. Sal spoke Hebrew, and he met with Israelis all the time—of course he was unusual in that respect, but because of that I thought it would be easy. I wanted to break down some stereotypes for her, my Israeli friend. She used the word "terrorism" liberally and said things like "Oh—why can't our peoples just get along?"

But that day, Sal had spoken in the Knesset and he was exhausted. He started cracking jokes. My Israeli friend and her husband sat with their arms crossed, not touching their drinks. Oh—you say your parents are from Russia? he said. Yes! Bring all of the Russians!

Ahlan wa sahlan, empty Russia and bring them to Palestine.

> It may be that the ancient Arabs sought to bring a balance to certain letters or, in other words, took care to give the opposite meaning full play too, for the letter *d* also encompasses many words indicating hardness, strength, and force, as in *ta'addud* ("harshness"), *ta'kīd* ("asserting"), *ta'yīd* ("confirming"), *jal'ad* ("hard and strong"), *jalmad* ("a rock"), *jamad* ("ice"), *ḥadīd* ("iron"), *suḥdud* ("strong and rebellious"), *sukhdūd* ("a man of iron"), *samhad* ("a thing hard and dry"), *tashaddud* ("harshness, severity").

When I next saw my Israeli friend, she'd Googled Salih and changed her mind.

"He'll be a leader," she said. "It's amazing. I can't believe all that stuff about him reading Gandhi and Nelson Mandela in jail—and how he taught himself English and Hebrew! Incredible. Is that what they all do in the prisons?"

He told me about the isolation, the hunger strikes, the beatings, the gassing—the onions they sniffed to keep conscious for as long as possible while the guards gassed their cells.

"You must make sure you have no *cut* or whatever on your body," he said. He was describing the times they knew for sure they would be gassed—such as during hunger strikes, and on the Prophet's birthday. "Because if you have any cut at all, it's going to sting really, really bad."

"My sentence was fifteen years. You know it was actually a joke, me and this other guy, he was twenty years old, and we both got our ages! *Yanni*, and then I was let out five years early for good behavior."

"What was it like when you were released?" I asked him.

"It was like . . . my mind was buzzing. I went straight to the sea, and I stood there by the water. It was like this buzzing inside my head."

I looked at his black curls, seeing bees.

*

275

A great blizzard came, and we were stuck in his apartment. The electricity was out all over Ramallah. I wore three pairs of trousers and two coats, and jumped up and down. The gas canister was empty, the shops were closed, we could not even make hot drinks on the stove. A neighbor had given us a candle. *One for me and one for you!* he had said, holding the hand of his child so I would not be afraid of him. Sal and I sat beside the lit candle and laughed. Outside, the snow was thigh-deep.

Al-Shidyaq:

> When I thought about the matter and looked into it in depth, I started to doubt that snow could be created by an excess of cold formed in the air. I decided that, on the contrary, it may well, in fact, be caused by the creation by excessive heat of an irritated patch on the air's breast above the inhabitants of the Earth plus a superabundance of ire inside its guts.

The ice cut gorges in the tarmac roads. In daylight we trod slowly into town, holding each other for balance. Still, we walked.

Even before the thaw, the time came when my visa would expire. My plan was to leave via Jordan, and then reenter through the Negev border.

Sal began to worry that he would never see me again.

"I have this bad feeling. I don't know why."

Ibn Battuta writes:

> *I* THEN *passed on to Jerusalem, and on the road visited the tomb of Jonas, and Bethlehem the birth-place of Jesus. But, as to the mosque of Jerusalem, it is said that there is not a greater upon the face of the earth: and in sacredness, and privileges conferred, this place is the third. From Jerusalem, I paid a visit to Askelon, which was in ruins. In this place was the meshhed, famous for the head of Hosain, before it was removed to Egypt. Without Askelon is "the valley of bees," said to be that mentioned in the Koran. I next proceeded to El Ramlah, then to Naplous, then to Eglon.*

*

Sometimes, when Sal talked, I knew he was giving me a version of one of his speeches.

"I say—I come with the land. That's the way I see it. You want the land, you have me. I am like the olive trees."

> *From this place I proceeded to 'Acca: in this is the tomb of Salih the prophet, which I visited. After this I arrived at the city of Tyre, which is a place wonderfully strong, being surrounded on three sides by the sea. Its harbor is one of those which have been much celebrated.*

No, I wanted to say, you are not a tree.

> *I next visited Sidon, and from this place went into the parts of Tiberias, which it was my wish to see. The whole was, however, in ruins, but the magnitude of it was sufficient to shew that it had been a large place. The place is wonderfully hot, as are also its waters.*

I told my Israeli friend about Ibn Battuta. From North Africa, I told her. I mean, this was centuries and centuries ago.

"Maybe there's some Jewish in you," she said.

"Oh, I don't know about that. But, yeah, I guess it's possible."

The next time I came to Jerusalem, I took a bus to her neighborhood. We met at her house and went for a walk out along the old railroad track into Sheikh Jarrah. We talked about my family, about her family, her children, my parents.

"Didn't we decide you were Jewish?" she said.

Al-Shidyaq:

> When an ugly, misshapen (*shawhā'*) woman looks at her face in the mirror, she says, "I may be ugly and misshapen to some but to others I am handsome," which is why the author of the *Qāmūs* [dictionary] says, "*Shawhā'* means both 'a woman who frowns' and 'a beautiful woman'; a word with two opposite meanings." When a man with a big nose looks at that crag on his face, he says, "It may well be that some good-looking women will desire it and see in it no crookedness or curve."

*

I was gone for only two weeks. I took a shared taxi one morning from Ramallah through Jericho to the King Hussein Bridge. The snow on the ground thinned as we traveled down to the center of the earth, until it disappeared entirely in the rocky valleys by the Dead Sea. The passage out was easier than expected; I took a taxi to Amman, and then a plane to Aqaba. I stayed there for a weekend, swam in the sea. The hotel was walking distance from the Eilat checkpoint, and on the following Monday morning I took my suitcase and wheeled it over.

They kept me there for only a few hours waiting, while they "checked" my passport. *And what is your father's religion?*

Al-Shidyaq:

> We see the sun as though it had risen, when according to the scientists it hasn't yet done so, and we see a stick in water as though it were crooked, though "there is therein no crookedness." A mirage shows a person as though double and certain colors appear in two different forms. Magicians make observers think they are walking on water or going through fire without being burned. To a person in a ship plowing along opposite houses and property, the part of the land closest to him appears to be moving and mobile, when it is unmoving and fixed.

If I am honest, I will say I deceived myself about our differences. I wanted badly not to make him other than me. He thinks like a Westerner! Honest, intelligent, seeing through it all; we can roll our eyes together and smile at that nonsense one-upmanship, people as boastful about steadfastness as others are about praying. How many years was your son in prison? How many tears shed for the homeland? But it was lighthearted mockery. We too wept, of course. And still he was gracious and full of forgiveness.

So in a way I did him an injustice. Projecting as I did.

But he also, he wanted me to be like him.

("*Be human*," he would tell me, when I said goodbye).

Too many times, he had said, "You know I never had sex with any

278

woman since I met you? This is not fair. These women, I *have* them, *yanni*, in the *palm of my hand*. If I want it, I can have it. You know, I'm charismatic. This prison story, what can I say, it's sexy. But you know what? I can't do it. Not since I met you."

O Men of Peace, Messiahs holding women in their upturned palms. When you strip off the arrogance, what are you leaving behind?

Naively, I thought I could teach him what openness he *hadn't* learned in his prison of men. And of course there were other reasons. Loneliness, that was one of the reasons.

> *ṣafīḥah* ("slab of stone"), *ṣaldah* ("wide stone"), *iṣlinṭāḥ* ("widening out (of a valley)"), *muṣalfaḥ* ("large headed"), *ṭaḥḥ* ("spreading"), *mufalṭaḥ* ("large headed"), *fashḥ* ("standing astraddle"), *faṭḥ* ("broadening"), *falṭaḥah* ("flattening"), and so on to the end of that rubric. To these may be added numerous words whose connection to the idea of amplitude and expansiveness is not obvious and can be detected only with careful scrutiny, such as *sujāḥ* ("air"), *tasrīḥ* ("divorce"), *samāḥah* ("generosity"), and *sunḥ* ("good fortune and blessing").

In my determination to overlook differences of education, upbringing, expectation, social formation, I had overlooked other things.

"I never get what I want," he said.

It was the day I said (again) I couldn't see him anymore.

"I *never get what I want*."

I had never seen him so angry.

"Did I ever tell you how they arrested me?" he said, and he stared. I shook my head.

"They put handcuffs on us. And they put us in the back of this car, where you can hardly breathe, and it's completely dark. Then they drove us around a lot so that we wouldn't know where we were. So we were completely lost. And then they took us into the fucking prison." He kicked the wall. "And how did I survive? *In my imagination.* That's how it was. I'm not making it up. I was far away. I was in Haifa by the sea, I was in Jaffa. I was in fucking Switzerland, *yanni*."

*

279

Isabella Hammad

And Ibn Battuta writes in his *Rihla*:

> *I left Tangier, my birthplace, on Thursday, 2nd Rajab 725 [June 14, 1325], being at that time twenty-two years of age [22 lunar years; 21 and 4 months by solar reckoning], with the intention of making the Pilgrimage to the Holy House [at Mecca] and the Tomb of the Prophet [at Medina].*

He did say he had learned some things from me. And I did learn from him.

> *I set out alone, finding no companion to cheer the way with friendly intercourse, and no party of travelers with whom to associate myself. Swayed by an overmastering impulse within me, and a long-cherished desire to visit those glorious sanctuaries, I resolved to quit all my friends and tear myself away from my home. As my parents were still alive, it weighed grievously upon me to part from them, and both they and I were afflicted with sorrow.*

NOTES.

Ibn Battuta, *The Travels of Ibn Battuta* (1355), trans. Samuel Lee (London: Oriental Translation Committee, 1829).

Shidyaq, Ahmad Faris al-, *Leg Over Leg : Volume One* (1855), ed. and trans. Humphrey Davies (New York and London: New York University Press, 2013).

The Spinal Descent
Tim Horvath

AS FAR AS LEONARD DAHL WAS CONCERNED, only Johannes Nachbor in his generation had been his equal, not to mention the only human being who'd been as loyal to him as the chills. He'd never taken a public shot at Nachbor, even as his friend began to do some of the very things he abhorred. Writing music for television shows. For a chain of waffle dives, the waffles flapping and grinning like giant mouths. For a period of time a few years after they'd graduated, Nachbor was *everywhere*. Leonard couldn't avoid his music—he'd flip on the radio and there would be the unmistakable strains, or he'd be watching some TV show and grow suspicious, and he'd force himself to scrutinize the credits, more often than not catching the tiny name as it flew by. That same name was so reliably on the Tanglewood program that he might as well have been some elite donor. On one occasion he and his dad were in the bleachers at Shea watching the Mets clobber the Cubs, and his dad, several beers in, was hugging him, which was embarrassing, but who was he to turn away such affection? And then, blaring from the speakers, came something decidedly Nachborean, and he stiffened and froze, nearly paralyzed, looking up as though he could see the music in midair, a plume wafting over Flushing. If Dahl could've penned a single musical instruction across Nachbor's work in italics, it would've been *Etcetera*—he seemed to have bottomless reserves. It was around this time that there was a painter in Soho who was reputed to hire others to do his paintings, and Leonard pictured a giant loft full of Nachbor's minions, awaiting instructions and then going off into their own corners to compose under his name. He wondered when he'd be able to go to the movies again, could board a plane without hearing the song that the airline had decided you should listen to while you were waiting on the runway for takeoff, a soothing piece that would stave off thoughts of an inferno of twisted metal and made it feel like the plane had started to rise, was already soaring. For this piece too was unmistakably Nachbor's, and if it wasn't, it was so blatantly influenced by him that that was almost worse. You'd overcome your fear of flight with this

281

transcendent music, and you'd know something too of what dying might be like, he thought, shedding your body, the soul unburdened at last. He plugged his ears and waited for cruising altitude and shitty wine and the oblivion of the plane's neutral gray hum.

Whoever'd decided to put them together in the same dorm room their freshman year, they determined right away, was either a genius who wanted to push them, neck and neck, to greater and greater feats, or else some sick prankster. Their room was a study in contrasts, Dahl's shit everywhere, while Nachbor's side could've almost passed for unoccupied. Nachbor would sit there composing at his desk in his neat, calligraphic hand, while Dahl would scrawl like a graffiti artist on any available surface—a carton of Cinnamon Pop Tarts or the wall itself. Nachbor actually made use of his closet for clothes. Hanging in that closet were all of the T-shirts from all of the music camps that he'd gone to—the North Country Harmony Camp, Interlochen, while Dahl was working summer jobs, moving corn dogs on the boardwalk at Coney Island and swabbing out instruments at a repair shop, the squeak of his rag in the belly of a horn till he could see his own zits reflected in it. Sometimes when Nachbor was in class, Dahl would open his closet and flip through those T-shirts—the Bach Festival with its chirping chickens, musical notes spelling out the name of the camp, and try them on like they were Brooks Brothers suits, carefully returning them to their hangers and hoping Nachbor wouldn't suspect a thing.

So diligently had they abided over the decades by the ironclad rule that they'd established for themselves in their first year together as roommates at the University of Hartford that they might as well have been shaggy, sheepish freshmen well into their forties, Dahl down to a single zit but still his deep-set eyes—he still imagined one as blackened from a childhood fight, though of course it had faded in the weeks after he'd gotten it. *And in this corner, Jo-hannes Nach-bor, doing everything he can to cover up the fact that he was raised in the posh-er parts of Stam-ford, Con-neC-ticut!* "Middle C," Dahl called him, part reference to the letter in the middle of his home state, part jab. The rule was this: they could talk about anything, absolutely anything under the sun, except music. The rule came about in the glimmer of a morning light during their second semester as roomies. They were staying up till dawn, arguing some arcane point without resolution—whether Webern owed more to Zemlinsky or to Schoenberg, or who was more *radically revolutionary*, Ligeti or Xenakis, or whether Stravinksy had not just lost his mojo but misplaced his ever-loving mind somewhere in the Swiss Alps during World War I, somewhere between the ambush of *The Rite of Spring* (how could it not have single-handedly won the war?) and the fussless, yawn-worthy *Pulcinella*, indistinguishable from a hundred other ballets. To an outside observer, they were just splitting hairs, goading each other on. That's what Maudsley would've said, a premed getting in his last bong hits while he still could, pounding on their walls in the dead of night, nary a sense of rhythm, as Dahl pointed out while pounding back in gradually shifting time signatures, which in turn caused Nachbor to guffaw as soon as he figured out what Dahl was up to. Maudsley's mean, heavily capillaried face in their doorway was enough to get them to knock it off, but not enough to keep Nachbor off academic probation, since he was sleeping through the nine thirty German class that his parents were making him take. He was supposed to be getting to know his roots. To justify it to himself, he'd claimed it was bringing him closer to Beethoven and Stockhausen, but at that hour he was more likely dreaming about them than learning their tongue.

If music was verboten, what else was there? Plenty of other fertile topics: June Finchner, Letitia Jablowsky, and Midge Archibald, among others, whether they were sleeping with classmates or professors, and professors themselves, but only about their beards, their blazers, and slumgullions of sweat, their crazed mannerisms, not their music. Later, when Nachbor went all Jesus-y for a while—his girlfriend's father was a minister, and he'd gone to her house over one vacation and come back brimming with the holy spirit—they'd talked about God. And once they'd graduated, when the meetings began to spread further and further apart, they caught one another up as best they could. They spoke of shitty jobs and first apartments and bodegas that were fronts for brothels; they spoke of sexual exploits and conquests and the relationship between pain and pleasure and pretentious artists and neo-hippies and road trips and movies—no, film—my God did they talk about *film*. They talked about shady landlords and academia and being outside academia and they used code words like *uptown* and *downtown*, and they talked about minimalists but only the painters and architects. Someone might have said that they were speaking of nothing but music. Occasionally one of them slipped and mentioned something—a commission he was hoping to get, a run-in with a famous musician who didn't give you the time of day—and they'd enter warily into the forbidden zone, their voices dropping a little bit as if to acknowledge that they'd crossed some border and now could be shot at on sight. But one of them would say, "The rule." And the other would respond, either in kind or "Fugga the rule." "Fugga the rule" usually led to verbal fisticuffs. They couldn't go far into any conversation without getting hung up on something or falling back into some conversation that they'd already had and agreed to disagree on years earlier. "This isn't even hairsplitting," Dahl said once. "It's splitting split ends."

"It's splitting atoms," Johannes shot back, his mouth approximating an explosion, his hands a billowing mushroom cloud.

It was easier, for them at least, to talk about God or the Middle East or the value and scourge of capitalism than about a single C-major chord, *simpliciter*; that they concurred on. They did the dance of visiting one another in various cities—Nachbor moved to San Francisco, where he met Lindsay, and then, as a couple, relocated, first to Portland, then back east to the Berkshires to be closer to their families.

Meanwhile, Dahl had never really left New York, though pinballing from the East Village to Nolita, Williamsburg to Greenpoint. With the exception of when he was out of town at a residency, he still strolled into his parents' walk-up Friday night for dinner, his mother's cooking surrounding him like some kind of salve after a week of the city's flagellations. The city, after all, took its toll on him. It gave and took away, always. Nothing was easy in or about it.

Occasionally they flouted the rule and always seemed to regret it. A few years after they'd graduated, Nachbor flew into New York to see him. They began drinking early in the evening while Dahl heated up some pierogi he'd picked up at a local Polish dive. After a few shots of cheap vodka, Nachbor brought up one of their contemporaries who had just started to achieve widespread acclaim, the kind that comes with a glossy spread in *The New York Times Magazine* sandwiched between an article about a golfer and another about artichoke dip. The guy was, Dahl was certain, a fraud, yet Nachbor somehow had been duped with all the others, fallen under his spell. "Were you high? When you first listened, I mean. Just tell me, I won't judge. If I sense a pattern, we'll revisit."

"No more high than you are now," Nachbor scoffed.

"I'm pretty fucking high right now," said Dahl. "I might smoke some pot just to come down a little."

"You really oughtn't dismiss it so a priori. *Maudsley*." This invocation of their old neighbor, still a running joke after all these years, was considered a low blow.

"'So a priori.' Listen to you. Save the dirty talk for your wife, OK?"

Then, after a moment, "Where do you think Maudsley is right now?" Dahl looked to the wall, as if he might be right there. "Is he practicing delicate surgery right now or lying in some gutter?"

"Seriously, will you suspend your cynicism for thirty seconds and give it a listen?"

"Are you proposing we make a Tower run?" asked Dahl. He motioned toward his stove, where pierogi were starting their boil, their scent holding their own in the general mustiness of Dahl's apartment. Nachbor's stomach groaned around a G, Dahl's started at A and curled into a chromatic half scale.

It happened that they knew the DJ who would be coming on at six. Neither of them liked him much, but that was no matter—he had, at his disposal, not only a record collection and the means to diffuse music throughout the entire city, but the record in question.

Nachbor got on the phone—it pained Dahl, the idea of giving this whippersnapper, this hype-ridden, derivative upstart, any recognition whatsoever, much less free airplay. The fact was, though, that since *The Times* article had come out, the station probably would've played him anyway.

"Hey, Richard," said Nachbor into the phone, "Johannes Nachbor here. Listening to you as always on a Thursday night. Sure, I'll hold." He covered the mouthpiece and said to Dahl, "He's busy. Says he's working or something. Something neither of us would know about, right?" The joke was that Dahl would be able to live off the proceeds from his Sousa number and that Nachbor had a sugar mama in his then-still-girlfriend Lindsay. A few minutes later, Nachbor announced, "He says he'll play it."

Dahl messed around on a few instruments, but the occasion seemed to call for the trumpet. He clicked open the case and screwed on the mouthpiece like an executioner readying himself for the task at hand. They sat there for a solid half hour playing Name That Tune until they were shaking drops out of the vodka bottle, and at last the station played something Dahl didn't recognize. Nachbor's face took on a knowing look, and Dahl, who'd insisted he'd be able to hear it with an open mind, waited a full two and a half minutes before hoisting the mouthpiece to his lips and forming an embouchure that, while not professional, was pretty good for someone who played only for his own ears. And then he began blowing the bejeezus out of it, cheeks flaring like Gillespie's, like a blowfish puffing itself up to fend off a shark. Nachbor was folded on the divan that, like most of Dahl's furniture, had been salvaged from the sidewalk, and he grew tighter and more involuted as the piece went on, Dahl's embellishments getting more and more outrageous, and then, suddenly, he yanked the cord out of the socket as if simply hitting "off" wouldn't be decisive enough, and Dahl was laughing, reaching for the cord like a dog off the leash. Nachbor grabbed too, and the trumpet came clanging to the floorboards with a dull crash.

"Fine, you fucking win," said Nachbor. "Why don't you call back and play along over the phone, so that all of New York can hear you? Better yet, go marching down to the studio with your fucking sousaphone. Where's your phone book?" He began picking up objects—books and unopened packages and filthy dishes—with exaggerated motions.

Lowering the instrument, Dahl laughed, thinking he'd done Nachbor a turn, that his friend was giving him a hard time because of their rule. This was the raison d'être of their little rule—to talk about music, well, bad enough, but to actually *play* it—well, that's a rabbi at a rib roast right there. But full minutes of this went by, Nachbor's jaw still clenched, unyielding. And at last he broke his silence. "That was the wrong piece. He misunderstood. Or did me a solid." The piece had been, Nachbor explained, Nachbor's own, released on a compilation by a small label alongside a handful of other contemporary American composers, all far more prominent than Nachbor, who packed quickly, perfunctorily, refusing apologies. Apologies from Dahl! Would that anyone in the world could have borne witness to this! Like a Sasquatch sighting.

After that, two years went whooshing by before Nachbor returned Dahl's phone call. No apology was ever granted, but if before that they'd sidestepped music like some shaky grating over the subway, afterward they avoided it as if they'd known someone who'd gone plummeting through one.

For longer than he'd care to remember, Dahl had lived from semester to semester, floating from residency to residency, landing artist-in-res gigs at colleges and weird high schools where he tucked away his misanthropy like a mild deformity and put on a happy face that convinced principals and music teachers and only the occasional student saw through it (but they still wanted to hear about the *March of the Cyclone*). In between he'd sniffed bowling shoes and loaded medical waste onto trucks, nervous for his hands lest a hypodermic come spearing through the bag. He'd apprenticed to a typesetter and answered phones for an architect. Every one of these odd jobs, every mundane thing he did, entered the bloodstream of his work, but mostly it allowed him to compose on company time, and he'd savored the whiff of incognito, a spy right under their noses. All the while, his parents kept the same lock on his childhood house, so he always had that to go back to. And then one day the locks were different—they were scaling back, headed south to North Carolina, warmer climes and more space, and they wanted rent, no more olly olly oxen free. He'd have to bank on fellowships. Someplace cold, where he could sit amidst the chills and maybe knock them out of his system, like some form of homeopathy. The envelope from McMurdo was distressingly thin, yet he felt relief, having had this image of his ass freezing to a sheet of ice while spooning watery fish soup into his mouth, the legendary *hoosh* he'd read about, a word he repeated aloud like a mantra, hoping he could trick it into a tune. Iceland, God bless their ethereal, elf-positive selves, took him. It would be his first gig since the accident. As the plane made its descent toward Reykjavik it felt as though someone had squinched gauze into one of his ears and was tugging it slowly out the other. This had happened to him after flights before, and it always went away, but on top of the chills, it would make life nearly unbearable.

He'd stepped off the plane and taken a cab into the heart of the city, where it felt like someone had wrapped his head in a plaster cast, and he'd barely been able to communicate with the driver, in spite of the guy's insistence that he spoke English. For the next couple of weeks, he made do, strolling up and down the wide streets, past the gray, red-roofed houses, tilting his head and muttering to himself and trying to convince himself his hearing wasn't permanently hampered. He sought out *brennivín* and shark meat in hopes that they'd jolt him back into the land of sound and maybe take out the chills as a convenient side effect. He underdressed severely, thinking maybe frostbite would issue his body an ultimatum: *Plan on keeping those fingers? Toe for a toe, both of them yours?* He found a composer who made instruments out of ice and who let him try out the frozen versions of the xylophone and trumpet. All was going well until the composer left the room to make them some tea, and Dahl, staring at the xylophone, the icy bars of its keys so perfectly aligned and spaced out, got the nearly uncontainable urge to climb upon it and lie down with his back against it. He was shaking—whether more out of terror that the thing would collapse beneath his weight or out of sheer cold was impossible to say—but he managed to get his butt

287

down and was about to lower his spine when the composer came back in sooner than he'd expected, horror in his eyes as though he'd come upon Dahl and his own wife in flagrante delicto, and—this was perhaps worse—Dahl's pleas that he might explain himself or that he'd pay for whatever damage he might have done, anything, anything to stay longer and keep discoursing, all falling flat. As he was racing out, chased by doorslam and what he surmised must be Icelandic curses, he wondered at the strangeness of his urge. Surely he could have just lain down on any old sheet of ice, any frozen patch. And yet something about the instrument, its painstakingly sculpted anatomy and pellucid overtones, had set off in him this aurora of momentary insanity. The rest of the trip was nondescript. Gradually, his hearing came back, but the chills refused to abate, and after another week of this he was heading home, citing medical complications that required he be a single Metro-card swipe from an orthopedic spine specialist, load of manure though this was.

North Carolina was the next nonstarter for him. The countryside his parents had moved to seemed to consist of one pig farm after another. Why couldn't they have gone to Florida? "You get used to it in a few days," his mother assured him.

You get to be happy as pigs in shit! is what he wanted to say.

They sounded happy, though, and he wanted to visit, but knew that even if he got used to it, the smell would be no less there: porcine fecal molecules—in the air, in your hair. Then he got something in the mail from his old alma mater—not the usual flier asking for money, but a pamphlet about his legacy, about preparing his will, and did he maybe want to think about the Hartford School of Music while he was doing so? He thought of Nachbor—at some point every day, Nachbor strolled through his mind, but this time he had a more specific image, of him tearing open the same envelope. He didn't know what Nachbor's bank account looked like, but given all of his successes, not to mention that he'd come from money, he figured not too shabby. Nachbor was the alumnus who such fliers were aimed at. He envisioned a concert hall with Nachbor's name on it, the acoustics peerless, the seats sublimely comfortable. The last thing he wanted to do was to ask *him* for help, but he felt like he was down to his last out, and maybe the bulletin was a sign, and he got on the horn. As it were.

Johannes, for his part, sounded delighted to hear from him.

"Did you get it yet?" Dahl asked.

"Did I get it?" Nachbor wondered. "Don't tell me you've sent me a recording, Leonard?" But he sounded, if anything, enthusiastic, or at least relieved, as if he had the inside track on Leonard's woes.

"*I* didn't send you anything, but our illustrious alma mater did. Let's just say that we're moving up in the reunion parade, getting closer to the dodderers and the ones who require someone to push them and have IVs in their arms. A few steps closer to the grave."

"I'm looking right now," Nachbor said. "Yes. Yes! I see what you're talking about. This is great! Don't tell me they've hired you to try to squeeze a few more dollars out of me. I give, I gave!"

"How about old Maudsley? Is anything left over after his monthly dubage order has been placed?"

Nachbor laughed. "What the hell are you doing these days?"

And Dahl explained that he was between places, between jobs, between relationships. Lots of betweens. He almost made a joke about microtones, which fell in the murky cracks between the ones generally recognized in Western music, the notes he'd gotten infatuated with in the second semester of his freshman year of college— the dark matter that dominated the universe, that lurked between pinprick stars. But the prohibition kicked in. He was like some Orthodox Jew who kept finding himself within sniffing distance of pork, tempted again and again, but always holding off.

He was more than welcome at their place, Nachbor said. At first, he offered Dahl the run of his house in the Berkshires, since they were going on their annual vacation. Did he remember Lindsay, his wife's, lake house in central Maine that they'd been fixing up for years? It was an eco-friendly place now, and only getting eco-friendlier. He could even dogsit, though on second thought Ralphie loved the lake. The idea of Nachbor's empty house seemed promising at first, but he saw himself naked and lonely in palatial sprawl in East Crunchboro, Massachusetts. There would be too much light and not even a dog to commiserate with. It felt like a vast chasm opening up in the earth, like the Antarctic ice sheet itself. Thankfully, Johannes went on. There wasn't a lot of extra sleeping room *in* the house, not with all of them there, but they did have an old Shasta camper, the giant tin can Lindsay had rattled around in for family vacations as a kid, now sitting in the driveway with Dahl's name on it.

"Lindsay makes me sleep in there anytime I screw up badly enough," Johannes said. "But, really, it's perfectly habitable. I'll be a little envious."

"Anytime you need to crash," said Leonard. "*Mi* Shasta *es su casa.*" The chuckle that came through the earpiece then must've traveled thirty-two years to arrive, and they could have been eighteen again, the Shasta just one more ridiculous sideshow, and somewhere beyond it the world waiting—biding its time, still patient, then—for whatever was roiling within them.

Need

Roberta Allen

AT EVERY PARTY ON SATURDAY night, the way she smiles, first at me, then at the Dutchman, you'd think we were lovebirds, a foot from the altar, honeymoon-bound. I see that smile whenever she mentions him—which is often, especially when she's in the car driving me on errands. Over and over, I've told her and other partygoers in this artsy upstate town that my relationship with the Dutchman is noncommittal, but they just don't seem to get it. Whenever her white-haired husband sees me alone, he asks, "Where's your guy?" I shrug and say, "I don't keep tabs on him." I remind him that the Dutchman I am dating stays with me only three days a week. The other days he's at home in the city. I could be prowling the weekend flea market in town, walking down Main Street, or looking in the bookshop window, which I was doing this morning, when he asks me for the umpteenth time.

Later, I run into the woman in the local health-food store whose spine is unusually curved. She says with a knowing smile, her voice full of innuendo, "How's your boyfriend?"

"Fine," I reply, my voice flat, as I recall her saying to him at a party: *I know you'd like to do me.*

These older, well-heeled partygoers, mostly from the city, smoke so much marijuana it must impair their thinking. Or else they're too old to remember open relationships, even though they once were hippies, like the aging, long-haired dropouts who congregate at the village square. Sleeping around is not something he and I do. In fact, we've been faithful ever since we met. At least, that's what we tell each other.

The wife of the white-haired man is unhappy, but she doesn't admit it. She and her husband still have sex once a month, she has said. I don't talk about my sex life. Nevertheless, she has often told me that regular sex has made my hair grow thicker. Once, I actually ran my fingers through my hair.

Why spoil her fantasies or the fantasies of other partygoers who spend time and energy wondering, or gossiping about, the sex they imagine other people are having, or not having, or about the sex they wish they were having, especially with the Dutchman. He is handsome and youthful despite his years. Who can blame them for flirting with him at Saturday night parties, given the scarcity of available older men without paunches draped over their pants and hairs sprouting like weeds from nostrils and ears. Like teenagers at synagogue dances, women dance with women at parties to Led Zeppelin, the Who, the Stones, and men stand on the sidelines and watch until booze, or pot, or both, give them courage enough to make their moves.

In summer, on Friday nights like this one, when local bands play sixties rock at a dance club in a nearby town, I miss the Dutchman. I grow tired of dancing with the same women, week after week, especially with the one who has an unusually curved spine, and shimmies on all fours when she's drunk enough. After plenty of booze, partygoers repair to the club gazebo, outside in back, to smoke marijuana. I follow after them.

What else can I do?

I depend on the party crowd. They fill in for the wife of the white-haired man when she's too busy to drive me. Without them, I am stuck in town, watching petunias grow on my porch.

I pray that I pass my driving test soon!

The gazebo is clogged with smoke when the club owner's wife, a judge, walks by, and looks the other way. None of the partygoers who drive me home from weekend soirees, often drunk, or impaired by drugs, or both, have ever been fined, or prosecuted, or had a license suspended or revoked—as far as I know.

Seated across from me in the gazebo, the stoned psychiatrist from the Bronx, nicknamed *The Receptacle* by those who follow her sexual escapades, stares at me with glazed eyes. "Whatsamatter you don' like me?" I recall how she tried to entice the Dutchman at a party by grinding the air in front of him, in time to the music, while he and I sat quietly talking. How annoyed he was by her interruption. She was too stoned to notice.

Driving me to the gym last week, the widowed redhead, desperate to find a husband, said, "I would never date a man as flirtatious as your guy." Why didn't I tell her his flirtations mean nothing?

The wife of the white-haired man has told me over and over how unhappy I was before I met the Dutchman.

Unhappy? I asked her. "Did you see something in me that made you say that? Something in my face? My voice? The way I carried myself?"

Her answer is always vague: "I could just tell."

Is it possible I *am* happier? Hasn't my relationship with the Dutchman made me less dependent on the party crowd? When he's here, he drives me in my Cabriolet convertible, the car I naively purchased before understanding how difficult driving would be for a woman my age. I am almost ready to take my test again.

When I pass, will I still need the Dutchman?

Will the wife of the white-haired man still tell herself she is better off married when she sees me driving wherever I please? How much safer it is for her to complain about his short-term memory loss, and how she has to run his bed & breakfast, curb his spending on collectibles, handle investments, pay bills, do household chores, prepare meals, entertain his ex-wife and their married children and grandchildren, and even entertain an ex-girlfriend, besides hosting parties on weekends for the local crowd. Even her cancer didn't stop him from depending on her. "No time out for cancer!" was her frequent refrain.

Nevertheless, she recovered.

This last time the wife of the white-haired man went on about how unhappy I had been, I changed the subject by telling her about the kids who continued eating ice-cream cones when their mother lost control of the car and crashed into a ditch, a story my driving teacher told me. I doubt she heard a word I said.

I've told her many times I don't want to be any man's wife, certainly not the Dutchman's wife. He has never married; he has lived alone all his life. Every so often, he talks about wanting to fall madly in love, something unknown to him. I hate to admit it, but sometimes I catch myself wishing we were Bill Holden and Jennifer Jones, picnicking under a large shade tree, in *Love Is a Many-Splendored Thing*.

Is there a picnic scene?

One night after a party, I was ready to call it quits. But he begged me not to end it. He had smoked pot like everyone else but me. All evening he had chased a beautiful blonde realtor from room to room. Her disinterest made him more persistent. "You better watch that man!" drawled a pretty southern transplant. Later, she would leave her boyfriend because he'd flirted with the same blonde.

Raucous laughter in the gazebo doesn't stop me thinking about the blonde realtor. Maybe she changed her mind. Maybe she's entertaining him now in her Chelsea loft. Another blonde comes to mind, a famous female artist I ran into with the Dutchman in the city. After learning that he lived in Soho, the artist looked up at him with big blue eyes and innocently, or maybe not, asked if he ever visited me upstate. He said he'd stayed with me several times. I wanted to say that if several times meant three days a week for nearly six months, then several times was correct, but I let it slide, said nothing.

In the gazebo, I let the white-haired husband interrupt my thoughts. In a loud, raspy voice, he is telling a story everyone but me is too stoned to remember hearing a thousand times before about a woman he dated forty-five years ago, who ended the relationship after telling him he would never make any money. "She's the one who spurred me on!" he says, laughing, phlegm catching in his throat. "She's the reason I became so successful. I found her on the Internet recently and told her so. But," he says, hysterical, barely able to get the words out, "she didn't remember who I was!" He doubles over in laughter. The others laugh hysterically too—except for his wife, whose smile is pasted on her face.

This night is going to be a long one.

I glance at couples talking and drinking quietly at outdoor tables nearby.

Goodbye, Mister Starfish
M. J. Rey

"THEY SAY THE MOST UNFREE souls go west. It's true, ya know, about the West; it's part of 'em—like a blood knowledge."

Tony paused for a moment, carefully stepped over a small tide pool, and then straddled the next, much larger one. With his left boot heel submerged and his right wedged into the exposed reef he stood straight up and scanned the horizon, and then the coastline. About fifty yards down the shore he could see Magdalena following Cosma, who had curled his little torso over another pool. It was difficult to tell from this distance, but it looked like the boy was gently poking a sea anemone and watching it shrivel.

"I remember when I first saw this beach, and these cliffs," and then Tony nodded toward the long breakwater and the large cranes that stood several miles away. "I remember when I saw the Port of Los Angeles too. I almost went to work in the tanker trade, ya know; this place was too barbaric for me, too many dead and unfree souls."

"You used to tell us this story when Francis and I were kids," Marina said. She was holding her dress up while she followed Tony across the exposed reef.

"I did? God, Rinka, it's been so long."

Tony smiled and then lunged across a small channel, where he nearly lost his balance; at low tide, thin skeins of water, which glistened like fat,covered the smoother rocks, but Tony's bad eyes had not noticed; he was also thinking about the stories he used to tell Marina, all those years ago.

When they were children, Marina and her brother, Francis,were Tony and Magdalena's neighbors, and even though Francis still lived next door, before today neither Tony nor his wife had seen Marina in twenty years. Stranger still, when Marina had knocked on their door not one hour ago and told them that she had just returned home, and that Francis had sent her to collect Cosma, who was his son but the old couple's near ward, both Tony and Magdalena seemed unsurprised to see her. And when Cosma told his "auntie Rinka" that he wanted to see the tide pools first,the four set out together, walking the half dozen blocks to the cliffs and then taking the easier, but longer, shore-bound trail. Minutes later they were picking up seashells, finding starfish for Cosma, and speaking in the casually disinterested tones of old friends. But that was their way, especially Tony's.

Tony was a seventy-year-old but still tall, still agile, and still broad-shouldered man from Picuris Pueblo, a small reservation in New Mexico's Sangre de Cristo Mountains. Tony had always enjoyed telling little Marina that when he was born his parents had not named him Tony but had given him a Tiwa-language name, and he would try to teach her the long word. *Pie-ate-see-oo-uh-ah-la*, he would say, exaggerating each syllable,but neither Marina nor Francis, nor even Magdalena, could ever pronounce it, and he would laugh good naturedly and then tell the children another Picuris folktale. He also used to tell them that his Tiwa name meant *Deer Yellow Willows*, but Tony would say this with a wry smile, as if *Deer Yellow Willows* was really not his name but something he had heard in a bad spaghetti western.

Marina only knew for sure that Tony had also been baptized at the Pueblo's modest adobe church, where a priest gave him his second, Spanish Catholic name—Antonio Archuleta—and that Tony thereafter moved through the world straddling two identities, just as he now straddled the rocks and the water as if he were the Colossus of Rhodes. *Straddling*, in fact, had become Tony's primary method for navigating life.

Marina watched his deft movements across the rocks. Tony's litheness betrayed his age and she was shocked by how similar he had looked when she was a child, only back then he was even taller, and even more broad shouldered. Tony's legs were thick and he always kept a wide stance, but he had curiously narrow hips that cinched in his waist so that he looked, at least in silhouette, like a living, breathing, sheaf of wheat. His preferred outfit had remained the same too: cracked-leather cowboy boots with thin arabesques stitched into the vamps, blue jeans, a long-sleeved flannel shirt, and sometimes a bolo tie, or sometimes a cowboy hat, but usually neither.

Nothing's changed, Marina thought, and she watched Tony's body turn black with shadow when he walked between her and the setting sun. Only his face, which was now beset with deep wrinkles, seemed to show his age, and his eyes, which were now a little duller and a little more sunken, and his long, beautiful hair, which had turned from a sable black to a heather gray.

"When was the last time you were here?" Tony said while inspecting another pool; he felt no need to lift his gaze.

"Thirty years, at least. Not since I left for the convent."

"It's beautiful, isn't it?"

Tony, loquacious but famously deferential, didn't press the issue. He knew that his former babysitting charge had joined a convent when she was eighteen to escape some great trauma—the rumors told of an unplanned, and later lost, pregnancy—but when Tony had opened the door this afternoon and saw her standing there, looking aged and wan but wide smiled, and wearing a strange sundress and jean jacket, he knew all that he needed to know. Once, he had loved this woman like a daughter, and all that mattered now was that she looked happy, which made him happy.

"It's stunning," Marina said, "but, more than anything, I forgot the sound."

Marina turned her ear to the ocean and listened to the water's rhythmic pulse; gently, but steadily, sets of waves reached the half-submerged rocks and reef. First they pounded, and then they effervesced, and then she heard the clicking of pebbles as each receding wave dragged some stones offshore. Looking down the shoreline, Marina saw Magdalena corralling Cosma, who had wandered off, and behind them she saw a brace of crows playing midair. They were darting, charging, and tumbling at one another, but the two birds mostly ignored a large flock of seagulls sunning below them, who glanced annoyedly upward like overtired parents.

Marina smiled. She'd forgotten how much she loved bird-watching, but watching these particular birds, less than a mile from her childhood home, soon made Marina think about her brother, who was not an avid bird-watcher but was obsessed with the mythical phoenix, which he had taken as his unofficial emblem, and this thought then triggered a new thought about Francis's wife, Norah, who always ridiculed and embarrassed Francis for this childlike fascination, and soon Marina's smile vanished, although she continued to watch the flock.

There were several dozen, pure-white seagulls, and apart from their occasional upward glances they were motionless, like so many teacups scattered on the ground, and Marina then realized, as she had periodically throughout the day, that she felt happier and freer and, strangely, closer to God, than she could ever remember feeling at the convent. She watched her little teacups and she listened to the raspy barks from a sea-lion rookery one cove over, and then she heard Tony's voice suddenly bellow.

"Cosma," he yelled, "starfish!" and Tony raised one hand from a pool and presented a spindly, squirming, bright orange creature.

Cosma, who was now walking hand in hand with somber Magdalena, broke free and began to run toward Tony, but he stopped almost as soon as he began. The seagulls had caught his eye, and he redirected his course and charged at them as fast as his six-year-old body would allow. The birds watched this little, brazen thing bear down upon them, and then, in perfect unison, they exploded off their orange webbed feet and let the updraft along the cliffs carry them skyward. Cosma, maintaining his youthful impetuousness, then turned around and continued sprinting toward Tony, as if his half-crazed detour were the most natural thing ever, almost perfunctory.

They gathered around the strange life and Tony handed it to Cosma.

"Careful now—you be very careful with it. Don't hold it too tightly—pretend like you're holding an egg."

The young boy sat mesmerized and Marina watched Cosma's strangely mannish way. His patient gestures and his outsized pride, even his coarse platinum hair, which stood heaped upon his head as if it were a rick of straw, seemed unusually refined. And while Cosma studied the starfish and Marina studied Cosma, Tony studied Marina, and in the raking evening light he finally saw just how much she too had aged. Strangely, Tony ultimately perceived Marina as Marina had perceived him, which is to say that while Marina's cloistered life had paled her Balkan skin, and networks of faint wrinkles had recorded the years, Tony still saw the little girl who he, so many years ago, had helped raise.

Tony also noticed that Marina's knees were still shapely, and her ankles too. In fact, all of Marina's most prominent bones still appeared effortlessly feminine—the cleft of her jaw, the ridge of her brow, the back of her wrist. Tony almost gasped when Marina grabbed something atop her head—a rubber band, he thought—and her hair tumbled out. *Rinka's back*, he thought.

It was only Magdalena who, unlike the others, had gracelessly entered old age. Her frame had always carried a little extra weight, but a sedentary lifestyle had not been kind. Her face was red and blustery now, like an alcoholic's, and she looked wholly uncomfortable on the rocky beach. Magdalena's manner was strangely noncommittal, but those who knew her well knew that she possessed one extraordinary gift: a near-limitless capacity for patience and love. Magdalena often struggled to express or harness this patience and love, but the capacity stood latent inside her. She, for instance, had a completely well meaning but slightly overbearing manner with little Cosma, as she once had had with little Marina. Magdalena was, in fact, now kneeling next to Cosma, who was holding the starfish six inches from his face.

"Why don't you show Auntie Rinka what you learned today, Cosi? I'm sure she'd love to see."

Tony, assuming that Marina must be lost, leaned over and whispered, "Every time we watch Cosma, Magdalena teaches him a poem," and then Tony laughed quietly. "The boy is very . . . *obliging* . . . with her. It's sweet."

Meanwhile Magdalena had continued her prodding.

"Come now, Cosi—show your Auntie Rinka what we've learned."

"Maggie!" Tony laughed. "Leave him alone—he's having fun!"

"I—I don't remember it," Cosma pasted in.

His eyes had not once left the creature. Its rough skin tickled his own as it slowly writhed around his hand.

"Come on, Cosi—we practiced all afternoon."

The boy sighed. Cosma, as young as he was, perfectly understood Magdalena's nature. She loved him, and he loved her, and he also knew it was useless to object. Cosma looked at Tony and offered him the starfish, but his gesture, almost quixotic, was one of intense solemnity and respect, as if he were returning a crown to a regent.

"That doesn't belong to me," Tony said. "Go put him back in that pool over there. That's his home."

Cosma dutifully crouched beside the chosen pool and slipped the bony star beneath the water, and then, again with great solemnity, he stood straight up and addressed the horizon.

"Goodbye, mister starfish," he said, *"you were my friend."*

Marina thought she heard the slightest tremble in his voice. *That poor child*, she thought, *growing up in that house. . . .*

Cosma then rejoined the adults.

"Come on now, show your auntie what we've learned."

Marina decided to join the game, although she doubted that they could goad this little boy into doing anything that he had no desire to do.

"Won't you show me what you've learned, Cosi?" she cooed. "I want to hear it."

He looked half desperately to Magdalena. "I told you, I forgot it."

"Well, do what you remember then."

He sighed again, and then he put his arms at his sides, raised his head, and slowly closed his eyes. Tony and Magdalena had grown accustomed to Cosma's great pride and earnestness, but it still shocked Marina. The boy, meanwhile, began to speak in a steady, rhythmic voice:

"Bred to a . . . ah . . . a harder thing than triumph, turn away, and . . . and laugh . . . laugh like a string where mad fingers play . . . amid the place of stone, be secret and exult—" and Cosma paused, then opened his eyes, "ah . . . be secret and exult . . . something something . . . that is most difficult."

The others burst into laughter and, slowly, as Cosma came to recognize his own unintentional joke, he laughed too, while Magdalena tried to frown.

"Cosi! We practiced so much!" But secretly Magdalena enjoyed his revision.

Cosma, however, had already stopped laughing. He approached Tony, looking solemn.

"Mr. Archuleta?"

"Yes?"

"Norah says she wants to send me away," Cosma began, calling his adopted mother by her given name—a convention Norah herself enforced. "I don't think she likes me. I don't think she likes Francis either. If she sends me away, can I stay with you and Mrs. Archuleta?"

Tony did not hesitate.

"You will always have a home with Francis. He loves you more than anything."

"But what if something happens?"

"Nothing will happen, but, God forbid you do need a home, you can always stay with us—can't he, Maggie?"

Magdalena nearly pounced on the child.

"Of course," and she smothered him in kisses, "of course of course of course."

"Or," Tony continued, "you can stay with your Auntie Rinka."

"Yes," Marina chimed on cue, "you can stay with me," and she too knelt before him.

Strangely, Cosma did not appear upset, more curious in a bored kind of way, like when a child asks why the sky is blue, or why the ocean is blue, or why the sky is blue because the ocean is blue. Marina could see that Cosma, like all those blessed with a natural stoicism, could not understand their concern.

"But, Mr. Archuleta, why *is* Norah so mean to Francis? I mean, she's mean to me because she doesn't want me. She told me so. But why's she so mean to Francis? Is it 'cause he wanted me?"

For the first time all afternoon Cosma showed his age. Collectively the other three wondered if they should tell Cosma that he already knew the answer: Norah was mean to Francis for the same reason she was mean to him—because she didn't *want* him.

Tony was about to speak when an egret landed several yards away. He then knelt beside the others.

"You see that egret?"

"Yes."

"Well, think about that egret for a moment."

"OK."

"Now think about mister starfish."

"OK."

"Now, what makes them different?"

Cosma paused.

"One lives in the water and the other lives in the air?"

"That's right, Cosi. You see, where I come from we believe that our home was placed in the exact middle of the world, and the rest of the world extends from this middle place in all six directions," and Tony placed one finger in a nearby tide pool. He began to trace a cruciform shape as he spoke.

"There is the North, the South, the East, and the West. But there is also the down," and Tony drew his finger into the pool. "My people have a word for it, but in English we call it the nadir. And there is also the up," and Tony raised his finger shoulder-high, as if he were about to bless someone, "and the up we call the zenith. My people believe that all creatures belong to a direction, just as the egret belongs to the zenith and the starfish belongs to the nadir.

"And, Cosma, it's the same with us: there are zenith people and there are nadir people. Francis is a zenith—he lives in the sky, he is hollow boned and light and belongs above the rest. Norah is a nadir—she lives in the underneath," and Tony glanced meaningfully at the others, "she belongs below the others, she is dense and strong."

"So, Francis is the egret and Norah is the starfish?"

"Yes. And this is why they don't always get along. One is the air and the other is the water—they move in opposite directions. It has nothing to do with you; it's not your fault."

"Oh. Well, OK," Cosma said rather cheerfully.

Marina and Tony stood up, proud of their proxy parenting, when Cosma silently untwined himself from Magdalena's arms and, without

301

hesitation, ran directly at the egret and unleashed a high-pitched, wild scream. The bird wheeled itself around, tore into the air, and began flying out to sea. Magdalena was the first to recover her speech.

"Cosma—why?—why in the world did you just do that?"

The boy walked back.

"I'm saving Francis," he announced with perfect nonchalance, and then continued, "I'm hungry. Can we please go home now and have something to eat?"

Moments later the four were walking toward the switchback trail that led up the shore's steep cliffs when Marina felt compelled to stop. She turned and faced the ocean one last time. Again she heard the caws and the barks and the effervescence and the clicks, and for a second she thought she saw the egret, silhouetted by the sun. It was heading west over the white-capped sea.

Four Poems
Elizabeth Robinson

RITUAL

Friendship is ritual as
ritual is a form of loyalty.

As ritual is intimate recall and information, also
a form of loyalty.

Encyclopedic even.
Where loyalty is much like scholarship.

Which requires initiation until the intricacies
of practice and performance

dwindle into familiarity.
Pleasure even.

Friendship is absurdity,
marking the absurdities

of time. Birthday,
holiday, the rituals

of mortality. Ritual is
a form of loyalty, that is,

commitment, that
circumvents

mortality, operating
through the meaning

of ritual rather than of time.
Friendship was circular

that way, intent on
conflating the terms

of itself. Intent on
abutting time and not

betraying it. A contract
much like a contraction,

loyalty closing around
its object, expelling time.

Elizabeth Robinson

VIRGINIA WOOLF SAYS GOODBYE TO LYTTON STRACHEY, THEN ROGER FRY

Always one thing left behind in a series.

We were counting, and then the increments changed.

Even—no,

odd—

integers.

I might have insisted that the sheer abstraction of numbers is ridiculous.

Yet here I am, counting breaths as I would count

waves breaking on the shore.
Expecting their tempo to remain steady.

Odd numbers, always,
weren't they?

Divided from each other, they have no natural parity.

Loss makes unnatural remainder.

Elizabeth Robinson

COMPETITIVE MOURNING

Each of us wants to take

a little piece of what isn't left of you.

Huff a little breath on the absence, shine
it on the sleeve, hold it up to the light.

A little opacity, yes, almost opaque, almost
opal, almost

anything one could purely imagine.

One walks away from what isn't there having

poached a bit of it, stuffed it in the pocket.

Slowly the sense of translucence, cloudy as it was,
becomes absolutely lustrous, a pearl through which

no light obtrudes.

Closeness, in the end—after the end—
does not conduct light, but deflects it.

Each of us has this conviction,
that we leave you
as you left us.

The pocket almost empty, but not quite.

A glance back over the shoulder, our breath
a vague smudge in the cooling air.

Elizabeth Robinson

MINA LOY WRITES TO JOSEPH CORNELL
ABOUT CHRISTIAN SCIENCE

My dear,

I have been thinking—health is the mundane, made of quotidian recognitions.

Magazines from which we clip pictures, the child's discarded marble flicked

to a crack in the pavement, parchment modeled, mottled, and curved

again as a lampshade, sheltering the light beneath it.

My dear friend,

I recognize you. I mean to say that we know the same illusions.

Snow is falling with its varnish of cleanliness. A white world. But soon,

traffic will dirty this surface too. I am tempted to say that by knowing

what is beneath, we transcend. What's underneath fails its own glow—for now.

One of my favorite words is "recognition." Its sacred modesty.

Ami, Amico,

Whatever anyone else may believe, isn't it the case that we know what we know,

and that creates the surfeit, the wholeness, that we call health? I am sure and

unsure. Fullness is theology that we reclaim and revise: all that discarded

surplus. Matter may be illusion, but at the same time, we know that theology at

its core is illuminated detritus. We, who are scavengers, are faith's adepts.

307

Mass

Matthew Cheney

THE BRIEF OBITUARY FOR WENDELL Hamilton that appeared in the September 30, 2015, issue of the *Coös County Democrat* was not entirely inaccurate, but it was far from complete. I expect he wrote it himself years ago. (Perhaps his lawyer submitted it as a requirement of probate.) Dr. Hamilton's life was significant enough that his obituary should have appeared at the very least in *The Boston Globe*, and it should have been noted by Cornell University, where he taught for nine years, and by Yale, where he earned his PhD, and by Dartmouth College, where he earned his BA. The only notice of his death that I have been able to find, however, is the one in the *Democrat*, the small weekly newspaper covering the northern region of New Hampshire where he was born and grew up, though not quite where he died.

When I tracked him down during the summer of 2007, Dr. Hamilton was living on a dirt road in the very small western town of Pike, New Hampshire, in a hundred-year-old house (little more than a cabin), where every spare bit of space was filled with books, journals, magazines, and newspapers. I was twenty-four, had just finished my second year as a PhD student at Boston University, and had been granted a modest research fellowship to study representations of mass murder in contemporary American fiction. Early in that research, I discovered that Randall Curry's best friend had been a literature professor.

Curry is hardly the most famous mass shooter in the United States. Indeed, he's been mostly forgotten, for though he shot seventeen people (killing nine) outside the Tip O'Neill Federal Building in Boston in 1994, his crimes were not extraordinary enough to last in the public memory, and he was killed by a security guard before he could be taken into custody, leaving little for the media to feast on later. My father worked for the Department of Housing and Urban Development at the time, and he had been in the O'Neill Building when the shooting occurred, so I had a particular interest in it, and my memory of that day remains vivid, though I was only ten years old at the time. (My father came home late, and afterward he never spoke about what happened or what he saw, if anything.)

Soon after meeting with Dr. Hamilton, I dropped out of my PhD program and worked odd jobs out west for a while, mostly in Montana and North Dakota. Eventually, I ended up here in New Mexico, teaching part-time at NMSU in Las Cruces, before recently feeling a need to move on again, somewhere farther away, beyond the borders of the United States, somewhere where the language is unfamiliar and I can't read any of the books I encounter.

I will leave this memoir behind with Ruben Trevino, a research librarian at Boston University's Mugar Memorial Library, who helped with so much of the work that led me to Wendell Hamilton, and who sent me the obituary. He will file it away somewhere where a researcher with interests similar to mine might find it, if such a person ever exists. There is some information here, and possibly even something more than information, but I am currently in no frame of mind to speculate on what that might be. I have learned what I can from this material.

If you, whoever you are, need final words for all this, then let them be these: do not try to find me.

I was working on my master's degree at Dartmouth when I first read one of Wendell Hamilton's essays, "Style as Substance at Century's End: *The Picture of Dorian Gray*, *The Wings of the Dove*, and *Three Lives*," published in a 1984 issue of *Modern Fiction Studies*. I don't remember how or why I encountered it. It had nothing to do with anything I was working on. I've long been interested in Wilde and Stein, so maybe that was it. (I've also long had an aversion to the writing of Henry James, which perhaps should have led me away from the essay, but didn't.) I doubt that I understood much of what Hamilton wrote, and none of his arguments are what stuck with me. Instead, it was the precision of the mind behind the words, the clarity and elegance of his writing, that fascinated me and compelled me to seek out everything I could find by him.

The list of his writings is not long. As far as I can tell, he never published a book of his own (oh for the days of more lenient tenure committees!), but he did coedit *Outside the (Meta)Text: Deconstruction and Twentieth-Century American Metafiction* with John W. Rye, published in 1989. Simply listing his bibliography solidified my fascination with his work and my curiosity about his fate:

- "Style as Substance at Century's End: *The Picture of Dorian Gray, The Wings of the Dove,* and *Three Lives,*" *Modern Fiction Studies,* 1984
- "*The Making of Americans* and the Making of the Twentieth-Century Novel: A Study in Discourse," *Modern Fiction Studies,* 1986
- "Obscene Harlem Unseen: Ford & Tyler's *The Young and Evil,*" *Studies in the Novel,* 1988
- "'A Squeeze of the Hand': Melville's Radical *Différance,*" *Social Text,* 1989
- "Cut-up as Self-Narrating Form in *Naked Lunch, The Ticket that Exploded,* and *The Wild Boys,*" *Outside the (Meta)Text* anthology, 1989
- "Fascist Aesthetics and the Adventure of History in Barry Sadler's *Casca* Novels," *Journal of Popular Culture,* 1992
- "John Rambo/John Barth: Lost in the Funhouse of *First Blood,*" *Journal of Popular Culture,* 1994

There is much that could be said about that bibliography, but what struck me immediately was the difference between the first five and last two items, the movement from the study of modernist and post-modernist texts (utilizing common theoretical lenses of the time) to the study of popular paramilitary fiction. I read each of the essays and was impressed by the sharp, unaffected writing in them, even when they relied on abstruse philosophical concepts that I've never been especially skilled at parsing. The 1990s essays were as beautifully structured and written as the earlier ones, but there was a difference in them too, a new sense of, for lack of a more precise word, *urgency.* The sentences were generally less complex than those in the earlier essays, the philosophy was less dense, and the insights led to an unsettling feeling that these items of popular culture matter in a way that everything else Hamilton had written about could not—that, in fact, some sort of life-and-death struggle was not just represented within books designed for quick and unreflective reading, but embodied by them.

And then Hamilton published nothing else that I or, later, various research librarians could find. Ruben Trevino did uncover his 1983 dissertation at Yale, *Oscar Wilde after Dorian Gray,* and I read it, though with disappointment. Its best passages were early drafts of ideas that would appear in some of the articles, and nothing that had

310

not later found its way into print seemed to me especially insightful.

After my brief original interest in Hamilton, I forgot all about him until I was a student in a seminar at BU on violence in contemporary American fiction. I grew curious to know whether anyone had fictionalized Randall Curry and the shooting at the O'Neill Building, thinking I could somehow turn the subject into a seminar paper, and in my general search on literary topics related to Curry, I quickly discovered a long profile of him in *The Globe*, published a year and a half after the shooting, which noted: "Curry's closest friend for much of his life until recently seems to have been the Cornell literature professor Wendell Hamilton. Dr. Hamilton declined to be interviewed for this article, and has never spoken publicly about the friendship." Suddenly my interest in Hamilton returned, I dug up all my old photocopies of his essays, and I searched everywhere I could for mention of him in connection with Curry. His name occasionally appeared, but no one had managed to get any more information than *The Globe*, and anyone's nascent interest in Hamilton (if there had been anyone with such interest) had vanished as other mass shootings grabbed headlines and, inevitably, fascination with Curry dissipated.

Now, though, knowing the connection between the two men, all of Hamilton's 1990s publications made more sense—or not sense, exactly, since I had no idea what the nature of their friendship was, but rather the change in Hamilton's work no longer seemed entirely, almost comically, random.

The newspaper and magazine articles about Curry said he was someone with paramilitary fantasies. He'd been raised in a basically middle-class family in Peekskill, New York (father an accountant, mother an insurance agent), though apparently there was significant tension between the parents; they divorced when Randall was young and he moved with his mother to central New Hampshire. They were, by all accounts, liberal in their politics. Randall was a stellar student, and easily earned a scholarship to a private school nearby, which is where he met Wendell Hamilton, who was one year behind him. Randall's life doesn't get interesting until after high school, however. He attended Harvard for a year and a half, pursuing a double major in computer science and political science. He never fit in at Harvard, kept dropping classes and failing the ones he didn't drop, until finally he just stopped attending, returned to New Hampshire, worked various low-wage jobs (many of which he got fired from; apparently he was especially unsuited for retail jobs), and finally ended up working at a small-engine repair shop in the southeastern part of

311

the state. Acquaintances said Curry was standoffish and often seemed to think he was superior to the people around him. He became interested in various conspiracy theories, and he developed an obsession with guns and militaria, spending the majority of his income on weapons, tools, accoutrements. He wore a camouflage cap and an olive drab coat he called his "Rambo jacket." He occasionally had contact with his parents, mostly to ask for money, but never talked about either his mother or father to anyone except to say that they were dead or, if the person knew they were not, that they were mentally unstable, especially his mother, whom he seemed particularly to despise. He subscribed to *Soldier of Fortune* magazine, and told more than one person that he wished he could become a mercenary; it seemed like a good way to see the world. On a Monday in the middle of April, he didn't go in to work, but instead drove to Boston, parked his 1989 Ford Bronco illegally outside the O'Neill Building, and started shooting at the building with an AR-15 semiautomatic rifle. He finished with the rifle, got out of his Bronco, walked toward the building with a Sig Sauer P226 pistol in hand, and shot three people at close range before a security guard was able to return fire, shooting him in the head, chest, and stomach, killing him.

Where had Wendell Hamilton fit into this life?

I wrote my seminar paper as a comparison between ideas in some of the *Casca* novels of Barry Sadler (tales of an eternal warrior) and Don DeLillo's *Mao II* and *Libra*—a terrible paper, really, but my goal wasn't so much to write a good paper as it was to think more about Hamilton and his ideas. It also let me put together the core of a research proposal for the summer. Though my ostensible topic was masculine, paramilitary violence in literature and society in the 1990s, my real interest was the connection between Randall Curry and Wendell Hamilton.

Mostly, I wanted to find Hamilton and talk to him. For reasons I couldn't possibly have explained at the time, I sensed that he might somehow offer a key not only to Randall Curry, but to some inchoate feeling lurking in the shadows of my own life. But how to find him? Cornell seemed a good place to start, and so I e-mailed every member of the English Department who had been there when Hamilton had also been on the faculty. Only one responded: Maxwell Corliss, a Milton scholar whose first two years at Cornell overlapped with Hamilton's final two. He replied to my e-mail and told me to give him a call, so I did. (With his permission, I recorded the phone call.)

"Wendell was not as odd as some people will probably make him out to be to you," he said. I told him that nobody so far had responded to any of my inquiries. Either they had no memory of Hamilton or didn't want to talk about him, at least to me. Corliss laughed. "Not surprising," he said. "Wendell was not the touchy-feely type, not at all. People liked him well enough—I don't think he had enemies, per se, at least not any more so than the rest of us—people who disliked something he said in a department meeting or something, certainly, but not more than that, and in any case, Wendell hardly ever spoke in meetings, at least that I saw."

"Did you know he was friends with Randall Curry?"

"Who?" Corliss said.

"The man who killed nine people outside a federal building in Boston. Nineteen ninety-four."

"Oh, right, yes," he said in the sort of tone that made me think he didn't remember it at all. "I can't say I paid much attention. Tenure was calling. But no, I had no idea Wendell was involved. How strange."

"He wasn't involved, but he knew the shooter somehow."

"I see." An awkward pause and then I asked if he could tell me anything else about Hamilton. "What do you want to know?" he replied. I said I didn't know anything about his personality, his likes or interests. "Oh," Corliss said, "well that's a bit difficult. A bit personal."

"Personal?"

"He's a very private man. There are so many things I never knew about him, things I don't know about him, and yet we were—well, I'm far less interested in privacy than Wendell, so I'll just tell you: he and I were in a casual, primarily sexual relationship for a lot of my time here. Wendell didn't have any interest in something more than that, at least not with me, but it was very cordial, and I honestly think back on it with fondness. He wanted to know about me, and he enjoyed talking about poetry and books and scholarship, but he rarely opened up much about himself."

"Did you keep in touch with him after he left Cornell?"

"Yes, for a year and a half, maybe two years. He returned to New Hampshire. I assume he's still there. He inherited a house, some money. He really didn't like academia. He liked scholarship, and in many ways I think he actually enjoyed teaching—I think he sees the sharing of knowledge to be a kind of duty, a moral duty—but he has little tolerance for bureaucracy, and even less for the corporatist *weltanschauung* that has so infected higher education, the, well, you know, the endless insistence on *usefulness*, the instrumentalizing

313

and marginalizing of the humanities, all that. So once he was able to, he left. Even when he was here, we'd meet in Manhattan, usually. There were some bars and clubs that he liked, some friends he had down there. This was the nineties, and New York was a different sort of world, a different place from what it's become. Now it's just a playground of the rich. But there was some life still there in the nineties. The last hurrah of the real New York, as it were. We had a nice time, always, but Wendell had become more interested in . . . well, in rougher trade than I. I'm rather bourgeois in my tastes, I'm afraid. He was not, at least not usually, and less so after he left here. There wasn't a lot remaining for us to talk about, it seemed, nor much passion in the sex, so we drifted apart, and I haven't heard from him in a while. I thought maybe you might have."

Corliss was willing to give me a mailing address he had for Hamilton, a post office box in Hanover, New Hampshire. "He said he checks his mail two or three times a week, and that it's a good half hour from where he lives. He may still be there, wherever it was. It's been almost a decade since I last heard from him, though."

I wrote a short, stiltedly polite note to Hamilton, explaining my research project, conveying my long interest in his work, and saying that I was planning on a trip to New Hampshire during the summer and wondered if he might be willing to talk to me. I included my address, phone number, and e-mail address. I mailed the note to the post office box and waited.

A week later, I received a response written elegantly in black ink on a small sheet of heavy, cream-colored stationery: "Dear Mr. Dalaria: Thank you for your kind letter. I will, indeed, be at home this summer. Please send me your essay, as I would like to have a sense of your work before I commit myself to meeting. Sincerely, Wendell Hamilton."

I read the note over again and again, my feelings a lightning storm of surprise, elation, terror. I had made contact with someone whose ideas had been important to me for many years, and he seemed willing to meet, but he wanted to read my own work—work I had little confidence in. I regretted even mentioning it to him. I spent the next few days revising my essay on *Casca* and DeLillo, trying to make it not quite so insipid, trying to show that I had thoughts of my own and wasn't merely repeating the insights in Hamilton's own essay. I wondered if he would respect me more if I was critical of some element of his work. There was nothing I particularly disagreed with in what he had written, though. I decided not to force it. Better to have him think of me as a naive sycophant than as an arrogant kid. Finally, I printed the paper out, stuck it in a large envelope, and mailed it to him.

A week and a half later, I received another letter: "Dear Mr. Dalaria: Thank you for sending your very interesting essay. I am generally at home and would be happy to meet you. If July 16 at 1:00 p.m. would be convenient, that would work well for me, and you do not need to reply, but simply show up. If it is not convenient, please reply with another date and time and I will make myself available. I have enclosed a map. Sincerely, Wendell Hamilton."

The map was hand drawn, simple and graceful, with clear indications of where highways turned into small roads, where pavement gave way to dirt, and where moose, deer, cows, chickens, geese, ducks, and dogs were most likely to walk in the road. I found an inexpensive hotel a few miles away from Hanover and booked a room, then spent the long days until our meeting rereading not only all of Hamilton's writings, but the various books and writers he wrote about. I was trying to shape my own knowledge to be similar to his.

And then I was driving through the back roads of New Hampshire, through forests and valleys so heavily wooded that I feared claustrophobia would overtake me. I got to the hotel, tried to read, couldn't concentrate, ordered a chicken sandwich from room service, could hardly eat it, tried to sleep, couldn't, took a bath, then spent much of the night lying in bed, staring at the ceiling, and running scenarios through my mind: Hamilton likes me and answers all my questions jovially, Hamilton hates me and doesn't answer any questions, Hamilton is demented and answers my questions in bizarre riddles, Hamilton is not home, Hamilton is a serial killer and slits my throat with a rusty kitchen knife. . . .

In the morning, I drove to Pike. Being nervous and excited, I was early. I think I allowed four hours to drive the forty miles from my hotel to Hamilton's house. I used the spare time to drive around the area until I understood how each road connected with the roads around it. It was a lovely day, sunny and not too hot or humid, so I parked my car and wandered through woods, stopped to look at rivers and ponds, letting myself take in the shape and smell of the landscape that Wendell Hamilton had made his own for more than a decade now. Places, I thought, could tell us about the people who chose them. What was this place—quiet, remote, somehow outside history—telling me about Wendell Hamilton?

I pulled into his driveway a few minutes before 1:00 p.m. He lived

315

on a dirt road off a dirt road, and his driveway was another sort of dirt road, though one with a bit more grass covering it. The driveway led down to a little gray house sitting on a ledge overlooking a brook. Beside the house stood a garage that looked barely large enough to hold one car.

Before I could knock on the front door more than once, it opened and a short, bald man smiled at me. "Mr. Dalaria, I presume."

"Dr. Hamilton."

"Nobody has called me 'Dr. Hamilton' in a long time. It sounds like an accusation. Call me Wendell, please, for the sake of my sanity. Come in."

I followed him into a closet-sized mudroom and took off my shoes. "And call me Ted. 'Mr. Dalaria' is not something I'm used to." He chuckled and led me to a living room where two whole walls were nothing but bookcases. Hundreds more books stood in stalagmite piles across the floor. The furniture (couch, two chairs, a coffee table) was old (but not antique); it made my own furniture, relics of yard sales past, seem fresh, modern, affluent. I noticed cobwebs in corners.

"I'm afraid I'm a bit of a Miss Havisham," Wendell said. "I used to be self-conscious about my indifference to housekeeping, but now I'm indifferent to my indifference. Entropy always wins."

He offered me a cup of coffee or a glass of lemonade, and I gladly accepted the latter, which it turned out he had squeezed himself that morning. It was sharp and sugary.

I scanned his bookshelves, stepping carefully between the piles.

"There's no real order to it all," he said. "There was once, but I found it oppressive and unhelpful. It is frustrating, I admit, to have to search when you are seeking one specific book, but I find the opportunities for serendipitous thinking far outweigh that occasional inconvenience."

Countless paperback mystery novels, many looking like they'd survived floods and beatings, mingled with pristine old hardcovers of Greek plays and French Enlightenment philosophy. New copies of recent novels sat beside old self-help books from the sixties and earlier. I took Norman Vincent Peale's *Stay Alive All Your Life* from a shelf. "I can't say I expected to find something like this in your collection," I said.

"Oh, Peale is one of my favorites. A blithering idiot and a snake-oil salesman, no doubt, but I can't help suspect he actually believed what he wrote, and I find something compelling in that, something even, perhaps, noble. A feeling that turns the laughter and scorn that fills me when I start reading to shame and then awe by the time I am finished."

I put the book back on the shelf, tucked between what looked to be a lovely illustrated volume of Rabelais and a home-repair manual from before I was born. "What do you read these days?" I said.

"Theoretical physics."

I laughed. He smiled. "Really," he said. "Not especially *detailed* theoretical physics, but introductory sorts of texts, popularizations, books for people who don't really ever have a hope of truly under-standing physics but nonetheless possess a certain curiosity. And its words are sometimes beautiful—a *tachyonic field of imaginary mass*—who couldn't love such a phrase? I find it all strangely com-forting, the more far-out ideas of quantum theory and such. It's like religion, but without all the rigmarole and obeisance to a god. Or perhaps more like poetry, though really not, because it's something somehow outside language, but nonetheless elegant, and of course constricted by language, since how else can we communicate about it? But it gestures, at least, toward whatever lies beyond Logos, be-yond our ability even to reason, though perhaps not to compre-hend. At my age, and having spent a life devoted to language, there is comfort and excitement—even perhaps some inchoate feeling of hope—in glimpses beyond the realm of words. There is, I have come to believe, very much outside the text. What is it, though? Call it God, call it Nature, call it the Universe, call it what it seems to me now to be—having read and I'm sure misunderstood my theoretical physics—call it: *an asymptote*."

I had not yet asked Wendell if I could record him, so the above is a reconstruction, but I feel I remember it almost perfectly, because I'd never heard anyone speak like him before. At first, I believed he must have prepared what he hoped to say to me in advance, or had said it to many other people over the years, turning it into a per-formance, a shtick. Maybe this was the case, but I prefer to think not. He enunciated carefully, his voice a bit high and almost, I thought, English in its accent, and he spoke without haste and without resort to the *umms* and *uhhs* and *like, you know, likes* that the rest of us so often succumb to in conversation. We talked for a while longer about nothing of any real import (certainly nothing I *remember* as having any import), and then I asked if he might be willing for me to record him.

"Why?" he said, suddenly suspicious. I said it was faster for me than taking notes, and that way I could forget about whether I was getting it all down and instead devote myself to listening, to conversation. He stared at me for a moment, then shrugged and said though he thought it a tad discomforting, he was sure it would be just fine. And so I began the recording. (My transcription here has cleaned up some of what I said, but I've hardly had to edit his responses at all. I have indicated where he took an especially long pause between words, as these silences seem to me as meaningful as what he spoke.)

Q: I'm most curious I guess why you switched, or changed—why you made the change from the sorts of essays you were writing in the eighties—right up through the William S. Burroughs piece—that essay—why after that—there's a break—a break in chronology as well as in subject matter—and that's probably the biggest thing that has stuck out to me over the years about your work, the question of why that shift.

A: Yes. There is a shift, certainly, obviously. I've thought about it a lot. [Pause.] At the time, I thought what had happened was that I had simply become bored. I had been doing the same sort of work, the same sort of writing, for a decade or so. I had been ambitious as a young man. I had seen academia as an escape from a fate—from a, though it will sound hyperbolic, a *doom*. It is the right word. I had felt doomed. I also felt that I was a fraud. Given the circumstances of my childhood, it is remarkable that I was ever able to imagine a life for myself different from the lives of the sorts of people with whom I attended public school, the sorts of people, in fact, that I now, once again, live among, and quite happily. But at the time of my childhood it was not happy. I was not happy. I dreamed of escape. School was the only thing I showed any talent for, and so school became my escape. Boarding school, then college, then graduate school. From each of which, of course, I also wanted to escape, because only new things offered the escape I sought, or at least that I thought I sought. It remained so even as I was hired by Cornell. The essays I wrote throughout the 1980s, the essays, we might say, of the Reagan years, those essays are written by a man who wants nothing more than to escape from a fate he cannot even quite articulate (if you'll pardon that unintentional rhyme), a fate that is, though unarticulated, though imprecise and vague and even perhaps mystical, a fate that is, as I said, a doom. The escape that man sought was an escape through literature, or, more accurately, an escape through the interpretation of literature. It was an attempt to get the stories right, to find, somehow, the right words, and, thus, salvation.

318

Q: But? What changed? What was the shift?

A: Not one thing, not one large crisis or such. A series of . . . it's hard to find the word. A series of insights. A series of catastrophes. Insights taken for catastrophes, catastrophes taken for insights. It was a long time ago. [Pause.] I will tell you this: people were dying. People I knew, acquaintances, and a couple of people I cared about very deeply. They died, slowly, horribly. They wasted away, sometimes neglected, all of them cast out by a society that declared them to be abject. Sinners, lepers. But not deserving of compassion, not even seen as human, at least not fully human. Untouchables. It is easy to forget now, seemingly so far away from it, what it was like for . . . us . . . to live then, to die then.

Q: AIDS?

A: Yes.

Q: But you weren't—

A: No. I used to get tested every six months, then every year, then . . . well, it's been a while. But there's no need. That part of life is over for me, and I will not pretend I'm not happy to be done with it. A friend once called me a Buddhist atheist, and I suppose the label is accurate for me, as I have spent many years now attempting to escape desire, though even as I say it I'm somewhat embarrassed as I know so little about Buddhism that my perception of its precepts, its antipathy to desire—even war against desire—may be a flight of my imagination. It doesn't matter, though. "Atheist" is accurate. Anything else is . . . noise.

Q: Why—OK, this is an impertinent question. I'm sorry. I—why do you think—why—I mean, your health, I assume—

A: Why did I not get sick?

Q: Yes.

A: Because most of my practices were not the ones that correlate with the highest transmission of the disease. I wouldn't want to give you the impression that I was *safe,* because I wasn't. I am, I expect, quite lucky, and perhaps even somehow immune. Or it may just be that since I've never really enjoyed anal sex, and haven't sought it out, and have rarely indulged in it, that I wasn't at as much risk as others. Oral sex, yes, some, certainly, but fundamentally I was interested more in touch than in penetration or the exchange of bodily fluids. I expect the reason, or *a* reason among a constellation of reasons, that I have been able to settle quite comfortably into celibacy is that I have always been somewhat, and sometimes quite strongly, disgusted by bodily fluids. You've seen *Dr. Strangelove,* I assume—

"precious bodily fluids," yes? (Is that the phrase?) Well, I'm quite the opposite. Nothing precious to me about bodily fluids. I all but faint at the sight of blood, for instance. But that's not quite disgust, not quite what I'm referring to. (I am, as always, circling my subject.) By disgust, I mean what has been inside the body and is expelled, secreted. Semen, saliva, sweat: they're all equally unappealing to me. To hold a hand, though, to touch a face, to kiss a cheek, to run hands through hair—to wake in the morning and look into someone else's eyes, or to watch them as they sleep peacefully, to listen to them breathe—that, for a while at least, was an exquisite pleasure, a privilege even.

Q: For a while?

A: Yes. Feelings change. Emotions fade. Desires fade, I'm sorry to say. I expect it was because certain people died.

Q: AIDS?

A: Mostly. Not entirely.

Q: Randall Curry?

(I had not planned how I would bring Curry up. In my memory, his name just pops out of my mouth, but I expect I was thinking that the time was right, or that there would, at least, not be a better time, given how honest and personal Wendell had become in our conversation.)

A: [After a long pause.] Yes. But. No. Not in the same way. Randall and I were not lovers, I should say that. We were friends, best friends for a time. When we were young. Our ideals were similar, if you can believe it. We wanted to be intellectuals, and we wanted to change the world, to make it a more just, more equitable place. We became embittered and disillusioned, but in different ways, toward different ends.

Q: Were you surprised by what he did?

A: What he did was a shock, and ghastly, and unforgivable. It was, in addition to being ghastly, and in addition to being unforgivable— it was, for me, personally—it was a . . . a disappointment. Randall was a brilliant man. My sense of escape was entwined with my sense of *his* escape. We were, I had thought, similar. I was wrong. Or perhaps not wrong. I have thought about it a lot over the years, of course. How could I not? I never wanted to talk about it at the time because I only wanted to reject him, to cast him out, to make him, as it were, my own abject. To keep him, and his beliefs, and his acts, to keep them outside, untouchable and, most importantly, untouching me. A foolish, if natural and understandable, emotion. In a narcissistic way, I saw Randall as a failed version of myself. There but for fortune go I. Our given names, after all, are so similar. Wendell. Randall. The same but for a few small letters. Surely, that must mean something? And yet it does not. Chaos torments the pattern-seeking mechanisms in our minds. Catastrophe brings out the fool in the best of us. And I am not the best of us.

Q: Did he have anything to do, for instance, with your interest in the *Casca* novels?

A: Yes, of course. He was one of the contributors to the shift in my thinking, my desires, my life. His was one of the later deaths, and an entirely different type than that of my friends who got sick. But his decline—I know no other word for it, though the word itself saddens me and, in fact, implicates me—his decline was clear for years, and viewed in retrospect it seems, to me at least, that only a moral monster could have seen it as anything less than a severe crisis. But that is in retrospect. Still, much was visible, even at the time. How could it not be? My inclination, though, was simply to create distance. To separate myself from him. To avoid contact. Do not touch. And yet I was fascinated. The fascination of the abomination.

Q: Did you think he would kill people?

A: No. Of that I am certain. (Or I tell myself I am certain.) I had no conscious idea it would take the final form that it did. Does that exonerate me? If anything, I think it shows how unperceptive I was. All the clues were there. I did not see them. I thought I was reading him with great insight, but I was terribly wrong. It's not that I was oblivious. I was afraid for him. But only for *him*, because in the darker moments of night when I thought about his fate, his doom, I thought only that he might kill *himself*. And he did. In the worst possible way, by bringing other people into his own despair.

—But you asked about the books. Indeed, the *Casca* novels were ones he loved, as was *First Blood*, though in his case the movie and not the novel, which I don't think he'd ever read. I tried to understand him by writing about them. I tried to write my way out of his doom. It was arrogant and stupid and the only thing I could, at that moment in my life, see to do. [Pause.] What I, in my self-absorption, could not see is that my writing those essays, my engaging with those thoughts, those patterns, would do nothing. And did nothing.

Q: The *First Blood* essay came out right around the time when he died.

A: A month or so after. Yes. Academic publishing is very slow. I had written it two years earlier.

Q: Is there a connection between his death and your not publishing again?

A: Yes. Of course. There is everything outside the text.

Q: The deaths? And?

A: Deaths and asymptotes. Chaos theory and lots of fractals. [Pause.]

Q: I . . .

A: The story is banal, I'm afraid. I inherited some money, I didn't enjoy academia anymore, I had no idea what to write about, I had little interest in sex and none in relationships, and so I came here. [Pause.] How is Max Corliss, by the way? You said he was the one who gave you my address?

Q: He seems to be well. I think he misses you.

A: And I him. I should send him a note. He was the least combative Miltonist I've ever known. They're a fighterly lot. Friendly, but fighterly. The nature of the subject, I suppose. What we study shapes us.

Q: He said you were good friends.

A: Well, yes, we were. We had sex, did he tell you that? Probably not. He was always so shy. I did something unpardonable, I'm afraid. When I didn't understand my own feelings well enough, and didn't understand why I wanted to get away, and mistook my desire for escape as a desire for escape from *him*—I lied to him. I told him a story. He was always so demure, it was easy to make up a story and make up a self. I wanted to believe I was the kind of person who could enjoy pain, who could find pleasure in inflicting and receiving violence. I told a story about that imagined self, and that story was my escape from him. I've always regretted it.

Q: He doesn't seem to hold a grudge against you. I think he'd like to know you're well.

A: Mr. Dalaria—Ted—let me ask you: *why* are you doing the work you are doing?

Q: Interviewing you? Because I found—I find—your work, your writings, fascinating and—

A: No, no, no. Forget about me. I'm flattered by your attention, certainly, and gratified that some things I wrote long ago have whatever ability to communicate still today, but no, that was not what I meant. What I meant was: why are you doing what you do?

Q: Getting a PhD?

A: In literature. Yes.

Q: It's work that I'm pretty good at. Work I enjoy. And I honestly don't really know what else to do. I mean, I'm not the best in my program, by any means, but I'm not bad, and I, well . . . it's something to do. I know that sounds pathetic.

A: No, not pathetic. I don't think so. My own reasons were similar. And you are not me and the world is different now and in any case numerous people in far more destructive careers have far more pathetic reasons for doing what they do than you have for what you do. But you must know—and yes, I will sound like a meddling scold when I say it—you must know that books and words will not save you, that they are not an escape from whatever you are seeking escape from, but rather an escape *into* something that . . . [Pause.]

Q: Something that . . . ?

A: [After a pause.] Hamlet: "Words, words, words."

He picked up my glass and carried it to the kitchen. "More lemonade?" he asked. I said no, I was fine. He asked me to wait a moment, then went to another part of the house. I heard some drawers open, some items shift around. I stopped recording. Then he came back and handed me a small envelope. "This is the note that Randall sent me before he died. I never showed it to the FBI. Doing so would feel like a violation. And there's nothing they could have used in it. But you should read it."

I didn't want to read it. Just holding it in my hands felt like a violation, like touching fire. Wendell did not move and would not look away. I opened the envelope.

"Dear Wendell," the letter began—handwritten in blue ballpoint pen, almost scrawled—"You will be very angry with me, and I understand that. I'm going to go do something I've wanted to do for a while now. We've become very different. I wanted you to understand me, and I couldn't figure out a way to make you understand. What I am going to do will not make you understand me. But it will do something. Action, not ideas. Reality, not fantasy. No stories, just lives. And deaths. All there ever is. Goodbye, my friend." He wrote his name like an official signature at the bottom of the page. Beneath the signature, with a red pen, he wrote: "Soldier, you are content with what you are. Then that you shall remain until we meet again."

Wendell gave me permission to copy the letter into my notes.

"If you want the answer to me, to my life, it is there," he said. "There is no explanation other than those words. There is no interpretation, no story. I made a life, and then I made what I hope will prove to have been a different life for myself than the life I led before."

"Have you," I asked after I finished copying the letter, "written anything recently?"

He sighed. He started to speak, stopped. Then: "You haven't understood a word I've said." He spoke quietly, without anger, without even disappointment. But his words were a wall suddenly between us. I had confirmed his doubts.

I tried to protest, tried to speak, to put words to it all. I don't remember what I said.

"Goodbye, Mr. Dalaria. It was nice to meet you. I wish you the best with your studies."

And so I left.

The sky had become gray, rain was moving in, and darkness shimmered through the hovering trees. I listened to the water in the brook below the house. I listened to birds, though I know nothing about birds and could not identify their calls. I stood in the driveway, fearing to leave. Mosquitoes found me, bit me. Misty dashes of rain touched my hands and nose. I got into my car. Soon, the rain poured down hard, torrential, pelting the metal of the car like pebbles on a steel drum, splashing—smashing—against the windshield in obscuring bursts so that I could barely see even a few feet ahead. The world was dark and the headlights could not penetrate the darkness. Now and then, the lights' glare flashed in the water on the windshield and the rain became a firefly, alive for a moment only. I kept moving forward, as slowly as the car would go, inches at a time, because the bare animal part of me insisted that if I stopped I would die, the car would wash away in a flood, and the flood was here and only here, and if I could get away from here then I could find some dry land, some place to stop and rest without fear. I imagined that the rain was not rain but mosquitoes and flies and june bugs, insect life lured to my headlights and splattered together into a mass and wiped away. I started laughing, nervously, then ghoulishly, and soon in my mind the water on the windshield was no longer bugs but birds and bats and then severed bits of bodies and then eyeballs and then, as somehow the night grew even darker, sprays of maybe ink or maybe blood, I didn't know, but surely not water, because how could mere water so menace me? I exhausted what laughter I had left. The night remained dark. The rain continued to fall. All I could do to stay alive was try to keep moving forward no matter how little, no matter how deafeningly the torrent attacked the car, no matter the floods beneath the wheels, and to hope that somewhere the rain would stop, day would erase the night, the quiet would return, and I could step outside.

Friend of My Heart
Joyce Carol Oates

AND NOW, AFTER THIRTY-TWO YEARS, seven months, three weeks, and a scattering of days we will meet again.

At least, you will have been met by *me*.

Not sure if I should announce myself too explicitly. If you recognize me, and remember what happened between us, you might call for help, or manage to flee, before I can act appropriately, as I have (meticulously) planned; but if I don't identify myself, so that you comprehend clearly the reason for my actions, there is hardly any point in my acting at all.

For what is *revenge* if it is not registered in the brain of the Other?

Like the proverbial tree that falls in the forest with no creature to hear it, *revenge* that is not made unambiguously clear to the subject is hardly *revenge* but mere catastrophe, which might happen to anyone, innocently/accidentally, to no purpose.

For weeks I have rehearsed my greeting. For weeks, what I must summon my courage to do publicly, to you.

Hel-lo! Do you remember me?

Or perhaps—*Hello Professor K_____. Do I look familiar to you?*

Or maybe I will say, simply—*Hello, Erica. Are you surprised that I'm still alive?*

"Excuse me. These seats are reserved for faculty."

"Excuse *me*. I am faculty."

A dramatic moment. I had not intended to call attention to myself at your lecture but somehow this has happened, and I cannot respond otherwise to such an insult.

The usher stares at me, in my soiled khakis, suede jacket worn at the elbows, baseball cap pulled low over my forehead, hiking boots. She must be mistaking me for a noncollege person, perhaps even a homeless person, with my grimy backpack, stringy hair, and truculent manner; she is uncertain how to react—whether to back off or

326

to call for reinforcements to prevent me sitting in a so-called "re-served" seat at the front of the five hundred–seat auditorium.

Not one of my students—ever. If she'd been, the little bitch would be respectful to Ms. Leeuwen.

For your much-ballyhooed "Gender/Language/Sexuality" lecture in Hill Auditorium all ushers appear to be undergraduate volunteers, and all appear to be female. Though our college has been coed since 1997 its (revered, inflated) history is that of a women's college (founded in 1883) and the great majority of our student body remains female; the abysmal quality of our male students is something of a joke but our administrators are desperate for undergraduates, any sex/gender/IQ will do. It would be hypocritical of me to criticize them since I am a longtime member of the faculty, as I am trying to explain to this dolt of a girl-usher.

How angry I am, at being treated so disrespectfully! My heart beats fast and hard and a taste of toad venom comes into my mouth.

You would be amused, I suppose. *You*, who have become an academic celebrity, a shameless plagiarist/charlatan, concocting a career out of the labor of others whom you've used, wrung dry, and discarded. The insults hurled at me in the ordinary course of my life would be a joke to you—the illustrious E____ K_____.

Another girl-usher comes tripping down the aisle to assist the first. Sheaths of fair, straight, identical-blonde hair falling about their blank-idiot faces. It's touching, I suppose—each girl-usher is wearing a fresh-ironed white shirt, hunter-green school tie, black trousers. Not the usual ridiculous pre-torn jeans and T-shirts or cutoffs showing their flawless skinny legs.

"It's undemocratic and elitist to reserve so many seats. Not all these 'VIPS' will show up for this meretricious lecture, I guarantee."

My voice is icy, calm. If the silly girl-ushers had any doubt that I am a faculty member they should be convinced now.

By this time I am sitting in defiance of the ushers, backpack on my knees. And I am not going to budge. In the very center of the first row in the choicest seat in Hill Auditorium directly below the podium and approximately twelve feet from the stage where you will be giving your lavishly "endowed" lecture within the hour.

Would you be apprehensive if you knew? In fear of—something happening to you in this public place?

The girl-ushers flutter nearby, uncertain what to do until one of the faculty arrives to whisper to them that, yes, the person whom they are regarding with such suspicion is indeed a faculty member.

327

It is a pleasure to see the girl-ushers' faces clot with chagrin! Not that they will apologize to me, of course.

And not that this person, one of the English faculty, that's to say the permanent faculty, knows my name. Though I have been an adjunct instructor in English and Communication Arts here for eleven years.

Strange, no one seems to know my name. Or will acknowledge my name. That is the pretense.

Should I be insulted, I will not be insulted. Not by pygmies.

Should I be wounded, I will not be wounded. I will not be *disrespected.*

There is nothing shameful in being an *adjunct instructor.* There is nothing shameful in having no car, in being obliged to bicycle to campus from (rented) quarters three miles away, even in rainy or snowy weather. There is shame only in the elitists who have denied me a permanent position at the college even as they have given themselves such positions, with tenure, and raises, and every kind of benefit—medical, insurance—denied to adjuncts; even as they are well aware of my superiority over them, as a scholar, and as a writer, and as a teacher.

Elitists who misuse their power to offer exorbitant lecture fees to individuals like *you.*

(Yes, the rumor is that E_____ K_____ is receiving, for a presentation of no more than fifty minutes at our college, as much as an adjunct instructor is likely to receive for an entire course in a twelve-week semester—outrageous!)

The auditorium is filling. Buzzing and murmuring like a hive. The largest crowd I've seen in years, since Oliver Sacks. Undergraduates clutching copies of *The Masks of Gender: Language, Sexual Deceit, and Subterfuge* they will ask you to sign, breathless and eager—*Oh please will you—? Professor K_____? And may I take a picture of myself with you? Gosh!*

Gradually the reserved seating is filling also. Colleagues of mine—to whom I am invisible, nameless. At first they avoid me, pointedly; for the tenured faculty avoids the untenured, if it is humanly possible, without being overtly rude or vicious. (They need us, after all. Or rather, the college needs us, to work for a fraction of the salary at which the permanent faculty works.) No one sits beside me until those seats are the only remaining, and two late arrivals have no choice but to take these.

It is amusing really. It is *laughable.* How stiffly aware of me these "colleagues" are. Though not knowing my name, knowing that I am *not one of them*. A plebeian, a prole, in their midst. A leper. Yet a *worker-leper*. Daring to sit amid the reserved for the fancy endowed lecture as if we are all equals.

But no need to worry. I am very well-behaved. When I wish to be. As you noted, thirty-two years ago. *Still waters run very deep. Still waters mined with explosives, deeper still.* (How shrewdly you knew my soul, dear Erica, though we were not yet twenty years old!)

Just sitting here innocently, backpack on my knees. No need for anyone to make awkward small talk with *me*.

Of course, no one else in the two front rows of the auditorium is an adjunct instructor. No one else would act so boldly—so brashly— as I have done. Indeed it's doubtful that any other adjuncts have come for your lecture—the majority of us are too exhausted from over-work. Rare for us to indulge in the luxury of a "cultural occasion," however bogus, as in your case.

When I'd first learned last spring that you, of all people, had been invited to give an endowed lecture here at our college, immediately I protested; it is my habit to protest against misuses of college funds, especially outlandish fees paid to ill-qualified academics. Then, when I was assured that the invitation had been accepted, and could not be rescinded, I volunteered to introduce you, on the grounds that I am prominent in your field, and I know your work thoroughly—of course. Though I did not emphasize this, for I am not a name-dropper, I ex-plained that you and I had been undergraduate friends, for a (brief) time while near roommates, at Champlain College.

I was unsurprised when my request was denied. Yet somewhat surprised that the request was denied so rudely, in a terse e-mail from the dean.

Yet it is my prerogative to sit here, in the reserved seats. Of all the faculty, it is I who most deserves to be here for it is I who knows you most thoroughly—*I alone who knows your plagiarist's sham heart.*

(In a lurid suspense film, the camera would linger on my unwieldy backpack. On my arms crossed over it to secure it in place and on my fingers clasped tightly together. The viewer would be provoked to think—*What does she have in the backpack? A weapon?*)

(If so, it would be the kind of low-tech weapon that must be used at close quarters. Not a weapon to be operated at a distance. For inti-macy is the point of the assault. Aristotle's *anagnorisis*—recognition!)

*

At last! You have appeared—yet, it is not *you.*

Walking with a cane? Your head shaved? In a bright, showy, kimono-like costume? *You!*

Twelve minutes after the hour, escorted onto the stage by an appa-ratchik from Gender Studies, a former PhD student of yours from Stanford, who will introduce you—you have entered the bright, blinding lights of acclaim from which there can be no retreat.

It is shocking to me—how you have changed. Older—*other.*

Seated on the stage smiling like a fat old eunuch Buddha with a bald-shaved head. A greedy look on your face as you listen to the fatuous introducer praise you with every sort of cliché, absurd un-warranted hype, lists of books, awards, and honors, visiting profes-sorships, MacArthur "Genius" Award—*Bold, original, outspoken, defiant. Bringing women's rights issues to a totally new plateau. Feminism as confrontational theater. Gender as deconstruction. Female speech/guerrilla speech. Politics of a New Radicalism. Courageous, pioneering* . . .

Shrewdly you are wearing oversized dark-tinted glasses so the audience can't see the crepey skin beneath your eyes—can't see your shiny little pig eyes darting about in glee at such comically inflated praise.

Must be pancake makeup slathered on your face—not that make-up can disguise the jowly sag, the creases, aptly named crow's-feet at the edges of your eyes. Eyebrows penciled in dark and given a curi-ous antic "arch"—ridiculous. Square-jutting jaw like Gertrude Stein, and with the heft of Stein's (sexless) body, in the famous Picasso por-trait. How different from the beautiful girl you'd been!

Then, you'd have shuddered at the sight you are now. You, who were so intolerant of *fat.*

Not that you are *fat*—exactly. Overweight by thirty pounds, per-haps thirty-five pounds, but you are a tall woman, large boned, and you carry yourself like an Amazon warrior, still. Though both your face and body exude soft-middle-age flaccidity you are not unattractive; in fact (one might say), you are exotic looking, weirdly seductive, for that has been a paradoxical cornerstone of your "perverse" feminism—the sexual body, the pansexual body, is not neglected or repudiated but rather celebrated. Even pornography in which women are objecti-fied is celebrated!—by a devious logic anathema to an earlier genera-tion of feminists. Shrewdly you'd calculated that you could hardly build a career by agreeing with the older, liberal-minded pioneer feminists who'd preceded you, who'd been your mentors when you were a graduate student; you could not build a career of any substance by acquiescence or compromise—certainly not common sense. And so E____ K_____ has made a career out of the inflammatory and provocative. *Sex is not political. Desire is not containable. What is is not what should be.*

Ideas you'd swiped from me, long ago when we were undergraduates. Papers I'd "vetted" for you for psychology, philosophy, linguistics, feminist studies.

A strange costume you are wearing for an academic setting: gold-spangled, quilted, a kimono with exaggerated shoulders, falling loosely over silky black trousers flared like pajamas. A crafty way of disguising your fifty-three-year-old body from the sharp eyes of the young.

(*Fifty-three!* Difficult to believe.)

(Fortunately, my lean, rangy, flat-chested, and flat-hipped body has aged very differently from yours; indeed, along with my mostly unlined face, it seems that I have scarcely aged at all and no one would guess me to be your almost exact age.)

On your feet (which had once embarrassed you, so *big, broad, flat*—size ten EEE) are square-toed black shoes graceless as cudgels, orthopedic shoes in disguise; seeping over the sides of the shoes are (puffy, swollen) ankles mostly hidden by the flaring pajama legs, which is a good thing.

And yet—amid thunderous applause you have heaved yourself to your feet. You walk with a slight limp, favoring your left side, but you maneuver your black-shellacked cane like a plaything.

"Thank you! I am very honored to be here. . . ."

A sugary voice! A ghastly smile! Fat, wetted lips like a sexual organ, distasteful to see.

Unctuous words. Clichés like faux pearls on a string. And so many pearls, and such a long string. How skilled in hypocrisy you've become, like a lyre you've learned to stroke in your sleep, designed to draw predictable responses from your credulous audience.

What a fraud you are—but a very clever fraud. Making a career out of exploiting the anxieties of *females* in a world of *patriarchal males.* Pretending to believe that there is a *radical female speech* inaccessible to the enemy, i.e., the *male*, that might unite us.

And then, I see that, for just an instant, you have glanced down into the front row of the audience—at me.

Yes, I am sure—at *me.*

For alone of the crowd I have not been applauding. Just sitting here with arms tight-folded and my backpack on my knees. And my hiking-booted feet flat on the floor. And my baseball cap—rudely, you might think—pulled low on my forehead, so that I can peer out at others without their easily seeing me.

You are startled by the sight of me, for a moment thrown off stride. Can't quite recall who I am—is that it? Or is it the intransigence of my being, my refusal to applaud you like the others?

And so, I allow myself a smile like a scissors flashing.

Yes. It is I, your closest friend you'd imagined you had outlived.

Kirkland, Erica A.

Leeuwen, Adra M.

Alphabetical destiny: abutting each other on lists in our freshman residence at Champlain College, Vermont. In a large psychology lecture in which seats in the steeply banked auditorium were assigned and attendance assiduously taken.

Not destined to be friends, obviously. For you were "popular"—drew friends like a magnet. When you walked into a room all eyes swerved onto you, conversations faded, as if you'd strode onto a lighted stage; within a few days of the first semester everyone knew your name. *Erica! Erica Kirkland.*

Of course, I took little notice of you. At first.

Vaguely aware of the tall, swaggering girl in our freshman residence with long, thick, streaked-blonde hair, shrill laughter, restless agate eyes and a face that "lit up" a room. Aggressively you recruited admirers, foolish girls trailed in your wake, for you did not like ever to be alone but rather surrounded by a circle of witnesses like handmaids holding mirrors to reflect your face.

Did I even know your name?—I'm sure that I did not. At first.

As a work-scholarship girl I had neither the time nor the inclination to linger in the dining hall after meals; I did not seek conversations, as I did not seek friends; I had a spare, single room on the top floor of the residence, which meant that I could work through the night if I wished, with no roommate to complain or distract me. I could not comprehend how others in the residence could so happily drift from room to room, smoking their perpetual cigarettes, laughing loudly, wasting hours of precious and irretrievable time in chatter. Fifteen hours a week I worked at the college library. My fitful, brief, self-punishing hikes in the pine woods above the college left me exhilarated and primed to return to my work. I cared only for my courses, my books, and my own writing efforts; the vicissitudes of my interior life—moods ever shifting like the sky above Lake Champlain.

Yet our names sounded alike.

"'Adra'—'Erica.' Separated at birth."

The first thing you said to me, with familiarity startling as a nudge in the ribs.

No one at the college had spoken to me with such intimacy, which suggested a kind of teasing; even my relatives didn't speak to me in such a way, for I never encouraged them.

I didn't know how to answer. I didn't know if I was offended by you smiling into my face as you were, or whether your attention was flattering.

"It's like we're twins—you know—'separated at birth.'"

You must have thought that I was slow-witted; you had to explain your remark.

You laughed, the twin notion was so extravagant. For obviously "Adra" and "Erica" hardly looked like twins: one so strapping blonde, gorgeous, and the other—well, not so.

I remember that we were in the residence hall, on the first floor by a stairway. I remember that you were standing discomfortingly close to me, and I stepped back. A hot blush had come into my face.

My eyes swerved aside, I would not look at you. Shrugged and murmured a vague *Yes, maybe*—as you'd murmur to humor someone who has tried to be clever but the effort has fallen flat.

Later, I would wonder if you'd meant to be cruel, ironic. And it was that intention that had fallen flat.

"D'you smoke, Adra? No?"

"No."

Hard to believe, this was an era in which everyone smoked. In our residence hall, in classrooms. Seminars in which our professors smoked, dropping ashes into Styrofoam coffee cups.

Your brand was Tareytons.

"You should try, Ad. It's like caffeine—it gives you a *charge*."

With time, you began to call me "Ad"—familiar.

With time, shyly, I began to speak your name—"Erica." The sound—the three quite sharp, distinctive syllables—felt strange on my lips.

Yes, I did begin to smoke. But only in your presence, at first, with cigarettes you gave me—"Here, Ad. You look like you could use a cigarette." Casually you'd hold out your pack of Tareytons to me, giving it a little shake.

It makes me faint to recall that gesture. I think that I don't want to recall that gesture, which was often made in the presence of other girls, as if to signal a special connection that excluded them.

(Eventually, I began to smoke alone. In time, by the end of college, and through the protracted misery of my twenties, I was smoking two to three packs of cigarettes a day, which I could not afford; each time I lit a cigarette I felt a wave of faintness, recalling *you*. Cursing *you*.)

(But I am over that now. It has been decades since I've thought that inhaling toxic fumes into my lungs was "romantic"—that anything passed from you to me might have been "romantic.")

"'Shy.' You wear shyness like armor, Ad."

Your strategy was to observe, to analyze. You were not being *critical*, you claimed. As a feminist, you were utilizing tools of *deconstruction*.

Where Adra was *shy*, Erica was *bold*.

Or rather, Adra was *shy seeming*.

Together we read the early feminists. Mary Wollstonecraft, Charlotte Perkins Gilman, Virginia Woolf. Simone de Beauvoir, spoiled for us by our discovery that she was in thrall to her longtime lover Jean-Paul Sartre, a walleyed gnome/womanizer whose infidelities de Beauvoir too readily forgave.

"If I'd caught Sartre being unfaithful to me, with someone young enough to be his daughter, I'd have stabbed the bastard. Right in the groin."

Like a child you spoke savagely. Others who were listening were taken aback by your vehemence but I just laughed.

"Would you do the same, Adra?"

"No."

"Why not?"

"Because I don't give a damn about men. Where men stick their penises is of no concern to me."

You laughed, startled. You were impressed by such words. Though you were a brash, bold, outspoken young woman you were yourself in thrall to men, or rather to sex; to the allure of sex that was a part of the air we breathed. You wouldn't have thought of dismissing, as I had, what seemed to mean so much to the human species.

334

For it was true, I didn't give a damn about men. I was tall, lanky limbed, with a plain, fierce, white-skinned face and a prepubescent body (at age eighteen), uninterested in attracting the attention of others except by way of my writing, and then it was only the attention of my professors that meant anything to me. And then, only a very few of my professors, for the faculty at Champlain College was not much distinguished.

You said, staring at me, "Of course. You're right, Adra. Only another female knows what a female wants, by instinct."

You could not have spoken more jubilantly if you'd made this discovery entirely by yourself.

Still waters run deep. Still waters mined by explosives, deeper still.

It seemed natural to me, to prefer my own company to the company of others. In high school I had mastered the art of *icy calm, detachment, indifference.*

For I did not trust you. Any of you.

Though most of the girls in our college residence had been afflicted with homesickness virulent as flu for the first week or two of the first semester, soon a bizarre change came over them, a rabid need to be together much of the time, to walk in braying packs to the dining hall and to gather in one another's rooms late into the night. Homesickness was forgotten in a compulsion to confide in one another, to talk wildly about things that should have been kept private, and to laugh at things that were not remotely funny, like getting drunk—"wasted"—and throwing up at a fraternity party—"making out" with some guy they scarcely knew—"flunking" an exam. And of course they talked about one another ceaselessly, with relish, with pity, with a pretense of outrage, with the most lurid and unapologetic curiosity—*My God have you heard!*

What they said of me, I could imagine. Or maybe it was mostly pity they felt for what they perceived as my *aloneness.*

. . . wouldn't be bad looking if she wasn't so sour.

. . . if she'd just smile.

(But why would I smile at them? It was enough that, by degrees, I was learning to smile at *you.*)

You liked to quote Sylvia Plath (whom, with your blonde hair and manic ambition, you resembled, to a degree)—"'I eat men like air.'"

Dropping by my room on the fourth floor of our residence when I was working late on a weekend night, in the aftermath of a fraternity party or a "date." Eyes dilated and mouth swollen, hair in a tangle, smelling of beer, male sweat, and (I imagined) semen—"Hi, Adra! Can I interrupt?"

You were very funny, very wicked, complaining of the guys you went out with. Wanting me to know both how popular you were, how every guy who saw you desired you, some of them even fought over you, and yet how bemused you were by them, their clumsiness and stupidity, how disdainful you were even of sex, unless it was *the very best sex.*

Did I want to hear this? No.

Did I want to hear—some of this? *No.*

And so one night when you came to my door to rap lightly with your knuckles and push it open and ask, *Can I interrupt,* quickly I stammered that I was busy, I had no time. Not at the moment, I did not want to be interrupted. *No.*

Seeing in your face a look of faint incredulity. That anyone would rebuff *you.*

But you went away. You did not insist. You laughed, you went away, gracious if a little drunk, a good sport. Never one to push yourself on another but rather one who calculates a new point of entry, a new strategy of triumph and revenge at another time.

(It was true, I worked late into the night, in a kind of fever. I believed that I did my most inspired work after midnight and I did not want to waste my waning energy listening to your droll tales told to impress me, to make me envious and jealous and yearning to be like you. *No.*)

How did I come to know your secret. One of your secrets.

I did not ever actually *know,* I think. But by accident hearing you in one of the bathrooms and knowing it had to be you, exiting at once when I heard what it seemed I was hearing and not wanting to know anything further. . . . Quickly disappearing into my room, and the door shut.

But soon, others knew. Began to know something. How you starved yourself, bloated your stomach with Tabs. And then, how you ate—ravenous as an animal. At the worst of times you hid away to eat. Campaigning for vice president of our class. Posters with your face everywhere on campus. (And some of us, overzealous on your behalf, having put up your posters, returned after dark to deface or tear down the less attractive posters of your rivals.) It began to be whispered how you crept away to vomit—to force yourself to vomit. Sticking a finger down your throat, quickly the reaction came, a nervous reflex, deftly executed. *Just this one time. I haven't done it in—months. . . . Just the pressure right now. Stuffed myself like a disgusting pig.* You could make a joke of it, almost.

Why are you telling me. Why, I don't want to know.

Embarrassed and ashamed for you. Stricken with concern for you.

Though we did not—yet—know the clinical term *bulimia.* Though we had heard—some of us—of *anorexia.*

(*Anorexia:* aversion to food. Fear of food, fear of "getting fat"— developing hips, breasts. Aversion to menstruating. How well I understood!)

But I don't want to share these secrets with you. Not with anyone. Even you.

Also: I have work to do. Always, I have work to do. Like saying a rosary, *work to do.*

Please don't knock at my door. Please don't interrupt.

Please don't make me feel sorry for you, fear for you, it is a way of seduction, I am not strong enough to resist.

And so: a girl in the residence was speaking of you, meanly, maliciously, and I overheard and came up to her and told her to shut her mouth—"It's none of your business, what any of us do." The girl— her name was Beverly Whitty—one of those who'd adored you and followed you around and was rebuffed by you—was shocked, and the expression on her face so inane, fatuous in alarm, I shoved her back against the wall as I'd never done before in my life to anyone—as I'd never imagined doing. *And yet it was easy!*

All who witnessed this were shocked. But no one dared protest as I strode away, tingling with righteousness, my blood beating in my veins as rapidly, happily, I ascended the stairs to my room on the fourth floor.

How easy, to shove another. What a surge of pleasure, one could become addicted.

It was at this time that fear of Adra Leeuwen began in the residence where before there'd been only a kind of wary disdain. I did not trouble to discourage it.

Our residence adviser, Miss Tull (as we called her), summoned me to speak with her. She was a nervous woman with a tenuous air of authority and a permanently strained smile (she knew how flighty,

337

fickle, febrile girls our age were, how swiftly they could turn upon even someone they claimed to adore). Of course, the silly, frightened girls had reported me, but it was not clear that they'd reported the reason for my having behaved as I had, my defense of *you*.

In Miss Tull's sitting room I was stony faced, unyielding. By the age of nineteen I had attained my full height of five feet ten but I was still lean, flat hipped as a boy, with close-cropped hair like a boy's, and a pale, somewhat sallow skin that was the very expression of adolescent *sulk*. My reputation in the residence was of a high intelligence linked to a sharp, sarcastic tongue. (But why was this? I rarely exchanged remarks with anyone in the residence except you, and I was never sarcastic with you.) I have no doubt I intimidated poor Miss Tull, who clasped her hands tightly together to disguise their shaking. This was not yet an era in which psychological counseling was recommended for students displaying the slightest "aberrant" behavior, so Miss Tull simply spoke to me, with a pretense of calm, drawing upon tactics very likely provided for resident advisers by their supervisors—"You are a very intelligent young woman, Adra. It is just surprising—it is unexpected—that you would behave as you did. . . ." Frowning and silent and staring at the carpet, I let Miss Tull speak for some minutes before I said, "What I did to—her—was morally justified. I would not have acted as I did to halt a malicious slander if it had not been justified."

"But we are hoping it won't happen again, Adra. . . ."

I had to smile. With Adra Leeuwen there is no *we*.

However, I didn't contradict Miss Tull. As a young child I'd learned the strategy of allowing my elders to think what they wanted to think while I did what I wanted to do as soon as their backs were turned.

When you found out, you squeezed my hand, and said, with rapidly blinking eyes, not quite looking at me, laughing—"Look, I don't know what the hell it was, what it's about, all I heard was—you stuck up for me. Thank you, Adra! Anybody else, they'd have said nothing. They'd just—wouldn't—have stuck up for me." Your words were halting, uncertain. Still you could not look at me. A hot blush came onto your face and seemed to spread to mine, to my chill, sallow cheeks.

All that I could think to say was: "Well, I'm not 'anybody else.'"

Stiff, trembling. Needing to run away.

"Well, I just wanted to—thank you. . . ."

"We don't have to talk about it. OK?"

"Well—OK"

Stiffly walking away. Feeling your eyes on the back of my head, quizzical, grateful.

Next time I saw you, in a public place, you were flushed with triumph. You were looking gorgeous—not like a girl who has been sticking a finger down her throat. Your friends crowded around you, to congratulate you for having won the "hotly contested" election for vice president of our class by a narrow margin—something like fourteen votes.

(Yes, it was a rumor that you'd cheated somehow in the election. Supporters of yours had rigged ballots. For you aroused such adulation, such loyalty. I did not wish to compete with these friends of yours; I kept my distance, aloof and uninvolved.)

"Friend of My Heart." The sentimental Irish song one of the girls in the residence played on the battered old piano in a corner of the living room. Unbidden, the melody comes back to me sometimes. Very ordinary, you'd have to say banal, yet the song had the power of burrowing into my brain. *Friend of my heart, where have you gone. Friend of my heart, I am alone.*

Driving my shuddering Honda Civic rarely less than one hundred miles a week when I was commuting to teach at two other colleges beside this college. And during these hours, it was "Friend of My Heart" that echoed in my brain.

To live as an adjunct instructor is to commute—if you are lucky enough to have more than one job. Because this college will not employ me as a full-time instructor, still less give me tenure, until my car broke down last year I was obliged to drive seventy miles to the state university at Troy, to teach a course that meets on Monday and Thursday evenings for ninety minutes; here, I teach on Tuesday and Thursday mornings. Fortunately, I can bicycle to my classes here; I can take a train to Troy. An adjunct instructor lives by her schedule, and the "schedule" is whimsical and wind driven as fate.

You would not understand. *You* who earn in a single cobbled-together lecture an adjunct's salary for an entire term.

Where have you gone. I am alone.

*

It was genuine, my indifference to you. At the start.

A giant icicle, a stalactite, strikingly disfigured, that begins to melt, and to drip, and by degrees loses even its disfigured shape. Melting, bleeding away.

For you were so very friendly to me. Waving to me, calling to me, inviting me to sit with you and your companions in the dining hall, and blinking in surprise when I declined. For truly, I had thoughts of my own to think, which I did not want scattered and broken.

Not thinking—*No! I will not be seduced by you, and dropped. I am not that lonely, and I am not that stupid.*

Yet, we became friends. Somehow that happened.

By degrees it happened, in the winter months of our freshman year. Hiking together in the pine woods above the college—just Erica and Adra. Brisk, exhilarating walks along snowy trails. You kept up a stream of excited chatter, your plans for a "fantastic future" to which I murmured assent, half humoring, half impressed. And so by spring a change had occurred between us. A quickening of my pulse when I saw you on campus, and an undertow of apprehension, dread.

"Adra! Hey. Wait. Walk with me."

I was a tall girl. Invariably I'd been the tallest girl in my class even in high school. One of the tallest persons in the class.

Yet, beside you, at Champlain College, I was not taller: we were of a height. (Though you wore heels, often high-heeled boots on your large, broad feet to boost your height; you did not shrink to make yourself smaller.)

Wanting to trust you. Wanting to believe you when you told me how special I was, like no other person you'd ever met before.

And how grateful you were, when I took time to help you with your class work. So very—flattering. . . .

"Ad! Thank you *so much.*"

And, "Addie! You're my *heart.*"

In such ways, my indifference melted. My resistance. An icy little puddle at my feet.

In our Introduction to Psychology class of 130 students it was our destiny to be seated side by side—*Kirkland, Leeuwen.* And so naturally you might ask me to explain, for instance, the distinction between Pavlovian and Skinnerian conditioning (a distinction you never could recall); you might ask me to help you prepare for quizzes, mid-term, and final, and your term paper on an overambitious subject ("Is there a 'female speech'?"), which, with your numerous campus activities you didn't have time to adequately research.

That first paper, for which you received a stellar grade—A+.

And how funny it seemed to us, that my grade for my paper, at least as solid as yours, received only an A.

Over a period of time it came to be that I "helped" you with vir-tually all of your academic work. Under the pretext of our studying together, working together, earnestly discussing issues together, your exploitation of me flourished. I am not claiming that it was system-atic—it was spontaneous, opportunistic. For you were a very bright individual, for one who was so gregarious: quick-witted, agile, and re-sourceful as any predator. Ideas flashed from your brain, half cracked, half inspired—few of them original, or even plausible—but the many distractions in your life made it impossible for you to sit still long enough to actually—what is the plebeian word?—*work*.

To explore an idea, to research and present an idea, to do the drudg-ery of footnotes, a bibliography—to write, write, and rewrite—that is *work*.

As I am an adjunct instructor seemingly by fate, so, by fate, am I obliged to *work*. While you—your inane "research"—are supported by a ceaseless succession of grants and appointments. Are you not ashamed to be so blessed while others, your peers, your superiors, are accursed?

Of course, it was flattering to me as an undergraduate that you so appreciated my help. And truly you did not ask of me that I con-tribute so much to your undergraduate papers, as I did; you'd only asked me to "skim"—to "make suggestions." But being generous as I was, that's to say besotted and foolish, I could not resist pouring out my brain, that's to say my heart.

Papers in feminist theory, literary theory, the philosophy of lan-guage, "gender studies" (new and revolutionary at the time, a bold anthropology of sexual identity)—how many times you squeezed my hand, or hugged me as no one had ever hugged me—*You are just so, so brilliant, Ad! Oh, God, what would I do without you.*

Strange that, beside yours, my own work seemed dull. Those papers that bore the name Erica Kirkland seemed (somehow) more exciting, more glamorous, than those bearing the name Adra Leeuwen.

In our classes, you spoke frequently. Bold, assertive, and seductive. I was apt to brood in silence, bent over a notebook in which (it would appear) I was taking notes earnestly. My face was stiff, impassive. It was not clear (even to me) if I was stricken with shyness in class, or with stubbornness.

Gnawing at my lower lip until it bled.

There are no new ideas. Only new appropriations.

This has been the cornerstone of your career. How convenient for a plagiarist to proclaim! An ideal way of obscuring the fact that you've stolen your ideas from others.

J'accuse: The core of *The Masks of Gender: Language, Sexual Deceit, and Subterfuge* was stolen from one of my papers, itself a masterwork of undergraduate pretentiousness—an application of Hegelian principles to ideas of intentionality in consciousness originally developed by Edmund Husserl, and all of it imposed upon the *female voice.*

Have you forgotten, this idea was originally *mine?* And how lavishly you thanked me for it, and praised me for it. . . . Yet in the acknowledgments to your "seminal" book there is no "Adra Leeuwen."

In none of your books. In none of your footnotes. Nowhere!—in more than thirty years.

The heartbreak of looking for my name. The futility.

(At least I don't buy your books. It is enough for me to stand in a bookstore and leaf through them checking the index, checking footnotes for my name, and hoping no one will discover me at this humiliating task.)

I did not want to acknowledge how shallow you were, enrolling in courses that would assure you high grades; avoiding the most rigorous courses, which, with typical recklessness I never hesitated to take—symbolic logic, phenomenology, cognitive psychology, Saussurean linguistics, Husserl and Heidegger, Lacan and Foucault. Which was why, at the time I withdrew from college in the spring of our junior year, my grade-point average was almost exactly the same as yours.

To you, appearances were all. Impressions were all. Whatever you wrote, or handed in as your writing, was a stratagem to be admired and an appeal for a high grade. Anything less than an A was distressing to you, and required emergency conferences with professors; if a professor did not appear to be utterly charmed by you, you dropped the course. *Look at me, admire me, are you impressed with me, love me. Surrender to me! Die for me.*

Later, I would learn that I wasn't the only person you flattered in this way. I wasn't the only naive "friend" you exploited. But I was the one who did the most for you, over a period of more than three years. Stupidly, I was the *friend of your heart.*

"Adra? Can I say something—personal? You won't be offended."

Won't be offended. Of course not.

It was a giddy prospect—not being offended. Dizzying, like standing at the edge of a deep ravine.

Out of your smiling mouth, these words: "What I really, really admire about you, Adra—I guess I'm envious!—is how you don't give a damn how you appear to other people—what they think of you. Like, guys."

A shrug of my shoulders. As if what you were going to tell me would not be wounding as it would be to another, ordinary girl.

"It's so cool, Adra. You don't even *try.* You let your hair go, sometimes you don't wash it for days. Looks like you barely comb it. You never wear makeup—of course. (You don't even own makeup, I'm sure.) Your face could be a boy's face, almost. A handsome boy's face."

You dared to touch my face, with your fingertips. For a long moment I did not flinch away.

Nearing the end of sophomore year you said, as if casually: "We should room together, Ad. Next year? OK?"

Like a blade these words cut into me. Thrilling, with an undertone of dread.

"No. I don't think so."

"What d'you mean—*no?* Why not?"

"I don't—want—to room with anyone."

You stared at me, wounded. *With anyone!* But how was Erica Kirkland—*anyone?*

The prospect of sharing a room in a residence hall with you filled me with panic. Like being pushed close to a mirror, so close that I could not see the reflection in the mirror, in this way blinded, suffocated. *No thank you. No.*

You went away. Furious. You were not so forgiving now for you had offered yourself, with rare openness. And in my shyness, in my fear of our intimacy, I had rebuffed you. It is likely that you were thinking *She will pay for this insult.* Though I could not have guessed at the time.

*

And then, in our junior year, the scales tipped away from me, and I became morbidly attached to you.

Your invitations to sit with you in the dining hall, to accompany you to events on campus, to receptions and parties, began to diminish. You dropped by to visit my room less frequently. (At a little distance I would see you, swaying drunk, giddy, and your face lit with merriment that excluded me, which seemed to me vulgar and foolish, shameful. And I retreated from you, and shut my door and locked it.) Rarely you invited me to walk with you in the woods above the college.

Suddenly you had no time for me.

You won an award for "outstanding citizenship," and others crowded around you to congratulate you. You published an essay in the school literary magazine, that I'd seen only in an early draft, which I had critiqued closely, but you had not returned it to me for a second reading.

Were others "vetting" your work now? I could only guess. Trying not to be sick with jealousy.

Covertly I watched you. I was edgy, anxious for your attention. Though I did not seek it. When you needed help with a paper on normative philosophy, the news came to me through another girl, a network of girls, each of them passing on the request—*Erica is worried to death she is going to flunk this course. But she doesn't want to ask you to help her, she feels that she has taken up too much of your time as it is.*

"That's silly. That's just ridiculous. Tell her to bring it to me. Of course, I'll be happy to help her."

And this was so. I was very happy to help you.

That paper, we received an A. Both of us quite proud!

Weekends when I was not working at the library, I had time to myself. Too much time perhaps. I had time for my own work, for my "creative" writing, and I had time for your work, which had begun to be more daring now, more original and imaginative, in ways I could not have foreseen. *As if she has swallowed me whole, and has grown around me.* I did not mind providing footnotes, combing research materials in the library while you were at fraternity parties, attending a conference in New York City. I took pleasure in knowing how it would surprise you, that I'd expanded your sparsely argued fifteen-page paper into a thirty-page paper, richly footnoted, brilliantly argued. One of your "pioneering" papers.

I did not "stalk" you—the very notion would have been repugnant to me. But sometimes it happened (by chance) that we were walking in the same dircction, onto the hilly campus, you in the lead and me trailing behind, like a dog that is dragging one of its feet, reluctant to be seen, and yet hopeful.

And you would see me, and wave to me. "Adra? C'mon, catch up and walk with me."

You laughed at me. (Did you?)

You took pity on me. You were pitiless.

With the innocence of the most profound cruelty you inspired others to laugh at your lanky-limbed disheveled friend. Your friend who was indeed "special" yet deeply unhappy.

Of course, it was not stalking. "Stalking" had not been invented.

And one day on the steps of Lyman Hall you said, "Look. I'm tired of you following me, Adra. It's boring. You're boring."

But it was a joke. (Was it?) I was shocked, but managed to laugh. Tears flooded my eyes, which often happens when I am taken by surprise, I cannot seem to *see* or even to *hear*, for my senses are blocked by the surprise.

"I'm not 'following' you. That's—that's ridiculous."

"You're acting like a damn *girl*."

"You! You're the damn *girl*." Suddenly stammering, "You—you bleach your *hair*. *You're the girl*."

Hated you! Could have flung myself at you and scratched and gouged your eyes you'd outlined in dark brown eye pencil and darkened with mascara that gave your lashes a stiff look like the legs of long-legged spiders.

You laughed at me, seeing the fury and misery in my face, which you knew I dared not express. Turning away, with a negligent gesture of your hand as if you were waving away an annoying fly—"Oh, go away. I'll see you later, Adra."

There are the exploited, and there are those who exploit.

The predator, and the prey.

The parasite, and the host.

It was a time when I walked often—alone—in the woods above the college. I did not really hike any longer—I did not have the time.

I had a fear too of getting lost in the trails for I did not have a strong sense of direction. The area of the brain that monitors spatial relations had not developed in my brain as it develops in others.

Walking with you, for the last time, in the fresh pine-sharp air, all of my senses alert to the point almost of pain, and my heart running rapid as a mountain stream, and you are breathing deeply and humming under your breath, which (you know) is distracting and annoying to me and suddenly you say, quizzing me, "Which way is the college, Adra? Just checking." And I am jolted from my thoughts and not immediately able to comprehend our location. For it is not a simple fact, that the college must be behind us; the trail has been curving, twisting, turning back upon itself, indeed we have turned onto several trails, and a panic comes over me that we are lost. . . .

"Don't be silly, Adra. Nobody gets lost *here.*"

You'd hiked long miles, five or six hours, seven hours in the Adirondacks. You'd belonged to a hiking club. Your leg muscles were hard and thick, stronger than mine. It was natural for you to become impatient with me, who had so poor a sense of direction.

In hiking boots your feet were large as a man's. The only feature of yours that truly embarrassed you, you'd said you *hated.*

But you liked it that my feet were the same size as yours, in length. In width, my feet were narrower than yours.

We sat on a fallen log. We noted how tiny ants swarmed beneath the bark, which we lazily picked off. Dreamily, you said, "Ants in a colony are like neurons in a great brain, but they are brainless."

Some of this I knew also, from our psychology lecture. In fact, I had been reading on the subject, and must have told you, in my fascination with the mysteries of evolution, and now you were quoting me back to myself, in a way that was impressive to me as if what I was hearing was entirely new.

With a shudder, I said that it was terrible to think of ants—"What they represent."

"What they 'represent'? What's that?"

"Ourselves. They are like ourselves."

"Oh, I don't think so. The ants are just *ants.*"

You laughed at me. At times you found my seriousness very charming but at other times you found my seriousness very boring.

Stubbornly I said, "Nothing is just what it is. It is also what it represents."

"No! An ant is an ant, and five ants are a single ant. A trillion ants are just one ant."

"That's what I meant. They are terrifying." I didn't know what we were talking about but I was feeling disoriented.

"Oh, I think they're wonderful. Just—ants."

Grinding the heel of your boot into a small anthill, crushing as many scurrying ants as you could. The look on your face!—murderous, grinning.

You were bored with me, and told me that you wanted to be alone for a while. It was an era before cell phones so I did not think that you would make contact with another person whose company you preferred, to laugh at me behind my back. I did not think this. You said for me to sit, and think my "deep boring thoughts," and you would return in a while; but you did not return, and I knew that you would not though I waited anxiously.

At the edge of a steep ravine I was sitting. By the ravaged anthill, about which hundreds of ants now scurried in a single, collective paroxysm of panic. I was afraid to stand, for my legs would tremble if I did. All that day, on the hiking trail, I had been feeling lightheaded, uneasy. I was wanting to cry, and clutch at your hand. Hoping that you would ask me to room with you next year—our senior year.

In my backpack I always carried supplies—water in a plastic container, plenty of tissues (for my eyes and nose watered badly in the cold air), a Swiss army knife.

Not for a long time had I hiked such a distance that these supplies were needed. Yet, I never went out without them. The Swiss army knife seemed particularly crucial should I want to slash my wrists or, better yet, slash another's throat on a remote trail.

In fact, I'd never taken the knife out of the backpack. Not once.

At last, I managed to stand, shakily. I could not see—my eyes flooded with tears. I was groping for the log, and sat down again, clumsily, weakly. I had not cried in such a way since childhood. And my vain, frayed life seemed to pass before me like a poorly executed film of jerky images. *You are not even brave enough to die here. She wants you to die, so she can be rid of you. But you are a coward. You will let her down. And she knew that too. You can only return to what you are, and what you will be.*

But I did not return to what I'd been. Soon after, I departed from Champlain College.

Nor did you return that day to find me where I was sitting weak legged, dazed by the edge of the ravine. Instead you would claim to have believed—to my very face!—that I'd taken another trail back down the mountain, and that we'd agreed to "each go our separate ways"—for this was something we'd done "many times before."

Your lies are melodic in sound. Each syllable a joy (to the ignorant ear) to hear.

My words are truths, harshly uttered. No one wants to hear such ugly words barbed with little hooks like the penises of cats.

In your mouth, honey. In my mouth, toad venom.

"And now, in conclusion . . ."

For the past fifty minutes I have been staring at you. We have all been staring at you. Stunned by the horror of you.

Few know, as I know, how you'd once looked. How vile you are now that your (ugly) soul has emerged. Your coarse, showy blonde beauty has faded as if it had never been and now you are revealed as a middle-aged woman who has let her body go and has become sexless, graceless. Over the years I'd observed your official photographs change with glacial slowness (for a feminist, you were certainly loath to acknowledge your aging); yet now, exposed on the bright-lit stage in your ridiculous tent-kimono, head hairless as soapstone and face sagging, you appear much older than your calendar age so that I am thinking—gloating?—that you must have a medical condition, or you'd had one; cancer, probably. (I wonder: do you still smoke? Do Tareytons still exist?) Chemotherapy has ravaged you, face, throat, body, and scalp. Perhaps you'd lost weight and have more recently packed on weight as a warrior might pack on armor for self-protection. Oh—it is upsetting to me, to see the change in you, who'd once been so—seductive. . . .

Especially I do not want to imagine what your ruin of a body looks like, hidden inside those silly clothes.

Friend of my heart—it is what you deserve.

". . . thanking you all for your kindness, and hospitality, and your warmth on this beautiful campus. . . ."

Each of your words, uttered with breathy insincerity, is a banality, a cliché. Yet, strung together, like cheap pearls on a cheap string, they bring to mind a memory of beauty. I shut my eyes so that I see only narrowly through my eyelashes, which shimmer with tears, and I scarcely see *you*—fat old woman with a Buddha face.

Instead I see that other. The girl you'd been.

When greed and ambition had not (yet) shone in your face.

Boring. You are boring. Go away.

Abruptly I'd withdrawn from college in March of our senior year. Returned home, so weak that I could not get out of bed some days but lay in a half sleep of fever and dread. Eventually it was diagnosed that I had infectious mononucleosis, which I'd thought was a mythical illness but turned out to be real. The transcript of my grades came to the house, a column of I's—Incompletes.

These would change automatically to F's if I did not return to complete the courses within a semester. But I did/could not return.

In this initial skirmish, you won. In subsequent skirmishes in the long battle, you have won. But your victories have been predicated on victims not fighting back.

Giving up. *But I did not give up.*

After I left Champlain College broken and ashamed we lost contact. I did not write to you, and out of shame and guilt you would not have written to me. Perhaps you forgot me! For I was but one of those whom you'd exploited, whom you might forget as one of those carnivorous insects that sucks frogs dry and leaves behind the frog husk would forget its succession of victims.

For several years I would live at home as one might live underground. For a while I stopped reading entirely—the "life of the mind" had nearly destroyed me. I would work at low-paying jobs including public-school substitute teaching. In my midtwenties I dared to return to college. This was not Champlain College where my tuition had been paid for me but one of the State University of New York branches, functional and charmless as an automat. Working days, attending classes at night, I eked out a beggarly master's degree in English and communication arts; eventually my PhD was earned with labor like the labor of one breaking rocks with a sledgehammer. But it was too late, I'd missed my time. Older than others on the job market by five, six years and soon then condemned to a lifetime of adjunct teaching—for which I learned to be grateful if at the same time spiteful. Yet I did not ever give up my intellectual aspirations—I will never give up. . . .

All the while I was keenly aware of you—who'd gone to Duke on a fellowship, then a first-rate department of stellar feminist scholars and critics. You were never a scholar, you hadn't the patience. You were never a true critic, you hadn't the taste. You were no kind of intellectual, for you hadn't the intelligence. But you had the seductive manner that, in academic circles, is a most effective substitute. Soon, you became the protégée of a famous feminist, coeditor of a massively successful anthology of women's literature from Sappho to the present time. You'd assisted in this project, one of the great curatorial projects in American feminist literary history—*you!*

From there, so launched, you were hired at Brown, and then hired away to Columbia; then, in a dizzying coup, you were summoned to Stanford, where you received a half-time appointment in gender studies and a half-time appointment at the Stanford Institute of Research. There, you cobbled together—you did not *write*: you are too wonderful for mere *writing*—the fandango of purloined material that would become *The Masks of Gender*. Your star ascended, brightly glaring with sparks, while mine smoldered, and nearly went out. (Indeed my star was hardly a star, rather an ember.)

Many times, pride swallowed like phlegm, I wrote to you—in appeal, in accusation, bemused, furious, matter-of-fact, and "nostalgic." Of course you did not answer—why would you answer? These were the days of (typed or handwritten) letters in envelopes, sealed and stamped, which shifted by degrees to e-mail, so fluid, so seemingly (though not actually) bodiless, anonymous. I would write e-mails to the editors of journals in which your work appeared, and to your publishers; I would write to the dean of the faculty at Stanford, and to your departmental chairs; I would write to feminist colleagues enclosing photocopied material that condemned you, often with zestful wit. Some of these colleagues were kind enough to respond to my appeals, but most were not. And those who were initially kind soon ceased communicating with me when I sent them more material, heavy packets of photocopied material, and demanded that they join with me in a "class-action suit" against you.

Every friend, I have come to see, is a fair-weather friend.

For years, as possibly you know, I have been publishing reviews of your work in quasi-academic journals, the most public being *The Women's Review of Books*; it has been my solemn task to eviscerate your (insipid, bestselling) books, your shoddy scholarship and questionable theories. Boldly I have dared to attack you as a plagiarist and thief—a betrayer of the heart. A *faux feminist* who sells out women.

You have won many awards, however undeserving. That is a matter of (shameful) historic fact. I have won no awards—I am not ashamed but, in a way, proud. *For I do not conform to the expectations of others.* My threadbare life does not make a striking résumé for a book jacket—I have yet to publish my first book—yet I am stubborn in resilience, I believe in myself—one day, my contribution to cultural studies will be appreciated.

Each semester it seems that I open my veins, and bleed. And I bleed, and I bleed. I teach the great texts—the *pre*texts of our debased era: Freud, Nietzsche, Dostoyevsky, Kafka, Sartre, Camus. And one or two students, perhaps, will appreciate me—in their student evaluations they will write, *Ms. Leeuwen is an excellent teacher, I think. She is very well knowledgeable and her tests are hard but not unfair. When I did not do like I thought I should, I went to talk to her and she went over my paper with me, and took time. She is not like some teachers, who are resentful of you when you come to their offices and the first minute you are there, they are waiting for you to leave.*

I feel sorry for Ms. Leeuwen, there is something sad about her. But she is excellent reading to us passages from Jean-Paul Sartre on disgust.

My friend said, Jesus I would slash my wrists if I turned out like her. But I do not feel this way. I think that my thinking has been sharpened by Ms. Leeuwen and I would take more courses from her if these existed.

Other evaluations, cruder, frankly stupid, scribbled by persons to whom I gave grades lower than A, I do not dignify by reading. Quickly shoving the forms into the unwieldy envelopes, and "filing" them in the trash.

At the start of my career at this college I was admired by many in the tenured ranks. Many times I was complimented on something I had written, published in an obscure journal, or online; not all of these compliments were insincere or hypocritical, though, this being academia, one should not be naive. But at departmental meetings, which I took care not to miss, though I was but an adjunct, I could not resist raising my hand to comment, to question, to object, and occasionally to ridicule; in this way, though many continued to admire me, and admire me still, after eleven intrepid years, the majority soon came to dislike me as one of those whom literary tradition has called the *plain dealer*—the individual who speaks her mind, all too bluntly.

Shamefully, though I am the most experienced, the most published, and the most intelligent of the small army of adjuncts who help keep the college afloat, like galley slaves hidden from the upper deck, there was a small cadre of colleagues who tried to terminate my contract just last year. Only my reasoned appeal, and my threat of bringing a lawsuit against the college, with a likelihood of sensational repercussions in local media, as in *The Chronicle of Higher Education*, thwarted this attempt to destroy me; but I do not trust anyone here now.

At last you have finished your "lecture." You are peering coquettishly over the rims of your dark-tinted glasses at the audience exploding in applause.

It is deafening—such applause!

And now—a standing ovation.

Stubbornly, I remain sitting. I am sure that some of my tenured colleagues will remain seated as well, for not all of them can have been persuaded by you, yet, by quick degrees, as if shamed by the younger persons behind them, my hypocrite colleagues rise to their feet, smiling and abashed like Chinese elders routed by the cudgels of the Red Guard.

At the podium you have the grace to remain standing, somewhat surprised looking, or so it seems, at the waves of warm applause washing over you; now, you are leaning your bulky body pointedly on your cane, and a look of fatigue has come into your face. Quickly the Gender Studies apparatchik comes to your side, to escort you from the stage.

Another time, your gaze drifts onto me—I think. As I sit here in the choicest seat in Hill Auditorium, stubbornly refusing to stand, arms crossed over my backpack as if to secure it.

And then, the unexpected occurs.

Though I have prepared, assiduously, for the next stage of my confrontation with E_____ K_____, steeling myself for the most demanding performance of my life, all is—suddenly, capriciously—changed; and what was to be, by my vow, is not to be after all.

At the conclusion of the program, there is to be a book signing. Many, many persons have lined up in the foyer, awaiting your arrival there, but I do not intend to be one of them.

Instead, boldly I leave my seat, and make my way up onto the stage. No one takes notice of me—the performance is over, people are milling about in the aisles, making their way to the exits. In my most pleasant voice I call your name—"Erica! Hello"—as I follow you and my colleague from Gender Studies, who is escorting you off stage; you turn to me, puzzled, with a half smile, and adrenaline rushes to my heart so powerfully that I nearly faint.

First glance, you'd think that I might be a graduate student—straggly hair, cap pulled low over my forehead, bulky backpack I am struggling to unzip, out of which I will probably (you assume!) tug a dog-eared copy of *Masks of Gender* to ask you to sign; your escort will frown in annoyance, but you, in your mode of noblesse oblige, will say, *Why of course! How shall I inscribe it?*

Second glance, you will see that I am not so young. Probably not a graduate student, and probably not a (full-time) faculty member.

Third glance, if there is time for a third glance, you will see that I am middle-aged, as you are; with a face less obviously ravaged and a body still lean, if perhaps too thin, and my skin papery pale, no longer the resilient skin of youth.

"Is it—Adrienne? Is it you?"

I almost can't *see*—you are so dazzling in the gold-glittering kimono.

And you are staring at me. An expression in your face of wariness, warmth—surprise. . . .

"Adrienne? It's you?"

On your cane you hobble toward me. This is so unexpected, I am unable at first to respond.

Your lips are parted, glistening. Your eyes inside the dark-tinted lenses are indeed pouched with tiredness, yet alert, fixed upon my face.

"Not 'Adrienne'—not exactly."

"You were my student at—Columbia?"

I don't correct you. At this moment my name seems laughably insignificant—*Adrienne, Adra.* How could it matter?

The shock is, you have recognized me. You have identified me— *friend.*

With seductive boldness you dare to take my hands, which are cold, and warm them between your palms, which feel almost hot, moistly hot, and comforting.

What a long time it has been!—through a buzzing in my ears I hear your throaty voice and the laughter in your voice. *Friend. Here is a friend.*

It is astonishing to me; you seem delighted to see me. Unless it is just a performance for several of my colleagues who have hurried to surround you—but I don't think so, I believe it is genuine; you are not pretending now that the lecture is over and the audience has departed. As you would to an old friend whom you had not seen in years, you complain of your "wreck of a knee" and the "mostly futile" surgery you'd had to correct it. Boastfully you say you'd decided just to "flaunt" your "ugly baldy head"—why not?

"So—you are teaching here, Adrienne? That's wonderful news. You're coming to dinner with us, I assume. . . ."

353

Glances among my colleagues. Eyes avoiding my eyes.

"I—I don't think that I've been invited. . . ."

"Of course you are invited! I insist."

You turn to the others, with an imperial look. Still you are grasping my hands, so strangely. Is it possible—I will think this much later, sleepless that night and in the throes of an enormous, burgeoning love like a great snake that has forced itself down my throat—that you do, in fact, recognize me?—Adra Leeuwen?

But no, this is not so clear. While recognizing me, my face, this look of yearning in my eyes, you have conflated me with another yearning girl, enough like me to be a substitute for me; but this does not invalidate the warmth with which you address *me*.

You seem shorter than I recall. There is sadness in that. Yet you are far heavier, and are leaning on me; I think it is a tremor I feel in your hands, and I wonder if you are overexcited as well as fatigued and unwell. The kimono is a brave, silly choice; the black slacks are more practical, hiding fat, quivery legs. You are making a fuss over me as—what is this?—lights flash, for a girl photographer from the student newspaper is taking pictures, and a professional photographer from the college development office.

Flashing lights! I am too confused to smile—overwhelmed—for it occurs to me that no one has taken my photograph in a very long time.

My colleagues are virtually tugging at you. Come with us!

Time for you, distinguished guest lecturer, to sign books. But there is a dinner to follow, at a local restaurant, and with dogged persistence, that steeliness that underlies your gregarious social manner, you say again to your hosts that you assume I've been invited; my face burns with a hurtful sort of pleasure. It is up to me to say, *Oh no, I'm very tired, I wasn't intending to come to dinner—but thank you so much;* yet, as my colleagues stare at me, embarrassed, glowering, I do not stammer these words; I will not stammer these words.

"Adrienne? You're coming, yes?"

"Yes. . . ."

"I'll see you at dinner then. Save me a seat!"

Save me a seat. So sweet of you, if ridiculous, hypocritical—you must know very well that as the guest of honor you will have a seat; in fact, it is the seat of the guest of honor, and if you want someone to sit close beside you, if you want someone, an old, dear friend, to clasp your hand, to drink with you, and reminisce with you, and laugh with you, it is your prerogative, and no one is likely to deny you who have been paid, for a fifty-minute lecture, in excess of an adjunct's salary for an entire semester.

In my soiled and ill-fitting khakis, in my hiking boots, worn suede jacket, baseball cap over straggly hair, with my wan, pale, truculent face I am not exactly dressed for the quasi elegance of either of our "good" restaurants; but it seems that I am invited, and that you will insist that I sit beside you, to the consternation of your hosts. For how sternly you address them, the middle-aged woman who is our new dean of the faculty, an avowed "fan" of yours (she has said), who will not fail to do your bidding; for you are complaining also, not gravely but pleasantly, with the air of a stand-up comedienne who is accustomed to getting both appreciative laughter and her own way, of the room you've been given in the alumni house—in fact, it is a suite, but it is not what you'd expected—you are hoping that some-one (the apparatchik?) can book a room for you in a "real hotel" with a large-screen TV and twenty-four-hour room service. Anything but this charming old "historic" house on campus. Of course, this will be executed.

An extra place at dinner, not so difficult. A hotel room at this time of evening, more difficult. But both demands will be met, for your hosts are eager to please you. The dean is particularly eager to please you for you are a famous person who will (very likely) write about them and the college, and it is to their advantage to please you, so far as they can.

Always, people have been eager to please you. Why?

The harder you are to please, the more eager they are to please you. It is something like a law of nature.

And it is a fact, or was—I loved you.

Might have died for you, if you'd explicitly requested it. As it was, your wish was too oblique out on the hiking trail. You'd allowed me to misinterpret. For which I am grateful—*I love you.*

Somehow then, you are gone—moving haltingly, using your cane. My colleagues have escorted you away with the intention of pro-tecting you from further interruptions; smiling after you, somewhat dazed, I am not sure what to do next—wishing that I had not brought my bulky backpack with me, damned awkward to carry on my bi-cycle, particularly in the rain.

Since approximately 4:00 p.m. it has been raining. When I'd made my way on my bicycle to campus, suffused with anticipation and de-termined not to fail.

What will be done that cannot be undone.

355

But now—all has been altered.

My pride is such, I will not run after my colleagues to ask which restaurant. Where is the dinner in your honor, at which I will sit close beside you, and clasp your hand?—where, in the night, in the pelting rain?

Pride too will not allow me to beg a ride with my colleagues. For these are not colleagues but rivals for the fickle admiration of under-graduates. Perhaps not rivals so much as enemies, who would be cheered if I died, or at least was grievously injured, in a bicycle mishap on the highway, in pelting rain on my way to the French Provincial restaurant at the edge of town—for I think it must be this, I think I overheard one of your hosts utter the name of the French restaurant in a low voice, hoping that I would not hear; of course, in the rain, as I pedal along College Avenue shakily, I am cursing myself for having come away without a raincoat crumpled and shoved into my back-pack with other supplies.

Headlights in my eyes, near blinding. Like the flashbulbs herald-ing a new life, which make me smile, and my breath catch in my throat.

Let's try that again, please. Both of you—eyes open and SMILE.

Now, however, my senses are on high alert. I am feeling good—uplifted. Very smart to wear my baseball cap; my hair will not blow wetly into my face. But I am hoping that it is the French restaurant at which the dinner will be held, and not the other—Carnival, it's called—on the other, farther side of town; if I arrive at the wrong restaurant, I will have to bicycle miles to the other, and even then, I can't be absolutely certain that the dinner for you will be at Carnival either, if not at the French restaurant; for there are one or two other possible restaurants to which the lecture committee might take you, one of them a steak house, the other a reputedly upscale Italian res-taurant, and each of them far too expensive for me to afford even if I were in the habit of going out to restaurants to eat, which I am not.

NOTES ON CONTRIBUTORS

ROBERTA ALLEN's most recent book is *The Dreaming Girl* (Ellipsis).

JOHN ASHBERY's newest collection of poems is *Breezeway* (Ecco/HarperCollins). A two-volume set of his collected French translations was published in 2014 (Farrar, Straus and Giroux).

JEDEDIAH BERRY's first novel, *The Manual of Detection* (Penguin), won the Crawford Award and the Hammett Prize and was adapted for audio by BBC Radio. His story in cards, "The Family Arcana," was recently published as a poker deck by Ninepin Press.

JONATHAN CARROLL (www.jonathancarroll.com) is the author of twenty books, most recently *Bathing the Lion* (St. Martin's). He lives in Vienna, Austria.

MATTHEW CHENEY is the author of *Blood: Stories* (Black Lawrence).

ROBERT CLARK has published nine books and has just completed a new collection, *Bayham Street: Essays in Longing*. He lives in New York.

ROBERT COOVER has published more than twenty books of fiction and plays, his most recent being *A Child Again* (McSweeney's), *Noir* (Overlook), and *The Brunist Day of Wrath* (Dzanc). His new book of fiction, *Huck Out West*, from which the excerpts in this issue are taken, will be published by Norton in January 2017.

ROBERT DUNCAN (1919–1988) was associated with movements including the San Francisco Renaissance, the New American Poetry, and the Black Mountain school. Called "one of the most accomplished, one of the most influential" of the postwar American poets by Kenneth Rexroth, he was also a pioneering figure in gay culture and politics, publishing the essay "The Homosexual in Society" in 1944. Recent editions of his work include *The H. D. Book: The Collected Writings of Robert Duncan* (University of California), *Ground Work: Before the War/In the Dark*, *A Selected Prose*, and *Selected Poems* (all New Directions).

RACHEL BLAU DuPLESSIS is the author of the multivolume poem *Drafts* (Wesleyan and Salt), *Interstices* (Subpress), *Graphic Novella* (Xexoxia), *Eurydics* (Further Other Book Works), and *Days and Works* (Ahsahta). "Useful Knots and How to Tie Them" is part of a new long poem, *Traces of Previous Formats*.

ANDREW ERVIN is the author of the novel *Burning Down George Orwell's House* (Soho), which was recently translated into French by Gallimard/Editions Joëlle Losfeld, and a collection of novellas, *Extraordinary Renditions* (Coffee House). He lives in Philadelphia.

357

MARGARET FISHER is the author of *Ezra Pound's Radio Operas, The BBC Experiments 1931–1933* (The MIT Press) and *RADIA, a Gloss of the 1933 Futurist Radio Manifesto* (Second Evening Art).

ELIZABETH GAFFNEY is the author of the novels *When the World Was Young* and *Metropolis* (both Random House). She lives in Brooklyn.

ISABELLA HAMMAD is an English writer based in Brooklyn. Her contribution to this issue marks her first appearance in print.

MICHELLE HERMAN's most recent books are *Devotion*, a novel, and *Like a Song*, a collection of essays. Her 2005 novel, *Dog* (MacAdam/Cage), will be reissued in 2016 (all Outpost 19). She directs the MFA program in creative writing at Ohio State.

BRANDON HOBSON is the author, most recently, of *Desolation of Avenues Untold* (CCM).

Cover artist ZACH HORN is a lecturer at the University of Massachusetts Boston. He lives and works in Dorchester, Massachusetts.

TIM HORVATH (www.timhorvath.com) is the author of *Understories* (Bellevue), which won the New Hampshire Literary Award, and *Circulation* (sunnyoutside). "The Spinal Descent" is excerpted from his first novel.

EMILY HOUK serves as coeditor of Ninepin Press and has just finished work on her first novel. This is her first appearance in print.

DIANE JOSEFOWICZ coauthored *The Zodiac of Paris* (Princeton) with Jed Z. Buchwald.

PAUL LISICKY is the author of five books, including *Lawnboy* (Graywolf), *Unbuilt Projects* (Four Way), and, most recently, *The Narrow Door: A Memoir of Friendship* (Graywolf). He teaches in the MFA Program at Rutgers University, Camden.

SPENCER MATHESON just completed his first novel and is writing a libretto for composer Patrick Zimmerli's opera about Lucia Joyce. He lives in Paris. This is his first appearance in print.

J. W. McCORMACK's work has appeared in periodicals including *Bookforum*, *Tin House*, *The New Republic*, *VICE*, *New Inquiry*, and *n+1*. He is a senior editor at *Conjunctions*.

RICK MOODY is the author of three collections of stories, a memoir, a volume of essays on music, and six novels, including, most recently, *Hotels of North America*. With Darcey Steinke, he edited *Joyful Noise: The New Testament Revisited* (both Little, Brown).

JOYCE CAROL OATES is the author, most recently, of the novel *The Man Without a Shadow* (Ecco) and the story collection *The Doll Master* (Mysterious Press). She currently teaches at UC-Berkeley and is a recent recipient of the President's Medal of Honor in the Humanities.

358

STEPHEN O'CONNOR is the author of five books, including the novel *Thomas Jefferson Dreams of Sally Hemmings* (Viking) and the fiction collection *Here Comes Another Lesson* (Free Press).

M. J. REY (mjrey.com) is an emerging writer based in Los Angeles. This is his first appearance in print.

ELIZABETH ROBINSON is the author, most recently, of *Counterpart* (Ahsahta) and *On Ghosts* (Solid Objects), a finalist for the Los Angeles Times Book Award.

DARCEY STEINKE is the author of the memoir *Easter Everywhere* and the novels *Milk* (both Bloomsbury), *Jesus Saves* (Grove/Atlantic), *Suicide Blonde* (Atlantic Monthly), *Up Through the Water* (Doubleday), and *Sister Golden Hair* (Tin House).

CHARLES B. STROZIER teaches history at John Jay College and the Graduate Center, CUNY, and is a practicing psychoanalyst in New York City. His contribution to this issue is an adapted excerpt from his forthcoming book, *Your Friend Forever* (Columbia). He is also the author of *Lincoln's Quest for Union: A Psychological Portrait* (Basic Books and Paul Dry Books), *Heinz Kohut: The Making of a Psychoanalyst* (Farrar, Straus and Giroux), and *Apocalypse: Fundamentalism in America* (Beacon).

Poet and translator COLE SWENSEN (www.coleswensen.com) teaches at Brown University. Her most recent book is *Landscapes on a Train* (Nightboat).

GILLES TIBERGHIEN is a philosopher and writer specializing in landscape theory and land art who teaches at the Université de Paris I Panthéon Sorbonne. His work in this issue was originally published in French in his 2008 book *Amitier* (Éditions du Félin).

SALLIE TISDALE's new collection of essays, *Violation*, was published in April by Hawthorne Books.

C.D. Wright

1949-2016

Poet and Mentor

Brown University Literary Arts

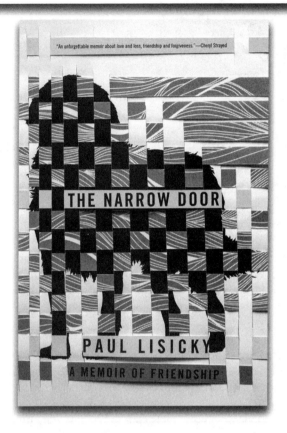

GRAYWOLF
PRESS

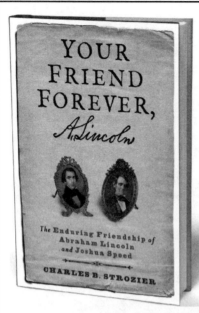

MARCEL BROODTHAERS:
MY OGRE BOOK, SHADOW
THEATER, MIDNIGHT

Translated by Elizabeth Zuba

Co-edited by Richard Kraft, Lisa Pearson & Elizabeth Zuba

This intimate and gorgeously produced book delves into the origins of the influential and elusive artist-poet Marcel Broodthaers whose works live in the interstices between language and image. Pairing two of Broodthaers's earliest collections of poetry—both previously unpublished in English—with an eighty-image projection work made toward the end of his too brief life, this collection reveals a dizzyingly prodigious interplay between the images and texts—particularly illuminating Broodthaers's use of the dark fairytale framework within (and against) which he plays with reflections and reproductions, inversions and fictions, body and shadow, decor and violence.

$39.95 · Cloth · 160 pages · 80 color & b/w illustrations · **www.sigliopress.com**

siglio

──uncommon books at the intersection of art & literature──

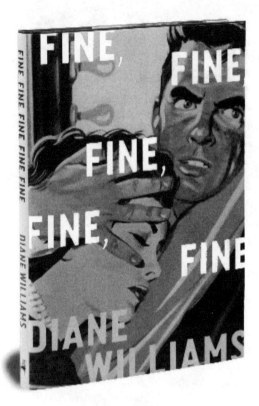

SOLID OBJECTS

Renee Gladman
MORELIA

Laura Mullen
*COMPLICATED
GRIEF*

Thalia Field
*EXPERIMENTAL
ANIMALS*
(A REALITY FICTION)

Miranda Mellis
THE SPOKES

Lisa Jarnot
*A PRINCESS
MAGIC PRESTO
SPELL*

Julie Carr
THINK TANK

www.solidobjects.org

The Ronald Sukenick/ FC2 Innovative Fiction Contest

$1,500 & publication by FC2

Entries accepted August 15, 2016 - November 1, 2016

Submission guidelines: www.fc2.org/prizes.html

 is among the few alternative, author-run presses devoted to publishing fiction considered by America's largest publishers to be too challenging, innovative, or heterodox for the commercial milieu.

FC2 & The Jarvis and Constance Doctorow Family Foundation

present the

FC2 Catherine Doctorow Innovative Fiction Prize

Winner receives $15,000 and publication by FC2

Entries accepted
**August 15, 2016 -
November 1, 2016**

Submission guidelines
www.fc2.org/prizes.html

FC2 is among the few alternative, author-run presses devoted to publishing fiction considered by America's largest publishers to be too challenging, innovative, or heterodox for the commercial milieu.

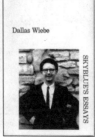

NOON

A LITERARY ANNUAL

1324 LEXINGTON AVENUE   PMB 298   NEW YORK NY 10128

EDITION PRICE $12 DOMESTIC $17 FOREIGN

THE PEOPLE IN THE CASTLE

SELECTED STRANGE STORIES

JOAN AIKEN

"The particular joys of a Joan Aiken story have always been her capacity for this kind of brisk invention; her ear for dialect; her characters and their idiosyncrasies. Among the stories collected in this omnibus, are some of the very first Joan Aiken stories that I ever fell in love with, starting with the title story "The People in the Castle," which is a variation on the classic tales of fairy wives."
— Kelly Link, from her Introduction

"Jeffrey Ford is a beautifully disorienting writer, a poet in an unclassifiable genre—his own."
Joyce Carol Oates

A NATURAL HISTORY OF HELL

STORIES

JEFFREY FORD

★ "Seamlessly blends subtle psychological horror with a mix of literary history, folklore, and SF in this collection of 13 short stories, all focused on the struggles, sorrows, and terrors of daily life."
Publishers Weekly (starred review)

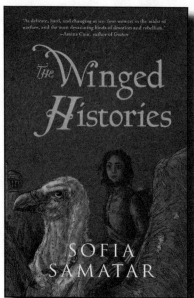

"As delicate, hard, and changing as ice: four women in the midst of warfare, and the most devastating kinds of devotion and rebellion."
—Amina Cain, author of *Creature*

THE Winged Histories

SOFIA SAMATAR

"Harrowing — and written in such heart-stoppingly beautiful language there's a good chance readers will ignore the plot and spend a few hours just chewing on the words, slowly, to draw out the flavor. Then they'll need to read it again. Fortunately, this is a short book; also fortunately, there's a lot of novel packed into relatively few pages. A highly recommended indulgence."
New York Times Book Review

TRIP THE DARK & LIGHT FANTASTIC.
SMALLBEERPRESS.COM

WORKSHOPS AT BARD COLLEGE

Sunday to Friday, July 10—15, 2016

The July weeklong workshops offer teachers and faculty an opportunity to develop an understanding of "writing-based teaching," its theory and practices, and its application in the classroom. Each workshop will focus on writing methods that deepen learning across all subject areas—literature, history, grammar and STEM.

TO REGISTER and FOR WORKSHOP DESCRIPTIONS
please visit _writingandthinking.org_

July Workshops Include:

- Writing and Thinking
- Writing and Thinking through Technology
- Inquiry into Essay
- Writing Retreat for Teachers
- Writing to Learn
- Poetry: Lyric Investigations across Disciplines
- Writing to Learn in the STEM Disciplines
- Applying the Practices
- Revolutionary Grammar
- Teaching the Academic Paper
- Thinking Historically through Writing
- Creative Nonfiction: Telling the Truth

The July workshops offer a retreat in which participants learn new writing practices, read diverse texts, and talk with teachers from around the world on the Bard College campus. The luxury of time helps us envision how we might make these new practices our own–how we might tweak the writing prompts, change the readings, figure out ways to accommodate collaborative learning in larger classes, and explore how poetry, for instance, might inspire students from ethnically and linguistically diverse backgrounds.

"I've seen 12 new ways to think about this text—as technology, as evolution, as modern art, etc. I've also seen how I can have deep conversations with the texts as a whole by looking at just one short passage." —participant in "Teaching the Academic Paper"

IWT Bard | 1982-2016
Celebrating More Than 30 Years of Writing and Thinking

Bard Institute for Writing & Thinking PO Box 5000 | Ludlow 105 | Annandale-on-Hudson, NY 12504

A Public Space, as you like it

print
online archives
e-editions

apublicspace.org

PEN AMERICA

A JOURNAL FOR WRITERS AND READERS

ISSUE #19: HAUNTINGS

Featuring Conversations, Essays,
Fiction, Poetry & Art by
Tom Stoppard
Yusef Komunyakaa
Joyce Carol Oates
Mona Eltahawy
Laura Esquivel
Edward Snowden
Kimiko Hahn
& many others

www.PEN.org/journal

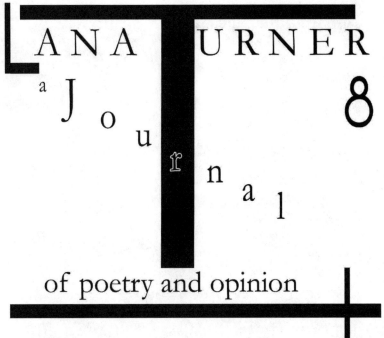

LANA TURNER

a Journal

8

of poetry and opinion

POETRY

JORIE GRAHAM, BRENDA HILLMAN, GEOFFREY G. O'BRIEN, CÉSAR VALLEJO, BIN RAMKE, ANNE BOYER, SANDRA SIMONDS, RAE ARMANTROUT, RUSTY MORRISON, MONICA YOUN . . .

PROSE

CÉSAR VALLEJO on ART AND THE SOCIAL SPHERE, GOPAL BALAKRISHNAN on THE MEANING OF MARXISM, COLE SWENSEN & ELENI SIKELIANOS on the EXPERIMENTAL LYRIC, a selection from JEAN FRÉMON'S NOVEL about LOUISE BOURGEOIS, ASAD HAIDER on BARAKA AND BLACK LIVES MATTER . . .

ART & REVIEWS ... see lanaturnerjournal.com.

READ TO LIVE

GOOD WRITING CAN CHANGE THE WORLD.

GREAT WRITING CREATES IT